Gerry Frank's Oregon

Gerry Frank's Oregon

Printed in the United States of America

ISBN: 978-1-879333-29-1
First Edition, 2012
Second Edition, 2014
Third Edition, 2016
Fourth Edition, 2018

No fees were paid or services rendered in exchange for inclusion in this book. Although every effort was made to ensure that all information was accurate and up-to-date at the time of publication, neither the publisher nor the author can be held responsible for any errors, omissions or adverse consequences resulting from the use of such information. It is recommended that you call before your visit to verify the information for individual business listings.

Gerry Frank's Oregon

Gerry's Frankly Speaking, Inc.

P.O. Box 2225
Salem, OR 97308
503/585-8411
800/692-2665
gerry@teleport.com
oregonguidebook.com

To the reader,

Gerry Frank is an Oregon treasure. Most people know that by now, but if you aren't convinced go to Salem, where his name will grace a new amphitheater and has been a fixture above his long-time restaurant, Konditorei, for 36 years. People within a five-mile radius of the statehouse know him simply as "Gerry."

I had lunch with Oregon's living legend at Konditorei the day he asked me to write this foreword. It was so crowded, even Gerry couldn't get a table.

No matter. There's no down time if you're Gerry Frank. During the 15-minute wait, he made the rounds to every corner of the restaurant, shaking hands and thanking guests. Everyone recognized him. Most knew him.

Gerry has built relationships with everyday Oregonians and the state's elite spanning more than 60 years. That's even more remarkable when you consider that Gerry doesn't stand still. He's been living out of a suitcase for decades. Always on the go. Always visiting someplace new. Always stopping by old haunts. That underscores his importance as a storyteller and an essential guide for readers. He knows every nook and cranny of our state. There is no better Sherpa to offer tips on the best restaurants, hotels, resorts or spas from Astoria to Ashland and from Lincoln City to John Day.

At 94 years young, Gerry is an inspiration. He shows no signs of slowing down. He's on the road every week writing reviews and offering suggestions to readers of his Sunday column that has graced the pages of *The Oregonian* for 31 years.

Gerry Frank's Guide to Oregon, written in partnership with The Oregonian/OregonLive, is now in its fourth printing, having sold more than 50,000 copies. If you bought an earlier version, thinking that would be enough, consider this: Gerry estimates that about half of his latest edition is different from the last. That's remarkable and important. It gives this book currency and relevancy. It is the ultimate guide to Oregon.

I hope you enjoy it.

Mark Katches
Editor and Vice President of Content
The Oregonian/OregonLive

Contents

About price categories

Most businesses are categorized by a price range. Here is a guide.

Restaurants/pubs/breweries

Based on the per-person cost of an entree plus appetizer; drinks and tip not included.

Inexpensive: under $15
Moderate: $15 to $29
Moderately expensive: $30 to $44
Expensive: $45 and up

Hotels/B&B/lodging

Assumes double occupancy and based on the nightly room rate; taxes and surcharges not included.

Inexpensive: under $125
Moderate: $125 to $249
Expensive: $250 to $399
Very expensive: $400 and up

Museums/parks/activities

Based on venue admission fee for one adult; fees for additional or optional activities not included.

Nominal: under $10
Reasonable: $10 to $19
Expensive: $20 and over

From the Author

Dear Readers,

I have been overwhelmed by the positive response to the first three editions of *Gerry Frank's Oregon* (2012, 2014 and 2016). The title has been a huge success! Wherever I travel throughout the state, longtime friends, former colleagues, retail associates and readers share heartwarming anecdotes and fond memories and suggest their favorite places to visit. The experience continues to be an exciting journey around Oregon and a wonderful trip down memory lane.

I have made lots of discoveries since the third edition was published. Many are being shared in this new book, and all entries have been updated. Again I am featuring "Gerry's Exclusive List," a comprehensive listing of the very best places to eat, drink and stay in Oregon. In contrast to previous editions, I have reorganized the Exclusive List into seven components, one for each chapter and region, which should make it even more useful to readers.

It requires a hard-working team to accomplish revisions such as this. I want to recognize the following individuals whose skills and diligence helped make this new edition a reality: Dan Bender, Nancy Burke, Nancy Chamberlain, Linda Chase and Olga Polyakova. Each of these people has my sincere gratitude for another job well-done.

I hope that you enjoy using this book as you explore Oregon's highways and byways, and if I am lucky, we'll meet along the way.

Gerry Frank, Author

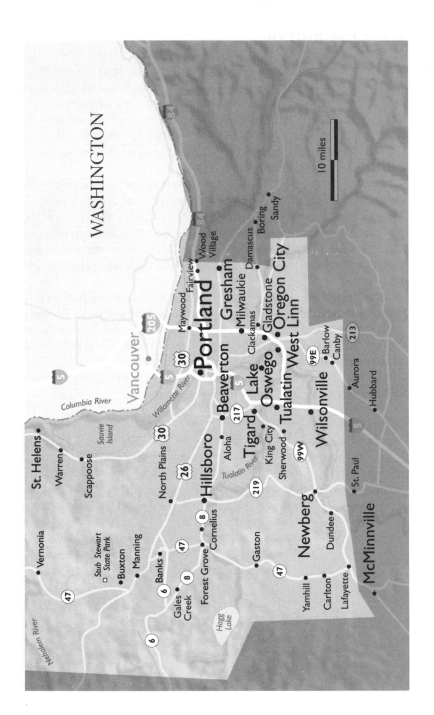

CHAPTER ONE

Greater Portland

BEAVERTON

Decarli

4545 SW Watson Ave   503/641-3223
Tue-Sun: 5-9 (extended bar hours)   decarlirestaurant.com
Moderate

Jana and Paul Decarli are talented and attentive hosts at their Italian ristorante. With a wealth of cooking experience, Chef Paul creates sophisticated and rustic dishes influenced by his Swiss-Italian-American background
and the fresh bounty of the Northwest. The daily-changing menu includes
wonderful salads and pasta, meat, fish and seafood entrees. Fascinating
and delicious ingredients and accompaniments turn ordinary offerings
into gourmet fare; happy hour selections and desserts receive similar
treatment. The warm dining room is lighted by a large brass chandelier
which, in another life, illuminated the historic Benson Hotel; private dining room available. Around the corner, the Decarlis have another business:
Watson Hall (12655 SW 1st St, 503/616-2416) is open for lunch, dinner
and Sunday brunch (closed Monday).

La Provence Bakery and Bistro

15151 SW Barrows Road   971/246-8627
(See detailed listing with Petite Provence, Portland)

Stockpot Broiler

8200 SW Scholls Ferry Road   503/643-5451
Mon-Fri: 11:30-2:30, 5:30-close;
Sat: noon, 5-close; Sun: 10, 5-close   stockpotbroiler.com
Moderate

When you want a delicious meal, don't forget the always-busy Stockpot Broiler for an elegant lunch or dinner. Chef Joshua Murphy features a consistently good menu using Northwest ingredients. You won't be disappointed with dinner from the grill, especially the tender, flavorful steaks. Entree salads are filling, soups are fresh and meals are made to order. In addition to sandwiches and burgers, you can also enjoy Korean tacos or seasonal seafood. On weekends, a trip to a buffet of fresh fruit, rich pastries and other treats accompanies brunch favorites like eggs and crab Benedicts, Pennsylvania pancakes, classic shrimp and grits and other creative vittles.

FOREST GROVE

Bites Restaurant

2014 Main St   503/746-6812
Mon-Fri: 11-9; Sat, Sun: 11:30-9   bitesrestaurant.com
Moderate

Bites is one of a handful of fusion restaurants that merges American, Mexican, Korean and Japanese flavors with ease, all while using local ingredients. Their colorful lineup include salads (ahi, lemongrass pork, house and cucumber); Thai, Korean and Japanese-style soups; Korean-style tacos; nachos; kimchi fries; signature wings with barbecue sauce; crab cakes with kimchi tartar sauce and more. Enjoy their small plates with your favorite cocktail, beer or wine. Larger plates include the Thai coconut risotto, salmon fish and chips, and burgers like the 808 (Oregon wagyu beef topped with spring mix, grilled pineapple and 808 sauce). House sauces and marinades and Bites apparel are available online.

Maggie's Buns

2007 21st Ave   503/992-2231
Mon-Fri: 6:30-4; Sat: 7-1   maggiesbuns.com
Inexpensive

The slogan at Maggie's Buns is "too hot to handle." The restaurant offers exciting full breakfast and lunch menus; breakfast to 11 midweek and until noon on Saturday. Sandwiches are made on Maggie's freshly-baked breads and salads are healthy and tasty; homemade soups change daily and lunch entrees run the gamut from pasta dishes to pork loin and salmon. Giant cinnamon buns are always served piping hot, straight from the oven — as advertised. Maggie's also offers catering and specializes in corporate and wedding events. Come as you are; this is a favorite "gal pal" coffee-and-more spot.

Montinore Estate

3663 SW Dilley Road   503/359-5012
Daily: 11-5   montinore.com
Inexpensive
Father and daughter team, Rudy and Kristin Marchesi, run this 210-acre certified biodynamic and organic estate. For those who are not familiar with biodynamic farming, it is said to be one of the most sustainable forms of agriculture resulting in healthier food. Their values lie in that of a well-lived life, which includes good food and wine with friends and family, as well as creating quality wine. Seven grape varieties are grown including pinot noir, pinot gris, Gewürztraminer, Riesling, Müller-Thurgau, Teroldego and Lagrein. For tastings, the current $10 flight features six wines that change with the seasons. The vineyard is located near the foothills of the Coast Range with views of the mountains; the beautifully appointed tasting room is perched overlooking a stretch of the lush grape vines. Grounds are spacious and picnics are encouraged if visiting on a nice day.

SakéOne

820 Elm St   503/357-7056
Daily: 11-5   sakeone.com
This is a different kind of craft brewery. SakéOne brews saké for America, based on more than 500 years of Japanese history and traditions. Production includes six traditional Momokawa Junmai Ginjo sakés (premium grade, including two organic), a super-premium saké brand called g Saké and a fruit-infused saké under their Moonstone brand. All are available nationally and, increasingly, internationally. In the tasting room, choose from three saké tasting flights and a food pairing; you will also find imported Japanese saké and saké serving sets. Complimentary brewery tours are offered 1, 2 and 3 p.m. Friday through Sunday and by appointment Monday through Thursday. Kanpai!

GALES CREEK

OutAZABlue Market & Cafe

57625 NW Wilson River Hwy   503/357-2900
Wed-Sun: 4-9 (cafe)
Daily: 9-9 (market)   outazablue.com
Moderate
If traveling alongside the scenic Wilson River Highway, and you find your-

AND NOW, THOMAS LAUDERDALE

Pink Martini (pinkmartini.com) is the musical vision of Portlander **Thomas Lauderdale**. While working in politics and attending lots of fundraisers, Thomas was inspired to form Pink Martini, his "little orchestra," with the goal of providing beautiful music for political events. The talented group features about a dozen musicians and lead vocalists China Forbes and Storm Large who perform a multilingual repertoire on concert stages and with symphony orchestras in Europe, Asia, the Middle East and North and South America. Their music crosses genres such as classical, jazz and old-fashioned pop. Thomas continues to support important causes such as the environment, civil rights, education, affordable housing and others.

self looking for a roadside mini-mart, a cafe, a family restaurant or even a fine dining restaurant, look no further than OutAZABlue. The name describes this all-in-one stop perfectly. Owner and award-winning Chef Gabriel Barber says that it was inspired by their "middle of nowhere" location, appearing almost "out of the blue." When asked what kind of food they prepare, "everything from A to Z and back to A again" tends to be the response. Menu offerings range from build-your-own pastas and burgers, pizzas, steaks, fish and poultry dishes all the way to salads, sandwiches, wraps and calzones fashioned on fresh pizza skins with unique ingredients. The cuisine is Mediterranean-focused, but also includes classic dishes with an AZA twist. Just as the restaurant always strives to use local, organic ingredients, the countryside market also sources take-home organic produce, breads and pastries. The wine list is extensive, reasonably priced and includes local and imported varieties; beer available. Monthly winemaker's dinners on the third Sunday of every month are posted on their website; call for reservations. Although you may not know it from the outside, this is much more than your typical roadside diner. Catering is available off-site and for intimate on-site events.

HILLSBORO

Copper River Restaurant and Bar

7370 NE Cornell Road   503/640-0917
Daily: 11-11 (Fri, Sat till midnight)   copperriverrestaurant.com
Moderate

I am a big fan of the two Oswego Grills, so it's no wonder I am now a devotee of Copper River, too. After all, they are locally-owned and -operated by the same Burnett tribe that so successfully runs the Oswego Grills. With the help of other members of the family and expert advice from David's mentor, the late Bob Farrell (of Farrell's Ice Cream Parlours), Christie and David Burnett operate a huge sparkling room in the shadows of Hillsboro's Intel and Nike. Copper River is a crowd pleaser with an attractive atmosphere, a huge and inviting menu and superbly-trained help, managed by Andy Tinling and Vice President of Operations and family member Kristen Burnett. The 300 seat facility includes a private dining area for any occasion and offers ample parking, two happy-hour menus and delicious food from the finest ingredients. Included on the menu are 21 appetizers, varying from traditional fried chicken tenderloins to corn fritters, 52 local craft beers on tap, a variety of canned and bottled beers, local wines that are sure to satisfy any taste, hearty salads, sandwiches and just about everything else a hungry family might want without spending a fortune. When customers are treated like family, as is the case with the Burnett tribe, success is assured.

Helvetia Tavern
10275 NW Helvetia Road   503/647-5286
Daily: 11-10; (Fri, Sat till 11)   Facebook
Inexpensive to moderate
Decades after opening up in 1946, beer continues to flow with domestic, imported, draft and micros by the pint or pitcher. While the rustic, rural locale is part of the draw, foremost are burgers, all made with freshly-ground beef, cooked to perfection and finished with the usual fixings and special sauce (bacon, jalapenos and ham are extra). But, it's the much talked about jumbo burger that sets them apart from the rest. They should really call it the no mumbo-jumbo burger, because a true quality burger doesn't hide behind its components and this one doesn't either. Don't pass on an order of hand-cut fries and onion rings (or both). If you visit on a warm day you'll want to sit outside on the patio. Note that this is a "cash only" business, but there is an ATM conveniently on-site.

The Reedville Cafe
7575 SE Tualatin Valley Hwy   503/649-4643
Mon-Thu: 6:30-10 (Fri till 11); Sat: 7-10; Sun: 7-9   reedvillecafe.com
Moderate
This institution started as the Shack Tavern in 1934 and has been owned and operated by the Van Beveren family since 1950. After a name change in 1990, the building has seen several remodels in order to serve an ever-growing number of loyal customers. Breakfast, lunch, dinner and happy hour menus are offered daily, and there is outdoor seating in season. For breakfast there's hearty, slow-roasted corned beef hash and eggs with

horseradish sauce along with plenty of other good options such as omelets, pancakes, French toast combos and biscuits with country gravy. The lunch and dinner menus feature backyard burgers and tasty seafood baskets. Monthly specials include Crabfest in January, Steakfest in April, Sizzlin' Summer BBQ in July and Oktoberfest in the fall. A full bar offers craft beers, wines and cocktails. It's no wonder this cafe continues to be a busy place.

Rice Northwest Museum of Rocks and Minerals
26385 NW Groveland Dr   503/647-2418
Wed-Fri: 1-5; Sat, Sun: 10-5   ricenorthwestmuseum.org
Nominal
What started as Helen and Richard Rice's personal and private mineral collection in their home basement grew into this beautiful public museum that holds a world-class collection of rocks, crystals, petrified wood, fluorescent minerals, fossils and more. Being a logger, Richard used rare Oregon woods during the construction of their home (now museum). Because of its unique architectural style and use of natural materials, the museum is listed on the National Registry of Historic Places. The working collection of over 20,000 specimens includes the "Alma Rose" rhodochrosite, dinosaur eggs, meteorites and an impressive chunk of gold and exotics. Don't miss what is perhaps the largest example of Oregon's state rock, a one-ton thunder egg. Being an affiliate of the Smithsonian Institution, visitors can expect a variety of events, site tours and educational opportunities that are open to the public. The gift shop is like no other museum outpost with high-end faceted gemstone jewelry as well as rare books and polished stones. Saturdays offer regularly scheduled guided tours (private group tours available by request).

Syun Izakaya
209 NE Lincoln St   503/640-3131
Mon-Thu: 11:30-10 (Fri till 11); Sat: noon-3, 5-10; Sun: 5-10   syun-izakaya.com
Moderate
The feature at this quaint Japanese pub-style restaurant in Hillsboro's former Carnegie Library is stupendous sushi. Lovers of this delicacy will find a large selection of dishes: raw fish, sashimi, sushi rolls, salads and delicious daily specials that include hot dishes and noodles; vegetarian options available. Patrons unfamiliar with the cuisine on this expansive menu are well-served by the knowledgeable and attentive staff; recommendations for food are on the mark. They'll also steer you toward fine sakés from their impressive inventory or you may opt for your familiar favorite from the full bar. Enter the brownstone under the green awning; seasonal outdoor seating.

Thirsty Lion Pub and Grill
2290 NW Allie Ave   503/336-0403
(See detailed listing with Thirsty Lion Pub and Grill, Tigard)

Topgolf
5505 NW Huffman St   503/549-5197
Daily: 9 a.m.-11 p.m. (Fri, Sat till midnight)   topgolf.com
Price category

Inject a little modern technology (plus drinks, food and marketing savvy) into the old-school idea of a driving range and you get Topgolf, among the latest in the immersive experience entertainment genre craved by the Millennial Generation. At Topgolf players use real clubs to swing at real but microchipped golf balls in one of its 100-plus climate-controlled bays. From there the balls score themselves while assessing the player's accuracy and distance. The games are geared to group play and competitions among groups, but individuals are welcome. A $5 membership card (which can be used every visit) will work as your score card and will be synced to your golf balls. Bays are priced by the hour, which can vary from $25 to $45, depending on the time of day. A bay can accommodate a group of six, so that could work out to less than $8 per person per hour during the most popular evening hours. Each bay has tables and chairs for your group as well as a TV; the setup is similar to a bowling alley's. Attentive servers keep an eye on your group. Menus include shareable, classic and creative cocktails, seasonal favorites, spirits, beer and wine, as well as fountain and energy drinks. Food offerings include cheesy fries, wings, burgers, nachos and flatbreads, as well as options like salads, hummus and sandwiches. Enjoy the whole show from the full-service restaurant and bar. Although guests under 16, or under 18 after 9 p.m., must be supervised by an adult 21 or over, this is a family-friendly establishment. Kids especially enjoy the KidZone, which keeps them entertained with video games, pool tables, board games and more. The fun does not have to end just because you've finished playing. Head to the rooftop terrace to enjoy the fire pit with friends.

LAKE OSWEGO

Baird's on B
485 2nd St   503/303-4771
Mon-Thu: 11:30-9 (Fri, Sat till 10)   bairdsonb.com
Moderate

Baird's on B is an attractive space in downtown Lake Oswego that includes a patio for outdoor dining. Baird Bulmore has put together an interesting, well-priced menu that includes smaller plates, snacks and fresh salads for those not wanting a full meal. Some offerings are seasonal. Items include crab cakes, fish and chips, mac and cheese, housemade fries and tater tots. For heartier appetites grilled salmon, seared scallops, linguine Bolognese, steaks and burgers are offered. The dessert menu changes regularly, and currently may include blueberry and white chocolate cheesecake, and chocolate caramel brownies with Tillamook Vanilla Bean Ice Cream.

La Provence Bakery and Bistro
16350 SW Boones Ferry Road   503/635-4533
(See detailed listing with Petite Provence, Portland)

Oswego Grill at Kruse Way
7 Centerpointe Dr   503/352-4750
Sun-Thu: 11-10 (Fri, Sat till 11)   oswegogrill.com
Moderate

Experienced local ownership is evident here with the winning ingredients of well-trained and friendly wait staff. The varied menu includes twice daily happy hour specials, fresh salads, burgers, first-rate prime rib sandwiches, pot pies, hand-selected steaks and more American classics. The hardwood grill's distinctive smoky mesquite and apple wood flavor is found on the romaine lettuce salad, meats, chicken and fish with Cajun, Southwest and Thai influences spicing up the menu. Desserts like warm, rich scratch-made doughnuts and hot-from-the-oven cookies and ice cream top off an amazing meal. Sister locations, Oswego Grill at Wilsonville (30800 SW Boones Ferry Road) and Copper River Restaurant and Bar (7370 NE Cornell Road, Hillsboro), are equally attractive and as charming as hardworking owners Christie and David Burnett and Kathy and Bud Gabriel.

St. Honoré Boulangerie
315 1st St   503/496-5596
(See detailed listing with St. Honoré Boulangerie, Portland)

Tucci Restaurant
220 A Ave   503/697-3383
Daily: 4:30-close   tuccirestaurant.com
Moderate

Tucci Restaurant offers Italian-inspired farm-to-table fare in a casually elegant dining spot. The seasonally evolving menu features house-made pastas, fresh and sustainable meats and seafood, a midweek prix-fixe menu, and always complimentary corkage. Alfresco dining is offered in the summer months, and the recently expanded Lido Bar features Hollywood-style booth seating.

LUXURIOUS DOWNTOWN LODGING

Portland offers many choices in luxury lodging, all with tastefully and magnificently appointed guest rooms and impeccable service. Some of the best include:

The Benson Hotel (309 SW Broadway, 503/228-2000): elegant landmark; El Gaucho Portland and The Palm Court Restaurant and Bar

Dossier (750 SW Alder Street, 503/294-9000): boutique hotel, art-filled rooms, locally-inspired amenities; intricately designed Opal restaurant and bar; Ranked No. 13 Hotel in the Pacific Northwest by Condé Nast Traveler in its 2017 Readers' Choice Awards

The Heathman Hotel (1001 SW Broadway, 503/241-4100): charming; 150 pet-friendly rooms; Headwaters restaurant

Hotel deLuxe (729 SW 15th Ave, 503/219-2094, 866/895-2094): retro-chic; classic fare at Gracie's restaurant; Manhattans in the iconic Driftwood Room

Hotel Eastlund (1021 NE Grand Ave, 503/235-2100): modern-chic Eastside boutique; rooftop Altabira City Tavern and bakery/cafe Citizen Baker

Hotel Lucia (400 SW Broadway, 503/225-1717): warm and contemporary; Chef Vitaly Paley's Imperial restaurant and The Crown Imperial pizza bar

Kimpton Hotel Monaco Portland (506 SW Washington St, 503/222-0001): classic tasteful Kimpton property, 221 guest rooms

Kimpton Hotel Vintage Portland (422 SW Broadway, 503/228-1212): boutique property; Italian-inspired Il Solito and Bacchus Bar, featuring Oregon wines and brews

Sentinel (614 SW 11th Ave, 503/224-3400): spacious guest rooms and suites, some with parlors and terraces; home to Jake's Grill and Jackknife, a hip, classic lobby lounge

Woodlark (813 SW Alder St, woodlarkhotel.com): 150-room lifestyle hotel slated to open fall 2018; will be home to Chef Doug Adams' highly-anticipated restaurant Bullard

MILWAUKIE

Bob's Red Mill Whole Grain Store

5000 SE International Way   503/607-6455, 800/349-2173

Mon-Sat: 6-6 (restaurant till 3)   bobsredmill.com

Since 1978 Charlee and Bob Moore have been grinding out flours, mixes, cereals, vegetarian-friendly products and other good-for-you eats (including gluten-free goods). The 15,000 square-foot red barn is a popular retail store that features all of Bob's Red Mill foods (packaged and bulk) and culinary-related items, a casual restaurant serving breakfast and lunch and in-house bakery. Nutritious recipes and essential techniques are taught in cooking classes also emphasizing whole grains. It's mighty difficult to resist the bakery which turns out dozens of healthy breads, muffins, cookies and vegan goodies; you'll spot them on the breakfast and lunch menus as well as other choices made with Bob's products. Beautifully landscaped grounds, super products, helpful suggestions and knowledgeable employees make this a true Oregon winner. The state-of-the-art milling, packaging and distribution operations are one mile down the road (15321 SE Pheasant Ct). Guests learn the ins-and-outs of the business with a smattering of the industry's history on a free tour of the facility conducted Monday through Friday mornings at 10.

Dave's Killer Bread

5209 SE International Way 503/335-8077
Mon-Sat: 7:30-6 daveskillerbread.com

Dave's Killer Bread (DKB) is the No. 1 organic bread in America. DKB revolutionized the bread industry in 2005 when it pioneered the organic seeded bread category at the Portland Farmers Market. Delicious slices are packed with nutritious grains, nuts and seeds and never anything artificial. Beyond baking the best bread in the universe, the brand believes in the power of Second Chance Employment: hiring those who have a criminal background and are ready to change their lives for the better. DKB's Healthy Bread Store is the place to find killer deals on loaves of DKB. Visit DKB's Healthy Bread Store for exclusive deals as well as a variety of DKB merchandise like t-shirts, reusable shopping bags and beanies.

Enchanté

10883 SE Main St 503/654-4846
Tue-Fri: 11-5:30; Sat: 11-4 Facebook

Enchanté is a Parisian-style chocolatier, located in the heart of historic downtown Milwaukie. Husband-and-wife duo Kim and Bill Cairo proudly handcraft their own chocolates in a tradition that has lasted 85 years. Additionally, several varieties of caramel corn are still made in a traditional copper candy kettle. When you visit this enchanting store you will be drawn in by exquisite displays that include confections from around the globe. There is a beautiful selection of gift items including treasures from Paris flea markets. USA Today named Enchanté one of the top ten candy stores in the country.

OREGON CITY

Stone Cliff Inn Restaurant & Bar

17900 S Clackamas River Dr   503/631-7900
Daily: 11:30-9 (Fri, Sat till 10)   stonecliffinn.com
Moderately expensive to expensive

Built from Douglas fir logs on the remains of a basalt quarry, Stone Cliff Inn Restaurant & Bar is a nod to the community of Carver and the rock quarry and logging industries. The menu options at Stone Cliff Inn are abundant and prepared from scratch. Smoked salmon chowder is always available as well as a soup of the moment followed by side and entree salads (Caesar, spinach, warm beet with goat cheese and more). Interesting and appetizing rubs, spices and glazes are used in steak and seafood preparations; favorites of the house include cioppino, baby back ribs, bacon-wrapped meatloaf and hazelnut chicken. Pasta dishes are laden with goodies from the land and sea with the option to add chicken, salmon, prawns or steak to an already hearty dish. Try the lamb shank or duck ravioli features if you are lucky enough to visit when these savory dishes are available. Lunch choices include many of the same items and a nice selection of sandwiches and entrees. If you have room, marionberries are in two desserts: crème brûlée and apple berry strudel. Be sure to check out the award winning wine list and the wonderful collection of craft cocktails. Twilight movie fans may recognize the property as a backdrop for several scenes.

The Verdict Bar & Grill

110 8th St   503/305-8429
Lunch, Dinner: Daily   verdictbarandgrill.com
Moderate to moderately expensive

Owner Ryan Smith remodeled Oregon's oldest commercial building and created his friendly Verdict restaurant across from the Clackamas County Courthouse. The reasonably-priced lunch and dinner menus are broken down as "Opening Statements" (delicious bacon-wrapped shrimp and hot artichoke dip), "Lighter Sentence" (soups and salads), "In the Jury Box" (classic sandwiches and burgers) and "Order in the Court" (fish and chips, fish tacos, pasta). "Night Court" options include braised pork osso bucco and black truffle scallops; "Guilty as Charged" refers to the fresh dessert options. Flat screen TVs, free Wi-Fi, hand-crafted cocktails and Oregon brews and spirits round out the docket. Smith's next door casual coffee shop, the Caufield House is convenient to downtown workers for breakfast, lunch and a quick cuppa joe. Banquet and private party space are available at The Verdict and The Holding Cell, appropriately named for its location between the two entities.

THE McMENAMINS EMPIRE

Mike and Brian McMenamin are Portland brothers who pioneered the brewpub business, starting with the Barley Mill, a pub that opened in Portland in 1983. Today the McMenamins (mcmenamins.com) brand operates historical hotels, restaurants, brew pubs, breweries, distilleries, movie theaters, bars, public houses and taverns, more than 60 in all, from the Seattle area to Roseburg along the I-5 corridor and stretching from the Oregon Coast to Bend. Yes, those terms can sometimes overlap, and as is often the case, many of these businesses are co-located. But that's sort of the point with McMenamins; a visit to one is not just a night out at a restaurant or a bar, it is a total experience. Perhaps no single venue epitomizes this better than **Edgefield**, in Troutdale (2126 SW Halsey St, 503/669-8610). Built in 1911 as the Multnomah County poor farm, Edgefield is a destination resort whose centerpiece is a historic hotel with more than 100 guest rooms and hostel accommodations. Here you'll also find The Black Rabbit Restaurant and Bar, Lucky Staehly's Pool Hall, The Loading Dock Grill (among about a dozen venues for food and drink), as well as the Power Station Theater & Pub, which combines casual dining with a modern cinema. Additionally you'll find lots of musical entertainment, extensive gardens, a glass blower and potter and artwork on walls everywhere on this 74-acre parcel about 20 minutes from downtown Portland. While each McMenamins has a unique vibe, a consistent theme runs throughout the empire: some of the best food, microbrews and wines (and sometimes tea and espresso) in the Pacific Northwest blended with a signature, but very un-corporate, quirkiness. For example, the Edgefield Hotel rooms have no phones or TVs. That's a selling point from the McMenamins viewpoint (and guests won't miss them anyway, given how much there is to do there). A typical McMenamins pub is often located in a restored historical (if not historic) building. Boon's Treasury in Salem, for example, is in one of the oldest buildings still standing in the city and is said to have the initials of Herbert Hoover carved into a brick wall (Hoover lived for a time in Salem as a teenager, and as you learned in school, he went on to become the 31st President of the United States). Not all McMenamins are listed in this book (they probably should be, but that would take its own chapter), so go to their website to see if one is in your area. If you are in Portland or the Willamette Valley, the answer is probably yes. Their fare is moderately priced, and the trip will be worth it.

3 Doors Down Café & Lounge

1429 SE 37th Ave 503/236-6886
Tue-Sat: 5-9:30; Sun: 4-9 3doorsdowncafe.com
Moderate to moderately expensive
This Italian sanctuary is serious about two things: wine and food. The list of imported and Northwest wines, sparkling wines and champagnes is impressive; specialty cocktails are artfully composed. Some wines by the glass are straight from the barrel and there are cocktails and cider on tap. You can cut to the chase and order full-bodied pasta dishes and entrees like the tender grilled pork chop or linger over reasonably-priced antipasto, appetizers and happy hour small plates while you navigate the bar offerings. Bring this bite of Italy to your next party with group-size appetizers, entrees and desserts (arrange in advance).

23Hoyt

529 NW 23rd Ave 503/445-7400
Dinner: Daily 5-10 (Sun till 9:30);
Brunch: Sat, Sun 10-3 23hoyt.com
Moderate to moderately expensive
Sophisticated New American tavern, 23Hoyt (so named for its location at 23rd and Hoyt), has a birds-eye view of this hip neighborhood. The two-story front windows bathe the first floor bar and upstairs dining room in natural light. It's no secret that this is a hot spot for daily happy hour snacks (priced between $2 and $9). Segue to dinner and choose from the chef's farm-to-table menu of interesting soups and salads, charcuterie made in-house and entrees accompanied by seasonal sides given an updated twist; the listing changes daily. Brunch kicks off with eye-opening $2 mimosas and delivers punched-up doughnuts, burgers, omelets, salads and sandwiches — all the more reason to brunch at 23Hoyt!

a Cena

7742 SE 13th Ave 503/206-3291
Lunch: Tue-Sat: 11:30-2:30
Dinner: Daily 5-9 (Fri, Sat till 10) acenapdx.com
Moderately expensive to expensive
Enjoy lunch or dinner at a Cena (Italian for "come to supper"), reminiscent of an Italian country kitchen. On a changing menu, freshly-baked focaccia bread, pizzas and cured meats are favorites. Fabulous pasta dishes are made in-house, lasagna varieties change daily and tender ravioli are

stuffed with housemade ricotta cheese. Second courses of duck, braised short ribs, lamb, trout and seafood are equally enticing with exquisite fresh ingredients. For the finale, enjoy espresso or after-dinner coffee drinks and savor affogato, cannoli or tiramisu; all desserts are made daily from scratch. A private dining room is available.

Alpenrose Dairy

6149 SW Shattuck Road   503/244-1133
Events are seasonal   alpenrose.com

One of the great family names in Oregon is Cadonau, who co-own and operate, along with the Birkland family, Alpenrose Dairy in Southwest Portland. Since its beginning in 1891 when Florian Cadonau began delivering milk in a horse-drawn wagon, this family has provided top-quality dairy products. In 1916, during the next-generation operation that included Florian's son, Henry, the business was officially named "Alpenrose" after the national Swiss flower. Family entertainment became an integral part of the business, including the annual Easter Egg Hunt that generations of children fondly remember; Dairyville is a replica frontier town; the Alpenrose Stadium provides baseball facilities for Little League and the girls' Little League Softball World Series; the Alpenrose Velodrome (bicycle race track) is Olympic-class and one of only 20 in the United States and a Quarter Midget Racing arena attracts speedster enthusiasts. All recreational facilities offer free admission (check with Alpenrose for a detailed calendar).

Andina

1314 NW Glisan St   503/228-9535
Lunch: Daily 11:30-2:30;
Dinner: Daily 5-9:30 (Fri, Sat till 10:30)   andinarestaurant.com
Moderate to moderately expensive

Andina is a standout Peruvian restaurant in the Pearl. Celebrating the country's culture and cuisine, the space is bold, warm and beautiful and masterfully appointed to showcase the atrium. A large menu lists various Andean tapas — meats, fish, vegetables and cheeses. Plates are offered in two sizes to savor or share. You won't be disappointed with the extensive wine list (Northwest, Spanish, South American) and imaginative cocktails served in the lounge or dining room. Dressed-up family recipes and traditional entrees are served for both lunch and dinner; each presentation is a visual masterpiece. Meat and fish headliners are deliciously married with herbs, spices, quinoa and sundry elements creating unforgettable flavors as in the double rack of lamb served with a Peruvian potato side and roasted pepper demi-glace. The wait staff is knowledgeable and gracious; their Spanish pronunciation of menu items is music to my ears.

Baker & Spice Bakery

6330 SW Capitol Hwy   503/244-7573
Tue-Fri: 6-6; Sat, Sun: 7-6   bakerandspicepdx.com

Sugar and spice and all things nice describe Baker & Spice's retail bakery operation and cafe in the Hillsdale Shopping Center. Breads, pastries and lunch items are made in small batches from scratch with European-style butter, Belgian chocolate and the best local, organic and imported ingredients. The displays are overflowing with hearty scones, buttery croissants, housemade granola, fruit-laden hand pies, cookies, tarts and daily variations of bread pudding. Pies are available Friday through Sunday or any day by pre-order. Baguettes, buns, rolls, loaves and rounds are baked daily. For lunch, enjoy savory meat or vegetarian sandwiches made with the fresh breads or homemade soups and salads. Grab-n-go sandwiches are available to pick up at 8:30 for later lunch. Visit their cake annex and retail bakeware store, The Cakery (6306 SW Capitol Hwy, 503/546-3737), just eight storefronts up.

Bar Mingo

811 NW 21st Ave   503/445-4646
Daily: 4-10 (Fri, Sat till 11)   barmingonw.com
Moderate

If you are looking for a bar that specializes in casual Italian fare, then look no further than Bar Mingo. There are plenty of easy-priced hot and cold sharable plates and daily happy hour specials between 4 and 6. Substantial dinner choices are listed on the giant chalkboard featuring several fresh pasta dishes. This attractive watering hole offers sidewalk seating, perfect on warm evenings. Come early, because it is always crowded. Next door, **Caffe Mingo** (503/226-4646) is open daily for dinner with comforting zuppa, pasta of the day and other tempting Italian plates.

Beaches Restaurant and Bar

Portland International Airport
7000 NE Airport Way   503/335-8385
Daily: 5 a.m.-11 p.m.   beachesrestaurandandbar.com
Moderate

For innovative and satisfying meals at the Portland Airport, step into Beaches. Owner/operator Mark Matthias has a superbly-trained staff that makes customers feel welcome. The tempting menu has something for anyone's taste: Asian, American and Italian choices, and an inexpensive kids' menu. The long hours accommodate travelers' breakfast (5 to 11 a.m.) and lunch/dinner (11 a.m. to 11 p.m.) appetites, ideal for surviving jet lag. If you're in a hurry, stop by the quick-service Beach Shack (5 a.m. to 9 p.m.) on the airport's main concourse for carry-on food. Both outlets have marvelous caramel corn made fresh daily. The main **Beaches Restaurant and Bar** is across the Columbia River in Vancouver (1919 SE Columbia River Dr, 360/699-1592).

Beast

5425 NE 30th Ave   503/841-6968
Dinner: Wed-Sun; Brunch: Sun   beastpdx.com
Expensive

Plan ahead for this one. Diners are offered a choice of two seatings Wednesday through Saturday, one seating on Sunday night and a six-course prix-fixe menu (one menu for the week; substitutions possible with a 24-hour advance notice) five nights a week. Scrumptious meals are inspired by fresh and intriguing ingredients from local sources. Main courses are at the chef's whim according to the season and are often meat-heavy. Vegetable garnishes and accompaniments are oh-so-good. Cheese and dessert courses warrant saving room and wine pairings are carefully chosen to best complement each course. Three-course Sunday brunches (10, 11:30 and 1) are similarly composed.

The Benson Hotel

309 SW Broadway   503/228-2000, 800/663-1144
Moderate and up   bensonhotel.com

Guests are greeted by professional doormen at the Benson Hotel, one of Portland's most elegant landmarks. For over 105 years it has been the "residence of the presidents," graciously accommodating each U.S. president from William Howard Taft to Barack Obama (and many celebrities, too). This elegant property features original Austrian crystal chandeliers, Italian marble floors and historic Circassian walnut imported from the forests of Imperial Russia. Guests unwind in 287 tastefully modernized and renovated guest rooms and suites completed in 2018, that still maintain The Benson's historic charm and allure. Most are outfitted with comfortable Tempur-Pedic sleep systems, as well as specially designed eight-foot pillow-top mattresses in select rooms and suites. Luxurious amenities by Gilchrist & Soames along with organic bamboo bathrobes and slippers, umbrellas, in-room safes and modern technology are included in every room. Lavish ballrooms have been the scene of memorable soirees for Portland's elite and the setting for impressive business meetings. El Gaucho Portland Steakhouse offers old-school tableside service perfect for special occasions, while The Palm Court Restaurant and Bar offers relaxing lobby dining, featuring sumptuous menu options for breakfast, lunch and dinner along with happy hour and live entertainment. Exemplary accommodations and service are first-class.

ACHIEVEMENTS IN ATHLETICS
Since its inception in 1978, the **Oregon Sports Hall of Fame**
(4840 SW Western Ave, Beaverton; 503/227-7466; oregonsportshall.
org) has recognized and honored Oregon's rich athletic history.
The achievements of Baker, Brooks, Buckwalter, Drexler, Fosbury,
Harrington, Jacobsen, Prefontaine, Salazar, Schollander, Schonely,
Simonton, Sitton, Walton and more are showcased at this museum
(call for days and times the museum is open). An annual induction
ceremony welcomes new honorees to Oregon's Sports Hall of Fame.
The organization is dedicated to education and continues to award
a number of collegiate scholarships annually with the underlying
message that hard work and dedication reap benefits for any life path.

Bluehour

250 NW 13th Ave   503/226-3394
Dinner: Sun-Wed 5-9; Thu-Sat 5-10
Brunch: Sat, Sun 10-3   bluehouronline.com
Expensive

Under the direction of restaurateur Bruce Carey, Bluehour continues to
wow patrons in a modern yet intimate setting. The Pacific Northwest seasonal menu with Mediterranean influences features the area's rich bounty.
Expect terrines, salads, pastas, fish and seafood, duck confit and more; opt
for a tasting menu for optimal flavor exposure. Happy Bluehour (Mon-Fri
4-6:30; Sat, Sun 3-6:30) eats are casual and range from fried green tomatoes to gnocchi with arugula and scallions to the restaurant's signature
burger. Satisfying desserts include plum and sour cream cake, citrus coconut macaroons and nectarine and berry sorbet. The bar lounge has extended hours.

Buffalo Gap Saloon & Eatery

6835 SW Macadam Ave   503/244-7111
Daily: 8 a.m.-2:30 a.m. (Sun open at 9; hours may vary)   thebuffalogap.com
Moderate

Every neighborhood deserves a place like the Buffalo Gap: fun, laid-
back, extended hours, consistently good food and jam-packed menus
for breakfast, lunch and dinner. Breakfast choices are hearty (housemade
biscuits and gravy) or sensible (Paleo breakfast tacos), and gigantic cinnamon rolls are baked each morning. Soups are made from scratch. Specialty salads are indeed special and laden with lots of tasty ingredients.
Intriguingly-named sandwiches and burgers are served with a choice of

OSU ENHANCES ITS PRESENCE IN PORTLAND
Oregon State University is making another big move into downtown Portland, offering great new degree options to students who want to live in the city while they work toward their degree. And it's breathing new life into the historic Meier & Frank Building, too, whose first five floors have been unoccupied since Macy's closed in 2017. But the building's second floor, about 40,000 square feet in all, has been completely renovated and as of Aug. 1, 2018, will be the university's Portland home of its hybrid option for degrees in business administration, psychology and human development and family sciences. The space's central location and access to transit will be a real convenience to students. Classes at the new location will be offered in a new hybrid format — part online and part on-site. This innovative approach pairs valuable face-to-face learning with the flexibility of Oregon State's online capability. The new space is an example of the effectiveness of **Dr. Mitzi Montoya**, who became dean of the College of Business in 2015 and since then has been a leader in OSU's Portland strategy. And it's a testament to the vision of OSU President **Dr. Ed Ray**, who is transforming OSU into a truly statewide university system.

sides. Not to be overlooked are pizzas, pastas and full-meal-deal dinner platters. There's plenty of seating inside and out, upstairs and down with live music Friday and Saturday nights, billiards and other games plus every saloon beverage you can think of. The Attic area is available for private parties and banquets.

The Cakery

6306 SW Capitol Hwy   503/546-3737
Tue-Sat: 9-6; Sun: 9-3   bakerandspicepdx.com

Baker & Spice's cake annex and retail bakeware store, The Cakery, might be considered the proverbial icing, or sprinkles, on the cake. This shop, eight doors down from the bakery, creates and sells lots and lots of cake — whole or by the slice. During the holidays they make an amazing Yule log as well as peppermint patties, marshmallows, caramels and killer ginger snaps. An assortment of their confections is available year round. The shelves are brimming with quality baking supplies (including sprinkles and edible decorations), aprons, tea towels, handmade candles, vintage kitchenwares and hand-selected baking books.

Castagna Restaurant

1752 SE Hawthorne Blvd   503/231-7373
Wed-Sat: 5:30-10   castagnarestaurant.com
Expensive

Monique Siu has created one of my favorite dinner houses in Portland. Elegantly-presented courses take center stage in this sleek, modern establishment where service reigns supreme. Choose from the seasonal tasting menu or the chef's tasting menu with optional wine pairings. The chef defines the cuisine as "seasonal and progressive" with unexpected twists created by incorporating uncommon ingredients.

Cool Moon Ice Cream Company

1105 NW Johnson St   503/224-2021
Daily: 11:30-11   coolmoonicecream.com

Cool Moon makes its ice cream right in the store, in small batches using only natural ingredients. Although they have a rotation of about 200 flavors, you can expect to see standards like the Belgian chocolate, salty caramel, coffee crackle, Oregon berry (marionberry, strawberry, blueberry), birthday cake and the popular kulfi, which is infused with rosewater, cardamom and pistachios. For something more interesting, keep an eye out for the much-talked-about Thai iced tea flavor. Cutting dairy? No problem. Their sorbets are dairy-free; the chocolate is a house favorite, but the fresh fruit sorbets are just as delicious.

Dan & Louis Oyster Bar

208 SW Ankeny St   503/227-5906
Mon-Thu: 11-9 (Fri, Sat till 10); Sun: noon-9   danandlouis.com
Moderate to expensive

Five generations of the Wachsmuth family have been shucking oysters at this landmark since 1907. A prominent green and red striped awning over the gleaming brass and glass front doors and large windows frame the interior. What to eat? Oysters, of course; on the half-shell, Rockefeller, in stew, as a sandwich, sautéed in a delicious burre blanc sauce, fried or combined with other fresh seafood like prawns, clams, cod or calamari. A specialty of the house is cioppino, which blends the best fresh fish of the ocean in a delicious broth. Delicious preparations of salmon, steak and authentic gumbo are not to be ignored. For decades, this has been a go-to restaurant for client dinners, company parties and celebrations; the future looks strong for the next generation at Dan & Louis.

PORTLAND AIRPORT HOTELS

Here is a sampling of the hotels conveniently located near Portland International Airport that offer frequent airport shuttle service:

Aloft Portland Airport at Cascade Station (9920 NE Cascades Pkwy, 503/200-5678): loft-inspired design
Clarion Hotel Portland Airport (11518 NE Glenn Widing Dr, 503/252-2222): free full breakfast, heated indoor pool
Courtyard Portland Airport (11550 NE Airport Way, 503/252-3200): fitness center, renovated guest rooms
Embassy Suites by Hilton Portland Airport (7900 NE 82nd Ave, 503/460-3000): free breakfast, indoor saltwater pool
Fairfield Inn & Suites Portland Airport (11929 NE Airport Way 503/253-1400): free breakfast, seasonal outdoor pool
Hampton Inn Portland Airport (8633 NE Airport Way, 503/288-2423): free breakfast buffet, long term parking

Departure Restaurant + Lounge

525 SW Morrison St   503/802-5370
(See detailed listing with The Nines)

Dossier

750 SW Alder St   503/294-9000
Moderate to expensive   dossierhotel.com
Dossier opened in August 2017 and was ranked as the No. 13 Hotel in the Pacific Northwest by Condé Nast Traveler in its 2017 Readers' Choice Awards. The hotel's intricately designed restaurant and bar, Opal, serves breakfast, lunch and dinner daily from a menu that ranges from avocado toast in the morning to delectable salads and sandwiches at midday to great cocktails, pastas and steaks in the evening. Branded by Provenance Hotels (provenancehotels.com), which also operates The Heathman, Hotel Lucia, Hotel deLuxe and Sentinel in Portland, Dossier is home base for connecting with the city's creative culture. The hotel serves a free daily craft beer and kombucha hour that features brews from Ferment out of Hood River. It also is a partner with **Knot Springs** (503/222-5668, knotsprings. com), a social club centered on health, wellness and good times. Guests enjoy Knot Springs' membership pricing on soaks, classes and treatments, and all guest room baths feature a Knot Springs salt scrub. Rooms start at

Hilton Garden Inn Portland Airport (12048 NE Airport Way, 503/255-8600): on-site restaurant

Hyatt Place Portland Airport/Cascade Station (9750 NE Cascades Pkwy, 503/288-2808): free breakfast

LaQuinta Inn & Suites Portland Airport (11207 NE Holman St, 503/382-3820): free breakfast, indoor pool

Radisson Hotel Portland Airport (6233 NE 78th Ct, 503/251-2000): on-site restaurant

Red Lion Hotel Portland Airport (7101 NE 82nd Ave, 503/255-6722): on-site restaurant and lounge

Residence Inn Portland Airport at Cascade Station (9301 NE Cascades Pkwy, 503/284-1800): free breakfast, indoor saltwater pool

Sheraton Portland Airport Hotel (8235 NE Airport Way, 503/281-2500); on-site restaurant, outstanding

SpringHill Suites Portland Airport (11922 NE Airport Way, 503/253-4095): breakfast buffet, indoor pool

350 square feet and have free Wi-Fi and a host of amenities aimed at getting a great night's sleep.

El Gaucho Portland

The Benson Hotel
319 SW Broadway   503/227-8794
Daily: 4:30-11 (Fri, Sat till midnight; Sun till 10)   elgaucho.com
Expensive

An extraordinary dinner at El Gaucho, where no detail is overlooked, will impress your clients or significant other. The well-orchestrated exhibition kitchen is in full swing turning out melt-in-your-mouth dry-aged prime steaks, meats, seafood and poultry expertly prepared on a charcoal grill or rotisserie. Elaborate tableside preparations include Caesar salad and carved chateaubriand. The showmanship continues with a flaming sword of brochettes of tenderloin. Flambéed desserts of Bananas Foster and cherries jubilee turn any occasion into a special occasion. A nice touch: a fruit and cheese dish served "on the house" after your table finishes their entrees. Enjoy nightly live music in the bar or retire to the clubby Cigar Lounge for single malt scotches, after-dinner drinks and imported cigars. The tab will be pricey, but visit this old-school destination when only the best will do.

Filson

526 NW 13th Ave   503/246-0900
Mon-Sat: 10-6; Sun: noon-6   filson.com

Since 1897, the creed and motto that this company has lived up to is "might as well have the best." Recreation enthusiasts or anyone whose profession puts them in the elements will find high-quality clothing and accessories at Filson's flagship store. Boots can be re-soled and garments repaired (contact customer service; 800/624-0201). Filson luggage is proudly handed down to next generations. Only the finest from Filson for canines, too: coats, beds, dog mats, leashes and even dog dishes are made from Filson's proprietary Tin Cloth.

Fink's Luggage & Repair Co.

517 SW 12th Ave   503/222-6086
Mon-Fri: 8:30-6; Sat: 9-5   finksluggage.com

For over 40 years travelers have been outfitted with Fink's savvy packing products. Luggage brands in every price range, wallets, briefcases, handbags and other travel necessities are offered, plus outstanding repair service, knowledgeable staff and personal attention. Alex Fink and crew repair all makes of luggage and leather jackets, replace linings, recondition leather items and work magic on handbags and briefcases. For excellent service, Fink's is the best!

Fogo de Chão

930 SW 6th Ave   503/241-0900
Lunch: Mon-Fri 11:30-2; Brunch: Sat-Sun 11:30-2
Dinner: Mon-Fri 4:30; Sat, Sun 2   fogodechao.com/location/portland
Expensive

This is not just an Americanized take on Brazilian cuisine; the founders of Fogo de Chão bring you authentic tastes straight from Southern Brazil, based on centuries-old traditions. The food is plentiful and unusual, the service friendly and efficient and the whole experience very pleasant, even if the tab is on the high side. Lunch is easier on the pocketbook. The Market Table is plentiful and fresh with special pricing available for a light lunch. Brazilian-trained gaucho chefs bring delicious skewers, including fire-roasted meats like filet mignon, ribeye, picanha, lamb chops, chicken, sausage and more. This is truly a feast for the eyes and the stomach.

Forktown Food Tours

503/234-3663
Office: Tue-Sat: 9-5 · forktownfoodtoursportland.com
Expensive

Rain or shine, Forktown Food Tours explore Portland's impressive food culture. The three-hour walking tours feature good eats with a side dish of commentary by restaurant owners, chefs and food crafters. Samples vary and may include microbrews or other libations, dishes made with locally-sourced ingredients, unusual desserts and only-in-Portland food cart cuisine. Current tours are North Mississippi Avenue, Downtown Portland, Division Street and Downtown Portland featuring the Farmer's Market (available seasonally); reservations necessary.

Gartner's Country Meat Market

7450 NE Killingsworth St · 503/252-7801
Tue-Sat: 9-6; Sun: 10-4 · gartnersmeats.com

Nearly 60 years ago, the late Jack Gartner opened his butcher shop with the mission statement of "People come for what's inside the case; they come back for the service behind the counter." From Jack's parents to his children, they all pitched in over the years; Jerry Minor came on as a business partner in 1965. The company has passed along generationally and today Sheri Gartner Puppo and Rick Minor (the "kids") continue this Portland institution with the same commitment. It's a busy and popular spot for always-fresh beef, pork, poultry, lunch meats and cheeses along with Traeger grills and pellets for just-right barbecuing; custom cutting and game processing are also offered. Three full smokehouses turn out the best handcrafted sausages (many also fresh or unsmoked), hams, bacon and specialties.

Gilda's Italian Restaurant

1601 SW Morrison St · 503/688-5066
Restaurant: Mon-Fri: 11:30-2 and 5-9 (Fri till 9:30),
Sat: 5-9:30; Sun: 5-9
Lounge: daily 4-11 (Fri, Sat till midnight) · gildasitalianrestaurant.com
Moderate

Grandma Gilda's home cooking influenced chef-owner Marco Roberti to pursue his passion for Italian food and entertaining. That enthusiasm led him to Italy where he immersed himself in cuisine, culture and cooking family dishes with his aunts and cousins, ultimately earning his master's degree in Italian Culinary Arts. With those experiences under his belt, he returned to Portland to open his own restaurant featuring his beloved grandmother's signature family dishes. Lunch features a number of smaller dishes, along with grilled paninis, pastas and risottos, plus a delicious lemon chicken breast with a dash of sherry. I like the Sformatino at dinnertime, a fabulous artichoke flan in a parmesan cheese sauce. The beloved Italian dish of prosciutto and melon is excellent; several veal dishes are house favorites and Italian black cherries served over housemade ice cream make a nice ending to a good meal. Gilda's Old World specialties will leave you satisfied and enamored with this family business which includes next-door Gilda's Lounge, a cozy spot for pizza, handcrafted cocktails and local beers and wines.

Goose Hollow Inn

1927 SW Jefferson St   503/228-7010
Daily: 11 a.m.-midnight (Fri till 1 a.m.)   goosehollowinn.com
Inexpensive

The history of the Goose Hollow Inn is as interesting as its proprietor, Bud Clark, Portland's mayor from 1985 to 1992. Bud's first tavern venture was the Spatenhaus (which was replaced by the Ira Keller Fountain). The Spatenhaus method, using a pizza oven to toast sandwiches, was developed with imagination by Bud and customers. The soul and simplicity of those days has been retained as Goose Hollow has evolved to match today's modern palates and interests. The Reuben sandwich is still referred to as "the best on the planet," vegetables, meats and other menu items are freshly-prepared on premise and there are no fried foods or hamburgers. Soups are homemade and fresh as are the salads (quinoa-beet, crab and shrimp Louis, spinach) with homemade dressings. Locally-produced hard liquor and wine join the lineup of 18 on-tap beers and ciders. Outside, the Portland Timbers Army has found a welcome watering hole on the deck; inside, framed historical photos and posters add to the cabin atmosphere. Bud's other notorieties are his enthusiastic "Whoop! Whoop!" greeting and as the trench coat-clad model for the famous poster entitled Expose Yourself to Art.

Grand Central Bakery

2230 SE Hawthorne Blvd   503/445-1600
3425 SW Multnomah Blvd   503/977-2024
7987 SE 13th Ave   503/546-3036
714 N Fremont St   503/546-5311
4440 NE Fremont St   503/808-9877
4412 SE Woodstock Blvd   503/953-1250
12595 NW Cornell Road   503/808-9878
Daily: Hours vary   grandcentralbakery.com

These artisan bakeries are conveniently situated around town. They craft breads to perfection: crusty on the outside, chewy on the inside and at their prime when eaten warm and generously buttered. Muffins, croissants, fruit tarts, cookies, pies and cakes are sweet choices; purchase one or be a hero and bring treats for the office. Ingredients for all breads and pastries are natural and top-quality. All locations serve sandwiches for breakfast and lunch, from-scratch soups, salads and seasonal specials; sack lunches are a specialty. Busy home cooks get a helping hand with balls of U-Bake pizza dough, rolls of puff pastry, pre-formed cookie dough and disks of pie dough ready to be transformed into "homemade" meals and desserts.

Headwaters
1001 SW Broadway   503/790-7752
Dinner: Daily 5-10 (Fri, Sat till 11);
Breakfast/Lunch: Mon-Fri 6:30-11/11-2
Brunch: Sat, Sun 8-3   headwaterspdx.com
Moderately expensive

Chef Vitaly Paley and his wife, Kimberly Paley, have opened Headwaters in the historic Heathman Hotel with the help of longtime manager and operations director Garrett Peck. The cuisine is focused on seafood and the fresh flavors of the Pacific Northwest. As is the restaurant, the dinner menu is modernized and may include catch-of-the-day seafood, paella and fish and chips, as well as offerings from land such as a half roasted chicken or New York strip steak. A sea bar welcomes guests to slurp raw oysters or indulge in caviar and smoked and kippered appetizers like house-cured salmon, sturgeon, sablefish and more. For breakfast choose among brioche French toast, huckleberry pancakes or a variety of omelets including Dungeness crab, among many offerings. The Heathman's weekend tea service lives on, but with a twist. Now known as the Russian Tea Experience (reservations required), the tradition stays true to Vitaly's roots.

FESTIVAL OF ROSES
Portland's annual **Rose Festival** (rosefestival.org) is a source of pride and community spirit. For over a century the event has kicked off each year in March with court selections from city high schools with one of the princesses named Queen of Rosaria at the highly-anticipated coronation event. Fun runs and walks, the Starlight Parade, dragon boat and milk carton boat races, fireworks, naval fleet participation, the Junior Parade and many more activities make up the four-month celebration, featuring the 4.2 mile Grand Floral Parade. Jeff Curtis, the chief executive officer, is an extraordinary leader. Check the website for schedules and other information.

The Heathman Hotel

1001 SW Broadway   503/241-4100, 800/551-0011
Expensive and up   heathmanhotel.com

The Heathman Hotel, a Portland cultural fixture since the day it opened in 1927, has undergone a full renovation of all 151 guest rooms and public spaces. Lighter, brighter and more contemporary, the new design is rooted in the building's unique history and pays homage to the hotel's role as muse to generations of guests. Those guests have included a literary who's who throughout the years and, over time, the hotel has amassed a 2,700-volume library of works signed by the authors that includes texts and novels by Pulitzer and Nobel Prize winners, past Presidents and U.S. Poet Laureates. The Heathman Hotel's library is the largest of its kind in the world. Upstairs, the guest rooms embrace the beauty of the Portland landscape with natural materials and reclaimed elements that create comfortable, sophisticated space for curling up with a good book surrounded by works from locally-based artists. Downstairs, Chef Vitaly Paley offers fresh Pacific Northwest cuisine at **Headwaters** (see detailed write-up), the hotel's restaurant, and weekend tea service known as the Russian Tea Experience (48-hour reservation required), in the renovated Tea Court Lounge. There are many more examples of culture and beauty at this ten-story brick landmark.

Hilton Portland & The Duniway Hotel

921 SW 6th Ave   503/226-1611
Moderate and up   hilton.com

Your author has spent many a night a guest in this downtown hotel. The management and staff are wonderful ambassadors offering exceptional world-class service. That is no small feat considering this is Oregon's largest convention hotel with 455 guest rooms. The building was constructed in 1963 and remodeled in summer 2017. The hotel boasts over 70,000 square feet of meeting space. In addition they offer a contemporary fitness center and complimentary Wi-Fi in the lobby. The on-site restaurant, **HopCity Tavern & Market**, is an American gastro pub that offers hearty comfort foods and seven local handcrafted beers on tap. It captures the spirit of Portland by supporting more than 16 local farmers, creameries, butchers and bakers. The restaurant and bar are open until 11:30 p.m. daily and offer a lavish happy hour. Across the street is **The Duniway**, embracing the artistic, creative and independent nature of Portland's trailblazing spirit. This bold boutique hotel delivers unscripted service and unexpected delights from an incredible staff. It has a pool and fitness center, and its brand new rooftop lounge, Abigail's Hideaway, offers a relaxing atmosphere with modern sofas and seating that is sectioned off by lush vegetation.

Celebrity chef Chris Cosentino's on-site restaurant, **Jackrabbit**, features an extensive raw bar, gin-centric cocktails, house-cured meats and dishes using local ingredients. Beyond the restaurant, the spacious upscale guest rooms are equipped with luxurious bath amenities, plush robes and Vittoria Espresso machines. The elegant Captain Gray ballroom and intimate conference rooms accommodate everything from corporate meetings to special events.

Hotel Eastlund

1021 NE Grand Ave   503/235-2100
Moderate to moderately expensive   hoteleastlund.com
Downtown Portland's Eastside neighborhood welcomes you to stay at their hotel located across from the Convention Center. This luxury boutique hotel is modern chic with many well-thought-out touches such as the beautiful art and faux fur throws in each room. Amenities and services are topnotch and include all that any full-service luxury hotel would have: high speed Internet, Keurig coffeemakers, smart refrigerators and HD television. Some rooms have soaking tubs. In addition, there's concierge service, a fitness center and plenty of meeting/event space. Within the hotel, restaurateur David Machado runs **Altabira City Tavern** (503/963-3600, altabira. com) and **Citizen Baker** (503/963-3610, citizenbaker.com). Altabira is a rooftop restaurant and bar perched above Portland's Lloyd district, a perfect match for the hotel's atmosphere. The panoramic views surround you as you lounge on outdoor sofas by the fire pits. Take a seat indoors in one of five private dining rooms and enjoy the same stunning views through floor-to-ceiling windows. The restaurant serves fresh, seasonal American cuisine. Extensive drink options include European and Northwest wines, locally-distilled spirits and 16 tap handles of local craft beers. Don't leave without stopping by the bakery for a fresh breakfast pastry.

Huber's Cafe

411 SW 3rd Ave   503/228-5686
Cafe: Mon-Thu 11:30-10 (Fri, Sat till 11); Sun 4-10   hubers.com
Bar: Mon-Thu till midnight; Fri, Sat till 1 a.m.
Moderate
Huber's was established in 1879 and is Portland's oldest-operating restaurant. The original location was at the corner of First and Alder and named The Bureau Saloon; this domain with a magnificent arched leaded-glass ceiling is on the ground floor of the Historic Oregon Pioneer Building. The history is an interesting read and stars Frank Huber, Jim Louie, turkey sandwiches, Prohibition and Spanish Coffee. The latest chapter of Huber's continues the Louie family's involvement, a tradition of turkey

---

GREATER PORTLAND B&Bs

If you are looking for a cozy lodging option when visiting Portland, here are some great bed and breakfasts:

Lion and the Rose (1810 NE 15th Ave, 503/287-9245): eight- room, 1906 Queen Anne mansion in Irvington District; seasonal services

Mayor's Mansion (3360 SE Ankeny St, 503/232-3588): four-room 1912 Albee House at Laurelhurst Park

Portland's White House (1914 NE 22nd Ave; 503/287-7131): luxurious 1911 Greek Revival mansion in Irvington District

---

(sandwiches and turkey cuisine are prominent on the menu) and Spanish Coffee (the signature drink) is still prepared tableside. Each week about 1,000 pounds of roasted turkey is served as entrees (picatta, marsala, enchiladas, wings, drumsticks) along with salads made with organic field greens, Certified Angus Beef steaks, seafood and pasta. Interesting fact: Huber's is said to use more Kahlua than any other independent restaurant in the United States.

Imperial

410 SW Broadway   503/228-7222
Dinner: Daily 5-10 (Fri, Sat till 11)
Breakfast/Lunch: Mon-Fri 6:30-11/11-2
Brunch: Sat, Sun 8-3   imperialpdx.com
Moderately expensive

It may have been the exceptional fried chicken that won me over to Imperial, another gem in Chef Vitaly Paley's crown. The menus change regularly with the season at this upscale restaurant at Hotel Lucia, but you will find that its "favorites" tend to be staples. Breakfast is simple with omelet variations, healthy small plates and favorites such as the Imperial French toast and pastrami hash. Fresh squeezed orange juice is always my go to, but fresh coffee and their morning cocktails are sure to wake you up. Lunch features a number of dishes including (but not limited to) a sausage soup, the signature Cobb salad, seasonal fish, a flat top burger, pasta, fresh oysters and other seafood. The dinner menu is a play off the lunch menu, but more extensive with several vegetarian, seafood, meat and poultry dishes. Local and imported wines, craft cocktails, ciders and beer complete the menu. Desserts include ports and dessert wines as well as warm chocolate chip cookies, caramel crème brûlée, the pie of the day (don't forget to make it a la mode) and more.

Irving Street Kitchen

701 NW 13th Ave   503/343-9440
Mon-Thu: 5:30-10; Fri-Sat: 10-2:30, 5:30-11;
Sun: 10-2:30, 5-9:30   irvingstreetkitchen.com
Moderate

Irving St. Kitchen is on the Pearl District's growing list of eateries. The space is large and airy and nice weather brings outdoor dining. Interesting snacks along with a reasonably-priced mix of charcuterie are good meal-starters. The New American menu includes about a dozen delicious first courses like meatballs with Yukon Gold mashed potatoes and sauce au poivre, barbecued shrimp or a tasty Bibb lettuce salad with Rogue blue cheese dressing. The menu changes regularly, but delicious fried chicken is always available. Desserts are inspired, including the ever-present butterscotch pudding with caramel sauce.

Jackrabbit

830 SW 6th Ave   503/412-1800
(See detailed listing with Hilton Portland & The Duniway Hotel)

Jake's Famous Crawfish

401 SW 12th Ave   503/226-1419
Mon-Thu: 11:30-10 (Fri, Sat till 11); Sun: 10-10   jakesfamouscrawfish.com
Moderate to expensive

Just the thought of Jake's crawfish makes my mouth water. If I've set my heart on a big 1½-pound bowl of the freshwater crustaceans boiled in a spicy broth, I call ahead to make sure they are fresh and on the menu (the season is roughly Easter to Halloween). Other delicious preparations are in pasta, cooked and chilled, Cajun-style or "popcorn" fried tails. The best, however, is the famous live crawfish boil. Lunch and dinner menus are printed daily to reflect the freshest bivalves, seafood and steaks; fresh catch is listed with the source of origin. Check out the daily Blue Plate lunch special and catch of the day priced at $10.95. Jake's clam chowder is legendary and you can't go wrong with a fabulous crab or shrimp cocktail or salad for lunch or dinner; sandwiches (turkey, crab, shrimp, chicken) are served for lunch. Dinner steaks are superb with the option of adding a lobster tail or jumbo scampi prawns to create a surf and turf combo to your liking. Chocolate truffle cake and bread pudding with bourbon anglaise have become famous in the dessert department. If you want just a bite, consider Jake's dessert trio with mini-portions of berry cobbler, truffle cake and crème brûlée. The bar is a popular after-work watering hole, as well as a great venue for groups and banquets. Jake's has rightfully earned a spot in the top ten seafood restaurants in America and has been a Portland fixture since 1892.

Kachka

720 SE Grand Ave   503/235-0059
Daily: 4-midnight   kachkapdx.com
Moderate to moderately expensive

Note: Kachka plans to open a new location in this same neighborhood in summer 2018, so please check the website for details.

Bonnie Morales, a 2018 James Beard finalist for best Northwest chef, is making a name for herself with her traditional Russian cuisine. The first things you're likely to notice on the dinner menu (served until 10 p.m.) are the hot and cold "zakuski" options (roughly translated as "drinking food," because these entrees and hors d'oeuvres are traditionally accompanied by a shot of vodka). These dishes include caviar varieties, an Eastern European-inspired meat and cheese board, cured duck breast and rabbit satsivi. Other items on the menu include chicken blinchiki (pot pie-inspired stuffed crepes), lamb skewers, dumplings, pickled vegetables and cabbage-wrapped meat. Also offered (until midnight) are about 50 different vodkas (Russian, European and American), housemade infusions, craft cocktails and Eastern European-focused wines and beers. Reservations are recommended.

Kenny & Zuke's Delicatessen

1038 SW Stark St   503/222-3354
Mon-Thu: 7 a.m.-8 p.m. (Fri till 9 p.m.); Sat: 8 a.m.-9 p.m.; Sun: 8-8
2376 NW Thurman St   503/954-1737
Mon-Fri: 8-3; Sat, Sun: 8-5   kennyandzukes.com
Moderate

There are delis, then there is Kenny & Zuke's. And now there are two locations. They arguably have the best pastrami sandwich in town, made with brisket that is cured for a week, smoked for ten hours and steamed for three hours. It is served between slices of housemade rye bread or toast, or with chopped liver and cole slaw. The most popular version is a glorious Reuben with sauerkraut, Swiss cheese and Russian dressing, then grilled and served with K&Z's pickles and potato salad. Other hearty hot and cold sandwiches (such as meatloaf and create-your-own double deckers) round out the lunch and dinner menu. There's much more: smoked and pickled fish, noodle kugel, rugelach, hot dogs, burgers and fries, salads and homemade desserts. Breakfasts feature deli case meats with eggs, bagels or in omelets as well as latkes, blintzes and weekend Benedicts and biscuits. Eat in, take out, rent the deli for your private event or arrange for the crew to cater your party; any way you slice it, these places are winners.

Ken's Artisan Bakery

338 NW 21st Ave   503/248-2202

Mon-Sat: 7-6 (Mon till 9:30); Sun: 8-5   kensartisan.com

Moderate

Boulangerie and patisserie proprietor Ken Forkish has honed his craft as an artisan baker exceptionally well and has justifiably been recognized in the local and national media for his rustic breads and luscious pastries. The latter are jaw-dropping creative works of art, handmade with real butter, fresh fruits, rich chocolate and other fine ingredients. Lunch fare (sandwiches, soups, salads) is served in the cafe in addition to the any-time bakery items and coffee drinks. Ken thoroughly researched flours and settled upon a local, sustainable product for his breads, croissants and pizzas. Pizzas are so popular that they have made Monday "Pizza Night" with extended hours to 9:30. You'll find Ken's breads on the tables of some of Portland's best restaurants and at select retailers; for the best selection, visit the bakery. **Ken's Artisan Pizza** (304 SE 28th Ave, 503/517-9951) was opened to accommodate the demand for the Italian pies — thin, crisp and baked in a wood-fired oven; open daily for dinner.

Kidd's Toy Museum

1301 SE Grand Ave   503/233-7807

By appointment   kiddstoymuseum.org

Free

Portlander Frank Kidd has amassed an enviable collection of vintage toys, mostly from the years 1869 to 1939. Mechanical coin banks, die-cast cars and trucks, Disney figurines, dolls, trains and toys from later years as well are displayed in glass-front cases. Kidd has traveled near and far to add to his collection and and has acquired pieces from friends. There's much to see and memories to recall. Tours are available by appointment.

Kimpton Hotel Monaco Portland

506 SW Washington St   503/222-0001, 888/207-2201

Expensive   monaco-portland.com

For a luxurious night in downtown amid museums, boutiques and large shops, amazing restaurants, nightclubs and entertainment, stay at Hotel Monaco Portland. A vibrant, ornate lobby, the site of morning coffee and tea service, greets guests at this Kimpton Hotel property. Each of the 221 rooms and suites are awash with a tasteful assortment of colorful furnish-ings and Italian Frette linens atop deep pillow top beds. Classy French doors separate sleeping and living areas in the roomy suites, a nice touch when enjoying in-room spa services. Standard conveniences include flat-panel TVs, private mini-bars, personal coffeemakers, laptop-compatible safes and fun animal print bathrobes. A hosted evening wine reception, 24/7 fitness center, PressReader digital newspapers, morning coffee in the lobby and use of bicycles are complimentary to guests. Four-legged companions are welcome on the pet-friendly floor with special services. Guests with allergies can enjoy one of three hypo-allergenic floors that have never seen a pet. These floors feature synthetic comforters and foam pillows (no down), special HEPA filter vacuums and room air filters and allergen- and scent-free cleaning products; hypo-allergenic toiletries are available on request. Adjacent to the Monaco, **Red Star Tavern** (503/222-0005, redstartavern.com) provides round-the-clock room service; but to experience the Portland vibe, head on over for phenomenal American cuisine with a twist; creative cocktails and an impressive whiskey selection.

Kimpton RiverPlace Hotel
1510 SW Harbor Way   503/228-3233, 800/227-1333
Moderate to very expensive   riverplacehotel.com
This is one of Portland's finest settings — downtown Portland along the Willamette River. The city and river vistas are stunning, but never more so than on a sunny day when watercraft navigate the sparkling waterway. Miles of walking paths front the RiverPlace connecting pedestrians with bustling or tranquil neighborhood eateries and shops (complimentary guest use of hotel bicycles). Consider staying here when you attend events at adjacent Tom McCall Waterfront Park or book a river view room for the annual parade of Christmas ships alternating between the Willamette and Columbia rivers. Luxury abounds in the 85 spacious rooms and suites at this Kimpton Craftsman-style boutique hotel; upscale in-room features are the norm as well as refrigerators stocked with local and organic snacks, yoga mats, umbrellas and electronic conveniences. Seasonal cooking has diners looking forward to breakfast, lunch, dinner and weekend brunch at **King Tide Fish & Shell** (503/295-6166; kingtidefishandshell.com).

Laurelhurst Market
3155 E Burnside St   503/206-3097
Restaurant: Daily: 5-10   laurelhurstmarket.com
Moderate
Butcher shop: Daily: 10-10   503/206-3099
Most of the day Laurelhurst Market is a first-rate butcher shop offering hormone-free and antibiotic-free meats. Choose from uncommon items such as cured meats, duck confit, housemade lard and 12 varieties of sausage. Special requests are not a problem. Tuesday is fried chicken day in the butcher shop (starting at 11 until it's gone) and deli-style and daily special sandwiches are prepared each day between 11 and 5 along with

soups and salads. The steakhouse-inspired brasserie serves an intriguing selection of hors d'oeuvres, including a charcuterie plate, marrow bones and beef tartare. Steaks and chops, though, are the signature dishes. The name is a bit deceiving; it is not where you shop for bread, butter or eggs.

Le Pigeon

738 E Burnside St   503/546-8796
Daily: 5-10   lepigeon.com
Expensive

True to Portland's persona, Le Pigeon is fine dining in a hole-in-the-wall establishment. Cuisine is French-inspired and features inventive game dishes such as rabbit, duck, pigeon and quail as well as beef and fish. Chef Gabriel Rucker offers five- and seven-course tasting menus. Every nook and cranny of the small restaurant is used with pigeonholed wine bottles becoming part of the decor. The open kitchen is in full view and best observed from the Chef's Counter. Craving breakfast or lunch? Visit their two sister restaurants. **Little Bird** (219 SW 6th Ave, 503/688-5952; littlebirdbistro.com) is open weekdays for lunch and daily for dinner — fine dining in more refined surroundings. **Canard** (734 E Burnside St, 971/279-2356; canardpdx.com), located next door to Le Pigeon, serves up breakfast, lunch and dinner daily with a focus on wine, cocktails and "wild French bar food"; weekend brunch available.

Made in Oregon

Pioneer Place, 340 SW Morrison St, Suite 1300   503/241-3630
Lloyd Center, 1017 Lloyd Center   503/282-7636
Washington Square, 9571 SW Washington Square Road   503/620-4670
Clackamas Town Center, 12000 SE 82nd Ave   503/659-3155
Portland International Airport, Oregon Market   503/282-7827
Portland International Airport, Concourse C   503/335-6563
Hours vary   madeinoregon.com

Since 1975 Made in Oregon has been the source for the best Oregon products under one roof: Pendleton blankets and clothing, gourmet foods (cheese, candies, nuts, salmon, cookies, jams and jellies), wines, jewelry, home accessories, books, T-shirts, Oregon State University and University of Oregon paraphernalia and souvenirs. The mix is extensive, and many items are assembled into attractive gift boxes and baskets. At the helm of Made in Oregon is legendary Sam Naito. The Naito family has a long history of community service, philanthropy and commerce in Oregon. Also find stores in Salem (Salem Center, 401 Center St NE, 503/362-4106); Eugene (296 E Fifth Ave, Suite119, 541/393-6891) and Newport (342 SW Bay Blvd, 541/574-9020).

Mama Mia Trattoria

439 SW 2nd Ave   503/295-6464
Daily: 11-9   mamamiatrattoria.com
Moderate

This busy downtown trattoria is located just off the Morrison Bridge. Crystal chandeliers, marble-top tables and gilded mirrors create a warm and inviting destination for the whole family. Food is traditional Italian — slow-cooked, made from scratch and plentiful. Housemade mozzarella and desserts are some of the many items that are prepared daily. Lunch choices include salads, sandwiches, pizzas and homemade pastas and potato gnocchi. As the sun sets, offerings include cioppino, chicken marsala, chicken and veal parmesan, jumbo prawns scampi and traditional pastas with pomodoro sauce simmered to perfection and married with cheeses, sumptuous meatballs and other fine additions. The extensive bar menu includes Chianti, Prosecco, Northwest wines, beers and specialty cocktails; happy hour eats are value priced. Try sinful amaretto cheesecake, rich cannolis or delicate sorbets for dessert.

The Meadow

3731 N Mississippi Ave   503/288-4633, 888/388-4633
Daily: 10-7
805 NW 23rd Ave   503/305-3388
Daily: 11-8   themeadow.com

Question: If you mix craft cooking and finishing salts, some of the world's great chocolates, throw in an interesting selection of Oregon and European wines, handcrafted bitters and fresh-cut flowers, what do you get? Answer: A very beautiful business called The Meadow. Mark Bitterman turned his love of food and travel into this unique shop. Exploring over 120 of the world's salt varieties, an array of more than 500 chocolate bars, 200 bitters for cocktails and delicious Oregon pinot noirs (so good with chocolate) makes for quite a mix-and-match experience. Tastings and classes are held at the shop from time to time. If you're in New York City, another Meadow location is in Manhattan's West Village (523 Hudson St, 212/645-4633); sans wine.

Mehri's Bakery & Cafe

6923 SE 52nd Ave   503/788-9600
Mon, Tue: 7-3; Wed-Fri: 7-7; Sat: 8-5; Sun: 8-2   mehris.com

Check out Mehri's for specialty cakes and desserts just like mom used to make: apple, berry and pumpkin chiffon pies; fruit cobblers and company's coming chocolate fudge cake. Not only does Mehri produce spectacular sweets (and custom wedding cakes), but she also offers the unusual twist of Persian delights (pomegranate chicken stew, shish kabobs and crusty bottom rice to name a few), along with more traditional fare for breakfast and lunch. At this time a large focus of the business is on wedding cakes and catering needs.

Mother's Bistro & Bar

212 SW Stark St   503/464-1122
Tue-Thu: 7-9; Fri: 7-10; Sat 8 10   mothersbistro.com
Moderate

Mother always said to clean your dinner plate before dessert. Fortunately, this mother does not make that admonishment! The oh-so-good pies vary according to the season and are baked fresh. In fact, all desserts are made with rich butter, cream, local fruits and quality ingredients. The devil's food cake with chocolate ganache is good and gooey! Mom would approve of the comfort food meals, often updated to appease more sophisticated tastes. For example; wild salmon hash, chicken salad, macaroni and cheese, meatloaf, beef pot roast and greens (salads and side dishes). Successful chef-owner Lisa Schroeder brings a wealth of experience from her training and experience on the East Coast, the Mediterranean and Europe. Specials change monthly to reflect the background cuisine of assorted mothers. This is a comfortable and dependable breakfast, lunch or dinner spot to take business associates, family and mom for people-pleasing meals "made with love."

Mucca Osteria

1022 SW Morrison St   503/227-5521
Mon-Sat: 5-10   muccaosteria.com
Moderately expensive

This is a success story about a native of Rome who relocated to Portland and opened an Italian restaurant featuring indigenous wines and authentic fare. The place is beautiful and welcoming and steeped in the aroma of fresh bread. An interesting side note is that they make their own natural yeast derived from the fermentation of raisins. Homemade pasta and rich seasonal dishes include winners such as slow-braised wild boar ragu, stewed rabbit, fish and seafood and poultry offerings. Multi-course tasting menus are served at dinner and are best enjoyed with outstanding wines or signature cocktails.

Multnomah Whiskey Library

1124 SW Alder St   503/954-1381
Daily: 4-midnight (Fri, Sat till 1 a.m.)   multnomahwhiskeylibrary.com

Portland has a very innovative whiskey bar, the inspiration of Portland real estate owner and civic promoter Greg Goodman and his nephew, Alan Davis. In a smallish upstairs space they have created one of the most appealing rooms in the city. With painted glass skylights, period pieces from abroad, historic pictures and leather banquette seating, the place is a real charmer. Along the walls are 1,600 whiskey bottles (including after-dinner drink selections) and wines and beers to choose from. Extremely polite mixologists will prepare your drink at the table. The menu includes plates to be shared like oysters, a salumi (pork cold cuts) board, fried cauliflower, pork and octopus along with razor clam linguini, a cheeseburger and steaks; all meant to be paired with fine libations and conversation. Memberships (at $650 per) sell out in a hurry; they allow the bearer to make reservations and access other perks. Otherwise, best you arrive before 4 p.m. Monday through Saturday, as the line is long. Educational seminars and special events (some for members only) are offered periodically.

New Seasons Market

7300 SW Beaverton-Hillsdale Hwy	503/292-6838
3495 SW Cedar Hills Blvd	503/641-4181
15861 SE Happy Valley Town Center Dr	503/558-9214
1214 SE Tacoma St	503/230-4949
6400 N Interstate Ave	503/467-4777
3210 NE Broadway St	503/282-2080
5320 NE 33rd Ave	503/288-3838
2170 NW Raleigh St	503/224-7522

DINING ALONG DIVISION AND CLINTON STREETS

One of the Portland's exciting dining areas is Southeast Division Street (and nearby Clinton Street) where you can find a variety of food options any time of day. Check out the area's tasty offerings at these restaurants:

Ava Gene's (3377 SE Division St, 971/229-0571): Northwest-inspired menu features produce and meats grown by local ranchers and farmers; dinner daily

Broder (2508 SE Clinton St, 503/736-3333): small Swedish restaurant, Scandinavian brunch

Fifty Licks (2021 SE Clinton St, 503/395-3333): scratch-made ice cream

Jacqueline (2039 SE Clinton St, 503/327-8637): seafood restaurant/oyster bar; dinner nightly

La Moule (2500 SE Clinton St, 971/339-2822): European-style bistro, frites, seafood; dinner nightly, Sunday brunch

Lauretta Jean's (3402 SE Division St, 503/235-3119): pie bakery; daily brunch (till 3) and cocktails

Little T. Baker (2600 SE Division St; 503/238-3458): breads, sweets, pastries; daily breakfast and lunch

4034 SE Hawthorne Blvd	503/236-4800
1954 SE Division St	503/445-2888
4500 SE Woodstock Blvd	503/771-9663
3445 N Williams Ave	503/528-2888
6300 N Lombard St	503/289-0834
14805 SW Barrows Road, Beaverton	503/597-6777
1453 NE 61st Ave, Hillsboro	503/648-6968
3 Monroe Pkwy, Lake Oswego	503/496-1155
7703 SW Nyberg St, Tualatin	503/692-3535
2100-B SE 164th Ave, Vancouver	360/760-5005
Daily	newseasonsmarket.com

On Leap Day 2000, Raleigh Hills welcomed an upstart grocer to their community. Now 18 New Seasons Markets in the Pacific Northwest are committed to providing an easy, fun and friendly neighborhood shopping experience — one that meets customers' needs for both national brand staples and local sustainable products. You'll find quality merchandise in all departments: bakery, beer and wine, bulk, cheese, deli, floral, grocery, meat, pastry, produce, seafood and wellness. But the neighborhood stores are about more than just groceries — they are about people. By supporting New Seasons and the local economy, they in turn, give grants and donations back to the area while their employees volunteer. In 2014

Nuestra Cocina (2135 SE Division St; 503/232-2135): old-peasant-style Mexican cooking; dinner Tuesday through Saturday

Off the Waffle (2601 SE Clinton St, 503/946-1608): daily breakfast of amazing liege waffle creations; interesting bathrooms

Pine State Biscuits (1100 SE Division St, Suite 100, 503/236-3356): biscuits and Southern cooking

Pok Pok (3226 SE Division St, 503/232-1387): Northern Thai food hot spot; lunch and dinner daily

Roman Candle Baking (377 SE Division St, 971/302-6605): plant-based, dairy-free, gluten-free, soy-free; daily till 4

Whiskey Soda Lounge (3131 SE Division St, 503/232-0102): serves Aahaan Kap Klaem (the drinking food of Thailand); across the street from sister eatery Pok Pok

Xico (3715 SE Division St, 503/548-6343): Mexican restaurant serving a fresh, seasonal menu, lunch Wednesday through Sunday, dinner nightly

New Seasons partnered with more than 900 local nonprofits dedicated to addressing hunger, public education and conservation.

The Nines

525 SW Morrison St   503/222-9996, 877/229-9995
Moderate and up   thenines.com

Of course I maintain a keen interest in the goings-on at Meier & Frank Square. After all, I spent a good part of my life there. The Nines opened as a modern luxury hotel in 2008, filling the floors above the former Macy's retail space with 331 guest rooms and 13 suites, meeting facilities, an atrium, fitness center, library and rooftop dining. It is spectacular and a great addition to Portland's downtown. Oregon artists are featured in the eighth-floor lobby, also the location of a charming library with more than 1,000 books from Powell's bookstore. Guest rooms and suites are tastefully appointed, sleek and tranquil. Guests on the 12th-floor club level receive light breakfasts, snacks and evening libations. The one bedroom Meier & Frank Suite affords spectacular city views from the comfortable living room; the dining room accommodates up to eight. During the summer, it's hard to beat the two view patios that add to the spectacular ambience at **Departure Restaurant + Lounge**. Here you can enjoy dinner or a late night visit in the rooftop setting; more private, classy seating is available inside. Small plates of sushi and dim sum, with specialties like Kobe meatballs and barbecue short rib buns are available. Chef Gregory Gourdet's kushiyaki grill and wok dishes feature a variety of chicken and meats; a favorite is Ishiyaki steak, a stone-grilled Wagyu strip steak served on a sizzling hot stone. The **Urban Farmer** is a first-rate steakhouse with inviting country-chic decorative touches. A huge table in the middle seats up to 16 diners; make a friend at breakfast, lunch, dinner or weekend brunch. Yes, my friends, the top floors of my family's department store have been spiffed up "to the nines."

Northwest Film Center

1219 SW Park Ave   503/221-1156
(See detailed listing with Portland Art Museum)

Nostrana

1401 SE Morrison St   503/234-2427
Lunch: Mon-Fri 11:30-2; Dinner: daily 5-10 (Fri, Sat till 11)   nostrana.com
Moderate

Nostrana is large and busy, with an energy level as high as any dining spot in Portland. This rustic Italian eatery, meaning "ours" in Italian, features a daily changing menu of simple homemade food from local sources. Resist filling up on the fresh baked bread and olive oil, because you'll want to save room for great starters like charcuterie and insalata. Interesting pastas are made in-house, and fish, seafood, chicken, pork and beef plates come with fingerling potatoes, lentils or other preparations. In traditional style, uncut pizzas are brought to your table along with a pair of scissors (fun for kids). Fine wines and baked-to-order seasonal fruit crisps complete the meal. Enjoy their open-air patio in season. Also check out Enoteca Nostrana, their wine bar that opened in May 2018 (daily 4 to midnight). It's a great place for private dining and events.

Oregon Historical Society Museum

1200 SW Park Ave   503/306-5198
Mon-Sat: 10-5; Sun: noon-5   ohs.org
Reasonable
For anyone wanting to understand the Oregon story, the Oregon History Museum, located in Portland's Park Blocks, is a required stop. Operated since 1898 by the Oregon Historical Society, the museum hosts an impressive number of permanent and temporary exhibits. A new $4 million "Experience Oregon" showcase exhibit will open on Oregon's 160th birthday — February 14, 2019. A recent addition is the "History Hub," an award-winning exhibit designed for families that highlights the histories of Oregon's diverse population. The museum has a research library that is home to the country's most extensive collection of maps, books, films and photographs relating to Oregon's rich history. OHS also sponsors an extensive array of programs and lectures. Executive Director Kerry Tymchuk is, like Oregon, one-of-a-kind.

Oregon Zoo

4001 SW Canyon Road   503/226-1561
Daily   oregonzoo.org
Reasonable
Lions and tigers and bears — oh, yes! You, your family and friends will want to visit all of the animal friends at the Oregon Zoo. Chimpanzees and elephants are especially popular, too. The zoo's origins date back to 1888 with a few animals collected from a Portland pharmacist's seafaring friends. Today, the menagerie has grown from one "she grizzly" to over 2,200 animals. The zoo encompasses 64 acres of exhibits (Great Northwest, Fragile Forests, Asia, Pacific Shores, Africa), exotic plants, a one-mile loop railway, eateries, gift shops and a petting zoo for the pint-size set. The zoo's focus centers on animal enrichment, zoological knowledge, education, sustainable operations and conservation. Over 1.6 million folks visit this animal kingdom each year; other popular events include summertime concerts on the lawn, camps and classes and the annual holiday ZooLights extravaganza. Keep an eye out for new zoo friends and

exhibits as big changes are under way at the Oregon Zoo between 2018 and 2020. Nearly half the zoo grounds will be getting an upgrade; paths will remain open.

The Original Pancake House

8601 SW 24th St   503/246-9007
Wed-Sun: 7-3   originalpancakehouse.com
Moderate
(See detailed listing in Salem, Chapter 2)

Otto's Sausage Kitchen

4138 SE Woodstock Blvd   503/771-6714
Mon-Sat: 9:30-6; Sun: 11-5   ottosausage.com
Since 1929 the Eichentopf family has produced smoked and fresh sausages; one of Portland's best sausage purveyors. Over 40 different kinds of sausage (including wieners and bockwurst) are made on-site including Otto's own recipes brought over from Germany. The neighborhood deli is a reliable source for imported cheeses, craft beers and wines, condiments, homemade salads, candies, sandwiches and catering. Both sausages and merchandise can also be purchased online.

Pacific Fish & Oyster

3380 SE Powell Blvd   503/233-4891
Mon-Fri: 9-6   pacseafood.com
You know the fish is fresh if you shop here. Begun by the Dulcich family more than 70 years ago, these folks showcase fresh local crab, salmon, oysters and shrimp. The business has expanded to nearly 40 fish and seafood processing and distribution facilities from Alaska to Texas. From those plants and worldwide imports, customers enjoy one of the largest selections in this area. In addition, they supply Dungeness crabs for fundraising crab feeds and ship Northwest fish and seafood across the country.

Pacific Pie Co.

1520 SE 7th Ave   503/381-6157
Daily: 11:30-9   pacificpie.com
Moderate
If you have a craving for pie, sweet or savory, head to Pacific Pie Co. The assortment of handmade savories includes classic beef (and mushroom variations), steak and cheese, creamy chicken and shepherds pies as well as a roast lamb version and spinach and cheese pasties. Order an outstanding pie floater which features your favorite meat pie or pastie floated in a bowl of homemade pea soup. Salads, potatoes and other sides com-

plete the hearty meal and it would be worth checking their website before you go for new and special offerings. But most importantly — those dessert pies! Fresh, local fruits are turned into delectable creations and sold whole or by the slice. A sample of the weekly selections includes apple sour cream streusel and key lime pies, chocolate salted caramel tarts, lamingtons (sponge cake covered in chocolate icing and coconut) and ANZAC biscuits (both are Australian favorites). Desserts are an integral part of many dinner parties; please give the busy bakers 48-hour notice ahead of time so you and your guests won't be disappointed.

Paley's Place

1204 NW 21st Ave   503/243-2403
Mon-Thu: 5:30-10; Fri, Sat: 5-11; Sun: 5-10   paleysplace.net
Moderately expensive to expensive
Culinary duo Kimberly and Vitaly Paley perfected their roles as general manager and executive chef at fine establishments in New York and France, then lure of the Northwest's sustainable and seasonal products brought them to Portland. Among this city's restaurants where they showcase their talents is Paley's Place, a beautiful house with two dining rooms and a wide front porch. Picture perfect charcuterie (order a single serving or tastes of three, five or one of each) and desserts are delicious. Superb entrees are planned around the availability of seasonal ingredients. To bring out the best flavors and qualities, preparations are braised, roasted or grilled. Relax and unwind at the cozy full-service bar with Oregon and French wines, handcrafted cocktails or an always-popular Paley's Burger; the happy hour menu is not to be missed.

The Palm Court Restaurant and Bar

309 SW Broadway   503/228-2000
(See detailed listing with The Benson Hotel)

Park Kitchen

422 NW 8th Ave   503/223-7275
Tue-Sat: 5-9   parkkitchen.com
Moderate
Located on the North Park Blocks in Portland's Pearl District, Park Kitchen provides inspired American fare utilizing the bounty of Oregon's own farms, ranches and fisheries to craft seasonal food and wine menus. Chef/ owner Scott Dolich is a true genius in the kitchen with original compositions as well as updated favorites. Small hot plates (chickpea fries with squash ketchup or sunchoke soup, hazelnut dukkah, truffle), small cold plates (duck ham, halibut carpaccio, lamb tartare), large plates (seared

salmon, sorrel, potatoes, leeks) and desserts (apple butter crepes or buñuelos with blood orange compote and chevre crème anglaise) are uniformly delicious. Visit on a warm evening when you can sit outside and enjoy a view of the park and busy bocce ball court.

Pearl Bakery

102 NW 9th Ave   503/827-0910
Mon-Fri: 6:30-4; Sat: 7-4; Sun: 8-3   pearlbakery.com

Fragrant fresh loaves of bread fill the space at family-owned Pearl Bakery, in business since 1997. Unique flavors and textures are achieved using different leavening methods to extend fermentation, and as a result, each variety of bread is unique. Pugliese is the signature variety, characterized by its chewy crust and dense holes and a hint of extra-virgin olive oil. Loaves vary in size and shape, from petite French rolls up to the four-pound walnut levain. Loaves are sold as baguettes, rounds and in decorative shapes and almost all breads are vegan. Over the years Pearl Bakery has received national attention for its artisanal breads, decedent chocolate chunk cookies and gibassier (a spiced French pastry). For lunch, hot sandwiches are made to order and cold sandwiches are available from the retail case. Both are made with Pearl's breads, natural meats, imported cheeses and organic greens.

Pearl Specialty Market & Spirits

900 NW Lovejoy St   503/477-8604
Mon-Sat: 9 a.m.-10 p.m.; Sun: noon-8   pearlspecialty.com

Talk about a liquor store on steroids! By the numbers it has over 1,000 spirits, 500 wines, 500 beers and 300 cigars. Those are labels, not actual pieces. They carry an impressive array of top-shelf bottles and imported and locally-produced wines, spirits and beers; champagnes; sakés; bitters; syrups and barware. The more exclusive (read very expensive) products, including a bottle of Remy Martin Louis XIII cognac, are in a specialty case behind lock and key; special orders are welcome. Unlike run-of-the-mill Oregon Liquor Control Commission outlets, Pearl Specialty stocks all these items including an extensive selection of craft beers, world wines, hard-to-find vermouths, mixers and bitters under one roof. They also have a glass-walled, temperature- and humidity-controlled walk-in humidor that pairs well with the extensive bourbon and scotch selection.

Pendleton Stores
Pendleton Woolen Mills

8500 SE McLoughlin Blvd   503/535-5786
Blankets, home, bags, accessories

WOOL & PRINCE

The creative force behind the Wool & Prince online clothing store (woolandprince.com, with a showroom in Southeast Portland) seems to know a lot about wool – as a fabric: its wearability, durability, functionality. The guy should. His name is **Mac Bishop**, of the same Bishop family that owns and runs Pendleton Woolen Mills. He's the son of Mort Bishop, who is now Pendleton's chairman. Mac Bishop launched the online business in 2013 in a Kickstarter campaign. It sells wool business attire, mainly button-down and dress shirts, but also underwear, T-shirts, Henleys, polos, boxers, socks and other items. The idea is that because wool is more durable and efficient than other fibers at evaporating absorbed sweat, it could be worn more often between washings, and thus last longer (and also thus justifying the now $128 price of a button-down). The media went gaga in 2013 about the original W&P pitch that you could wear one of its shirts 100 times before it needed a wash. That may be debatable, but the marketing has evolved. It appears now that, at least from looking at the website, what Wool & Prince really is selling is a lifestyle – with a dress shirt attached to it. That's a different approach to business than the one his ancestors took when they started Pendleton Woolen Mills. But hey, it's all good. Both may wind up at the same place: as purveyors of first-rate quality merchandise. Those shirts really do look snazzy. The showroom is at 2505 SE 11th Ave, Suite 339. Hours are 2 to 5 p.m. Thursdays and Fridays (or schedule an appointment online).

Mon-Sat: 10-5:30; Sun: 11-4
Pendleton Home Store
210 NW Broadway   503/535-5444
Clothing, blankets, home, bags, accessories
Mon-Sat: 10-5:30
Pendleton Portland Airport
7000 NE Airport Way   503/282-1235
Clothing, blankets, home, bags, accessories
Daily: 6-9
Pendleton Park Avenue West
825 SW Yamhill St   503/242-0037
Clothing, blankets, home, bags, accessories
Mon-Fri: 10-8; Sun: 11-7   pendleton-usa.com
Pendleton is one of the best known brands to come out of Oregon. Founded in 1909, Pendleton Woolen Mills still does its own manufacturing at its

Pendleton mill, and in Washougal,Washington, too. The foundation of Pendleton Woolen Mills is its vertical manufacturing — controlling the process from wool purchase to finished product. Its signature product is the Pendleton blanket, and it's hard not to see the intense colors and layers of Oregon's Painted Hills reflected in many of the multi-stripe designs. There are other blanket variations, of course, including those with Native American and Western motifs, and contemporary designs as well. Pendleton is also known for men's tough woolen shirts, and today the company has branched out into clothing more generally, as well as home furnishings and linens, accessories and more. The company was founded by Clarence, Roy and Chauncey Bishop, and today a sixth generation of the family leads this privately-held business. John Bishop is currently president and CEO. Admired for their corporate citizenship and participation in countless civic activities, the Bishop family and the Pendleton brand are true Oregon treasures. In addition to stores listed here, you'll find Pendleton stores or outlets in Lincoln City, Seaside, Medford, Eugene, Woodburn, Bend, Troutdale and Pendleton, and products online and at select retailers throughout Oregon and worldwide.

Petite Provence/La Provence

1824 NE Alberta St	503/284-6564
4834 SE Division St	503/233-1121
7000 NE Airport Way	503/493-4460
Daily: Hours vary	provencepdx.com

Originally from France, the owners of these bistros strive to create a nostalgic French atmosphere in their establishments, and they have become an integral part of their neighborhoods. Menus are similar at each location, but chefs operate in their own creative styles. Omelets, French toast, Benedicts, hash and more are available for breakfast; lunch patrons enjoy salad, sandwich and soup choices. The dinner menu includes salads and a vari-

ROBERT MILLER

Robert G. "Bob" Miller knows the retail and grocery business like the back of his hand. That's not surprising since he's been in the retail business, specifically the grocery industry, for over half a century, working his way up the ladder to manage the likes of Albertsons Companies, Inc., Fred Meyer, Inc. and Rite Aid Corporation. With his keen business acumen he led exponential growth, acquisitions and turnarounds of several companies. Back home in Portland, he is a well-respected civic leader and he and his wife, Sharon, are extremely generous contributors to myriad causes.

ety of small plates featuring classic French specialties such as Boeuf Bourgignon and Coq au Riesling. La Provence is the ideal happy hour meeting place with outstanding wine, beer and cocktail selections. Throughout the day enjoy wonderful fresh bakery goods from cases filled with yummy croissants, chocolate treats galore and fruit tarts. Additionally, check out sister locations **La Provence Bakery and Bistro** (16350 SW Boones Ferry Road, Lake Oswego, 503/635-4533; 15151 SW Barrows Road, No. 153, Beaverton, 971/246-8627) and **Petite Provence of the Gorge** (408 E 2nd St, The Dalles, 541/506-0037).

Piazza Italia

1129 NW Johnson St   503/478-0619
Lunch: daily 11:30-3
Dinner: Sun-Tue 5-9:30; Wed, Thu 5-10; Fri, Sat 5-11   piazzaportland.com
Moderate

For an authentic Italian meal, visit this fun Pearl District eatery. In 2000, the late Gino Schettini and Kevin Gorretta, a fellow Italian descendant, realized their dream for their own restaurant. Now members of Gino's family (Amy and Brian) carry on his vision of providing fantastic food from a large menu. Start with bruschetta with sauteed mushrooms, pancetta, fresh garlic, parsley and white wine. Order sauces like garlic marinara and wild boar meat sauce to accompany your chosen pasta. Linguine squarciarella is highly recommended. Adding to the appeal is good friendly service, lively Italian conversations and a bent for celebrating soccer. You can easily stock your fridge with the large selection of Italian wines and meats and cheeses from the deli counter. Ciao!

The Picnic House

723 SW Salmon St   503/227-0705
Lunch: Mon-Sat 11-3
Dinner: Mon-Thu 5-9 (Fri, Sat till 10)   picnichousepdx.com
Moderate

Picnic House, in the nearly century-old lobby of the original Heathman Hotel, is the project of Aaron and Jessica Grimmer. The classical two-story interior boasts the original hand-tiled floors and rich wood. Colorful mosaics of old printing plates embellish the walls and stair risers and retain the historical local flavor. Choose a seat at a table or the bar where locally-influenced and -named cocktails are crafted with regional spirits. The lunch menu lists interesting homemade soups, salads (green, vegan and pasta) and seasonally rotated sandwiches (buffalo chicken, Reubenesque or charred tomato and fresh cheese). Small plates and appetizers include seasonal roasted vegetables, charcuterie and artisanal cheeses, as well as

salmon poke and bruschetta. Dinner entrees include savory grilled offerings like vegetable skewers, salmon, sirloin and more.

Pine State Biscuits

2204 NE Alberta St	503/477-6605
1100 SE Division St, Suite 100	503/236-3356

Mon-Wed: 7-3; Thu-Sun: 7a.m.-11 p.m.

125 NE Schuyler St	503/719-9357
Daily: 7-3	pinestatebiscuits.com

Inexpensive to moderate

Don't miss the sumptuous buttermilk biscuits at Pine State Biscuits. Order
just one (I dare you) or a dozen, then slather on butter, honey or jam. The
sausage gravy is out of this world, and so are the biscuit sandwiches made
with bacon, housemade sausage, ham, fried chicken, brisket, eggs and
assorted greens, cheeses and sauces. You'll probably tackle your towering
concoction (multi-layers dripping with melted cheese atop creamy gravy)
with a knife and fork. Southern food extras like fried green tomatoes and
hush puppies or desserts baked on-site like pecan pie and bourbon cinnamon rolls are hard to resist.

Pine Street Market

126 SW 2nd Ave	pinestreetpdx.com

Daily (vendor hours vary)

Pine Street Market is Portland's new food hall just blocks from the waterfront in the historic Carriage & Baggage Building. Nine food shops from
some of the best local chefs and restaurateurs (in other words, they were
not randomly chosen), fill the market in a casual, open layout. Here's a look
at a few of my favorites:

Pollo Bravo (503/987-1500, pollobravopdx.com): This tapas bar may be
the most interesting place of all. The Spanish-style rotisserie chicken is absolutely delicious, as is the rotisserie roast beef sandwich with olive oil and
sea salt. A selection of wines, beers, ciders and cocktails complete the menu.

Checkerboard Pizza (503/299-2000, trifectapdx.com): Owner, baker
and James Beard Award-winner Ken Forkish offers a lineup of 18-inch pizzas (whole, by the slice, to go or eat in) that combine New York and Italian
styles. This place also sells pastries and breads from its sister bakery, **Trifecta Tavern and Bakery** (726 SE 6th Ave, 503/841-6675).

Wiz Bang Bar (503/384-2150, saltandstraw.com/wizbangbar): This is
the newest creation of Salt & Straw (see separate write-up in Portland),
one of the most popular scoop ice cream shops in the area. Wiz Bang Bar
offers soft-serve cones, sundaes, milkshakes, floats and sodas. Toppings
are homemade, as are the decadent mix-ins. It comes as no surprise that

the chocolate fudge is my favorite.

In addition to those described above, Pine Street Market features these fine food purveyors:

Bless Your Heart Burgers (byhpdx.com): classic American cheeseburgers and fries

Brass Bar (baristapdx.com): Serving tea and coffee from a proprietary roast.

Kim Jong Smokehouse (kimjongsmokehouse.com): Korean street food meets Southern-style barbecue smoking techniques

KURE (kurejuicebar.com): organic juices, smoothies, tonic shots and more

OP Wurst (opwurst.com): being rebranded as Olympia Provisions Public House

Marukin Ramen (marukinramen.com): This popular Tokyo noodle shop is now stateside.

Podnah's Pit

1625 NE Killingsworth St   503/281-3700
Mon-Thu: 11-9 (Fri till 10);
Sat: 9 a.m.-10 p.m.; Sun: 9-9   podnahspit.com
Moderate

Podnah's (Texan for partner — after the nickname of owner Rodney Muirhead's grandfather) offers authentic Texas pit barbecue cooked low and

---

WASHINGTON PARK

This Southwest Portland gem, located between West Burnside Street and Highway 26, offers something for everyone: recreation, trails, picnic areas and attractions plus some of the best vistas in town. Entrance to the park is free, although some of the major attractions charge a fee. Visit the park's website, explorewashingtonpark.org, for complete information. You'll definitely want to check out these activities:

Archery Range: free, bring your own equipment

Children's Playground: free

Hoyt Arboretum: free; 12 miles of trails, 2,000 species

International Rose Test Garden: free, 7,000 rose plants

Memorials and statues

Oregon Zoo: admission fee

Portland Children's Museum: admission fee

Portland Japanese Garden: admission fee

World Forestry Center: admission fee

slow over oak hardwood (not charcoal). Rodney never precooks the meat; it's guaranteed cooked start to finish right there in the pit. The downfall? Meats sometimes sell out before closing, but this place is worth a stop anyway. Fully loaded plates of brisket, pulled pork, spare ribs, trout and chicken come with two sides and cornbread. Other items include pulled pork and brisket sandwiches (served with one side), a la carte meats and a variety of sides and appetizers, and a Tex-cobb salad, too. Breakfast (served Saturday and Sunday 9-1) features in-house smoked bacon and sausage, biscuits and gravy, a breakfast platter (smoked brisket, eggs, potatoes and a biscuit) and other popular items like breakfast tacos on fresh, housemade flour tortillas. There's also a host of daily specials (after 5 p.m.) and weekend brunch specials. Cocktails, wines and draft and bottled beers are offered all day. For dessert consider the pecan pie or banana pudding.

Pok Pok
3226 SE Division St	503/232-1387
Daily: 11:30-10	
Pok Pok Noi	
1469 NE Prescott St	503/287-4149
Daily: 11:30-10	
Pok Pok NW	
1639 Marshall St	971/351-1946
Daily: 11:30-10	pokpokpdx.com
Moderate	

Accolades to Chef Andy Ricker who mastered the art of Thai cooking during a lengthy sojourn in Southeast Asia. His hard work has not gone unrecognized; he earned the James Beard Award for Best Chef Northwest and continues to add to his realm. Specialties of the house at his Portland locations include flavorful rotisserie-roasted game hen, papaya Pok Pok salad and deep-fried Vietnamese fish sauce wings; all are best enjoyed with sticky rice. Other authentic dishes utilize pork belly and ribs, sausage, boar collar and fish; preparations may be grilled or incorporated into noodle dishes. Find Pok Pok locations in Manhattan and Los Angeles, too.

Portland Art Museum
1219 SW Park Ave	503/226-2811
Tue, Wed, Sat, Sun: 10-5; Thu, Fri: 10-8	portlandartmuseum.org
Reasonable	

Oregon's premier art museum just happens to be the Pacific Northwest's oldest art museum and is an anchor in Portland's Cultural District in the South Park Blocks. Founded in 1892, there are over 42,000 items. The majority of the gallery spaces contain pieces from the impressive permanent collections of modern and contemporary art, English silver, graphic arts and art of the native peoples of North America. Check the schedule for interesting and stunning exhibitions and public tours; free to members or with paid admission. The **Northwest Film Center** (503/221-1156, nwfilm.org) is also a part of the Portland Art Museum and is home to a variety of festivals, exhibitions and a film school. Museum Director Brian Ferriso is a treasure.

Portland City Grill

111 SW 5th Ave, 30th floor   503/450-0030
Mon-Thu: 11 a.m.-midnight; Fri: 11 a.m.-1 a.m.;
Sat: 4 p.m.-1 a.m.; Sun: 9:30 a.m.-11 p.m.   portlandcitygrill.com
Moderate and up
The Portland City Grill is one of Portland's most popular award-winning restaurants, and if you've seen the breathtaking views then you know why. Atop the 30th floor of what is one of downtown's tallest towers are panoramic views of the city and the Cascade Mountains; there are not many places you can access these great views. This grill is famous for much more. It has one of the busiest happy hours in the city with cheap eats and delicious cocktails, just in time for the sunset. Diners also enjoy their Sunday buffet brunch. Their menu primarily consists of fresh seafood prepared with Northwest, Island and Asian influences and steak as well as soups, salads and appetizers. The signature dish is a chili-rubbed Kobe flat iron steak with poblano romesco, mustard marble potatoes and creamy charred corn with citrus. Their extensive drink menu features wines, cocktails and an assortment of beers; Wine Enthusiast magazine crowned them as one of the best 100 wine restaurants in the country and Restaurant Business Magazine crowned them as one of the top 100 independent restaurants.

Portland Marriott Downtown Waterfront

1401 SW Naito Pkwy   503/226-7600
Moderate to expensive   portlandmarriott.com
For those visiting downtown Portland for business or pleasure, this luxury hotel is an excellent choice. The hotel is ideally located in the heart of the city at the waterfront with easy to-and-from freeway access. Modern amenities include movable desktops, walk-in showers, ambient lighting, flatscreen TVs and Thaan natural bath products. Large windows afford picture postcard views of the Willamette River, Mt. Hood and the City of Bridges. A selection of rooms with bike storage is also available. The property offers a completely new, modern fitness center and M Club Lounge, Marriott's new 24/7 concierge lounge. **Truss** restaurant is open for breakfast, serving a "Purely Portland" inspired buffet including a fresh selection of fruits, made-

PITTOCK MANSION

Magnificent **Pittock Mansion** (3229 NW Pittock Dr, Portland; 503/823-3623; pittockmansion.org) was completed in 1914 for Henry Pittock, Portland businessman and founder of The Daily Oregonian. The French Renaissance house is furnished with 18th- and 19th-century European and American antiques. Sitting atop 46 acres, it offers panoramic views of the city. Self-guided tours take visitors through the mansion, Gate Lodge and stunning grounds; periodic Behind the Scenes guided tours allow glimpses of basement passages, the Otis elevator machine room and other places not on the general tour. Christmas is a particularly festive time to visit as rooms are filled with holiday decorations, lights and Christmas trees. Reasonable admission fee.

to-order omelets, waffles and local jams and butters. Visit **Proof•Reader Restaurant and Bar** a "Whiskey + Craft + Kitchen" for lunch and dinner that features the bounty of the Northwest and over 150 whiskies from Portland and around the globe. Enjoy a Purely Portland experience with their daily complimentary 5 p.m. microbrew toast in honor of the city. The hotel offers over 45,000 square feet of meeting space, of which over 2,000 square feet on the second floor is complemented with outstanding views; very nice, indeed.

Powell's Books

City of Books, 1005 W Burnside St   800/878-7373 (all stores)
Books on Hawthorne, 3723 SE Hawthorne Blvd
Books for Home and Garden, 3747 SE Hawthorne Blvd
Books at PDX, 7000 NE Airport Way
Cedar Hills Crossing, 3415 SW Cedar Hills Blvd, Beaverton
Hours vary   powells.com

One could say if it is printed on paper, it may just be at Powell's. Founded in 1971, Powell's Books remains a family-owned and -operated business, with Emily Powell serving as the company's third-generation leader. This Northwest Portland fixture has expanded numerous times to make room for more shelves of every type of book — new and used, fiction, nonfiction, hardcover, paperback, rare, reference, collectible, signed, and audio, plus toys and gifts. Over 1 million tomes are housed in the Burnside flagship location; each genre is shelved separately in the labyrinth of rooms. Over the years, the popularity of Powell's and its burgeoning supply necessitated expanding to other Portland buildings; additionally, the Beaverton store has over a half million selections. Travelers appreciate the three shops at PDX for last-minute reading material before boarding flights or to grab a quick gift on the way in or out of town. Two neighboring businesses are on Hawthorne Boulevard, one dedicated to home and garden materials as well as cooking utensils, accessories and related merchandise, while the other store carries a full spectrum of reads. Powell's is a leader in book buying and selling, in stores and online. This is another quintessential Portland institution.

Proof•Reader Restaurant and Bar

1401 SW Naito Pkwy   503/226-7600
(See detailed listing with Portland Marriott Downtown Waterfront)

RingSide Fish House

838 SW Park Ave, mezzanine   503/227-3900
Mon-Sat: 5-10; Sun: 5-9
Bar: Mon-Sat: 3-11; Sun: 3-10   ringsidefishhouse.com
Moderate and up
This business branched out from its historic Portland custom of providing the "best steaks in town" to celebrate Oregon's proximity to fresh fish and seafood with the creation of RingSide Fish House in the Fox Tower downtown overlooking Director Park. You'll find a raw bar, seafood platters and changing entrees of halibut, cioppino, lobster, trout and many other fish choices with a sprinkling of beef, pasta and poultry. This space is warm, classy and inviting and offers early and late happy hours in the busy bars; private dining.

RingSide Steakhouse Uptown

2165 W Burnside St   503/223-1513
Mon-Wed: 5-11:30; Thu-Sat: 5-midnight; Sun: 4-11:30   ringsidesteakhouse.com
Expensive
The RingSide Steakhouse Uptown has been a Portland tradition for 75 years. For decades they have been providing great steaks, fabulous onion rings and other delectables. The evolving menu features select steaks that are dry-aged and carved on-premises. The space is airy and cozy with a welcoming fireplace. Service, as always, is highly professional. The 10,000-bottle wine cellar is fabulous. In an era of chain restaurants, it is refreshing to boast about a homegrown winner. Great credit goes to the members of the Peterson family who keep watchful eyes on every phase of the business.

Roe

515 SW Broadway, Suite 100   503/232-1566
Wed-Sat: 5:30-10   roepdx.rest
Expensive

Roe has moved to the mezzanine level inside the historic Morgan build-ing downtown. Chef Trent Pierce remains laser-focused on using only the freshest and finest seafood in menus that change frequently. Roe offers two menus: a four-course prix-fixe menu with choices (Wednesday through Friday); and the full Roe Experience, a seasonal seven-course sea-food tasting menu (Wednesday through Saturday). An elegant caviar ser-vice is offered in-house along with wine, sake and spirits. Regardless of your choice, you're sure to find uniquely prepared sashimi, fin fish, shellfish and desserts. Reservations are recommended.

Ruth's Chris Steak House

850 SW Broadway   503/221-4518
Mon-Sat: 5-10; Sun: 4-9   ruthschris.com
Expensive

This prestigious steakhouse chain does things in a big way, and Portland's warm yet spectacular location is no exception. Classic seafood appetizers are the perfect way to start dinner. The beefsteak tomato salad is superb, baked potatoes are gigantic and other potato dishes are more than gen-erous. Beef lovers have their choice of USDA Prime cuts; tender, juicy and delicious every time. My preference, though, are the grilled lamb chops; cut extra thick and very flavorful. Fresh lobster is always on the menu as are other seafood and fish selections. Desserts include homemade cheese-cake, crème brûlée, chocolate cake, bread pudding and seasonal berries with cream. Weekday happy hours are between 4 and 7, a very pleasant way to ease into the evening.

Salt & Straw

2035 NE Alberta St   503/208-3867
Daily: 11-11
3345 SE Division St   503/208-2054
Daily: 11-11
838 NW 23rd Ave   971/271-8168
Daily: 10-11
100 A Ave, Lake Oswego   503/305-8267
Daily: 11-11   saltandstraw.com

Salt & Straw is a farm-to-cone ice cream shop which makes small batches of seasonal and classic flavors. Each scoop is chock-full of real ingredients; no artificial flavorings or manufactured particles are to be found. Savor the goodness in winning combinations of pear with blue cheese, strawberry with cracked pepper, chocolate with brownies, almond brittle with salted ganache or single-origin Woodblock chocolate ice cream. For a distinctive touch to any party, Salt & Straw's website offers catering options or order a five-pint gift pack delivered to your door. Also, find fresh spins on the childhood swirl, sundaes, novelties and more at Salt & Straw's **Wiz Bang Bar** (126 SW 2nd Ave, 503/384-2150) at the Pine Street Market.

Salty's on the Columbia

3839 NE Marine Dr   503/288-4444
Lunch: Mon-Fri 11:15-3; Brunch: Sat 9:30-1; Sun 9-1:30
Dinner: Mon-Thu 3-8:30; Fri 3-9; Sat 4-9; Sun 4:30-8   saltys.com/portland
Moderate

The mighty Columbia flows past this local landmark restaurant. With a beautiful Mt. Hood backdrop, the view doesn't get much better than this. Alfresco dining on the wraparound deck is spectacular in summer and window seats are coveted when the Christmas ships sail past in December. Salty's arguably presents the busiest and best weekend champagne brunch buffet in the state. Prawns, Dungeness crab, salmon, clams, mussels, made-to-order omelets, crepes, waffles, fruits, cheeses, baked ham (excellent), prime rib and much more make choosing a real dilemma. A Bloody Mary bar invites guests to make-their-own creations, while a four-foot tall fountain of gurgling chocolate sauce is irresistible for dipping fruits and lady finger cookies (kids love to swirl marshmallows). The impressive sea and land lunch and dinner menus feature entries such as sustainable seafood, live Maine lobster, cioppino and Certified Angus beef. Lighten up during the bar's weekday happy hours with great bar eats and drinks or join in the fun at Salty's entertaining cooking classes and special events.

Sayler's Old Country Kitchen

10519 SE Stark St   503/252-4171
Mon-Thu: 4-10; Fri: 4-11; Sat: 3-11; Sun: noon-10   saylers.com
Moderate and up

For years, wise steak lovers have made one-of-a-kind Sayler's Old Country Kitchen crowded every day of the week. Reasonable prices for top-quality meals bring customers back again and again. Although steaks are in the main here, those who prefer seafood or chicken can find a number of entrees. The crab Louis salad is especially appealing and delicious. Don't miss the fabulous onion rings — right at the top of any offered in the Portland area. Steak offerings include filet mignon, top sirloin, T-bone, porterhouse, ribeye (bone-in or not), New York and ground sirloin. Since 1948, the 72-ounce top sirloin dinner ($70.00) has been served free to anyone who can eat the steak and trimmings within one hour (weekdays only). Why (or how) anyone could do this is beyond me. Value-priced senior dinners are offered as well as prime rib plates and sandwiches. Sayler's is a true quality Portland tradition.

Seres Restaurant and Bar

1105 NW Lovejoy St　　　　　　　　　　　　　　　　971/222-7327
Mon-Sat: 11-10; Sun: 4-10　　　　　　　　　　　seresrestaurant.com
Moderate

This Pearl District restaurant serves tasty multi-regional Chinese cuisine with a NW twist. The surroundings are modern, neat and clean and the staff is informed. Start your meal with Dungeness crabmeat wontons or chicken and shrimp shumai — delicious. Classic dishes, like Peking duck or Mongolian lamb, are made with fresh, locally-sourced ingredients (free of hormones, antibiotics, MSG) and prepared on flaming woks. Eat in, take out or have your order delivered. While you're in the area, enhance your cultural experience with a visit to the remarkable Lan Su Chinese Garden in Old Town Chinatown before or after your meal.

Serratto

2112 NW Kearney St　　　　　　　　　　　　　　　503/221-1195
Mon-Thu: 11:30-10 (Fri, Sat till 11; Sun till 9)　　　　　serratto.com
Moderately expensive

Serratto is a busy Alphabet District favorite recognized for Mediterranean and Northwest fare. The extensive, eclectic menu features homemade pastas, family-pleasing delicious pizzas, risotto and locally-sourced meats, seafood and produce. Portland's best artisan bakeries provide the breads. A bittersweet chocolate cobbler served warm with vanilla bean gelato is on the dessert menu; other seasonal sweets and housemade gelato and sorbetto are also satisfying. You'll feel like part of the neighborhood at this cozy corner spot; the outside tables are charming.

Sheraton Portland Airport Hotel

8235 NE Airport Way　　　　　　　503/281-2500, 800/325-3535
Moderate　　　　　　　　　　　　　　　　sheraton.com/portland

The guest rooms, meeting facilities and the restaurant at this convenient hotel are most inviting. Rose & Compass Restaurant offers appealing meals from 6 a.m. to 10 p.m. and a limited menu to midnight; room service is available until 10 p.m. with a limited menu until midnight as well. Complimentary Wi-Fi is available for all guests throughout the 215-room hotel. The Sheraton also features great Starwood amenities such as the Sweet Sleeper Bed, Sheraton Fitness by Core Performance and the Sheraton Club which offers continental breakfast and evening reception for a nominal fee. Hardworking, civic-minded hotelier Harold Pollin's portfolio includes two other airport properties. Next door to the Sheraton is **Hampton Inn Portland Airport** (8633 NE Airport Way, 503/288-2423, hamptoninn. com) and **Aloft Portland Airport at Cascade Station** (9920 NE Cascades Pkwy, 503/200-5678, aloftportlandairport.com). Complimentary shuttle service to the airport runs 24/7 making these convenient stays for travelers in and out of PDX; also great as jumping-off-points for exploring Southwest Washington or the Gorge.

Slappy Cakes

4246 SE Belmont St	503/477-4805
Mon-Fri: 8-2 (Sat, Sun till 3)	slappycakes.com
Inexpensive	

Scratch pancakes are the order of the day here. Guests have the option of making their pancakes on tabletop griddles or leaving the cooking to the kitchen. Pick a batter (buttermilk, chocolate, peanut butter, vegan/gluten-free and seasonal); then the fixins (chocolate or butterscotch chips, fruits, nuts, mushrooms, avocado, chorizo, cheese, bacon, vegan sausage). Add a topping (lavender honey, peanut butter, lemon curd, whipped cream, chocolate hazelnut, caramel or maple syrup); and you'll have a memorable pancake breakfast. Additional breakfast choices include Benedicts served on housemade English muffins, country-fried steak, seasonal vegetable scrambles and a classic egg breakfast. Emphasis is on organic, and all produce comes from a local source. There's plenty of vegan and gluten-free items and dairy-free alternatives such as hemp, soy and almond milk for Bob's Red Mill slow cooked oatmeal. They also offer handcrafted cocktails and organic local juice.

St. Honoré Boulangerie

2335 NW Thurman St	503/445-4342
Daily: 6:30 a.m.-8 p.m.	
501 SW Broadway St.	503/954-3049
Daily: 6:30 a.m.-8 p.m.	
3333 SE Division St	971/279-4433
Daily: 7 a.m.-8 p.m.	
315 1st St, Suite 103, Lake Oswego	503/496-5596
Daily: 6:30 a.m.-7 p.m.	sainthonorebakery.com

The wonderfully rustic establishment sets the stage for specialty items (raisin and fennel benoitons, rolls, the signature Miche Banal loaves and cranberry hazelnut bread and rolls), baguettes and other breads. Not to be overlooked are the pain au chocolat (chocolate-filled croissant) and other decadent pastries. Croissant and other sandwiches, quiches, soups, salads and oh-so-good desserts are served in these neighborhood cafes at communal harvest or Parisian-style tables; the atmosphere is truly delightful. Whether you're looking for something elegant like Dominique Geulin's Lake Oswego cafe or for outdoor patio seating like at the Division Street store, there's likely a location that will best suit you.

St. Jack

1610 NW 23rd St   503/360-1281
Dinner: daily 5-10
Bar: daily 4-11 (Fri, Sat till midnight)   stjackpdx.com
Moderately expensive to expensive

This is the place for regional French cuisine. The marvelous food is matched by excellent service and a pleasant atmosphere. Begin with a decadent cheese plate assembled from nearly a dozen choices of cow, sheep and goat fromage, skillfully paired with wine, of course. Although the wine list is somewhat limited, the restaurant makes up for it with cognac, brandy and classic French-style cocktail offerings. For dinner, choose from delicacies such as tablier de sapeur (fried tripe), the classic steak frites with shallots and red wine demi-glace, or other entrees, salads and small plates on a menu that can change daily based on seasonal ingredients. Don't forget to stick around for dessert and their housemade ice cream.

Stammtisch

401 NE 28th Ave   503/206-7983
Mon-Thu: 3 p.m.-1:30 a.m.; Fri: 11:30 a.m.-1:30 a.m.;
Sat, Sun: 11 a.m.-1:30 a.m.   stammtischpdx.com
Moderate

Some of the best beers in the world come from Germany, and Stammtisch offers perfect examples of the craft. It's also a great place to experience German culture. This brew pub carries a large selection of traditional German beers, brandies and liquors, and it offers truly authentic German food such as Bretzels (Bavarian pretzels) and Hausgemachte Wurst (bratwurst, weisswurst or knackwurst with sauerkraut and house mustard). Now that's a mouthful. Some of the more popular beers include Andechs Hell and Ayinger Bräu Weisse with hints of floral to citrus to vanilla. The open-yet-cozy atmosphere is welcoming, staff friendly and attentive and the restaurant is very upbeat — as if it were Oktoberfest every day. You can also fill your stein at sister location **Prost** (4237 N Mississippi Ave, 503/954-2674).

SPORTS TOURISM
For more than two decades, **Oregon Sports Authority** (503/234-4500, oregonsports.org) has tirelessly served the state in the field of sports tourism. The goal of this nonprofit organization is to enhance Oregon's economy and quality of life by securing amateur and professional sports events and franchises. The foundation provides grants and conducts programs to support youth sports activities, with an emphasis on both underserved youth and increased physical activity. Kudos to CEO Jim Etzel, the board and the more than 150 members for their ongoing efforts.

Stepping Stone Cafe

2390 NW Quimby St   503/222-1132
Mon-Tue: 6 a.m.-7 p.m.; Wed, Thu: 6 a.m.-9 p.m.; Fri: 6 a.m.-3 a.m.;
Sat: 7:30 a.m.-3 a.m.; Sun: 7:30 a.m.-9 p.m.   steppingstonecafe.com
Inexpensive
Breakfast at all hours, every day. Here's another Portland eatery that has earned a national reputation. Casual Stepping Stone is famous for its dinner plate-sized mancakes (aka pancakes). One will probably do; order a stack if you dare. Otherwise, opt for the popular banana walnut French toast. There are plenty of other choices, some with interesting names like the Neo Bobcat (tomato, avocado, choice of cheese) and the Smothered Badass (chicken-fried steak, hash browns, onions, jalapeno, cheddar and smothered in gravy) omelets and One-Eyed Jack (fried egg) burgers. Lunch sandwiches, soups and salads are served starting at 10:30 and comfort food dinners begin at 5; meatloaf and chicken-fried steak are full-meal deals. You'll probably need a shoe horn to get into this small quirky cafe on weekends.

Sushi Mazi

2126 SE Division St   503/432-8651
Tue-Fri: 11:30-3, 5-close; Sat, Sun: 4:30-6   sushimazi.com
Moderate
Chef Marc takes great pride in preparing and presenting sushi using fresh fish and vegetables to create culinary works of art. The coconut shrimp roll, real grasshopper sushi and Buddha crunchy roll with mango, asparagus and avocado are appealing and interesting. Platters of sushi and hot foods such as chicken teriyaki are served with miso soup; beer, wine and saké are available. Expect friendly service at this casual and quiet restaurant.

OREGON CULINARY INSTITUTE
In addition to providing professional training in restaurant
management, the culinary arts, baking and pastry programs, the
Oregon Culinary Institute (1701 SW Jefferson St, Portland;
503/961-6200; oregonculinaryinstitute.com) has a fine-dining
restaurant open to the public Monday through Friday when school is
in session. Students participate in all aspects of the meal planning,
preparation and presentation. The three-course $12 lunch (noon) or
four-course $22 dinner (7 p.m.) is a fun opportunity to interact with
enthusiastic young chefs while enjoying a tasty, reasonably-priced
meal. Reservations required.

Toro Bravo

120 NE Russell St   503/281-4464
Sun-Thu: 5-10; Fri, Sat: 5-11   torobravopdx.com
Moderately expensive
This vibrant Spanish tapas restaurant offers plenty of choices. For tiny bites,
order toasted almonds, cheese and salads from the Pinchos section. Tapas
selections change daily and might include braised lamb, roasted cauliflower, grilled flat bread and other small plates great for sharing or a light meal.
Several whole meals are offered; paella, meatballs, fish and seafood and
vegetable options. For a special evening, order the chef's choice for your
party, complemented with Spanish wine and desserts such as sorbet and
ice cream or churros and chocolate.

Truss

1401 SW Naito Pkwy   503/226-7600
(See detailed listing with Portland Marriott Downtown Waterfront)

Urban Farmer

525 SW Morrison St   503/222-4900
(See detailed listing with The Nines)

Verdigris

1315 NE Fremont St   503/477-8106
Tue-Sun: 5-close; Sat, Sun: 9-2   verdigrisrestaurant.com
Moderate
Whether you are looking for a warm and cozy restaurant or somewhere
more intimate, the candlelit dining room, casual elegance and minimalist
decor of this funky French-inspired restaurant is sure to please. The menu

and the wine list are ever-changing, making for a new, refreshing experience each time. The rotating selection of appetizers and entrees includes items such as housemade pork terrine, Idaho trout, grilled top sirloin steak and crispy pork confit. A recent vegetarian option was delicious potato gnocchi. The cuisine doesn't skip steps either; every dish is cooked to order and breads made in-house and local produce help ensure freshness. Verdigris is ideal for a brunch with friends or a classic dinner.

Voodoo Doughnut

22 SW 3rd Ave   503/241-4707
1501 NE Davis St   503/235-2666
Daily: 24 hours   voodoodoughnut.com

It seems the whole world knows about Voodoo Doughnut, thanks to social media and faithful foodies. These are no ordinary doughnuts; probably the best known here is the signature Voodoo doughnut: a raspberry jelly-filled, raised yeast doughnut in the shape of a Voodoo Doll, frosted with chocolate icing, embellished with details and presented with a pretzel stake to the heart! It has a cult following. There are over 50 more varieties, from plain to over-the-top creations, some with names and descriptions inappropriate for this book. When you visit one of these almost-anything-goes shops, keep in mind that they accept cash only (ATM inside). Look for the Voodoo Doughnut pink cart in Cartlandia (8145 SE 82nd Ave); open daily, but with limited hours. Eugene also has an outpost (20 E Broadway, 541/868-8666). One more thing: they also perform legal and non-legal wedding ceremonies at all locations.

Willamette Jetboat Excursions

1945 SE Water Ave   503/231-1532, 888/538-2628
Daily: 9:30-4:30 (May-Sep)   willamettejet.com
Expensive

Take a thrilling trip up to Oregon City Falls or a shorter tour of the downtown area and harbor. Portland's version of jet boating gives guests a different perspective of the city's bridges by passing under a dozen bridges. Tour prices range between $21 and $55 (lower prices for kids), varying between scenic and downtown/harbor tours. Special packages include an all-inclusive lunch on the Columbia River.

Zama Massage Therapeutic Spa

2149 NE Broadway   503/281-0278
Daily: 9-9   zamamassage.com

Zama Massage Therapeutic Spa offers a wide variety of spa packages and bills itself as having the only therapeutic salt caves in Portland. Hair care, nail treatments, men's services, body wraps, facials and more than a dozen relaxation and deep tissue massages are available, so what more could you ask for? Book your treatment in a halo-therapy room (the salt caves), and you're body and mind will thank you (especially during allergy season). Or go for the unique HydraFacial, which restores and replenishes the skin with essential nutrients. Zama is the perfect place to pamper oneself before that special occasion. Sip on champagne, indulge in decadent truffles and enjoy a couple's massage or a side by side foot treatment. For a more hands on experience, bring your partner to learn the ways through a couples massage class.

Zupan's Markets

2340 W Burnside St	503/497-1088
7221 SW Macadam Ave	503/244-5666
16380 Boones Ferry Road, Lake Oswego	503/210-4190
Hours vary by location	zupans.com

Founded by the late John Zupan in 1975, Zupan's is a locally- and family-owned market that serves Portland's food-loving community. Likened to farmers markets, Zupan's focuses on quality, selling everything from the best meats and wines to the freshest produce, baked goods, gourmet deli products, specialty foods, flowers and more. Touting a unique grocery shopping experience, Zupan's stores are meant to indulge the senses, inviting customers to see, smell, taste and learn. Regularly scheduled beer, wine and cheese tastings are among customer favorites. Full-service floral departments have beautiful fresh-cut flowers year-round and provide custom design, wedding and event services. The deli features handmade, homestyle items with grab-n-go meals, gourmet sandwiches and catering. Bakery items are delivered from 35 of the best bakeries around the Portland area.

SAUVIE ISLAND

Blue Heron Herbary

27731 NW Reeder Road	503/621-1457
Fri-Sun: 10-5 (Mar-Oct)	blueheronherbary.com

Take a trip to Sauvie Island and explore the meandering roads passing by farms and wildlife refuges. Blue Heron Herbary is worth a stop to learn about the magic of herbs. Nearly 300 unusual and household herbs are planted in specialty beds: Mediterranean, salad, tea, bee and butterfly, Shakespearean and more. You'll find great-smelling lavenders of varying sizes, colors and shapes, medicinal herbs, culinary additives and ornamentals grown under the loving care of the Hanselman family. In the gift shop you'll find herbal plants for growing at home (over 350 varieties of herbs and more than 100 lavender variations), plus pottery, wind chimes, bird-houses, honey, spices and seasonings. Herbal and/or lavender wreaths, bath and beauty products, herbal cookies for dogs, catnip for felines and home decor and accessories (many items also available online) are crafted at the farm. Plan a visit to the beautiful grounds that are abuzz with bees, butterflies and songbirds. See their website for holiday hours.

SHERWOOD

Handel's Homemade Ice Cream and Yogurt

21300 SW Langer Farms Pkwy   503/822-5142
Daily: 11-10   handelsicecream.com

What started in 1945 as a small operation in Ohio has grown to multiple locations in nine states. This is Oregon's first location, and you're going to want to stop in. National Geographic recently recognized Handel's for having the best ice cream in the world, taking the number one spot on their feature *The 10 Best of Everything*. If that isn't reason enough for a visit, then generous portions, affordable prices and freshness should be. Small-batch ice cream, low-fat yogurt, ices and sherbets are made daily at every location, using fresh, quality ingredients and exclusive techniques. Blend-ins include nuts, creamy caramel, real vanilla beans, fruits, fluffy marshmallows, dark chocolate and more. Chocolate is my go-to, but you will be amazed at the extensive offerings and seasonal flavors available. Cinnamon sticky bun, dolce de leche, butter pecan, coconut cream pie and red velvet are just a few you can expect to see.

FAVORITE FULL-SERVICE PIT STOP

Since 1952 a favorite stop of truck drivers for fuel, truck services and other services has been **Jubitz Travel Center** (10210 N Vancouver Way, Portland; 503/283-1111; jubitztravelcenter.com) – but it's not just for truckers. Travelers are welcome at the 100-room Portlander Inn, restaurants, digital cinema and marketplace, too. The center's amenities include a laundromat, barber shop, shoe repair shop, arcade, postal service and outpatient medical center. Cascade Grill is a 24/7 full-service restaurant with homestyle food and daily specials cooked to order, stop in for a drink and entertainment at Ponderosa Lounge and Grill or grab a sandwich from Moe's Deli. Big riggers can take care of service and repairs at the truck service center or visit the driver lounge or convenience store. Fred Jubitz heads up this family endeavor which was founded by his father, Moe Jubitz.

Sleighbells Gift Shop

23855 SW 195th Pl   503/625-6052
Daily: 10-5 (Jul-Dec), trees cut till 4   sleighbellsgiftshop.business.site

Although the name implies Christmas, this shop is packed with attractive displays of decorative (traditional, whimsical, stylish) merchandise for other occasions like Halloween and Thanksgiving as well, but especially Christmas. Lines represented: Christopher Radko, Department 56 Villages, Tree Farm, World Christmas, housemade fudge and more. A tradition for many families is searching the 75-acre tree farm for the perfect Frasier fir tree. Early birds can call to preselect trees and have them ready on the pre-determined day; of course, tromping through the farm with kids and dog in tow and saw in hand is also an option. Sleighbells is a delightful stop; note their seasonal hours.

ST. HELENS

Nob Hill Riverview Bed and Breakfast

285 S 2nd St   503/396-5555
Moderate and up   nobhillbb.com

Three luxurious guest rooms at this bed and breakfast are descriptively named the Paris Apartment, French Suite and Casablanca Retreat. Accommodations in the turn-of-the-century Craftsman-style home vary and may include a private entrance, fireplace, jetted tub, kitchenette or separate living or dining area. Standard features include robes, lavish linens, down comforters and refrigerators. Relax on the front porch with views of the mighty Columbia River, passing ships and romantic sunsets or enjoy complimentary afternoon tea or beverages in the parlor. Each morning, the organic gourmet breakfast is served in the formal dining room or, upon prior request, in your suite. To augment your stay, choose from additional specials and packages. Keep in mind, this B&B gets quite popular in October, because it was the filming location for Grandma Aggie's house from the movie Halloweentown.

TIGARD

Bridgeport Village

7455 SW Bridgeport Road   503/968-1704
Daily   bridgeport-village.com

Bridgeport Village is one of the Northwest's premier shopping and dining destinations. Located just 15 minutes south of downtown Portland, this outdoor location offers mega retail therapy with over 75 stores and restaurants to explore. It is home to Oregon's only Crate & Barrel, Tommy Bahama, Eileen Fisher, Z Gallerie, Container Store and Saks Fifth Avenue OFF

5th. Hungry visitors have a dozen sit-down eateries from which to choose including PF Chang's Bistro, McCormick & Schmick's Grill, California Pizza Kitchen and Twigs Bistro & Martini Bar. First-class amenities include valet parking, free Wi-Fi, strollers, wheelchairs and an outdoor playground for kids. Catch a first-run flick at Regal Cinema; 18 screens and a 3-D IMAX. Additional big-name shopping venues are in the immediate area.

The Grand Hotel at Bridgeport

7265 SW Hazel Fern Road   503/968-5757, 866/968-5757
Moderate to very expensive   grandhotelbridgeport.com

Travelers and shoppers call The Grand Hotel their home away from home in this Portland suburb; the location is ideal for business or pleasure. Package deals combine superb lodging with wine tasting, shopping and romantic stays. The 124 luxurious rooms and suites offer first-class service and amenities with complimentary covered parking, Internet service, shuttle service and a delicious hot breakfast buffet. Nearby Bridgeport Village and adjacent complexes offer splendid local, regional and national retailers and irresistible boutiques. Unwind after a flurry of activities in comfortable rooms, conveniently furnished with leather couches and coffee tables, microwaves, refrigerators, coffee stations, work desks with ergonomic chairs and the outstanding hospitality of The Grand Hotel. Steve Johnson, president of parent company VIP's Industries, is an expert in the hospitality arena.

iFLY

10645 SW Greenburg Road   971/803-4359
Mon-Thu: 9-8; Fri, Sat: 8 a.m.-9 p.m. (Sun till 8)   iflyworld.com

Head to iFLY for indoor skydiving. This all-ages experience starts with training from certified flight instructors. They will teach body positioning and hand signals to help get you through the vertical wind tunnel smoothly. You'll enter the flight chamber wearing a flight suit, helmet and goggles — just as you would doing the real thing. The instructor will then spot you as you lean in and take flight. Although you may feel silly and uncomfortable the first time, the more you fly the better you'll get. For kids and teens age 4 to 16 who take a particular liking to this indoor sport, flight school is available with weekly sessions and a chance to compete quarterly.

Thirsty Lion Pub and Grill

10205 SW Washington Square Road   503/352-4030
Daily: 11-11 (Fri, Sat till midnight)   thirstylionpub.com
Moderate

Head here if you are hungry as a lion. Burgers start with a half-pound of

FAMILY ACTIVITIES IN AND AROUND TOWN

GASTON

Tree to Tree Adventure Park (2975 SW Nelson Road, 503/357-0109, tree2treeadventurepark.com): seasonal zip lines and aerial obstacle courses; reservations required

HILLSBORO

Rice Northwest Museum of Rocks and Minerals (26385 NW Groveland Dr, 503/647-2418, ricenorthwestmuseum.org): over 20,000 specimens

Topgolf (5505 NW Huffman St, 503/549-5197; topgolf.com): 100 hitting bays, restaurant and bars, rooftop terrace with fire pit

MILWAUKIE

North Clackamas Aquatic Park (7300 SE Harmony Road, 503/557-7873, ncprd.com/aquatic-park): wave pool, toddler splash zone, diving and lap pools, water slides, 29-foot rock wall

PORTLAND

Lan Su Chinese Garden (2239 NW Everett St, 503/228-8131, lansugarden.org): traditional garden, koi pond, tours, teahouse

Lloyd Center Ice Rink (953 Lloyd Ctr, 503/288-6073, lloydcenterice.com): public skating, lessons, parties

Oaks Amusement Park (7805 SE Oaks Park Way, 503/233-5777, oakspark.com): amusement park rides, roller skating, miniature golf, carnival games, picnicking; seasonal

OMSI (1945 SE Water Ave, 503/797-4000; omsi.edu): five halls of science exhibits, labs, planetarium, science playground, theater and USS Blueback submarine; something for any age group

Oregon Historical Society Museum (1200 SW Park Ave, 503/222-1741, ohs.org): permanent and temporary exhibits

Oregon Maritime Museum (503/224-7724, oregonmaritimemuseum.org): ship models, maritime artifacts, memorabilia, sternwheeler (Portland Waterfront Park; SW Naito Parkway at Pine St)

Oregon Rail Heritage Center (2250 SE Water Ave, 503/233-1156, orhf.org): exhibits, locomotives and railroad equipment,

Oregon Zoo (4001 SW Canyon Road, 503/226-1561, oregonzoo.org): 64 acres of exhibits, one-mile loop railway

Pittock Mansion (3229 NW Pittock Dr, 503/823-3623, pittockmansion.org): 1914 home of Henry and Georgiana Pittock; tours

Portland Aerial Tram (503/494-8283, gobytram.com): connects the South Waterfront to Marquam Hill

Portland Art Museum (1219 SW Park Ave, 503/226-2811, portlandartmuseum.org): galleries, 42,000 works of art, Northwest Film Center

Portland Children's Museum (4015 SW Canyon Road, 503/223-6500, portlandcm.org): playful learning experiences

Portland Japanese Garden (611 SW Kingston Ave, 503/223-1321, japanesegarden.com): cultural village, demonstrations, tea ceremony

Portland Police Museum and Historical Society (1111 SW 2nd Ave, 503/823-0019, portlandpolicemuseum.com): permanent and rotating exhibits such as photos, badges, uniforms, firearms, old jail cell

Portland Saturday Market (2 SW Naito Pkwy, 503/241-4188, portlandsaturdaymarket.com): vendors, food, live music

Portland Spirit River Cruise (503/224-3900, portlandspirit.com): sightseeing, lunch, brunch and dinner excursions; boarding at Salmon Street Springs Fountain, Tom McCall Waterfront Park

Portland Walking Tours (503/774-4522, portlandwalkingtours.com): downtown, ghost, food, libation, chocolate tours; departure locations vary

Powell's Books (1005 W Burnside St, 503/228-4651, powells.com): over a million books

Shanghai Tunnels/Portland Underground Tours (503/622-4798, portlandtunnels.com): heritage, ghost and ethnic history tours; ages 4 and above; meet outside Hobo's Restaurant (120 NW 3rd Ave)

World Forestry Center Discovery Museum (4033 SW Canyon Road, 503/228-1367, worldforestry.org): educational exhibits highlighting local and global forests and sustainable forestry

SAUVIE ISLAND
Sauvie Island (sauvieisland.org): wildlife refuge and recreational area; ten miles north of Portland at junction of the Columbia and Willamette rivers

TIGARD
iFLY (10645 SW Greenburg Road, 971/803-4359, iflyworld.com): indoor skydiving

ground beef, then grilled and dressed with different cheeses, sauces, on-ions, bacon, guacamole, peppers or mushrooms. Slaw, salad or hand-cut fries accompany burgers and other great sandwiches (chicken, turkey club, French dip, Reuben) with delicious components. Fresh entree salads (ahi, chicken Caesar, Cobb) are a full meal. Eclectic sharable appetizers in-clude Scotch eggs, garlic sesame edamame and favorites like pretzels and artichoke spinach dip. Entrees are also varied: mac and cheese, artisan piz-zas, pastas, chicken and fish dishes, ribs, steaks and more. Fare is seasonal and made from scratch; daily specials emphasize local ingredients. They pride themselves on a large offering of craft beers; signature cocktails are pretty tasty, too. A second gastropub is located in Hillsboro (2290 NW Allie Ave, Hillsboro; 503/336-0403).

TUALATIN

Cabela's

7555 SW Nyberg St	503/822-2000
Mon-Sat: 9-9; Sun: 9-7	cabelas.com

Cabela's is the mega-sporting goods emporium along I-5 just south of Portland. You'll find everything related to the good ol' outdoors, plus a wide assortment of museum-quality wildlife displays, an indoor ar-chery test area, a gun library and an aquarium stocked with local fish. Even if you're not an outdoorsman, you may be tempted to take up an activity just so you can amass the latest and greatest equipment, clothing and accessories for yourself, home, cabin, tent or pet. Cabela's has over 60 stores throughout the country; each one a bit unique to fit the location.

Fiorano Ristorante

18674 SW Boones Ferry Road	503/783-0727
Mon-Thu: 11-2:30, 5-9 (Fri till 10); Sat: 5-10	fioranos.com
Moderate	

Inviting Tualatin Commons Lake is the setting for this traditional and in-fused Italian ristorante. For starters, order one of Chef Shan's daily appetiz-er specials. Robust pasta dishes are enhanced with traditional red or cream sauces, garlic, chili flakes or optional chicken, shrimp, Italian sausage or meatballs. Otherwise, all pasta dishes are vegetarian. Try the lamb ragu or medallions of filet mignon with creamy madeira sauce. A sunny midday or a balmy evening is the perfect time to enjoy Fiorano's lakeside dining; catering at your site or theirs. Reservations recommended.

Hayden's Lakefront Grill

8187 Tualatin-Sherwood Road   503/885-9292
Mon-Thu: 6 a.m.-10 p.m.; Fri: 6 a.m. -11 p.m.;
Sat: 7 a.m-11 p.m.; Sun: 7 a.m.-9 p.m.   haydensgrill.com
Moderate

Hungry? Step into Hayden's for quality meals in a relaxed atmosphere (inside or outside seating along the man-made lake). Breakfast choices appeal to light or hearty eaters; lunches include meal-sized salads and generously-portioned sandwiches with fries. Dinner offerings run the gamut from Certified Angus Beef steaks and burgers to locally sourced seafood dishes and Latin inspired tapas, all made with fresh ingredients and updated for today's palates. Hand-crafted cocktails and award-winning happy hour offered daily. Full or mini-sized housemade desserts are the perfect finale.

VERNONIA

Coastal Mountain Sport Haus

66845 Nehalem Hwy N   503/429-6940
Moderate   coastalmountainsporthaus.com

Load up your friends and bikes for a great escape to this European-style inn, located on the Nehalem River, offering four spacious guest rooms, a bunk room, custom outdoor soaking spa and a yoga session. A mile long trail is open for walking or biking or opt to simply enjoy the peaceful surroundings; laid-back or active — you choose. Built in 2008, this locale easily accommodates retreats, girls' getaways, man-cations and family groups. The tariff includes well-prepared breakfasts and dinners using fresh and local ingredients. (Two-night minimum May 15 to September 15; children 14 and older; no pets.) Recognized by Travel Oregon as "Bike Friendly" and "Oregon Forever" sustainability practices.

WEST LINN

(five-O-three)

21900 Willamette Dr, Suite 201   503/607-0960
Tue-Thu: 11:30-9 (Fri, Sat till 10); Sun: 4-9   restaurant503.com
Moderately expensive

A lunch or dinner at (five-0-three) is a pleasant experience. Note that the restaurant's name is its area code and represents their commitment to source local ingredients. Not only is the food very good, but the service is personal, the atmosphere cordial and the prices are reasonable. The menu changes seasonally and many favorites come and go. At lunch try the grilled Asian salad, lobster enchilada or chile verde. Recommended dinner entrees include the glazed pork chop with truffle mac and cheese, the signature Delmonico steak or the signature burger (house-ground chuck, white cheddar, housemade bacon and caramelized onions on an artisan bun). For dessert, try a deep dish chocolate chip cookie with salted caramel ice cream made in-house.

CINDY'S ANTIQUES

Dynamic **Cindy Day,** the wife of the late state Senator L.B. Day, acquired legions of followers when she had her Et Cetera Antiques store. Formerly of Salem, Day has now relocated her business to Portland in the **Stars Antiques Mall** (7027 SE Milwaukie Ave, Portland; 503/235-5990), joining over 200 dealers in Portland's biggest antiques, collectibles and home decor mall. Her interesting inventory showcases glassware, china, silver, collectibles and many other pieces that are sure to add just the right touch to one's home or office.

Gerry's Exclusive List

BBQ
Podnah's Pit (1625 NE Killingsworth St, Portland; 503/281-3700)
Reverend's BBQ (7712 SE 13th Ave, Portland; 503/327-8755)

Bars and Pubs with Good Eats
23Hoyt (529 NW 23rd Ave, Portland; 503/445-7400)
Bar Mingo (811 NW 21st Ave, Portland; 503/445-4646)
Buffalo Gap Saloon & Eatery (6835 SW Macadam Ave, Portland; 503/244-7111)
Deschutes Brewery & Public House (210 NW 11th Ave, Portland; 503/296-4906)
McMenamins (mcmenamins.com): throughout the Northwest
Stammtisch (401 NE 28th Ave, Portland; 503/206-7983)

Best Sleeps
The Benson Hotel (309 SW Broadway, Portland; 503/228-2000)
The Heathman Hotel (1001 SW Broadway, Portland; 503/241-4100)
Sentinel (614 SW 11th Ave, Portland; 503/224-3400)
Sheraton Portland Airport Hotel (8235 NE Airport Way, Portland; 503/281-2500)

Breads and Bakery Goods
Baker & Spice Bakery (6330 SW Capitol Hwy, Portland; 503/244-7573)
Bob's Red Mill Whole Grain Store (5000 SE International Way, Milwaukie; 503/607-6455)
The Cakery (6306 SW Capitol Hwy, Portland; 503/546-3737)
Grand Central Bakery (numerous locations, Greater Portland; grandcentralbakery.com)
Lovejoy Bakers (939 NW 10th Ave, Portland, 503/208-3113; 33 NW 23rd Pl, Portland, 503/467-4067): breakfast, lunch and weekend brunch at Uptown location
Mehri's Bakery & Cafe (6923 SE 52nd Ave, Portland; 503/788-9600)
Pearl Bakery (102 NW 9th Ave, Portland; 503/827-0910)
St. Honoré Boulangerie (numerous locations, Greater Portland; sainthonorebakery.com)

Breakfast/Brunch
Beast (5425 NE 30th Ave, Portland; 503/841-6968): weekend brunch
Besaws (1545 NW 21st Ave, Portland; 503/228-2619): daily brunch

Imperial (Hotel Lucia, 410 SW Broadway, Portland; 503/228-7222): breakfast, brunch, lunch, dinner

Irving Street Kitchen (701 NW 13th Ave, Portland; 503/343-9440): brunch

The Original Pancake House, Portland (8601 SW 24th Ave, Portland; 503/246-9007)

The Palm Court Restaurant and Bar (The Benson Hotel, 309 SW Broadway, Portland; 503/228-2000)

Portland City Grill (111 SW 5th Ave, 30th floor, Portland; 503/450-0030): weekend brunch

Salty's on the Columbia (3839 NE Marine Dr, Portland; 503/288-4444): weekend brunch

Slappy Cakes (4246 SE Belmont St, Portland; 503/477-4805)

Stockpot Broiler (8200 SW Scholls Ferry Road, Beaverton; 503/643-5451): weekend brunch

Tasty n Alder (580 SW 12th Ave, Portland; 503/621-9251): daily brunch

Tasty n Sons (3808 N Williams Ave, Suite C, Portland; 503/621-1400): daily brunch

Verdigris (1315 NE Fremont St, Portland; 503/477-8106): weekend brunch

Burgers
Helvetia Tavern (10275 NW Helvetia Road, Hillsboro; 503/647-5286)
Canyon Grill (8825 SW Canyon Road, Beaverton; 503/292-5131)

Casual Dining/Casual Prices
Buffalo Gap Saloon & Eatery (6835 SW Macadam Ave, Portland; 503/244-7111)

Copper River Restaurant and Bar (7370 NE Cornell Rd, Hillsboro; 503/640-0917)

Goose Hollow Inn (1927 SW Jefferson St, Portland; 503/228-7010)

Oswego Grill at Kruse Way (7 Centerpointe Dr, Lake Oswego; 503/352-4750)

The Reedville Cafe (7575 SE Tualatin Valley Hwy, Hillsboro; 503/649-4643)

Stepping Stone Cafe (2390 NW Quimby St, Portland; 503/222-1132)

Cheese
Cheese Bar (6031 SE Belmont St, Portland; 503/222-6014): 200 local and imported cheeses

Coffee and Tea

Clockwork Rose Tea Emporium (12412 SW Broadway, Beaverton; 503/739-5120): whimsical atmosphere, steampunk tea room; reservations required

Coco Donuts (4790 SE Milwaukie Ave, Portland, 971/302-7445; 33 N Skidmore St, 971/279-4858; 2735 NE Broadway St, 503/477-9824; 814 SW 6th Ave, Portland, 503/505-4164; 709 SW 17th Ave, Portland, 503/360-1456)

Cup & Bar (118 NE Martin Luther King Jr. Blvd, Portland; 503/388-7701): coffee and chocolate tasting room

Steven Smith Teamaker (1626 NW Thurman St, Portland, 971/254-3949; 110 SE Washington St, Portland, 971/254-3935): tasting rooms and retail

World Cup Coffee & Tea (1740 NW Glisan St, Portland, 503/228-5503; Powell's City of Books, 1005 W Burnside St, Portland, 503/228-4551, ext.1233)

Confections

Candy Basket (1924 NE 181st Ave, Portland; 503/666-2000)

Chocolates by Bernard (440 5th St, Unit A, Lake Oswego; 503/675-7500)

Enchanté (10883 SE Main St, Milwaukie; 503/654-4846)

Ladybug Chocolates (266 NW 1st Ave, Canby; 503/263-3335)

Moonstruck Chocolate Co. (Factory Store: 6600 N Baltimore Ave, Portland, 503/247-3448; numerous retailers, 800/557-6666; moonstruck-chocolate.com)

Puddin' River Chocolates (1438 S Ivy St, Canby; 866/802-2708)

Doughnuts

Coco Donuts (4790 SE Milwaukie Ave, Portland, 971/302-7445; 33 N Skidmore St, 971/279-4858; 2735 NE Broadway St, 503/477-9824; 814 SW 6th Ave, Portland, 503/505-4164; 709 SW 17th Ave, Portland, 503/360-1456)

Voodoo Doughnut (22 SW 3rd Ave, Portland, 503/241-4707; 1501 NE Davis St, Portland, 503/235-2666): 24/7

Fireside

RingSide Steakhouse Uptown (2165 W Burnside St, Portland; 503/223-1513)

Fish and Seafood

Dan & Louis Oyster Bar (208 SW Ankeny St, Portland; 503/227-5906)

Jake's Famous Crawfish (401 SW 12th Ave, Portland; 503/226-1419)
Newman's Fish Co. (City Market, 735 NW 21st Ave, Portland; 503/227-2700): retail store
RingSide Fish House (838 SW Park Ave, mezzanine level, Portland; 503/227-3900)
Roe (515 SW Broadway, Suite 100, Portland; 503/232-1566)

Foreign Flavors

BRAZILIAN: Fogo de Chão (930 SW 6th Ave, Portland; 503/241-0900)
CHINESE: Seres Restaurant and Bar (1105 NW Lovejoy St, Portland; 971/222-7377)
FRENCH: St. Jack (1610 NW 23rd St, Portland, 503/360-1281); **Verdigris** (1315 NE Fremont St, Portland, 503/477-8106)
GERMAN: Stammtisch (401 NE 28th Ave, Portland; 503/206-7983)
ITALIAN: a Cena (7742 SE 13th Ave, Portland, 503/206-3291); **Gilda's Italian Restaurant** (1601 SW Morrison St, Portland, 503/688-5066); **Mama Mia Trattoria** (439 SW 2nd Ave, Portland, 503/295-6464); **Mucca Osteria** (1022 SW Morrison St, Portland, 503/227-5521); **Nostrana** (1401 SE Morrison St, Portland, 503/234-2427); **Piazza Italia** (1129 NW Johnson St, Portland, 503/478-0619); **Tucci Restaurant** (220 A Ave, Lake Oswego, 503/697-3383)
JAPANESE: Syun Izakaya (209 NE Lincoln St, Hillsboro; 503/640-3131)
MEXICAN: Amelia's Restaurant (105 NE 4th Ave, Hillsboro; 503/615-0191)
PERUVIAN: Andina (1314 NW Glisan St, Portland; 503/228-9535)
RUSSIAN: Kachka (720 SE Grand Ave, Portland; 503/235-0059)
SPANISH: Toro Bravo (120 NE Russell St, Portland; 503/281-4464)
THAI: Pok Pok (3226 SE Division St, Portland, 503/232-1387, 1469 NE Prescott St, Portland, 503/287-4149, 1639 Marshall St, Portland, 971/351-1946); **Thai Bloom** (3800 SW Cedar Hills Blvd, Beaverton, 503/644-8010)

Game

Beast (5425 NE 30th Ave, Portland; 503/841-6968)
Le Pigeon (738 E Burnside St, Portland; 503/546-8796)

Ice Cream and Other Frozen Treats

Cool Moon Ice Cream Company (1105 NW Johnson St, Portland; 503/224-2021)
Handel's Homemade Ice Cream and Yogurt (21300 SW Langer Farms Pkwy, Sherwood; 503/822-5142)
Salt & Straw (2035 NE Alberta St, Portland, 503/208-3867; 3345 SE Divi-

sion St, Portland, 503/208-2054; 838 NW 23rd Ave, Portland, 971/271-8168; Pine Street Market, 126 SW 2nd Ave, Portland; 503/384-2150); 100 A Ave, Lake Oswego, 503/305-8267)

Liquid Libations
Multnomah Whiskey Library (1124 SW Alder St, Portland; 503/954-1381)
Pearl Specialty Market & Spirits (900 NW Lovejoy St, Portland; 503/477-8604): retail store
SakéOne (820 Elm St, Forest Grove; 503/357-7056): saké

Meats
Gartner's Country Meat Market (7450 NE Killingsworth St, Portland; 503/252-7801)
Laurelhurst Market (3155 E Burnside St, Portland; 503/206-3097): butcher shop all day; dinner after 5
The Meating Place (6495 NW Cornelius Pass Road, Hillsboro; 503/533-0624): butcher shop, sandwiches
Otto's Sausage Kitchen (4138 SE Woodstock Blvd, Portland; 503/771-6714)

Personal Favorites
Ava Gene's (3377 SE Division St, Portland; 971/229-0571)
Beaches Restaurant and Bar (Portland International Airport, 7000 NE Airport Way, Portland; 503/335-8385)
Copper River Restaurant and Bar (7370 NE Cornell Road, Hillsboro; 503/640-0917)
Fogo de Chão (930 SW 6th Ave, Portland; 503/241-0900)
Imperial (Hotel Lucia, 410 SW Broadway, Portland; 503/228-7222)
Jake's Famous Crawfish (401 SW 12th Ave, Portland; 503/226-1419)
Le Pigeon (738 E Burnside St, Portland; 503/546-8796)
Mother's Bistro & Bar (212 SW Stark St, Portland; 503/464-1122)
Multnomah Athletic Club (1849 SW Salmon St, Portland; 503/223-6251): private club
Paley's Place (1204 NW 21st St, Portland; 503/243-2403)
Portland City Grill (111 SW 5th Ave, 30th floor, Portland; 503/450-0030)
Q Restaurant and Bar (828 SW 2nd Ave, Portland; 503/850-8915)
RingSide Steakhouse Uptown (2165 W Burnside St, Portland; 503/223-1513)
Sayler's Old Country Kitchen (10519 SE Stark St, Portland; 503/252-4171)

Pie
Baker & Spice Bakery (6330 SW Capitol Hwy, Portland; 503/244-7573)
Mother's Bistro & Bar (212 SW Stark St, Portland; 503/464-1122)
Pacific Pie Co. (1520 SE 7th Ave, Portland; 503/381-6157)

Pizza
Apizza Scholls (4741 SE Hawthorne Blvd, Portland; 503/233-1286)
Ken's Artisan Pizza (304 SE 28th Ave, Portland; 503/517-9951)
Nostrana (1401 SE Morrison St, Portland; 503/234-2427)
Via Chicago (2013 NE Alberta St, Portland; 503/719-6809)

Sandwiches
Buffalo Gap Saloon & Eatery (6835 SW Macadam Ave, Portland; 503/244-7111)
Kenny & Zuke's Delicatessen (1038 SW Stark St, Portland, 503/222-3354; 2376 NW Thurman St, Portland, 503/954-1737)
Pine State Biscuits (2204 NE Alberta St, Portland, 503/477-6605; 1100 SE Division St, Suite 100, Portland, 503/236-3356; 125 NE Schuyler St, Portland, 503/719-9357)

Southern
Pine State Biscuits (2204 NE Alberta St, Portland, 503/477-6605; 1100 SE Division St, Suite 100, Portland, 503/236-3356; 125 NE Schuyler St, Portland, 503/719-9357)

Steaks
El Gaucho Portland (The Benson Hotel 319 SW Broadway, Portland; 503/227-8794)
Fogo de Chão (930 SW 6th Ave, Portland; 503/241-0900)
RingSide Steakhouse Uptown (2165 W Burnside St, Portland; 503/223-1513)
Ruth's Chris Steak House (850 SW Broadway, Portland; 503/221-4518)
Sayler's Old Country Kitchen (10519 SE Stark St, Portland; 503/252-4171)
Tasty n Alder (580 SW 12th Ave, Portland; 503/621-9251)

Sushi
Sushi Mazi (2126 SE Division St, Portland; 503/432-8651)
Syun Izakaya (209 NE Lincoln St, Hillsboro; 503/640-3131)

View Restaurants
Chart House (5700 SW Terwilliger Blvd, Portland; 503/246-6963)

Portland City Grill (111 SW 5th Ave, 30th floor, Portland; 503/450-0030)
Salty's on the Columbia (3839 NE Marine Dr, Portland; 503/288-4444)
Stone Cliff Inn Restaurant & Bar (17900 S Clackamas River Dr, Oregon City; 503/631-7900)

Notes

Notes

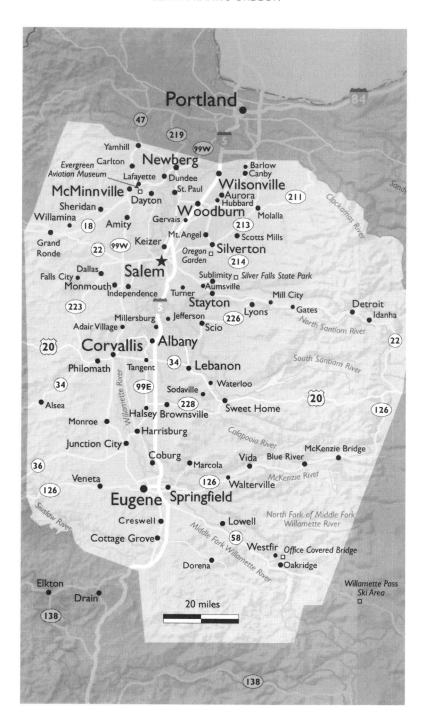

Portland

47

219

5

84

Sandy

99W

Yamhill

Evergreen Carlton
Aviation Museum   Lafayette ● Dundee
McMinnville ●   St. Paul
         Dayton

Newberg

Barlow
● Canby
Wilsonville

211

Clackamas River

Sheridan ●
Willamina ●
18   Amity   Gervais ●
Aurora
Hubbard
Woodburn   ● Molalla

Grand
Ronde   22   99W   Keizer   Mt. Angel   ● Scotts Mills
213

Oregon □
Garden   Silverton
214

Salem ★

Dallas ●
Falls City ●
Monmouth ●
Independence   Turner ●
Sublimity □ Silver Falls State Park
● Aumsville
Stayton
223   Millersburg ●   Jefferson ●   226   Lyons   ● Gates   Detroit ●
Adair Village ●   Scio   ● Idanha

20   Corvallis ● Albany
Mill City

North Santiam River

22

Philomath ●   Tangent   34   ● Lebanon
South Santiam River

34   99E   Sodaville ●   ● Waterloo
● Alsea   228   Sweet Home   20   126
Monroe ●   Halsey Brownsville
● Harrisburg

Junction City ●
Calapooia River

36   Coburg ● Marcola   Vida   Blue River   McKenzie Bridge ●

Veneta ●   126   ● Walterville   McKenzie River

126   Eugene Springfield

Siuslaw River   Creswell ●   ● Lowell
North Fork of Middle Fork
Willamette River

Cottage Grove ●   58   Westfir   Office Covered Bridge
Dorena ●   ● Oakridge

Elkton ●
Drain ●

138

Willamette Pass
Ski Area □

20 miles

138

CHAPTER TWO

Willamette Valley

ALBANY

First Burger

210 1st Ave W
Tues-Sat: 11-8
Inexpensive

541/704-1128
thefirstburger.com

First Burger is a casual outpost for hand-formed, made-to-order hamburgers. There are a dozen choices with names like The Smokestack, The Uncle Sam, The Iron Woman and The Whole Farm. If those don't strike your fancy, build your own from a list of patties made with house-ground beef, chicken, buffalo or half bacon and half beef; fresh, grilled or pickled vegetables; cheeses and such. The more you add, the more you pay. All sandwiches are served with hand-cut French fries. In addition, there are shakes, malts, soups, salads, onion rings and deep-fried pickles.

The Depot Cafe

822 SE Lyon St
Mon-Thu: 11-9, Fri, Sat: 11-10; Sun: 11-8
Inexpensive to moderate

541/926-7326
depotrestaurantinc.com

Since 1976, The Depot has been a landmark in town and known to have the best fish and chips around. The atmosphere is casual with a quirky interior; it resembles a cafe you might find at the coast. Menu options range from fish and fresh-cut fries to shrimp salads, award-winning housemade chowder and a variety of delicious appetizers. Aside from the best fish and chips and chowder, Bonnie's shrimp crunch salad is a crowd pleaser; a mix of shredded carrots, celery and green onions blended with tender shrimp, mayo, crunchy noodles and sunflower seeds. Beer and wine options are available including an array of bottled beers, rotating taps of domestic and craft beers and varietal wines of Riesling, chardonnay, cabernet and pinot gris.

Nichols Garden Nursery

1190 Old Salem Road NE   541/928-9280, 800/422-3985
Mon-Sat: 10-4   nicholsgardennursery.com

Three generations of this family business continue to take pride that they never buy or sell genetically-engineered seeds or plants. All garden varieties are home tested so vegetables grown from Nichols' seed or stock are delicious and healthy. In addition to new and unusual seeds (vegetable, herb and flower), plants, bulbs and roots, Nichols maintains many discontinued varieties of seeds, lawn mixes and other garden essentials. Non-garden products include supplies for making beer, wine and cheese; herbs; spices; oils; soaps and lotions.

Novak's Hungarian Restaurant

208 2nd Ave SW   541/967-9488
Mon, Wed-Fri: 8-8 (Fri till 9:30);
Sat: 7:30 a.m.-9:30 p.m.; Sun: 7:30-4   novakshungarian.com
Moderate

Guests are treated like family at Novak's Hungarian Restaurant where traditional European fare is featured for breakfast, lunch and dinner. Ukrainian pancakes, späetzle and gravy, homemade sausages and egg and griddle dishes make up the breakfast menu. Lunch specialties include savory cabbage rolls, chicken paprika, pork schnitzel sandwiches and vegetarian specials; combination plates, specials and an expanded list of entrees are served for dinner. If you'd like to sample a bit of everything, opt for the buffets: dinner Monday through Thursday and brunch on Sunday. Irresistible Dobosh torte, crème horns and other rich pastries and eye-popping desserts are made on-site.

Sybaris Bistro

442 1st Ave W   541/928-8157
Tue-Thu: 5-8; Fri, Sat: 5-9   sybarisbistro.com
Moderate to moderately expensive

Sybaris Bistro is a spacious, upscale dining establishment in what was once a historic downtown industrial building. Chef Matt Bennett creates a new menu each month using the freshest goods from growers and farmers in the heart of the Willamette Valley. The Northwest cuisine is an innovative and eclectic interpretation of classic meat, seafood and poultry dishes. Seasonally-adapted choices may include green bean almondine, duck breast stroganoff with wild mushrooms or slow-cooked smoked pork osso buco and burnt apples. Housemade is the rule, not the exception, right down to catsup and daily bread. The restaurant's decor is always fresh, too; partner and wife Janel Bennett arranges displays of local artists' works.

Vault 244

244 1st Ave SW   541/791-9511
Mon-Thu: 4-10; Fri, Sat: 4-11   vault244.com
Moderately expensive
Vault 244 has settled into a popular cocktail and dining gathering spot that feels much more metro than one would expect in Albany. You can readily make a meal from a dozen tapas choices or go for full entrees of salads, pastas, land and sea items; vegetarian, too. The wine and cocktail menu is extensive and the chocolate flourless torte is indeed as decadent as advertised. Plan to visit on a warm summer evening; outdoor seating is delightful.

ALSEA

Leaping Lamb Farm Stay

20368 Honey Grove Road   541/487-4966
Moderate   leapinglambfarm.com
Scottie and Greg Jones continue the original 19th-century Honey Grove Farm homestead tradition as a working farm and grow hay, corn, raspberries, blueberries, grapes, plums, pears, apples, and a variety of vegetables for themselves, their families, farm animals and guests to enjoy. During your visit you'll likely come in contact with chickens, turkeys, sheep, horses, a donkey and a peacock. A unique aspect to this farm is the two-bedroom farm stay cottage and the four-bedroom farmhouse for bed and breakfast guests. The cottage sleeps up to six people; a flat rate is the same for parties of two or six. The large, recently remodeled farmhouse sleeps up to ten guests, with a flat rate that increases per person over four. The kitchens in both units come fully stocked with breakfast items (seasonally fresh) for guests to prepare as they wish; they can even source eggs straight from the henhouse. Guests have the option to help feed the farm animals, buy fruits and vegetables, collect fresh eggs or wander the trails throughout 64 acres. If the weather allows, lazing by the creek or hunting for mushrooms is always an option.

AMITY

The Blue Goat Restaurant

506 S Trade St   503/835-5170
Wed-Fri: 5-8; Sat, Sun: 11:30-8 (seasonally adjusted)   amitybluegoat.com
Inexpensive to moderate

At this 50-seat restaurant, owners Cassie and Dave VanDomelen source local products for the daily-changing menu. At lunch, you'll find soups, salads and other starters, plus sandwiches, burgers and pizza. Dinner brings some of the same with added entrees (seafood, wood-fired tacos), along with weekly specials. Frequent desserts include their decadent chocolate hazelnut torte, classic bread pudding and seasonal fruit-driven specialties. In addition to Oregon wines and beers, there are house-crafted cocktails and a full bar.

Blue Raeven Farmstand

20650 S Hwy 99W   503/835-0740
Mon-Sat: 9-5:30; Sun: 10-5   blueraevenfarmstand.com

Step inside this farmstand and you'll be greeted by tantalizing aromas of freshly-baked cinnamon rolls, cookies and pies. Owners Jamie and Ron Lewis bring fresh berries from their 140-acre berry farm three miles down the road. For pie-lovers, dozens of varieties of five- and nine-inch pies will fulfill the hankering; many are seasonal to capture the essence of the freshest fruits enveloped in golden crust, sometimes solo or in interesting and delicious combinations. There is also a generous list of cream pies; on request, most pies can be prepared sugar-free. (It's best to call ahead if you're craving a certain flavor.) Fresh produce, jams, jellies, syrups, gifts and other local products round out the merchandise selection.

BROWNSVILLE

The Living Rock Studios

911 W Bishop Way   541/466-5814
Wed-Sat: 10-5 (or by reservation)   livingrockstudios.org
Free (donations accepted)

The Living Rock Studios offers a look back into history with a fabulous showing of rocks, historic artifacts, carvings of Oregon native woods, life-size bird paintings, hundreds of mineral specimens and other fascinating objects. Visionary artist and naturalist Howard B. Taylor spent over 30 years creating this unique attraction, made with more than 800 tons of stone and concrete. Visitors marvel at seven biblical scenes made of translucent rocks, perhaps more beautiful than stained glass windows. A tree of petrified wood pieces, lined with sparkling Oregon crystals, reaches two stories high, crowned by a fiber-art canopy. Look high and low as many items are built into walls, ramps and the stairway; flashlights are provided to highlight special details and to make agates glow.

CARLTON

Abbey Road Farm

10501 NE Abbey Road   503/852-6278
Moderate to very expensive   abbeyroadfarm.com
Sandi and Daniel Wilkens preside over an 82-acre farm, offering guests a choice of five tastefully appointed "silo suites" or a newly renovated three-bedroom farmhouse which works well for families or couples traveling together. The suites are unique in that they are built into grain silos with windows on the curved walls that open to stunning views of vast grass seed fields, a neighboring vineyard and the Silo Garden. A gourmet, locally-sourced breakfast is served in the beautiful dining room. As they explore the property, animal lovers will be entertained with the collection of llamas, sheep, goats, miniature donkeys and chickens.

Carlton Winemakers Studio

801 N Scott St   503/852-6100
Daily: 11-5 (Dec-Feb till 4)   winemakersstudio.com
Visit this innovative winemaking collective where over a dozen small, independent vintners produce and sell bottles of some of the best that

---

HISTORIC COVERED BRIDGES

With only hand tools, Oregon's pioneers began building covered bridges around 1850. There are 51 covered bridges; most are located in Lane and Linn counties although since 1900, most of them have simply worn out. They were first covered to keep the huge truss timbers dry because the wet climate could take out a wooden bridge in just a few years, while a covered bridge could last for 80 or more years. In Linn County, there is a scenic loop to see many of these covered bridges. It begins near the town of Scio; just follow the Covered Bridge Tour Route (exit off I-5 to Albany and take Highway 226 east of town). Further south, in Lane County, exit off I-5 to Cottage Grove to see other covered bridges. For additional information about these historic treasures around Oregon, visit covered-bridges.org.

Oregon wine country has to offer. Represented wineries may be as small as operations producing only 200 cases a year, and some are exclusive to this location. The large selection of red and white wines range from $20 to $75 a bottle. Creative uses of repurposed, recycled and green materials in the building's design and construction led to its impressive status as the first winery to be registered with the U.S. Green Building Council. You'll see many of these features in the state-of-the-art tasting room and in the production areas.

Cuvee

214 W Main St   503/852-6555
Wed-Sat: 5:30-9, Sun: 5-8 (summer);
Fri, Sat: 5:30-9, Sun: 5-8 (winter)   cuveedining.com
Moderately expensive

Chef-owner Gilbert Henry wanted to find a place reminiscent of his home region in Alsace, France where he could set up a fine country French restaurant. He decided that Carlton was just that locale. So he set to work to create a dinner house with a distinct French accent, a large wine list (French imports and Oregon favorites), classic cocktails and a restaurant drawing diners to his tables because of its sophisticated ambience. Lovers of true French cuisine will appreciate many traditional favorites such as bouillabaisse, escargots, coquille St. Jacques, steamed mussels and boeuf bourguignon with ingredients sourced from local farms and vendors. Two signatures of a real French dinner house are crisp pomme frites and warm, crunchy French bread with that just-out-of-the-oven aroma. In both cases, Cuvee excels. Informed diners visit Cuvee on Wednesday, Thursday and Sunday evenings for Chef Henry's scrumptious three-course prix-fixe dinner; it's a real bargain at $35 per person.

Equestrian Wine Tours

6325 NE Abbey Road   503/864-2336
Year round, by reservation   equestrianwinetours.com
Prices vary

Head to the Dundee Hills for a memorable adventure with friends or romantic outing exploring the wine country via horseback or carriage. If you'd just like to sit back and enjoy yourself, opt for a carriage ride wine tour and tasting; choose from a white "Central Park" carriage (also perfect for weddings or engagements), or a 12-passenger surrey carriage (ideal for small groups). If you are more ambitious, ride one of their well-trained Tennessee Walkers and wind your way between vineyards for a guided tour and wine tasting. Saddle up, sip and ride where wine meets fun in Oregon wine country.

The Horse Radish

211 W Main St   503/852-6656
Sun-Thu: noon-3; Fri, Sat: noon-10   thehorseradish.com
Inexpensive to moderate

Superb artisan cheeses from around the Northwest reign at this restaurant and wine and cheese bar The knowledgeable staff assists in creating custom meal and cheese platters from any of the offerings to take along on a wine tasting sojourn or enjoy in-house with wine or a meal. Soup, salad and sandwich fare prevails on the lunch menu, and dinner specials are offered Friday and Saturday nights in conjunction with weekly live music performances.

R.R. Thompson House Bed & Breakfast

517 N Kutch St   503/852-6236
Moderate   rrthompsonhouse.com

This stately 1930s Colonial Revival estate is within walking distance of over two dozen Carlton wineries and tasting rooms plus restaurants and shops. The historic home features five floral-themed guest rooms and suites with private marble and granite bathrooms, whirlpool tubs and luxurious mattresses for restful slumber. Breakfast in the dining room is a feast for the senses and morning appetites; the signature brie cheese omelet or French toast with homemade fruit compote may be the choice du jour. A thoughtful selection of light beverages from the well-stocked dining room refrigerator is handy for guests to raid day or night.

Republic of Jam

211 W Main St   503/395-5261
Daily: noon-5   republicofjam.com

The artisan spreads at Republic of Jam are not your mother's preserves. Jam master Angie Holt has paired local fruits, herbs and spices to create gourmet combinations such as blackberry lime, chocolate cherry, cranberry ginger, plum cinnamon walnut and raspberry anise. On an inspired whim, she'll toss in bacon, tomatoes, figs, mint and whatever else is in the kitchen to make outstanding jams and syrups. Lemons preserved in salt, spices and lemon juice are a staple in Middle Eastern dishes; delicious with salmon and vegetables, too. Shaw freely dispenses samples, recipes and serving suggestions. The tasting room serves swanky tastes on weekends (sweet and savory tidbits, drinks and flights of jam) using her products; check the schedule for occasional cocktail parties in the compact Main Street store.

CORVALLIS

Big River Restaurant

101 NW Jackson Ave   541/757-0694
Mon-Thu: 11-9:30 (Fri till 10:30); Sat: 4-10:30, Sun: 4-9   bigriverrest.com
Moderate

A big hit since it first opened, Big River features eclectic, fresh Northwest cuisine using local organic produce, natural meats, sustainable seafood and Big River artisan breads from the on-site bakery. Award-winning pastry chef Loretta Verdugo also creates hard-to-resist desserts. Sandwiches made on these breads and stuffed with pulled pork, turkey or house-cured beef brisket layered with sauerkraut are extra delicious. Specialty martinis, single malt scotch and local and regional wines are featured at the bar. The crew strives to bring good, honest food directly from the Valley with the menu supporting many of the area's hard-working farmers, ranchers and foragers.

Block 15 Restaurant & Brewery

300 SW Jefferson Ave   541/758-2077
Daily: 11-11 (Fri, Sat till 1 a.m.)   block15.com
Inexpensive

Located on a busy corner in downtown Corvallis with well over a dozen specialty and seasonal lagers, IPAs, stouts and barrel-matured ales always on tap, it's no wonder this is a well-known and popular hangout. The menu features casual pub food with a few twists to the usual offerings. Instead of a BLT sandwich, try the BMT—bacon, mozzarella, tomato and hazelnut pesto on grilled sourdough; all sandwiches and burgers are accompanied by beer-battered fries, salad or soup. Great tasting salads can also be found on the menu; dress them up with housemade dressings and the addition of chicken, salmon, pulled pork or smoked tempeh which can also be added to pasta dishes. Monthly and weekend specials feature the best local bounty. At Block 15, they are always evolving and constantly searching for new and effective ways to bring the highest quality beer and food in a more sustainable manner.

The Broken Yolk Cafe

119 SW 3rd St   541/738-9655
Daily: 7-3   broken-yolk.com
Inexpensive

The Broken Yolk Cafe is a home-style breakfast spot until 3 every afternoon. Eggs, of course, take top billing in skillet and scramble dishes or alongside or atop crispy chicken-fried steak or corned beef hash. Creamy sausage gravy and other sauces complement just about any entree, and Grandma Dale's strawberry jam is the perfect topper for toast or fluffy hotcakes. Homemade "cinn-ful" cinnamon rolls are always an option. Gramps built a fun play area for young kids in this family-friendly and collegiate favorite.

Caves Bier & Kitchen

308 SW 3rd St   541/286-4473
Tue-Thu: 4 p.m.-midnight (Fri till 1 a.m.);
Sat, Sun: 9 a.m.-1 a.m.   biercaves.com
Inexpensive to moderate

The owners of Block 15, Kristen and Nick Arzner, also operate this European bier tavern, located next door above Block 15's barrel cellar. Belgian beers are on tap as well as Block 15 brews, rotating local and imported craft beers and an impressive selection of bottled beers and bourbons. Regional farms are tapped to provide food offerings for the European/ American dinner menu. Because nearly everything is prepared fresh daily, the menu varies with the season. A sampling includes house-pickled vegetables served with bread and cheese, housemade pretzels with bier cheese, grass-fed beef burgers, salads and pastas. Brussels-style waffles with fried chicken, classic Benedicts and other hearty breakfasts and morning drinks are weekend brunch favorites (until 2 p.m.).

Del Alma Restaurant

136 SW Washington Ave   541/753-2222
Mon-Thu: 5-9:30 (Fri, Sat till 10)   delalmarestaurant.com
Moderate

At this contemporary Latin fusion restaurant and waterfront bar, the tapas menu is anything but boring. Guacamole is made with house-cured bacon, chipotles and hazelnuts and served with homemade chips; albóndigas are delicious ground beef and pork meatballs with spices, pine nuts, cheese and raisins. You could have a very satisfying and tasty meal from the tapas menu or select entrees such as Yucatan-style barbecue pork, grilled filet mignon or Oaxacan-style roasted vegetable tamale. Three-course dinner specials are the order of the day on Wednesdays; choose from three first and second courses and dessert, specially priced at $30 per person. Owner Kinn Edwards has assembled a notable wine list featuring selections from Spain, Portugal, South America and the Pacific Northwest; most are sold by the bottle and a limited number are poured by the glass. Frequent dinners with wine or cocktail pairings are delightful additions to this intimate, fine dining venue. The adjoining Dulce del Alma wine bar offers a casual venue for wine, tapas and desserts (dinner from the restaurant upon request).

FESTIVALS AND FAIRS IN THE VALLEY

MARCH
McMinnville Wine & Food Classic (McMinnville, sipclassic.org)

APRIL
Wooden Shoe Tulip Fest (Woodburn, woodenshoe.com)

MAY
McMenamins UFO Festival (McMinnville, ufofest.com)

JUNE
Oregon Garden BrewCamp (Silverton, oregongarden.org)
World Beat Festival (Salem, salemmulticultural.org)

JULY
Oregon Country Fair (Veneta, oregoncountryfair.org)
Salem Art Fair & Festival (Salem, salemart.org)
Benton, Lane, Linn and Marion county fairs are held. Check oregonfairs.org for dates and details.

AUGUST
Northwest Art & Air Festival (Albany, nwartandair.org)
Oregon Jamboree (Sweet Home, oregonjamboree.com)
Oregon State Fair (Salem, oregonstatefair.org): runs through Labor Day
Silverton Fine Arts Festival (Silverton, silvertonarts.org)
Willamette Country Music Festival (Brownsville, willamettecountrymusicfestival.com)
Polk and Yamhill county fairs are held. Check oregonfairs.org for dates and details.

SEPTEMBER
Corvallis Fall Festival (Corvallis, corvallisfallfestival.org)
Mt. Angel Oktoberfest (Mt. Angel, oktoberfest.org)
Sublimity Harvest Festival (Sublimity, sublimityharvestfest.com)

DECEMBER
Magic at The Mill at Willamette Heritage Center (Salem, magicatthemill.org)

Hanson Country Inn

795 SW Hanson St   541/752-2919
Moderate   hcinn.com

One of the Valley's oldest country inns enjoys a charming knoll-top setting. The five-acre estate was built in 1928 by J.A. Hanson and also functioned as a poultry breeding ranch. The home has been brought back to its original style and class by the Covey family and adorned with attractive antiques, art and a well-stocked library. Four spacious guest rooms feature original built-ins, sitting rooms and private baths; a cozy two-bedroom cottage is equipped with a private kitchen and modern electronic conveniences. Each morning, the aroma of homemade muffins entices guests into the sunny dining room for a full gourmet breakfast. The facilities are ideal for garden receptions, parties and meetings.

McMenamins Corvallis

420 NW Third St   541/758-6044
Daily: 11 a.m.-1 a.m. (Sun, Mon till midnight)   mcmenamins.com
Moderate

Locals frequent this English-style pub because of the fresh, seasonal food, awesome drink specials and cozy atmosphere. Outdoor seating is available in summer, and it's a great venue for "tailgate parties" before Oregon State University football games. (For a detailed description of the McMenamins brand, see Page 12)

Monroe

2001 NW Monroe Ave   541/758-0080
Sun, Mon: 11-11 (Tue, Wed till midnight; Thu-Sat till 1 a.m.)   mcmenamins.com
Moderate

The neighborhood meeting spot for students, faculty, staff and townies alike. Play a few rounds of pool, check out the onsite brewery, wonder at all the sinks on the wall or just grab a seat at the bar. (For a detailed description of the McMenamins brand, see Page 12)

Nearly Normal's

109 NW 15th St   541/753-0791
Mon-Thu: 8-8 (Fri, Sat till 9)   nearlynormals.com
Inexpensive and up

This handcrafted vegetarian restaurant has been evolving to "nearly normal" since 1979, producing "gonzo cuisine" — the outcome of using the freshest, often organic, ingredients; many original recipes "born from chaos;" and careful preparation and presentation of dishes. The large menu offers eggs, potatoes or pancakes for breakfast; soups, salads, veggie burgers (try the famous Sunburger), falafel and a "nearly nasty" burrito; kids' menu, too. Pasta dishes, Thai and Indian curries and enchiladas are popular dinner entrees. Enjoy your meal in either the upstairs or downstairs dining rooms or outside in good weather with beer, wine or a cocktail.

New Morning Bakery

219 SW 2nd St   541/754-0181
Mon-Sat: 7 a.m.-9 p.m.; Sun: 8-8   newmorningbakery.com
Inexpensive to moderate

Tristan and Keara James have tried to enhance New Morning Bakery as the "go to" downtown bakery spot; breakfast is available until 1 p.m. The oversized iced cinnamon rolls are irresistible along with tantalizing pecan sticky buns, scones, bear claws, coffee cakes and several varieties of quiche. The lunch and dinner menus include homemade soups, stews, chowders, sandwiches (made on freshly-baked bread), salads and plentiful entrees. Since a common dilemma is what to order; try a salad sampler plate for lunch—two or three salad choices plus delicious bread. There is a long list of entrees such as lasagna, roasted vegetable polenta casserole, wraps and daily specials with local beers and wines also available. Complete your meal with a decadent piece of cake, seasonal tarts and pies, cream puffs, bread pudding, cookies and cheesecake. Thursdays offer a $9.95 three-course dinner option. When holidays roll around, the bakers pull out all stops to turn out magnificent Irish soda bread and Christmas creations like rich fruitcakes, German stollen, candy cane-shaped coffeecakes, sweet breads and gingerbread houses and kits.

COTTAGE GROVE

Buster's Main Street Cafe

811 Main St   541/942-8363
Sun-Thu: 8-2; Fri, Sat: 8-7   bustersmsc.com
Inexpensive to moderate

Cottage Grove and vicinity have been on the silver screen as early as 1927 when Buster Keaton starred in The General. Thus, the name Buster's Main Street Cafe pays homage to this great comedian. Breakfast offerings include traditional, griddle and plenty of egg dishes plus blood orange mimosas and white peach bellinis. Sandwiches, burgers, homemade soups and salads are on the lunch menu. Of particular interest is the selection of craft sodas served by the bottle or glass or made into a float. The entire menu plus dinner specials are available on Fridays and Saturdays when Buster's remains open until 7 p.m.

Stacy's Covered Bridge Restaurant & Lounge

401 E Main St   541/767-0320
Mon-Wed: 11:30-8; Thu, Fri: 11:30-9; Sat: 4-9   Facebook
Moderate

Stacy's operates next to the Centennial Covered Bridge in a building that originally housed the Bank of Cottage Grove. With just 14 tables, the dining area fills up quickly. Owner Stacy Solomon prides himself on good service, comfortable prices and a menu of fresh seafood, prime rib, pastas and fresh salads. A good selection of appealing lunch sandwiches, reasonably-priced early-bird dinner specials and warm-weather outdoor seating add to the appeal.

DALLAS

Latitude One

904 Main St   503/831-1588
Thu-Sat: 4-close   latitudeonedallas.com
Moderate to moderately expensive

This delightful dinner spot is housed in a historic 1892 downtown Dallas building. A somewhat limited menu includes a variety of food from the land, sea and garden as well as weekly specials. Small plates and shareables include crab-filled mushroom caps, fish tacos, artichoke dip, prime rib sliders and more. Fresh Northwest entrees include locally sourced pork chops, chef's choice beef, steamer clams and pasta variations such as their five layer signature lasagna, a classic fettucine alfredo, mushroom fettucine and sweet pepper and sausage pasta with garlic and herbs. Entrees are accompanied by a fresh side salad or housemade soup. Seasonal specials and desserts are ever-changing to ensure the freshest ingredients are used. Arrive early enough to assure a seat on Friday evenings for live music entertainment.

DAYTON

Red Ridge Farms

5510 NE Breyman Orchards Road   503/864-2200
Store: Daily: 10-5   redridgefarms.com
Lodging: Expensive to very expensive

The Durant family began growing wine grapes in the early 1970s; today they farm over 60 acres of prime wine grapes and tend to approximately 13,000 olive trees. In 2005, they began growing cold-hardy olive trees. The Oregon Olive Mill building houses a state-of-the-art Italian Alfa Laval press and bottling facilities where olives are pressed mid- to late-November. The weekend before Thanksgiving, the Durants host a public Olio Nuovo party with tastings of fresh olive oil, bruschetta and samples of their wines. Visit the Red Ridge Shop and nursery for specialty vinegars, gourmet salts, teas, wines, local products, houseplants, lavender and rosemary plants, perennials, annuals, herbs, shrubs and trees. Lodging accommodations include a charming Garden Suite above the store and beautiful Stoneycrest Cottage situated in the vineyard.

Stoller Family Estate

16161 NE McDougall Road   503/864-3404
Lodging: Expensive to very expensive   stollerfamilyestate.com
Stoller Family Estate is one of Oregon's most highly regarded vineyards and wineries. Pioneering Oregonian and founder Bill Stoller purchased his family's second-generation farm in 1993 with the vision of cultivating an enduring legacy for the land and Oregon's wine industry. Over the last 25 years, he has patiently transformed the 399-acre property into the largest contiguous vineyard in the Dundee Hills that has become synonymous with exceptional wines. Longtime winemaker Melissa Burr works in concert with vineyard manager Jason Tosch to oversee the site's continued refinement. Stoller Family Estate features the world's first LEED Gold certified winery, three guest homes and a state of the art tasting room with panoramic vineyard views.

DUNDEE

Black Walnut Inn & Vineyard

9600 NE Worden Hill Road   503/538-8663, 866/429-4114
Expensive to very expensive   blackwalnutvineyard.com
The Black Walnut Inn is a boutique nine-room inn located in the heart of

---

WILLAMETTE VALLEY CASINO

There's plenty of gaming in Oregon for folks who want a chance at Lady Luck. Casinos are operated by individual Native American tribal councils and have been successful in bringing additional revenues and jobs to Oregon. Here's a brief overview of the Willamette Valley:

GRAND RONDE

Spirit Mountain Casino (27100 SW Salmon River Hwy, 503/879-2350, spiritmountain.com): 2,000 slots, table games, bingo, over 250 rooms, RV parking, dining (casual, buffet), concerts and special events

the Dundee Hills where luxury accommodations offer an intimate and comfortable elegant experience focused on connecting guests to the soul and bounty of Oregon's wine country. The location offers easy access to many world-class wineries. Breathtaking views across the Willamette Valley to Mt. Hood and Mt. Jefferson can be enjoyed from balconies, patios and garden areas throughout the inn and gardens.

Dundee Bistro
100-A SW 7th St   503/554-1650
Daily: 11:30-9   dundeebistro.com
Moderately expensive

Fratelli Ponzi Fine Food & Wine
         503/554-1500
Daily: noon-close   fratelliponzi.com
Mention the name Ponzi in Oregon and it will probably receive instant recognition as one of the leaders in the Oregon wine industry. It is no surprise that Ponzi's Dundee restaurant and wine bar are winners as well. With more than two decades of success hosting locals and the ever-increasing number of wine country visitors, the Bistro's kitchen continues to present fresh ideas and casual dishes inspired and executed by Executive Chef Ryan Clark. The Bistro consistently sources ingredients from neighboring farms, ranches, orchards, fishermen and wild mushroom foragers; the result is a seasonal and fresh menu. Designed and built by the Ponzi clan, the Italianate complex features murals and artwork by Oregon artists. Guests enjoy cozy fireside seating and summer courtyard dining; a private dining room accommodates up to 50 people. At the adjacent **Fratelli Ponzi Fine Food & Wine,** an Italian-inspired wine bar and retail shop, explore and taste the carefully curated selection of pinot noir and Italian varietals from Oregon and Italy. Olive oil, coffee, chocolate and other specialty Italian products offer wonderful take home items or gifts. Small plates, three wine flights daily and wines by the glass make up a comprehensive wine tasting experience and a comfortable place to relax or enjoy a pre-dinner aperitivo. For olive oil aficionados, here is where you can buy the Ponzi's extra virgin olive oil direct from their Italian estate in the Le Marche region.

Dundee Manor
8380 NE Worden Hill Road   503/554-1945, 888/262-1133
Expensive   dundeemanor.com
Well-traveled hosts Brad Cunningham and David Godfrey put fond memories and experiences from around the globe to good use in their 1908 Edwardian estate. Accommodations consist of four rooms with Asian,

European, African and North American motifs and accessories acquired on their journeys. Upon arrival, guests are welcomed with a glass of local wine. In-room snacks and refreshing beverages are offered nightly with turndown service. Carve out some time to take in views of Mt. Hood, Mt. Jefferson and Mt. Bachelor and enjoy the wooded and landscaped areas with gazebos, pergolas and private sitting areas, complete with attractive lighting and soothing music. En suite amenities are sure to please even finicky guests: down comforters, extra comfy queen beds, luxury linens, fleece spa robes and daily fresh flowers. The seemingly unending pampering continues at candlelit breakfasts — wonderful gourmet courses, beautiful presentation and special attention by your hosts.

Joy's Uptown Style
110 SW 7th St   503/223-3400
Mon-Fri: 10-6; Sat: 10-5   joysuptown.com

Joy Walker has an eye for fashion, especially beautiful casual wear with lovely accessories to match. Most ensembles may be ordered in a full spectrum of bright or subdued colors. Mother-of-the-bride (or groom) dresses and formal attire are available with more limited choices. An expert seamstress can take a tuck here or there, reposition buttons, raise hemlines or modify sleeves and collars to customize the piece for the desired look. At Joy's the seemingly lost art of personalized customer service is superb! Conveniently located next to Ponzi's Dundee Bistro.

Tina's Restaurant
760 Hwy 99W   503/538-8880
Daily: 5-close   tinasdundee.com
Expensive

Dwight McFaddin and Michael Stiller combine their passion for food in this small 50-seat restaurant, whose customers often return to the two intimate dining rooms and familiar bar. Dinner entrees include duck breast, halibut, rack of lamb, beef or pork tenderloin and vegetarian or shrimp risotto. Most dishes are prepared using European techniques. Menus are developed around organic, healthy, high-quality, fresh and regional foods from nearby farmers and neighbors. A substantial wine list is offered from vintners just a stone's throw away; spirits and beer, too. Tina's also offers a beautifully renovated one-bedroom cottage with a full bathroom, kitchen and living area — perfect for a weekend of wine touring. See their website for details. Booking is handled through vacasa. com.

EUGENE

Caddis Fly Angling Shop
168 W 6th Ave   541/505-8061
Mon-Fri: 9-6; Sat: 9-5; Sun: 10-3   caddisflyshop.com
Since 1975, novice or professional fishermen (and fisherwomen) have been visiting this amazing 4,000-square foot emporium for fishing gear. This Eugene institution not only offers the best brands of equipment (Echo, Orvis, Winston, Bauer, Rio, Sage and more), but also provides advice on just about anything you'd want to know about one of Oregon's great recreational activities. As a fly-fishing shop, they specialize in flies for all types of fish and stock all necessary supplies and materials if you choose to tie your own. Don't go near the water without the appropriate waders, inflatable watercraft, clothing, books and accessories that you may not have known even existed (convenient online shopping, too). Lastly, book a trip with one of their licensed and experienced guides for an unforgettable experience — rain or shine.

Café 440
440 Coburg Road   541/505-8493
Daily: 11-9 (Fri till 10)   cafe440.com
Moderate
When you're in the mood for a relaxed lunch or dinner at a friendly place, head to this stop on busy Coburg Road. You'll find topnotch comfort food like burgers, meatloaf and other sandwiches, delicious salads with housemade dressings, soups and "gourmet" mac and cheese. The dinner menu expands to include steaks, Northwest salmon, pastas and more. The sizable menu is bursting with old-standbys, many given updated treatment with unexpected and tasty ingredients. Owner Todd Schuetz adheres to his philosophy "keep it simple and make it better than everyone else." Sounds like the right idea.

Café Soriah
384 W 13th Ave   541/342-4410
Daily: 5-10 (dinner); Wed-Fri: 11:30-2 (lunch)   cafesoriah.com
Moderately expensive
This longtime establishment continues to please patrons with Mediterranean dishes. Old World spice blended with Northwest-fresh is Soriah's trademark on its varying menu. You might find Greek and Middle Eastern favorites like souvlaki (marinated beef skewers) or fattoush (romaine lettuce mix) that pairs nicely with chicken, steak, fish and seafood, lamb entrees or vegetarian plates of spanakopita (spinach pastry) and aubergine

(eggplant). Chef Ib Hamide enjoys mingling with his diners; order a flambé entree or dessert and he will dazzle you tableside (any day except Sunday and Monday). The cafe's backyard garden provides a great seating venue (heated to ward off a bit of chill if necessary).

Cascades Raptor Center

32275 Fox Hollow Road   541/485-1320
Tue-Sun: Hours vary   cascadesraptorcenter.org
Nominal

Take your children to this nature center and wildlife hospital for educational fun. Some 50 resident birds of nearly 30 species are viewable in roomy outdoor aviaries as part of the permanent exhibition. Other injured, ailing or orphaned birds of prey are elsewhere on the property and away from public view. These birds are rescued, rehabilitated and released back into the wild. A combination of special permits, exemplary medical care and adherence to stringent standards has allowed the dedicated staff and volunteers to provide individualized care to over 300 birds a year, with a goal of returning as many as possible to their rightful environments.

East 19th Street Cafe

1485 E 19th Ave   541/342-4025
Mon-Sat: 11 a.m.-1 a.m.; Sun: noon-midnight   mcmenamins.com
Moderate

This brew pub has a hippie vibe emanating from the University of Oregon campus just a block away. In addition to signature brews and grub, the pub offers pool tables, shuffleboard, pinball and darts. (For a detailed description of the McMenamins brand, see Page 12)

Eugene Science Center

2300 Leo Harris Pkwy   541/682-7888
Tue-Sun: 10-4 (Daily: July, Aug)   eugenesciencecenter.org
Nominal

Kids will want plenty of time to navigate and discover the fascinating planetarium (seasonal star gazing shows and full dome movies), educational exhibits and educational hands-on programs at Lane County's only science center. Located in Alton Baker Park, activities are continuously rotating to encourage youngsters' formative minds as they explore science, technology, engineering and math. The museum offers science camps, classes and special events delving into a wide variety of scientific disciplines specifically for children and their families; a fun birthday party locale.

Fiddler's Green

91292 Hwy 99N   541/689-8464, 800/548-5500
Daily: Hours vary   fiddlersgreen.com

If it is golf-related, it can be found at this family-owned and -operated business. Since 1976, Fiddler's has been a golfer's "candy store" with 250 models of demo clubs; 20 fitting specialists assure the best fit. Everything you might possibly need for this sport is here: carts, balls, bags, books; well-priced lines for novices and pros. A full array of men's and women's apparel, shoes, rainwear and accessories help you dress the part. To play the game, sign up for individual or group lessons, participate in popular clinics or initiate customized instructions. The on-property par-3 course and driving range are open year round; ideal for testing the latest equipment. Fiddler's also provides service, repair and an online store.

Fisherman's Market

830 W 7th St   541/484-2722
Daily: 10-8   eugenefishmarket.com
Restaurant: Moderate

Ask about the catch of the day and you're sure to hear where it was caught, by whom and perhaps a fish tale or two. The owners, Debbie and Ryan Rogers, have long been part of the Alaskan fishing scene and are proud to have supported local fishing families for over 30 years. They know fresh fish and the best ways to prepare cod, halibut, salmon, clams, oysters, scallops and other ocean denizens. The market serves tasty appetizers, fried or grilled combos with criss-cut fries, tacos and chowders. Crab salads are loaded with succulent Dungeness morsels and fresh veggies accompanied by housemade Louis dressing. Several types of fish and chips and Cajun crawfish pie are customer favorites. If you'd rather prepare fish your way, shop at the well-stocked fish counter; there are plenty of options for seafood gift baskets and samplers.

High Street Brewery & Cafe

1243 High St   541/345-4905
Mon-Thu: 11 a.m.-midnight (Fri, Sat till 1 a.m.);
Sun: noon-midnight   mcmenamins.com
Moderate

This first microbrewery in Eugene since the days of Prohibition features a shady backyard beer garden plus McMenamins' signature grub and limited release beers brewed on-site. (For a detailed description of the McMenamins brand, see Page 12)

Inn at the 5th

205 E 6th Ave   541/743-4099
Moderate to expensive   innat5th.com
The Inn at the 5th is ideally positioned across a courtyard from the 5th
Street Public Market, a crafter's destination since 1976 and home to unique
local shops and eateries. The sophisticated and sumptuous decor in this
70-room boutique hotel features Oregon artworks melded with interesting glass fixtures and artfully rustic furniture. Window seats and balconies
afford striking views of the Emerald City and grounds; gas fireplaces are
thoughtfully placed in most guest quarters. Room service is proficiently
handled by the neighboring **Marché** (541/342-3612) restaurant through
an unobtrusive butler door. If that isn't enough pampering, rejuvenate at
Gervais Salon and Day Spa (541/334-6533) in the hotel's lower level
for professional body, hair, nail, waxing and makeup treatments; in-room
services also offered. The staff is extra friendly.

King Estate Winery

80854 Territorial Road
Tasting Room: Daily: 11-8   541/942-9874
Restaurant: Lunch: Mon-Fri (11-4);   541/685-5189
Dinner: Daily (Sun-Thu: 5-8; Fri, Sat till 9);
Brunch: Sat, Sun (10-4:30)   kingestate.com
Moderately expensive to expensive
For a special occasion in a very impressive Oregon setting, make plans to
enjoy this family-owned, 1,000-plus-acre certified biodynamic wine operation. The main facility of the stunning European-style winery sits on the
rolling south Willamette Valley hills offering breathtaking vistas. Sustainable farming practices are used in the vineyards and also in fruit, vegetable and flower gardens to protect and nourish this prime agricultural land.
Daily informative tours of the production facilities depart on the hour from
the restaurant or you may choose to settle into the expansive tasting room
to sample flights of award-winning wines. The culinary end of the business
turns out superlative gourmet fare incorporating estate and local ingredients. What a winning combination: excellent food, a phenomenal setting
and world-class wines.

Made in Oregon

5th Street Public Market
296 E Fifth Ave, #119   541/393-6891
(See detailed listing with Made in Oregon, Portland)

Marché

5th Street Public Market
296 E 5th Ave   541/342-3612
Daily: 8 a.m.-11 p.m. (Fri, Sat till midnight)   marcherestaurant.com
Moderate (breakfast, lunch), Expensive (dinner)

Marché is the place to go for French market fare that is well-prepared, beautifully presented, fresh, healthful, seasonal and regional. Start with a signature artisan cocktail or glass of European or American wine and perhaps share a Provisions charcuterie plate while choosing from the mouthwatering fish, seafood, duck, beef and pork entrees flavorfully seasoned and accompanied by special vegetables, roots, grains, pastas and cheeses. The house steak dish is superb and the likes of mussels, steelhead and pizzetta are even better when prepared in the wood-fired oven. The expanded bar serves a casual bar menu all day — a smashing success. Next to the fountain in the market, sister business, **Provisions Market Hall** (541/743-0660, provisionsmarkethall.com), encompasses an artisan bakery and emporium for wines, gifts, cookware, fresh produce, meat and fish, specialty foods, pantry goods, a casual eatery (morning pastries, pizzas and more) and a fun spot for popular cooking classes. At the **Jordan Schnitzer Museum of Art** (541/346-3027, jsma.uoregon.edu) on the UO campus, **Marché Museum Cafe** (541/346-6440) is the scene of a small plate, quiche and sandwich casual eatery and a convenient meeting place for espresso and dessert. Bon appétit!

North Bank

22 Club Rd   541/343-5622
Daily: 11-11 (Fri, Sat till midnight)   mcmenamins.com

This McMenamins restaurant and pub has tiered inside seating and an outdoor deck overlooking the Willamette River. (For a detailed description of the McMenamins brand, see Page 12)

Off the Waffle

2540 Willamette St   541/515-6926
840 Willamette St   541/632-4225
Daily: 8-2   offthewaffle.com
Inexpensive

Waffle lovers take notice! Two brothers were introduced to Liège waffles while living in Belgium, and their desire to recreate this flavorful experience resulted in Off the Waffle. Richer and sweeter than your normal Belgian waffle, variations of Liège treats can make a complete and satisfying meal. Beyond the expected accompaniments of bacon and maple syrup, request organic toppings of avocado, fresh basil, goat cheese, housemade sauces and more. A local favorite, Goat in the Headlights, includes organic avocado, goat cheese and two over easy eggs, garnished with fresh basil, paprika and olive oil. Or try the sweeter "fruit party" waffle with a selection of fresh organic seasonal fruits topped with whipped cream. Leave all of your troubles behind and come to a place where waffles roam free and taste buds are a-frolicking. The menu also lists omelets, tea infusions, wood-roasted coffee and freshly squeezed orange juice. There is a satellite location in Southeast Portland (2601 Clinton St, 503/946-1608). These are one-of-a-kind restaurants.

WILLAMETTE VALLEY FAMILY ACTIVITIES

ALBANY
Albany Historic Carousel & Museum (503 1st Ave W, 541/497-2934): carousel rides, museum, special events

EUGENE
Eugene Science Center (2300 Leo Harris Pkwy, 541/682-7888, eugenesciencecenter.org): planetarium (seasonal star gazing shows and full dome movies), educational exhibits and educational hands-on programs

McMINNVILLE
Evergreen Aviation & Space Museum (500 NE Captain Michael King Smith Way, 503/434-4185, evergreenmuseum.org): home of Howard Hughes' Spruce Goose; inspires, educates, promotes and preserves aviation and space history
Wings & Waves Waterpark (460 NE Captain Michael King Smith Way, 503/434-3390, wingsandwaveswaterpark.com): ten water slides departing from the rooftop Boeing 747, pools, a play structure and educational H2O Hands-on Science Center

MOLALLA
Molalla Buckeroo PRCA Rodeo (503/829-8388, molallabuckeroo. com): PRCA rodeo, parades, fireworks, live music; four days surrounding July 4
Molalla Train Park (31803 S Shady Dell Road, 503/829-6866, pnls. org): free rides on the 7.5" gauge railroad running through four acre park; Sundays May through October (noon-5)

Oregon Electric Station

27 E 5th Ave   541/485-4444
Lunch: Mon-Fri (11:30-3);
Dinner: Mon-Fri: 5-close; Sat, Sun: 4-close   oesrestaurant.com
Moderately expensive to expensive
When you have a yen for juicy prime rib or fresh seafood, the Oregon Electric Station will fill the bill. The large menu offers much more, from starters such as seared scallops or coconut prawns to soups, salads, poultry and pasta. For those who are interested in a more casual dining experience, the bar offers this as well as happy hour cocktails and appetizers.

Rosse Posse Acres (32690 S Mathias Road, 503/829-7107, rosseposseacres.com): elk ranch and petting zoo; tours by appointment only

PHILOMATH
Philomath Frolic & Rodeo (philomathrodeo.org): NPRA rodeo, lumberjack competition, classic car show; July

SILVERTON
The Oregon Garden (503/874-8100, oregongarden.org)
Silver Falls State Park (503/873-8681, oregonstateparks.org)

ST.PAUL
St. Paul Rodeo (503/633-2011, stpaulrodeo.com): PRCA rodeo, parade, carnival, Western art show, entertainment, fireworks, barbecue cook-off; four days around July 4

WILSONVILLE
Family Fun Center & Bullwinkle's Restaurant (29111 SW Town Center Loop W, 503/685-5000, fun-center.com): bumper boats, rock wall, arcade, batting cages, go karts, miniature golf and more
World of Speed Motorsports Museum (27490 SW 95th Ave, 503/563-6444, worldofspeed.org): about a dozen unique exhibits, some permanent, others rotating or temporary; nearly 100 displayed cars, motorcycles and boats on loan

Generously portioned desserts are homemade; warm fruit crisps and decadent cheesecakes are worth the extra calories. Warm brick and paneled walls, gleaming brass and replica light fixtures evoke memories of the station's heyday; dine next to and inside of an antique railcar. Located in Eugene's historic depot area, the Oregon Electric Station served the Great Northern and Northern Pacific Willamette Valley electric train system, circa 1912.

The Original Pancake House
782 E Broadway Ave   541/343-7523
Mon-Wed: 6-3; Thu-Sun: 6 a.m.-8 p.m.   originalpancakehouse.com
Moderate
(See detailed listing in Salem)

The Oval Door Bed and Breakfast Inn
988 Lawrence St   541/683-3160
Moderate   ovaldoor.com
Innkeepers Nate and Brian Foster oversee The Oval Door, which is within easy walking distance of downtown restaurants and shops. The six spacious guest rooms with private bathrooms are well appointed. A warm welcome begins with tea and homemade cookies by the fireplace or on the front porch with a cool drink, depending on the weather. Soda, beer and wine are complimentary and a hospitality refrigerator holds other goodies for guests to enjoy. Breakfast features three main entrees daily, all made with seasonal, organic and local ingredients whenever possible. Every effort is made to accommodate dietary needs/restrictions.

Owen Memorial Rose Garden
300 N Jefferson St   541/682-4800
Daily: 6 a.m.-11 p.m.   skinnersbutte.com/rose-garden
Flower lovers can enjoy over 4,000 specialty roses at one of Eugene's major flower parks. The collection includes around 400 varieties (modern, hybrid, heritage). About 8.5 acres have been dedicated to the roses, the state heritage Tartatian cherry tree, walking paths, a picnic area, a gazebo and a beautiful pergola-lined walkway. Find this oasis nestled next to the Willamette River to give your senses a relaxing treat.

Prince Pückler's Gourmet Ice Cream
1605 E 19th Ave   541/344-4418
Daily: noon-11   princepucklers.com
Inexpensive
Sprint, don't walk, to this longtime really cool ice creamery that has been

satisfying locals since 1975. Top quality ingredients are blended into just over 40 best-selling and unusual gourmet ice cream flavors such as Galaxy and Muddy River (both chocolate malt ice creams), fresh banana brownie, raspberry truffle, espresso, Oregon Chai and green tea ice creams. Euphoria Chocolate Company's dark chocolate hot fudge sauce is the crowning touch to just about any ice cream dish or sundae that you concoct.

Sweet Life Patisserie
755 Monroe St   541/683-5676
Mon-Fri: 7 a.m.-11 p.m.; Sat, Sun: 8 a.m.-11 p.m.   sweetlifedesserts.com
Sweet Life Petite
1609 E 19th Ave   541/683-5676
Mon-Fri: 7 a.m.-10 p.m.; Sat, Sun: 8 a.m.-11 p.m.
As the sole judge of the annual chocolate layer cake contest at the Oregon State Fair, I feel somewhat qualified to pass opinion on sweets throughout the state. This bakery passes muster, in spades. There are magnificent handmade cakes, tortes, scones, sticky buns, muffins, croissants and other delectables (gluten-free, too) that help make life a bit sweeter. Favored cake flavors include chocolate fudge, champagne chiffon, orange sour cream, pistachio nut and caramel. Each month features a quartet of specials: cakes, cheesecakes, petits sweets and pies or tarts that are often made with exotic or only-in-season ingredients. A few savory choices complete the menu. The bakery also accommodates the wedding cake part of the business providing topnotch service to couples planning one of the most important occasions of their lives.

Voodoo Doughnut
20 E Broadway   541/868-8666
Mon-Wed: 6 a.m.-midnight; Thu-Sun: 24 hours
(See detailed listing with Voodoo Doughnut, Portland)

FALLS CITY

The Bread Board
404 N Main St   503/787-5000
Fri, Sat: 10-2; 4-9   thebreadboard.net
Falls City may be a trek for a loaf of bread, but this artisan bakery is worth the detour if you're in the vicinity. The ever-changing varieties are made with the owners' special wild yeast sourdough starters. Country sourdough, roasted garlic and sundried tomato, olive and rosemary, walnut sourdough and fennel with raisins loaves are frequently in the rotation.

Mid-day choices include breads, pastries, espresso, a light lunch menu and local beers and wines. The restaurant reopens at 4 p.m. serving thin crust wood-fired pizzas paired with other Bread Board favorite dishes. The owners claim to bake the goods in Oregon's largest wood-fired bread oven. You may also find The Bread Board's hearth-baked products at select farmers markets throughout the Valley.

GERVAIS

Bauman's Farm & Garden
12989 Howell Prairie Road NE   503/792-3524
Mon-Fri: 9-6, Sat, Sun: 9-5 (seasonal)   baumanfarms.com
This is a year-round operation, with each season showcasing the best there is to offer. The original buildings contain mouthwatering displays of fresh fruits and vegetables; shelves of fresh baked pies, breads, muffins and cookies; flavorful fudge and tempting doughnuts (apple cider, strawberry, pumpkin or other seasonal flavors). Tastes of the bakery's freshest goods are strategically placed for sampling and bites of fudge are cheerfully offered at the fudge and coffee counter. Packaged gourmet products and a vast array of gifts and housewares are integrated throughout. Step into the greenhouse for an overwhelming profusion of colorful seasonal plants, already planted in attractive containers and ready to dress up patios and porches or buy individual plants for do-it-yourself gardening. Exciting and fun family events are scheduled throughout the year with something for everyone: classes, Easter egg hunt, pancake breakfast, fall harvest events, holiday activities and so much more.

INDEPENDENCE

Mangiare Italian Restaurant
114 S Main St   503/838-0566
Mon-Sat: 11-9; Sun: 3-9
Moderate
Whether you opt for traditional spaghetti and meatballs or special pasta preparations, you'll find something to satisfy on the menu. Lasagna and baked sausage with penne pasta are hearty with robust flavors. Mangiare alla Casa (shrimp in a lemon and white wine sauce with capers and artichokes over linguine) and chicken picatta liberally seasoned with garlic are delicious; vegetarian choices are equally appetizing. Portions are more than adequate and prices are good. A short list of beers, wines and desserts complement the menu. Outside seating is available in warmer months.

The Pink House Cafe

242 D St   503/837-0900
Wed-Sat: 7 a.m.-9 p.m.; Sun: 7-7   Facebook
Inexpensive to moderate

Just across from the Independence Cinema is a charming pink and white Victorian house adorned with gingerbread trim. Inside several rooms create an intimate, relaxing ambience. The appealing, consistently good menu is filled with hearty breakfasts (a generous side of pan-fried spuds is included), lunches, dinners and desserts. Exceptional soups, salads, sandwiches and burgers are offered for both lunch and dinner; a serving of a green or homemade potato salad accompanies sandwiches. Movie patrons will find other tasty comfort food choices for date night such as fish, bratwurst, ravioli or short rib entrees; save room for berry cobbler, bread pudding or other desserts.

LYONS

Opal Creek Ancient Forest Center

End of Forest Service Road 2209
Seasonal   opalcreek.org

Take a one-hour, scenic drive east of Salem for an old-growth experience at Jawbone Flats, a historic 1920s mining town owned and operated by this local nonprofit group. In the heart of the Opal Creek Wilderness and Scenic Recreation Area, hiking, swimming, backpacking and kayaking opportunities beckon in the largest remaining low-elevation old-growth forest left in Oregon. Rusty remnants of the mining era are still visible along the 3.1-mile hike to Jawbone Flats, nestled at the confluence of Battle Axe Creek and Opal Creek. The 15 acres are host to science-based outdoor school programs, a slate of overnight workshops for a range of ages, weeklong summer youth backpacking camps, wilderness medicine trainings and private cabin rentals. Call ahead to register for programs or to book seasonal lodging in the rustic cabins (sleeping for two to 16 and equipped with kitchens and bathrooms; not accessible by vehicle); or visit year-round for day hiking and backpacking (depending on the weather). For additional information contact the administrative office in Portland (503/892-2782).

MARQUAM

MarKum Inn

36903 S Hwy 213   503/829-6006
Tue-Sun: 11-9   markuminn.com
Moderate to moderately expensive

Fabulous comfort food is what you'll find at the rebuilt (after a fire in 2014)

MarKum Inn, in the tiny crossroads community of Marquam (about seven miles north of Silverton on Highway 213). Try the famous MarKum burger (jumbo/double jumbo) or the Horse Shoe, a huge open-faced sandwich with your choice of meat or grilled veggies served on Texas Toast with piles of fries and smothered in a secret cheese sauce. I recommend coming in on a Tuesday after 4 p.m. for the hand-battered fried chicken special with honey bourbon glaze served with a potato gratin and fresh seasonal vegetables. Of note is the restaurant's 750-degree, wood-fired oven that turns out a variety of pizzas, calzones and warm desserts. Other favorites include the ranchers' meatloaf, spaghetti with signature red sauce, locally sourced steaks, salads, soups and a variety of hearty sandwiches. Prime rib Sundays are quite popular, although you'll likely find a mob. Thirsty? Try the Butte Creek Blond Ale, a restaurant exclusive, or several other regional and national brews on tap. There's also lots of local wines by the glass or bottle.

McMINNVILLE

3rd Street Pizza Co.

433 NE 3rd St   503/434-5800
Daily: 11-9 (Fri, Sat till 10)   3rdstreetpizza.com
Inexpensive to moderate
These New York-style pizzas are cooked in a traditional hearth stone oven. House specialty toppings are added to create Thai, Mexican, Greek and barbecue flavors, but pizza aficionados can choose more traditional alternatives. The expanded menu includes salads, sandwiches on homemade bread, calzones and chicken wings. You might choose to enjoy your pie while watching a movie in the on-site Moonlight Theater. There are three showings daily; Tuesday is bargain night with $6 tickets.

1882 Grille

645 NE 3rd St   971/261-2370
Daily: 11-9 (Fri, Sat till 10)   1882grille.com
Moderate
Head up to the third floor for casual pub fare, including pizza baked in a stone hearth oven (build your own by selecting your favorite sauce and toppings). Sandwiches include a variety of burgers with options and add-ons, a Portobello panini, Philly cheese steak and the 1882 Cubano with slow roasted pork, smoked ham, cheese and pickles. Salads and appetizers such as beer-battered onion rings and calamari are delicious on their own or shared with your meal. Prawn primavera and fish and chips are especially good on chilly autumn days, and the nearly 20 rotating beers on-tap are sure to please. Check their website for the current menu, beer selections and special events.

Bistro Maison

729 NE 3rd St
503/474-1888
Brunch, Lunch: Wed-Fri (11:30-2), Sun (noon-3);
Dinner: Wed, Thu (5:30-9), Fri, Sat (5-9), Sun (3-7)
bistromaison.com
Expensive

A visit to this tiny bistro in the heart of Oregon wine country is reminiscent of a quaint French countryside lunch of classic French onion soup gratinée, a Croque Monsieur sandwich and a glass of wine. European-influenced entrees are enhanced with seasonal elements and Northwest flavors such as Emmentaler and Tillamook cheddar cheeses in an Oregon white truffle fondue, classic Coq au Vin, freshly caught wild Chinook salmon and cassoulet. Profiteroles au chocolat and tarte tartin are standout desserts. An unlikely but yummy treat is the build-your-own s'mores (customer participation required). The charmingly updated home-turned-bistro is furnished with comfortable banquettes and chairs; the front porch and garden patio are equally appealing.

Community Plate

315 NE 3rd St
503/687-1902
Daily: 7:30-3
communityplate.com
Inexpensive to moderate

This is the type of place to settle into whether you're a solo diner or are accompanied by your cadre of best friends. The restored space includes a long wooden communal table and classic counter seating—step up to take a seat on swivel stools or secure a spot at the front window counter and enjoy the street scene and breakfast and lunch menus available all day. A rotating seasonal menu includes breakfasts of buttermilk pancakes with local fruit compote, pork hash with caramelized onions and braised greens, a daily scramble creation, housemade granola, quiche and more. For a special treat, order a latte prepared by an experienced barista or a breakfast cocktail to go with a pastry from the tempting bakery case. At lunch, choose from updated sandwich favorites: chicken salad, chickpea or grass-fed beef burger or a twist on the BLT. And there are always hand-cut fries, homemade soups and fresh baked breads. A monthly supper club features seasonally-inspired three- or four-course dinners with beer and wine pairings; by reservation.

Crescent Cafe

526 NE 3rd St
503/435-2655
Mon-Fri: 7-2; Sat, Sun: 8-2
crescentcafeonthird.com
Inexpensive to moderate

Wheel in to this wonderful breakfast, brunch and lunch spot for fine daytime cuisine. Crescent Cafe is family-owned in a refined setting with fresh flowers, classical music and attention to detail. To get the day properly started, try an amazing mimosa, chicken hash (a plate of crispy potatoes and large, tender pieces of chicken), an omelet or Benedict, fresh coffeecakes, buttermilk pancakes, pastries, breads and incredibly flaky and flavorful biscuits. The same attention is given to homemade soups and unusual sandwiches for lunch. Be patient, there are only about a dozen tables which fill quickly (alas, they don't accept reservations), but you will be treated well in this ultra-friendly and popular downtown neighborhood destination.

Evergreen Aviation & Space Museum
500 NE Captain Michael King Smith Way 503/434-4185
Daily: 9-5 evergreenmuseum.org
Expensive
The home of Howard Hughes' Spruce Goose is one of Oregon's premier family attractions which inspires, educates, promotes and preserves aviation and space history. Besides this mammoth plane, there are other historic collections of general aviation, military aircraft (SR-71 Blackbird), space flight (replicas of the Lunar module and Rover), helicopters and more. Tours are self-guided or docent-led; knowledgeable docents are also stationed throughout the museum to enlighten visitors about these prized beauties. Continuing in a big way, the nearly five-story tall digital 3D theater engrosses viewers with daily aerospace and educational-themed showings (one movie included with admission).

Golden Valley Brewery & Restaurant
980 NE 4th St 503/472-2739
Daily: 11-10 (Fri, Sat till 11; Sun till 9) goldenvalleybrewery.com
Moderate
This brewery-eatery sits in a historic setting with a gorgeous bar purported to be from Portland's famous Hoyt Hotel. Sixteen house beers on tap are named with seasonally descriptive and local connections. Choose from a large selection of appetizers, soups and salads, sandwiches, seafood, pork schnitzel, pastas and hand-cut steaks; the cuisine is fresh, local and made in-house. Owners Celia and Peter Kircher's 76-acre Angus Springs Ranch provides much of the restaurant's meat and produce. A second location with similar offerings is in Beaverton (1520 NW Bethany Blvd, 503/972-1599).

FIELDS IN BLOOM

The beautiful colors of Oregon's flower industry are manifested in these Willamette Valley fields; some farms celebrate the peak of the season with special events. Cut flowers are for sale during bloom season, and bulbs and tubers to grow your own are available for sale at the farms and online.

BROOKS
Adelman Peony Gardens (5690 Brooklake Road NE, 503/393-6185, peonyparadise.com): May to mid-June

CANBY
Swan Island Dahlias (995 NW 22nd Ave, 503/266-7711, dahlias.com): August to Labor Day; festival end of August

SALEM
Schreiner's Iris Gardens (3625 Quinaby Road NE, 503/393-3232, schreinersgardens.com): May to early June

TURNER
Frey's Dahlias (12054 Brick Road, 503/743-3910, freysdahlias.com): mid-August to mid-October

WOODBURN
Wooden Shoe Tulip Farm (33814 S Meridian Road, 503/634-2243, woodenshoe.com): Tulip Fest in April

La Rambla Restaurant & Bar

238 NE 3rd St   503/435-2126
Daily: 11:30-9 (Fri, Sat till 10)   laramblaonthird.com
Moderate to expensive

This culinary gem blends Spanish influences with a Northwest twist where hot and cold tapas and paella are specialties. Spanish-style flatbread pizzas, salads and several large entrees round out the menu with quite a few vegetarian and gluten-free options. The wine list is extensive with both Oregon and Spanish wines. Retire upstairs in the luxurious two-bedroom La Rambla Loft (VRBO #381644; expensive) with many amenities, including a gourmet kitchen, two fireplaces and laundry facilities. This is an ideal stay for four to six people touring the wine country. Owner Kathy Stoler provides more fun times next door at the **Gem Creole Saloon**

(236 NE 3rd St, 503/883-9194, mcminnvillegem.com) where the cuisine is creole with a Northwest flair. Specialties include delights such as fresh local oysters, crawfish étouffée and gumbo accompanied by regional wines and beers, whiskey flights, local distilled spirits and crafted cocktails. Let the good times roll.

Nick's Italian Cafe
521 NE 3rd St   503/434-4471
Daily: 5-9   Facebook
Moderately expensive and up
At this renowned pasta house you will not go away hungry. Local, sustainable produce and hormone- and antibiotic-free eggs and meats dominate the menu at Nick's. You'll likely rub elbows with local vintners; they know that dinner choices from the a la carte fare will be excellent and satisfying. Select from ragùs, pastas, seafood and vegetarian dishes or ask about the daily wood-fired oven lamb or pork preparations. An amazing wine list features Northwest and Italian tastings. Enter through the back door for the ambience of the comfy bar to enjoy wine, antipasti and perhaps a game of pool. It's no wonder that Nick's has been an integral part of McMinnville's dining scene since 1977.

Pura Vida Cocina
313 NE 3rd St   503/687-2020
Mon-Sat: 11-9   puravidamac.com
Moderate
Pura Vida Cocina serves up colorful Latin American-style dishes using fresh, locally sourced ingredients. Begin your meal with fresh chips served with housemade salsa and guacamole (there is a charge, but it's worth it). Move on to delicious enchiladas with your choice of chicken, sauteed vegetables or sauteed shrimp on handmade tortillas. Smaller dishes like empanadas and taquitos are also popular. For dessert try fresh churros served with a decadent chocolate dip. Beer and wine selections rotate but maintain a local focus. Quality cocktails are concocted with agave, fresh fruits and herbs. Pura Vida Cocina has turned into quite a local hotspot and although it can get crowded, with no reservations available, it's still worth the stop. Pura Vida Cocina diners who stop by Xicha Brewing in West Salem (find a detailed description in this chapter), may detect a similar vibe, at least with the menu. That's because owners Margarita and Ricardo Antunez are co-owners of Xicha Brewing, and Ricardo is the chef.

Red Fox Bakery

328 NE Evans St   503/434-5098
Mon-Sat: 7-4   redfoxbakery.com

This artisan bakery uses local fresh ingredients as much as possible (even growing many of their own herbs), offering housemade jams and hand-crafting breads and pastries. Flour is milled, produce grown and butter churned within miles of the bakery. The breakfast menu (7 to 10:30) is centered on egg and grain options and the lunch menu (11 to 3) offers filling sandwiches, soups and salads. The bakery turns out coconut macaroons, with daily fresh batches sold on-site or shipped; brownies, too. Cinnamon rolls, coffee cakes and more make up the daily-changing pastry menu and "everything" scones are baked only on Thursday.

Ribslayer BBQ to Go

575 NE 2nd St   503/472-1309
Tues-Sat: 11-7   ribslayer.com
Inexpensive to moderate

You'll know that you're near Ribslayer by the mouthwatering aroma emanating from the 9,000-pound custom-built behemoth smoker. This is one of the largest smokers in the area and can cook over 1,000 pounds of chicken, beef or pork at one time; all carefully seasoned and roasted long and slow. Homemade slaw, chips and pickles accompany orders of a half or whole bird, Carlton Farms pulled pork and award-winning beef brisket tri-tip and beef ribs. If you're really famished, sink your teeth into the "XXX" sandwich: a juicy combination of thinly sliced beef brisket, pulled pork and corned beef. Housemade sides and salads round out the menu. Owners Theresa and Craig Haagenson also operate Haagenson's Catering (503/550-7388), a full-service (and barbecue) catering business.

Serendipity Ice Cream

502 NE 3rd St   503/474-9189
Tue-Thu: 11:30-8 (Fri, Sat till 10); Sun: noon-8   serendipityicecream.com
Inexpensive

Serendipity is much more than an ice cream shop! They have homemade waffle cones, baked-from-scratch cookies, sundaes and shakes made from hand-dipped Oregon ice cream. The diet-busting sundae surprise is made with a warm chocolate brownie, two scoops of ice cream, two toppings and mounds of whipped cream. An interesting sidebar: this business is owned and operated by MV Advancements which provides training and jobs for persons experiencing developmental disabilities. Their hard work pays big dividends!

Thistle Restaurant & Bar

228 NE Evans St   503/472-9623
Tue-Sat: 5:30-close   thistlerestaurant.com
Moderately expensive
The ambience is warm and cozy in this smallish downtown storefront location, which is both eclectic and classically appointed. The compact kitch-
en is visible from the front window where nose-to-tail meat preparations
are underway; a seat at the chef's bar offers a similar view accompanied
by tantalizing aromas. A chalkboard lists the daily dinner menu as well
as the source from local farmers. The bar features classic cocktails and a
smattering of Oregon's finest beers, wines and ciders. Seasonal entrees
may include elk with winter squash and kale, pork with mushrooms and
onions or seafood choices; surprisingly, bread is served with lard rather
than butter. Thistle also offers a multi-course option, appropriately named
the Chef's Whim, and requires participation of the entire party. Reservations are recommended.

Wings & Waves Waterpark

460 NE Captain Michael King Smith Way   503/687-3390
Daily: 10-6 (Memorial Day-Labor Day)   wingsandwaveswaterpark.com
Reasonable to expensive
Wings & Waves Waterpark, next door to the Evergreen Aviation & Space
Museum, has ten water slides (appropriately named Tail Spin, Sonic Boom,
etc.) departing from the rooftop Boeing 747, pools, a play structure and
educational H2O Hands-on Science Center. This attraction is open during
the summer season and additional days and hours vary.

Youngberg Hill

10660 SW Youngberg Hill Road   503/472-2727
Daily: 10-4 (tasting room)   youngberghill.com
Moderate to very expensive
Youngberg Hill creates authentic wines and experiences in its tasting room
and inn. One of Oregon's premier wine country estates, it is set on a 50-
acre hilltop surrounded by an organic vineyard that produces award-winning pinot noir, pinot gris and chardonnay. The nine-room inn provides
the perfect retreat. A two-course breakfast is included and features dishes
such as salmon scramble, pancetta tarts, cornished baked eggs and pinot
poached pears. There are over 200 wineries and tasting rooms within a
20-minute drive.

MILL CITY

Giovanni's Mountain Pizza

146 NW Santiam Blvd   503/897-2614

Daily: 11:30-9 (Fri, Sat till 10)   Facebook

Inexpensive

For over 20 years Kathy and Jim Flack have been feeding hungry travelers in the picturesque Santiam Canyon. Customers return regularly for the New York-style pizzas made from fresh hand-rolled dough and plenty of tasty meat, vegetable and cheese toppings. The house specialty pizza, Fat Roman Delight, includes almost everything except the kitchen sink. Lasagna, spaghetti, calzones, homemade minestrone soup, salads, sub sandwiches and breadsticks round out the menu. This is a popular stop for recreationists heading back to the Valley after a day in the snow or on the lakes, rivers and trails.

MONROE

The Inn at Diamond Woods

96096 Territorial Road   541/510-2467

Moderate   theinnatdiamondwoods.com

This large facility features four en suite bedrooms and meeting rooms. Views of the Willamette Valley and Diamond Woods Golf Course are captured through soaring windows and from the expansive patio and sprawling lawn (ideal for large weddings or corporate events). Individual, group and whole-house reservations are accepted with special rates for several couples who would like to have the entire place to themselves for a football weekend, wine excursion or special occasion. Catering is available for guests, weddings and special events. Guests receive a 50% discount on golf at the 18-hole, 7,100 yard championship golf course, Diamond Woods.

MT. ANGEL

Glockenspiel Restaurant & Pub

190 E Charles St   503/845-6222

Daily: 11-8 (Fri, Sat till 9)   glockenspielrestaurant.net

Moderate

Hopefully you have experienced Mt. Angel come alive in September for its annual Oktoberfest and German cultural activities. Traditional cuisine, however, is not just autumnal fare in this Bavarian-themed village. Start your meal by sharing a pot of fondue and then move onto wursts. Sweet and savory braised red cabbage accompanies platters of schnitzels, späetzle, wursts, potato pancakes, steaks, seafood and other specialties. While German lunch selections are hard to beat, salads, hearty homemade soups and sandwiches (Reuben, sausage and burgers) are equally as tempting, especially when washed down with German and Northwest brews and wines. Fish lovers show up on Friday evenings for Glockenspiel's popular weekly Fish Fry featuring beer-battered fish, German slaw and fries. It goes without saying that any time is the right time for delicious apple strudel. Before leaving, be sure to notice the unique clock tower; bells periodically chime as figures dance above the entrance. It's quite a place.

Mt. Angel Sausage Co.

105 S Garfield St   503/845-2322
Restaurant: Daily: 11-8   ropesausage.com
Inexpensive to moderate
Retail Store: Daily: 10-8

Robust Old World-style artisan sausages are expertly handmade by the Hoke family and served on-site at their restaurant. Chicken, beef, pork and assorted spices, cheese and loads of garlic are added before the curing process to create distinctly flavored sausages. Only high-quality natural products are used; no chemicals, fillers or by-products. This casual eatery offers 25+ varieties of wursts in sandwiches or on a stick, schnitzel entrees, fondue, hearty dinners, German and domestic brews, wines and cocktails. Mt. Angel's oldest Bavarian restaurant and meat shop attracts patrons to the comfortable outdoor deck on warm summer afternoons and evenings; customers also come for European shopping. Their products are a staple at many nearby fairs and events. And if you're not in the area, but need a bratwurst fix, they gladly fill and ship orders each week.

NEWBERG

The Allison Inn & Spa

2525 Allison Lane   503/554-2525, 877/294-2525
Expensive to very expensive   theallison.com

Words cannot adequately describe this magnificent haven built by Oregon entrepreneurs Ken Austin and his late wife Joan. The genius of this world-class retreat is in the attention to details. For instance, comfy throws on "living room" couches and fireplaces on automatic timers. There is a fabulous spa with every amenity, including a treatment room with an overhead "rain" feature. Every guest room in this 85-room wine country boutique resort has an outside view terrace; gorgeous landscaping blends with the setting. The casually elegant in-house **JORY Restaurant** (503/554-2526) is of the same high caliber and honors Oregon's wine, microbrew, hand-crafted distilled spirit and agricultural industries with outstanding Oregon garden-to-table cuisine. For special occasions there are private dining rooms to accommodate small gatherings; the chef's table for ten boasts a customized menu; counter seating offers a view into the open kitchen. Any meal of the day is a guaranteed palate pleaser, especially the brioche French toast with berry compote at breakfast or midday interesting salads and charcuterie; the dinner menu's wood-grilled Wagyu striploin with cream-braised lobster mushrooms is as good as you will find anywhere.

Chehalem Ridge Bed and Breakfast

28700 NE Mountain Top Road   503/538-3474
Moderate   chehalemridge.com
Perched high above the Willamette Valley floor is this appropriately named bed and breakfast with inspiring vistas. The five bedrooms offer private baths (some with jetted tubs and fireplaces) and private decks. If you oversleep or depart early you'll miss the three-course breakfast extravaganza. Experienced as a professional chef and baker, Kristin Fintel is busy each morning baking pastries, preparing fresh fruits and impressing guests with hazelnut waffles, crepes, salmon quiche or amazing Benedicts. No worries if you have special dietary needs; food allergies are pleasantly accommodated. The library offers reading material and HDTV (if you must); but first make a slight detour to the cookie jar full of home-baked goodies.

Critter Cabana

516 E 1st St   503/537-2570
Mon-Sat: 10-7; Sun: noon-5   crittercabana.com
You'll be absolutely amazed when you walk into this pet-and-more store. It is a charming place full of interesting products and lovable pets. You'll find dogs, cats, birds, fish, snakes, frogs, tortoises, lizards, teddy bear hamsters and rabbits, plus other curious creatures. There is no shortage of high-quality pet supplies for your critters including food, toys, treats and everyday necessities. You have to see this menagerie to believe it; and keep your eyes open for the giant strolling tortoises. Here's a great idea for birthday parties: they will take their pets on the road. In Wilsonville, visit their second location (8406 SW Main St, #200, 503/682-9812).

Honest Chocolates

312 E 1st St   503/537-0754
Tue-Sat: 11:30-6   Facebook
At Honest Chocolates candies are crafted using high-quality, taste-tested chocolate, cooked in small batches and hand-dipped. What's not to love

about chocolate (dark or milk) honey caramels with French sea salt or rocky road with handmade marshmallow? A niche they have deliciously filled is crafting chocolates to pair with Oregon's special wines. Dark chocolate ganache with berries and pinot noir is the candy to accompany a glass of pinot noir or your favorite wine. There is no fancy packaging or expensive marketing campaign here, which means prices are kept reasonable. Visit them when you are in Carlton (217 E Main St, 503/474-9042).

JORY Restaurant

2525 Allison Lane   503/554-2526
Daily: Breakfast (6:30-10:30); Lunch (11:30-2); Dinner (5:30-9);
Brunch (Sunday 9-2)
Expensive
(See detailed listing with The Allison Inn & Spa, Newberg)

Le Puy A Wine Valley Inn

20300 NE Hwy 240   503/554-9528
Expensive   lepuy-inn.com
A transitional contemporary bed and breakfast is the brainchild of owners, Lea Duffy and Andy Kosusko, who used their architectural backgrounds to build a holistic, sustainable inn incorporating the principles of feng shui. Le Puy has eight en suite guest rooms with magnificent views of Chehalem Ridge and picturesque vineyards, with peeks at the Coast and Cascade Range mountains. A restful night is nearly assured on king- or queen-size beds with luxurious Tempur-Pedic mattresses; your room choice may include a balcony or patio, spa tub or gas fireplace. A private outdoor hot tub is featured with the Mountain Suite, the Thunder Suite is fully accessible and the Lake Suite is spa-inspired and contains both a jetted tub and separate double-headed shower. Breakfast is served between 9 and 10:30 a.m.; guests may filter in at their convenience during that time and enjoy local and organic specialties, homemade scones and other treats. A two-night minimum stay is required and seasonal discounts are available December through April. The electric car charging station is a thoughtful convenience.

The Painted Lady

201 S College St   503/538-3850
Wed-Sun: 5-10   thepaintedladyrestaurant.com
Expensive
Great things often come in small packages and this Willamette Valley dinner house is arguably one of the best in all of Oregon (awarded four stars from Forbes in 2013). Classy consistency with innovative cuisine and

topnotch service continue to make this tiny Victorian home a huge winner. Owners Jessica Bagley and her husband Allen Routt are a model team: Jessica mainly takes care of the front of the house and Allen does magical things in the kitchen creating classic dishes updated for a modern, refined palate. Everything in the intimate 35-seat home-cum-gourmet-restaurant, from the initial greeting to the superb service, makes for a special experience. The Painted Lady offers a nightly eight-course seasonal tasting menu.The menu can be modified to accommodate both vegetarians and pescatarians.Optional local and international wine pairings are available with all menus. Signature dishes include potato gnocchi and miso custard; grounded on seasonal, local, quality ingredients; you won't be disappointed. Reservations are nearly a must unless you are very lucky … and tell Jessica and Allen that Gerry sent you.

The Painted Lady Guest Cottage

205 S College St   503/516-4382
Expensive   thepaintedladycottage.com
Following an excellent meal at The Painted Lady, opt to spend the night in a charming two-bedroom home next door, ample for four guests. You will find a comfortable living area, modern technology and many other amenities including proximity to the downtown area and Dundee Hills' wine country. The gourmet kitchen is fully stocked; help yourself to the restaurant's garden for herbs, berries and vegetable bounty. Additional culinary packages are available.

Rain Dance Vineyards

26355 NE Bell Road   503/538-0197
Visit website for hours   raindancevineyards.com
Today, Rain Dance is home to 120 acres of farmland including 73 under vine, wildlife corridors, preserved native trees and over 100 llamas who add a unique twist to their sustainability program. Enjoy homegrown wines and gracious hospitality in the elegant country setting complete with tranquil views from the covered porch and patio, and a selection of artwork and estate woodwork.

Storrs Smokehouse

310 E 1st St   503/538-8080
Wed-Sun: 8-8   storrssmokehouse.com
Inexpensive to moderate
This Newberg barbecue joint serves a full breakfast menu (until 11) that includes homemade biscuits with creamy gravy loaded with chunks of sausage and brisket. The remainder of the day, Storrs, a "child" of the city's

famous The Painted Lady restaurant, is the place for Texas-style beef brisket, Southern-style pulled pork, ribs with a Midwest spice rub and saucy
chicken wings. Meats are slow-cooked until they are fall-apart-tender and
are accompanied by a choice of sauces: sweet pinot noir-laced Texas-style,
soy-based Asian and vinegary Carolina-style. Meals are served with cole-
slaw, bread and pickle; optional side dishes include favorites such as mac
and cheese, mashed potatoes and soup. Everything is homemade from
family recipes including salted caramel and whiskey brownie ice cream and
an excellent ice cream sandwich (peanut butter ice cream with chopped
peanut butter cups sandwiched between slices of chocolate chiffon cake).
Takeout orders and catering are also available; prepared meats are sold by
the pound.

OAKRIDGE

Brewers Union Local 180
48329 E 1st St   541/782-2024
Daily: noon-8 (Fri, Sat till 9)
(Closes one hour later in summer)   brewersunion.com
Inexpensive to moderate
This Anglo-American public house, which bills itself as Oregon's only real
ale pub and brewery, produces ales that are conditioned in firkins (casks)
and pumped from six beer engines. Other beers, wines, ciders and brewed
soft drinks are tapped from a keg or sold in bottles. For nourishment, try
fish and chips, assorted sandwiches, soups and salads, vegetarian options
or satisfying daily specials from the seasonal menu. Families and kids are
welcome until 9 in the pub or on the outdoor patio. Come on in, lift a pint,
tell a tall tale and enjoy free pool, books and games.

RAINBOW

Holiday Farm Resort
54791 McKenzie Hwy   541/822-3725
Moderate to expensive   holidayfarmresort.com
Ideally situated on the scenic McKenzie River, the secluded resort is a
mecca for fly-fishing, drift boating, bird watching, hiking and nearly un-
limited outdoor recreation. Most are riverfront cabins and homes less than
four miles from Rainbow; many are pet-friendly. Each accommodation is a
bit different and individually named to reflect its character: log house, historical, Mediterranean-style, rustic, cozy or spacious; capacity ranges from
two to ten occupants. Wood-burning fireplaces, kitchenettes, Wi-Fi and
decks are standard in most units. Golfers may want to book a tee time at

the 18-hole Tokatee Golf Club (tokatee.com), a Giustina family enterprise; views are incredible when not eyeballing your shot. Just a mile from the McKenzie Bridge, this stretch of the river is dotted with little burgs, parks and trails; a splendid region to explore for a day or longer.

SALEM

22 Below
4155 Rickey St SE 503/602-7502
Daily: noon-9 (Fri, Sat till 10) my22below.com
22 Below serves Thai rolled ice cream, very trendy stuff, but what is it? Start with a liquid ice cream base, spread it across a super-cooled metal pan, let it freeze, then scrape it off, rolling it up into little logs in the process. Well, your server does that. Your job is to choose flavor combinations and add-ins like a mad chef in an ice cream test kitchen. Menu combos include green tea and Oreo, mango and passion fruit, strawberry and cheesecake and many more. Finish off your creation with any number of yummy toppings. The process is as much fun to watch as it is delicious to eat. 22 Below uses a gluten-free and lactose-free ice cream base whose main ingredient is coconut oil. The final outcome depends on what you add in. Also in Eugene, where it started in 2017 (501 Valley River Center, 541/799-3734), and Portland (1728 SW Jefferson St, 503/509-6434).

Annette's Westgate
1311 Edgewater St NW 503/362-9588
Mon-Sat: 6 a.m.-9 p.m.; Sun: 7-2 annettesofsalem.com
Inexpensive to moderate
Housed in the historic Kingwood Building, Annette's still holds the same old-fashioned charm that the building has held since 1928, but with many renovations. Tasty American cuisine is served up for breakfast, lunch and dinner in a casual, family-friendly environment. The breakfast menu will especially delight foodies with an impressive selection of sweet and savory items, not to mention their generous portions. Lunch and dinner offerings are equally impressive. Breakfast entrees include a large selection of egg omelets, traditional breakfast items such as eggs Benedict, waffles, French toast, pancakes and more; lunch items include massive burgers made with 1/3-pound char-broiled beef patties, sandwiches, a salad bar and housemade soups. For dinner they serve it all; chicken, beef, pork or seafood, and the chicken-fried steak is a must-try. Make a meal with the all-you-can-eat salad bar with plenty of veggie, fruit, protein and crunchy choices; plus hearty clam chowder or housemade soup and bread. You can also find desserts, local wines, beers and cocktails on their menu.

SALEM AREA FAMILY ACTIVITIES

Enchanted Forest (8462 Enchanted Way SE, Turner; 503/371-4242, enchantedforest.com): amusement park for families; fairy tales, nursery rhymes and stories come to life; spring to fall; check web calendar for schedule

Gilbert House Children's Museum (116 Marion St NE, 503/371-3631, acgilbert.org): three historic Victorian-style houses with over a dozen interactive exhibits, a 20,000-square-foot outdoor discovery center

Kroc Center (1865 Bill Frey Dr NE, Salem; 503/566-5762): The Salvation Army Ray & Joan Kroc Corps Community Center features swimming and leisure pools, game room, climbing wall, classes, camps and more

Powerland Heritage Park (3995 Brooklake Road NE, Brooks, 503/393-2424, powerlandheritagepark.com): campus of museums dedicated to preserving Oregon's agricultural heritage including the Antique Powerland Museum (April through September), Great Oregon Steam-Up (July/August)

Riverfront Park (200 Water St NE, 503/588-6336, cityofsalem.net): carousel, heritage village, amphitheater, covered pavilion, picnic tables, boat dock, miles of walking and biking paths; connects Minto-Brown Island Park to West Salem via pedestrian bridges; seasonal festivals and ice rink

Salem's Riverfront Carousel (101 Front St NE; 503/540-0374, salemcarousel.org): indoor carousel with 46 hand-carved horses, gift shop, party room

Willamette Heritage Center (1313 Mill St SE, 503/585-7012, willametteheritage.org): oldest remaining wooden frame houses in the Northwest; the only woolen mill museum west of Missouri; library, archives and collections; interpretive displays; self-guided tours

Willamette Queen (Riverfront Park, 503/371-1103, willamettequeen.com): departs from Riverfront Park; lunch, dinner and brunch cruises; special events

Archive Coffee & Bar

120 Liberty St NE, Suite 120   971/701-6266
Daily: 7 a.m.–midnight   archivecoffeeandbar.com
Coffee: 7-6; Lunch: 11-4; Dinner and Bar: 4-midnight
Inexpensive to moderate

There are many good coffeehouses and bars in Salem but none quite like this one, bringing a fresh approach to downtown Salem. In fact, this is more of a coffee bar that you would expect to find in Portland. The atmosphere is youthful and laid back while remaining sophisticated. Creativity and passion are evident in all corners of the space from the decor and menu design to food and drink presentation. Archive prides itself on making high-end espresso as a form of art; no sugar-coating here. So, if you pride yourself on being a coffee connoisseur, your senses and taste buds will be highly satisfied. What sets them apart? Archive roasts and serves specialty coffee and a selection of fine teas; by night, they shift gears and feature quality spirits and innovative cocktails, food, wine and beer pairings — all of which have been carefully thought-out and concocted. Menu options are seasonal, ever-changing and feature Northwest-style cuisine.

Bentley's Grill

291 Liberty St SE   503/779-1660
Mon-Fri: 11:30-10; Sat: 3-10; Sun: 5-9   bentleysgrill.com
Expensive
(See detailed listing with The Grand Hotel, Salem)

Bo & Vine Burger Bar

176 Liberty St NE   971/301-2584
Mon-Sat: 11-10   boandvine.com
Moderate

At Bo & Vine you can build your own burger or choose from creative menu variations that start with chicken or locally sourced grass-fed beef. There are vegan options, too, such as a sweet potato and black bean patty or a balsamic glazed Portobello mushroom cap. Guests may recognize the Mad Hawaiian (beef with grilled pineapple, Spam, jalapeno-cilantro slaw, sriracha, onion, Swiss cheese, teriyaki glaze and mayo) from what once was offered by the Patty Wagon food truck. A restaurant signature is the Pitmaster burger, (with smoked ham, bacon, hefeweizen-battered onion strings, cheddar cheese, housemade sriracha mayo and Adam's Ribs barbecue sauce on a freshly baked, cheddar-crusted bun). Salads, fries, tots and tempting fully loaded "piles" served nacho style are also on the menu. On hot summer days a cold-brew mocha, Jones Soda float or a Stout & Cream (served shake-style with Irish cream, chocolate and whipped cream) may be all you'll need.

Boon's Treasury

888 Liberty St NE   503/399-9062
Mon-Thu: 11 a.m.-midnight (Fri, Sat till 1 a.m.; Sun till 11)   mcmenamins.com
Moderate

A McMenamins pub featuring handcrafted beers, spirits and wines, pub grub and live music most nights, offered in a historic (one of Salem's old-est) building. (For a detailed description of the McMenamins brand, see Page 12)

Café 22 West

5152 Salem-Dallas Hwy   503/363-4643
Mon-Thu: 7:30-2; Fri, Sat: 7-7;
Sun: 7:30-6:30 (some seasonal variations)   cafe22west.com
Inexpensive to moderate

For over 100 years the Aspinwall clan has tended the soil on this 40-acre prop-erty. Hard-working Clyde Aspinwall combines fresh produce from his next-door market with great comfort food. For hearty breakfasts, try fruit-topped pancakes and waffles with a mound of whipped cream or a heaping platter of chicken-fried steak with taters. Lunch and dinner options include a vari-ety of wraps, grilled sandwiches, fresh handcrafted burgers, crisp chopped salads and fish and chips. On weekends, the star attraction is the slow-roast-ed baby back ribs dinner special; sides of mac and cheese and baked beans can't be beat. If you're still hungry, there is always dessert, or saunter across the parking lot to Aspinwall's Nursery & Produce for summertime-favorite strawberry shortcake and ice cream. The restaurant is open year round and the market and greenhouse are seasonal. Aspinwall peaches are topnotch.

Court Street Dairy Lunch

347 Court St NE   503/363-6433
Mon-Fri: 6-2   Facebook
Inexpensive

Pop in any weekday for breakfast or lunch and you'll see folks from every walk of life ordering their "regular." Breakfast, served until 11, consists of sweets, omelets, fresh cottage-fried potatoes and egg dishes. Soups are homemade; one for each day. Great juicy burgers and special sandwiches are served with a choice of sides. There are also daily lunch specials, such as oven-roasted turkey on Thursdays, and satisfying fried ham and egg, meatloaf (warm or cold) and PB&J sandwiches. Sweet goodies include ice cream, sundaes, milkshakes, malts, ice cream sodas and floats; dairy prod-ucts were the mainstay of this business when it was founded in 1929.

E.Z. Orchards

5504 Hazel Green Road NE   503/393-1506
Mon-Fri: 9-6; Sat: 9-5; Sun: 11-5 (Oct only)   ezorchards.com

On the eastern outskirts of Salem, friendly John Zielinski leads his capa-ble team and family business at E.Z. Orchards farm store. Much of the fresh produce comes from the family's orchards and other farms from around the Valley. Smart retailer that he is, upon entering the store customers are assailed with the aroma and samples of just-out-of-the-fryer seasonal doughnuts (apple cider, strawberry, raspberry, blueberry, pumpkin or marionberry). The merchandise displays are full of mixes, sauces, preserves, seasonings, ingredients, condiments and gourmet staples to stock your pantry, plus housewares and gifts to outfit any kitchen. Cidre, a tasty Normandy French-style hard cider, is made by his brother, Kevin Zielinski. Outside, the Shortcake Stand (open May to October) is a beehive of activity selling strawberry, raspberry, blueberry, marionberry and peach desserts with hand-scooped ice cream and/or whipped cream. Events are held throughout the year; the harvest festival with a corn maze, pumpkin patch and lots of wholesome fun is many a family's tradition. Try to score a ticket to one of their five-course, farm-to-table alfresco meals in the orchards; space limited to 80 people. You can count on John for great customer service and a willingness to accommodate special orders.

Fitts Seafoods

1555 12th St SE   503/364-6724
Mon-Sat: 9-6   fitts.net

Fitts began retailing fresh seafood to the Willamette Valley from downtown Salem in 1901. Still family owned and operated, the shop specializes in fresh and frozen seafood from the Northwest and around the world (including live lobsters and crabs). Fitts makes its own smoked salmon spread, clam dip, crab dip, lobster spread, smoked oyster paté, shrimp dip, seasonings, and clam chowder and salmon chowder bases. They also carry a wide variety of spices, rubs, marinades and local wines; and also carry and can special order free range game and poultry.

Gamberetti's Italian Restaurant

325 High St SE   503/339-7446
Mon-Thu: 11:30-9 (Fri till 10); Sat: 4-10; Sun: 3-9   gamberettis.com
Moderate

Warm and affordable, robust Italian flavors emanate from the kitchen of this downtown restaurant. Big winners include molte carne tortellini (Bolognese sauce, marinara, Italian sausage and meatball on cheese tortellini), fra diavolo ravioli (shrimp, lobster and marinara over shrimp and leek ravioli) and grilled pizzas. Lunch selections, including specials, are available Monday through Friday from 11:30 to 3. Macaroni and cheese is featured on Monday evenings; not just any mac and cheese, but gourmet concoctions with steak, lobster, chicken or sausage. Tuesday night specials include soup or salad, a choice of entree and tiramisu for $14.95. Beer, wine, a full bar and outside seating attract diners to this popular location.

Gerry Frank's Konditorei

310 Kearney St SE   503/585-7070
Mon: 8 a.m.-9 p.m.; Tue-Thu: 8 a.m.-10 p.m.;
Fri: 8 a.m.-11 p.m.; Sat: 8:30 a.m.-11 p.m.; Sun: 10-9   gerryfrankskonditorei.com
Moderate

My good friend, the late Barney Rogers, and I opened this full-service restaurant in 1982, and I recently sold it to longtime manager Linae Sielicky and bakers Valerie and Mike Schultz. Cake lovers have descended upon the 40-seat cake shop for over 30 years. Many customers linger at the display cases to make the biggest decision of their day: choosing from the 55 available layer cakes, cheesecakes and mousse cakes. Choices include Gerry's chocolate, Barney's blackout, carrot, champagne, Mounds, poppy seed and seasonal preferences such as pumpkin, strawberry and others. Additional temptations made with the finest ingredients include cookies, bars, tortes and other baked goods; all made with the finest ingredients. In addition to sweet goodies, cakes by the slice and whole cakes, there are espresso drinks, light breakfasts, lunches, dinners, beers and wines. The famous Meier & Frank Cobb salad is a Konditorei exclusive. The menu always includes daily quiche and soup specials, sandwiches, lasagna and more. Call ahead for special requests, orders to go or box lunches.

Gilbert House Children's Museum

116 Marion St NE   503/371-3631
Tue-Sun: 10-5 (see website for seasonal hours)   acgilbert.org
Nominal

The nonprofit, hands-on Gilbert House Children's Museum is named for Salem-born A.C. Gilbert, an Olympic athlete, prolific inventor and creator of the iconic Erector Set. The museum, at the north end of Riverfront Park, is comprised of three historic Victorian-style houses filled with over a dozen interactive exhibits, as well as a 20,000-square-foot outdoor discovery center.

Gilgamesh Brewing

2065 Madrona Ave SE   503/584-1789
Mon-Thu: 11-10; Fri, Sat: 11 a.m.-midnight; Sun: 11-9   gilgameshbrewing.com
Moderate

The campus includes the brewery and a craftsman-style restaurant pub and plays host to a variety of fun activities throughout the year. The grounds have an atmosphere similar to a beer garden with the option of long picnic tables or small tables and plenty of room to mingle. While there is a fabulous cabin-like interior, the action continues outdoors right by Pringle Creek when weather permits; the large patio is covered and heated during

VOLCANOES STADIUM

Professional baseball had been part of Salem-Keizer community since at least World War II. But when the Salem Dodgers left for Yakima, Washington, in 1990, the area was without a team. That changed in 1997 with the construction of Volcanoes Stadium in Keizer, the home of the **Salem-Keizer Volcanoes**, a Class A short season affiliate of the San Francisco Giants. Since then the Volcanoes have won five Northwest League championships and have sent 95 players on to the Major Leagues, according to the team's history. The Giants have benefitted greatly from the Salem-Keizer team. After the Volcanoes most recent championship, in 2009, the Giants won the World Series in 2010, 2012 and 2014 with rosters full of former Volcanoes, including stars such as Buster Posey. Following its inaugural season, the natural turf stadium won a design award from the America Institute of Architects, and it has been modified and expanded several times since then. Today it can seat 4,254 fans with standing room for more. The stadium has 11 concession stands, a sports bar, playground, entertainment deck, 13 luxury suites, a home run porch, and is home to the Volcano Burger. Volcanoes Stadium is 6700 Field of Dreams Way, just north of the Keizer Station shopping center. The Volcanoes season runs from mid-June through Labor Day. Go to volcanoesbaseball.com for ticket and schedule information.

the colder months, too. The food choices include tasty burgers, variations of mac and cheese, pulled pork and Cuban sandwiches, steaks, chicken quesadillas and more. You won't go away thirsty either as Gilgamesh claims to have a refreshing beer for everyone. In addition to year-round and seasonal brews, you'll find wines, spirits, cocktails and seasonal ciders.

The Grand Hotel

201 Liberty St SE   503/540-7800, 877/540-7800
Moderate to expensive   grandhotelsalem.com

Grand it is, and provides Salem's most elegant lodging and flawless customer service under the direction of the extremely capable Steve Johnson. The prime downtown location, opened in 2005 and renovated in 2017, is contiguous to the Salem Convention Center; this combination is a major draw for visitors, meetings and conferences throughout the year. The nearly 200 rooms and suites are spacious, classically appointed and very comfortable. Suites are thoughtfully planned with separate bedrooms, microwaves and refrigerators; some suites have gas fireplaces and Jacuzzi tubs. A complimentary hot breakfast buffet is included with an overnight stay.

Sharing the complex, **Bentley's Grill** (503/779-1660, bentleysgrill.com) offers Northwest ingredients on its regional fine dining and bar menu. Light appetizers, salads, pizzas and sandwiches are served beginning at lunch, with fresh seafood a prominent element; steaks, chops, chicken, pasta and ocean fare are on the dinner menu.

Hallie Ford Museum of Art

Willamette University
700 State St   503/370-6855
Tue-Sat: 10-5; Sun: 1-5   willamette.edu/arts/hfma
Nominal (free on Tue)

Explore permanent galleries that feature works by Pacific Northwest and Native American artists and travel through time with the museum's diverse collection of traditional European, American and Asian art and artifacts that date from antiquity. Willamette University has a long presence in Salem, founded in 1842 by Methodist missionaries as the first university in the West. The inviting campus is between the Willamette Heritage Center and the State Capitol.

Kwan's Original Cuisine

835 Commercial St SE   503/362-7711
Daily: 11-9 (Fri, Sat till 10)   kwanscuisine.com
Moderate

My long association with Bo and Kam Sang Kwan goes back to the 1960s. Kwan's roots and work ethic started in Asia well before he ran the household of yours truly. In 1976 Kwan's Kitchen debuted in Salem's Civic Center; six years later his restaurant moved down the street to a new 300-seat restaurant with a landmark pagoda, new name and banquet facilities. The extensive menu is excellent and full of curry, Szechuan and garlic options in vegetable, rice and noodle dishes combined with meats (chicken, beef, seafood, emu, lamb and pork) and prepared with mild, medium, hot or super-hot spice levels. The results are interesting, flavorful (without chemicals like MSG) and attractively presented. Special dietary requests such as gluten-free are honored to nourish the soul and body. Hard-working Kwan is always on the job taking only four days off each year: Memorial Day, Independence Day, Thanksgiving and Christmas! One of Kwan's many talents is deboning a chicken with a meat cleaver while blindfolded!

Made in Oregon
Salem Center Mall
401 Center St NE   503/362-4106
(See detailed listing with Made in Oregon, Portland)

Marco Polo Global Restaurant
300 Liberty St SE   503/364-4833
Mon-Thu: 11-9; Fri: 11-9:30; Sat: noon-9:30; Sun: 11:30-8   mpologlobal.com
Moderate
Aptly named, this restaurant enjoys spacious downtown quarters. Proprietors Jackey and Cathay Cheung serve a full slate of Chinese-Asian fare, European specialties such as pastas and raviolis, vegetarian and vegan offerings, tofu entrees and American favorites such as burgers; gluten-free selections are also available. Garlic green beans with choice of chicken, prawns or beef and the Marco Polo special crispy pan-fried egg noodles loaded with chicken, barbecue pork and shrimp with a substantial portion of good-for-you vegetables are especially satisfying.

The Original Pancake House
4685 Portland Road NE   503/393-9124
4656 Commercial St SE   503/378-0431
Daily: 6-2   originalpancakehouse.com
Moderate
The Original Pancake House now boasts about 130 franchised locations in the U.S., plus more in Japan and South Korea. Founded in Portland in 1953 by Erma Heuneke and Les Highet, these breakfast houses have long been a Frank family favorite. Whether you call them pancakes, griddlecakes, flapjacks or hotcakes, the menu offers almost every concoction of pancake imaginable: buttermilk, potato, buckwheat, sourdough, Swedish or wheat germ finished with fruits, nuts, bacon or other goodies. Add crepes, waffles, egg dishes, omelets, cereal and specialties such as the Dutch Baby (an oven-baked soufflé, served with lemon, whipped butter and powdered sugar) and, man oh man, you have breakfast for everyone. (Also in Portland, Bend, Eugene and Redmond; menu and prices may vary.)

Riverfront Park
200 Water St NE   503/588-6336
                                          cityofsalem.net
Now a beautiful downtown greenspace along the Willamette River, Riverfront Park was formerly industrial ground for a flour mill and more recently Boise Cascade's paper and cardboard-manufacturing plant. In the

mid-1980s the City of Salem purchased the property and cleared the way for a carousel, heritage village, an amphitheater, covered pavilion, picnic tables, boat dock and miles of walking and biking paths. The park is host to numerous annual events like The Bite & Brew and World Beat Festival. One lasting vestige of the industrial past is a large pressurized acid ball which held acids for processing wood chips. A five-year endeavor transformed it into an artistic world globe depicted through 86,000 hand-crafted tiles. On the north end of the park a defunct railroad bridge is a popular pedestrian walkway across the river to West Salem and through Wallace Marine Park. The southern terminus of the park is connected via the Peter Courtney Minto Island Bridge to Minto-Brown Island Park. The delightful result is 29 miles of trails bypassing busy downtown traffic. Winter 2017 debuted a seasonal outdoor ice skating rink to the park, which will return in future winters.

Roth's Fresh Markets

Vista, 3045 Commercial St SE	503/364-8449
Sunnyslope, 4555 Liberty Road S	503/370-7833
Lancaster, 702 Lancaster Dr NE	503/585-5770
Hayesville, 4746 Portland Road NE	503/393-2345
West Salem, 1130 Wallace Road NW	503/370-3790
Daily: 6 a.m.-10 p.m.	roths.com

Roth's Fresh Markets has been striving for and providing excellence since it was founded in 1962 by the late Orville Roth, a visionary leader, philanthropist and community supporter. Son Michael Roth continues the traditions of personal cheerful service and a high-quality product mix in well-maintained, modern stores. The company provides valued jobs to the area and has been a huge supporter to a myriad of good causes — all part of Roth's original mission. Currently there are five Salem stores and additional locations in Independence, McMinnville, Silverton and Stayton. The Roth family is outstanding.

Rudy's Steakhouse

350 Chemeketa St NE	503/399-0449
Mon-Thu: 11-9; Fri, Sat: 11-10; Sun: 9-9	rudyssteakhouse.com
Moderately expensive	

Previously located at the Salem Golf Club, the new downtown location has been quite the hit, especially with their recent remodel. They've really livened up the restaurant and it fits in wonderfully with the upbeat scene downtown. More importantly, they have not let down on food quality, preparation or presentation. Lunch includes over a dozen sandwich and burger variations, entrees such as Dungeness crab cakes, fish and chips,

STATE CAPITOL

Any description of Salem would be incomplete if it were not noted as Oregon's capital city. And any tourism visit to the city would be incomplete if it did not include a trip to the state Capitol. The building's art, architecture, history and grounds (an official state park) are worthy of many visits. The Capitol currently is amid a nearly $60 million construction and maintenance project designed to improve access and safety which will continue into 2019. Visitors, however, should not be intimidated by all the temporary chain-link fencing and construction vehicles surrounding the building and grounds. The building is open for tours, although portions of the grounds may be inaccessible for some time. Generally speaking, guided tours are available weekdays through November, although special events may limit access. Capitol building tours start at the state seal in the rotunda. Knowledgeable guides share information about the history of Oregon, the Capitol and the legislative process. Walk-in visitors are welcome, and there are always opportunities for self-guided tours. From mid-June through early September, guided tours to the top of the Capitol tower, immediately below the Oregon Pioneer statue, are available weather permitting. Your guided tour departs from the rotunda on the first floor and climbs 121 steps to the observation deck. From there, the birds-eye view of Salem is grand. Visitors should always call ahead for precise tour schedules and other information, 503/986-1388, Monday-Friday from 8 a.m. to 5 p.m. You can also find an event calendar and other information online at oregonlegislature.gov/capitolhistorygateway. The state Capitol is at 900 Court St NE. Admission is always free.

and quality filet mignon medallions served with tasty char-grilled asparagus as well as soups and fresh crisp salads like the apple gorgonzola creation. Dinner options are plentiful and include juicy ribeye as well as a ribeye burger, slow roasted prime rib, chicken Marsala, halibut Parmesan, pastas, soups, salads, and a variety of add-ons and gourmet sauces. Make sure to save room for their famous marionberry cobbler or delicious blueberry bread pudding as well as a marionberry-infused cocktail. Sunday breakfast at Rudy's is a special treat and features scrambles, Benedicts, steak and eggs plus mimosas and Marys. Banquet facilities are across the street.

Salem Ale Works

2315 25th St SE   503/990-8486
Mon-Thu: noon-10 (Fri, Sat till 11; Sun till 8)   aleinsalem.com
Moderate

The new and expanded Salem Ale Works now features its own food menu in addition to its hand crafted beers. Choose locally sourced salads, burgers made from Oregon pasture-raised beef, build-your-own hot sandwiches, appetizers and dessert. On tap you'll find 12 beers and two guest ciders. If beer is not your forte, opt for a local wine, soda, lemonade or kombucha. The expansion doesn't mean a change in quality. Beers will still be brewed on site, in small batches, using fresh and local ingredients.

Salem's Riverfront Carousel

101 Front St NE   503/540-0374
Daily (seasonal hours)   salemcarousel.org
Nominal

A trip to the Riverfront Park is not complete without a ride on the locally hand-carved indoor carousel where 46 horses and friends prance to calliope music. The piece has become a Salem landmark and source of community pride. The adjacent gift shop is filled with unique and magical items.

Thompson Brewery & Public House

3575 Liberty Road S   503/363-7286
Sun-Tue: 11-10; Wed, Thu till 11; Fri, Sat till 1 a.m.   mcmenamins.com
Moderate

Another McMenamins brew pub featuring pub grub, sandwiches, burgers and salads; Edgefield wines, spirits and a host of full-bodied beers brewed on site in this house built for a Civil War veteran. (For a detailed description of the McMenamins brand, see Page 12)

Wild Pear Restaurant & Catering

372 State St   503/378-7515
Mon-Sat: 10:30-6:30   wildpearcatering.com
Inexpensive to moderate

Sisters and owners, Jessica Ritter and Cecilia Ritter, are known by their family as the "wild pair," hence the name of their restaurant. Walking in, you are welcomed by colorful and bold oil paintings of pears on the walls of this restaurant/catering establishment. The sisters take pride in bringing you flavorful American dishes made with Pacific Northwest bounty with a Vietnamese twist. Their selection of lunch items spans appetizers, soups, salads, sandwiches, wraps, pizza and the traditional Vietnamese pho dish (a family recipe). Popular dishes include an open-face lobster and seafood melt and the Wild Pear chicken pizza topped with pears, candied pecans, blue cheese crumbles, mozzarella and pesto. For more of a sampling across their menu, try one of their combinations varying from quiche with soup or salad, a salad and soup or even two soups with a salad. Decadent desserts, specialty cocktails, wine and beer are also highlighted on the menu. Sister restaurants include **Ritter's Housemade Foods** (102 Liberty St NE, Suite 100, 503/339-7928, ritterseatery.com) serving breakfast, lunch and dinner with an outstanding selection of cocktails and **Acme Cafe** (110 Hansen Ave S, 503/798-4736, acmecafe.net), a South Salem neighborhood lunch and dinner restaurant with weekend breakfast.

Willamette Heritage Center

1313 Mill St SE   503/585-7012
Mon-Sat: 10-5   willametteheritage.org
Tours: nominal

This history complex that began in 1896 as the Thomas Kay Woolen Mill, is a forerunner of the famous Pendleton Woolen Mills label. Restored, refurnished and moved to the manicured grounds are the oldest remaining wooden frame houses in the Northwest (the Jason Lee House and Methodist Parsonage), Salem's oldest single family dwelling (the John D. Boon house) and Pleasant Grove Church (the oldest remaining Presbyterian Church in Oregon). The mill, which closed in 1962, is the only woolen mill museum west of Missouri and was the last direct water-powered factory in the U.S. when it closed. In 2010, Mission Mill Museum Association merged with the Marion County Historical Society and established library, archives and collections divisions to oversee the combined collections and provide a vision for the future. The center has created interesting interpretive displays illuminating the area's history, from the days of interaction between Euro-American missionaries and Native Americans, to the time when blankets and textiles were made at the mill. A rushing millrace and the thump-thump sound of looms is part of the re-created working ambience. Self-guided tours for individuals and small groups and guided tours for larger groups are available. The warehouse building is home to several businesses, a cafe and orientation center.

Willamette Valley Pie Company

2994 82nd Ave NE   503/362-8678
Mon-Fri: 8-6; Sat: 9-5   wvpie.com
Check website for extended seasonal hours

This farm store not only offers fresh baked pies whole and by the slice, but frozen fruit, pastries, coffee and espresso, ice cream, smoothies and much more. They produce thousands of handmade pies that are sold locally and shipped throughout the western states (and beyond via their online store). Up to 30 local growers funnel fruits through this family-owned business to be used in not only pies, but cobblers, jams and jellies, freezer jams and syrups. The store offers other gourmet products, gift and garden items, home decor, lunch fare and more. Call-in orders are accepted for a pie baked fresh for you. With a new indoor seating area, as well as being surrounded by farm fields, a manicured lawn and play structure for kids, this is a beautiful destination between Salem and Silverton any time.

Word of Mouth Neighborhood Bistro

140 17th St NE   503/930-4285
Wed-Sun: 7-3   wordofsalem.com
Moderate

There is almost always a waiting line for a table on the enclosed front porch, at the bar or in the main floor dining areas at this small house. Until mid-afternoon, owners/chefs Becky and Steve Mucha turn out seductive breakfast winners such as Benedicts, the incredible flying biscuit (buttermilk biscuit, fried chicken, fried egg, melted cheese, bacon and sausage gravy with breakfast potatoes), omelets, hash (veggie, corned beef or filet mignon), housemade sausage and crème brûlée French toast (thick slices of custard-like challah bread with a caramelized crunchy topping, ordered a la carte or with eggs and bacon). Complement your order with a

---

FRIENDS AND SALEM PHILANTHROPISTS

I've been surrounded by movers and shakers from around the country my entire life and I'm especially proud to call these Salem businessmen true friends. If there is a worthwhile cause in the local area, and sometimes beyond, you will oftentimes find them leading the charge.

Jim Bernau: Founder Willamette Valley Vineyards; wine pioneer, entrepreneur and industry supporter
Scott Casebeer: President, Capitol Auto Group, a top auto dealership in sales and awards; reputation for community involvement
Michael Roth: President, Roth's Fresh Markets; continues family's legacy
Larry Tokarski: President, Mountain West Investment Corporation; committed to helping the youth and elderly
Dick Withnell: Chairman of the Board, Withnell Motor Company; generous with every good cause

Bloody Mary or freshly squeezed mimosa for a special treat. Lunch service begins at 11 with soups, chowders, fresh salads (spinach, chicken bistro or chopped chicken), burgers and hearty specialty sandwiches with a nice assortment of sides.

Xicha Brewing

576 Patterson St NW, Suite 140   503/990-8292
Daily: 11-9 (Fri, Sat till 10)   xichabrewing.com
Moderate

Freshness is evident at Xicha (pronounced Chee-chah) Brewing, where all the handcrafted beers are said to pair nicely with the Latin American cuisine (also housemade, colorful and beautifully presented). The queso fundido (broiled three-cheese mixture with house chips and salsas) is a great start to crispy pork belly tacos. The more adventurous may opt for the aguacate frito (fried avocado with greens, black beans, chipotle aioli and cotija cheese) followed by a handheld costillas (guava-chipotle barbecue spare ribs, cabbage slaw and cilantro). Other taco variations (including chicken, braised beef and seafood), sandwiches (or "handheld items" as they are called), starters and salads round out the menu, which is rather focused, but that should leave plenty of room for the beer (this is a brewery, after all). Traditional styles (for Northwest breweries) such as IPA, porter, pale ale and hefeweizen share the tap row with a Kellerbier Mexicano (a light lager) and staff favorite Märzen, among others. Growlers are gladly filled. Don't overlook this new brewpub (it opened in late 2017) just because it's in West Salem's industrial area.

SILVERTON

The Chocolate Box

301 E Main St   503/873-3225
Tue-Sat: 11:30-5; Sun: noon-4   silvertonchocolateboxshop.com

This boutique is all about my favorite food: chocolate. You'll find artisan handmade chocolates by award-winning Oregon chocolatiers including Moonstruck, Ladybug Chocolates and The Brigittine Monks under one roof. Buy these luscious chocolates by the piece or as many as you wish; custom gift baskets and boxes are no problem. The folks here will skillfully design a chocolate buffet or favors for weddings, showers, anniversaries and other celebrations. Dairy-free and vegan chocolates, chocolate sauces and gourmet hot cocoa are also featured.

Creekside Grill

242 S Water St   503/873-9700
Daily: 11:30-9   creeksidesilverton.com
Inexpensive to moderate
Silverton has an allure and charm all its own; small businesses are the fabric of downtown, colorful wall murals depict the town's history, and there is a sense of pride throughout the community. Creekside Grill is one such business that fits right in. Located beneath street level in the Hartman Building, the restaurant is situated along Silver Creek. On nice days, enjoy the delightful outdoor balcony. There are over a half-dozen items to choose from for lunch, such as BLT with avocado as well as a classic cheeseburger, banh mi chicken tacos and popular fish tacos. Flavorful dinners include several fish and seafood entrees, pork chop with seasonal tapenade, hickory-smoked pork ribs, grilled chicken breast with artichoke hearts and mushrooms as well as steak and pasta inventions; soups are made fresh daily. The unique zombie fries are made with tempura-fried Portobello mushrooms dusted with parmesan, chili flakes and truffle oil, accompanied by chipotle aioli dipping sauce. Meal-portioned salads include assorted delectable tidbits and the quinoa is locally grown, tossed with jicama, corn and cilantro.

Edward Adams House Bed & Breakfast

729 S Water St   503/873-8868
Moderate   edwardadamshousebandb.com
In one of Oregon's most picturesque towns, this cozy inn welcomes you to one of three lovingly restored bedrooms. Built by Swedish master craftsman Magnus Ek, the 1890 home is listed on the National Registry of Historic Places and is a Silverton Heritage Landmark. The home features antiques, a 1920 Steinway grand piano and vintage furnishings. Updated private baths are individualized with a whirlpool tub in the octagonal turret, vintage tub or a walk-in shower; all are stocked with sumptuous bathrobes and towels. Mornings start with a silver tray of coffee and tea placed outside your bedroom door, followed by a delightful breakfast of homemade goodies, fruits and varying entrees (special dietary needs can be accommodated) in the dining room.

The Oregon Garden

879 W Main St   503/874-8100, 877/674-2733
Daily: 9-6 (May-Sep); 10-4 (Oct-Apr)   oregongarden.org
Nominal to reasonable
Be sure to include time to admire the gardens, waterfalls, ponds and fountains at The Oregon Garden if you are planning a visit to the Silver-

ton area. Since its opening in 2001, more than 20 themed gardens have been developed. Each season brings new vistas with blooming annuals, perennials, trees and shrubs. In addition, this is a prime venue for festivals, weddings and a full spectrum of special events on the grounds or in the J. Frank Schmidt Pavilion. Between April and October, a tram conveys visitors throughout the 80 glorious acres. **The Gordon House** (503/874-6006, thegordonhouse.org), Oregon's only Frank Lloyd Wright-designed home, was relocated to The Oregon Garden (tours available by reservation). The house's Usonian design is characterized by an open floor plan, cantilevered roofs and floor-to-ceiling windows.

Oregon Garden Resort

895 W Main St   503/874-2500
Moderate   oregongardenresort.com

Several Northwest-style buildings contain 103 guest rooms (some pet-friendly); all include private patios or decks and fireplace, complimentary breakfast and admission to The Oregon Garden. The resort includes a full-service, moderately-priced restaurant with tables situated to enjoy the expansive Valley views. The resort also features full-service Moonstone Spa and the Fireside Lounge which hosts live music every evening. A seasonal outdoor pool and year-round hot tub are on the property.

Seven Brides Brewing

990 N 1st St   503/874-4677
Tue: 3-8; Wed-Sun: 11:30-9 (Fri, Sat till 11)   sevenbridesbrewing.com
Lunch: Inexpensive; Dinner: Moderate

When three proud dads and two uncles made the move from brewing in the garage to the pros, Seven Brides Brewing resulted. Born from the idea of paying for all those daughters' weddings, a brewery rooted in family tradition and committed to Oregon was born. Beer offerings range from pub classic styles such as Becky's Black Cat Porter to barrel-aged sours using local peaches. Food at the tap room has something to please everyone from the West Coast foodie to a family of five looking for a bite after hiking at Silver Falls State Park. There are full meals, salads, sandwiches, burgers and steaks.

Silver Grille

206 E Main St   503/873-8000
Wed-Sun: 5-9:30   silvergrille.com
Moderate and up

Chef Jeff Nizlek is in command of the Silver Grille, a charming and intimate contemporary bistro. His travels and experiences have honed his desire to offer fresh and savory first-class Willamette Valley cuisine. Appetizers, salads, entrees and desserts are artfully plated, each as pleasing to the eyes as to the stomach. The menu is ever-changing as Jeff incorporates the wide variety of products grown and raised in the Willamette Valley. Seasonal entrees are prepared for hearty winter appetites and include vegetarian options. Overall, everything is beautifully executed and surprisingly affordable; the environment comfortable and relaxed. World-class wines from the Valley's best wineries are also available.

Silverton Inn & Suites

310 N Water St   503/873-1000
Inexpensive and up   silvertoninnandsuites.com
A stay in one of the 18 accommodations may bring a quaint European town to mind. All suites (one, two or three beds; one or two bedrooms) are outfitted with full kitchens or kitchenettes. Each room is named after a portion of Silverton's rich history. For additional glimpses of the town's history, wander through town to view the dozen or so colorful murals.

SPRINGFIELD

McKenzie Orchards Bed & Breakfast

34694 McKenzie View Dr   541/515-8153
Moderate   mkobb.com
Get pampered in the countryside on the lower McKenzie River at this boutique bed and breakfast. Just 15 minutes from Eugene, this ADA-accessible, modern accommodation houses five guest rooms; four rooms offer tranquil river views. Wine and hors d'oeuvres are served each evening as guests regale one another with accounts of fly-fishing, bicycle touring or day trip excursions. Pampered overnighters are on the receiving end of hosts Karen and Tom Reid's culinary expertise for morning breakfasts; if you'd rather stay in and enjoy the solitude, inquire about light evening bistro fare. Check with the Reids for a seat at their popular cooking school (by appointment only) held at the inn; hands-on demonstrations (elegant but easy, French, Mexican, Italian, etc.), paired wines and a delicious dinner with fellow classmates make for a great and entertaining evening.

The Pump Cafe

710 Main St   541/726-0622
Mon-Fri: 7-2; Sat, Sun: 8-2   Facebook
Inexpensive
Spend a little time in downtown Springfield and you'll garner a glimpse of Springfield's historic past. Colorful murals depict The Oregon Trail, turn

of the century commerce, McKenzie River scenery and more. This breakfast and lunch gathering spot was previously a service station. The eclectic decor is accented with signage and artifacts befitting the former business. Although raspberry cream cheese French toast is the specialty of the house, corned beef over hash browns and potato pancakes are tasty, too. The lunch menu consists of sandwiches, homemade chili and soups and a variety of salads; lighter choices plus kids' and seniors' portions are also available. Since this is a popular spot, you may have to wait for a table; the food is good and so are the prices.

ST. PAUL

French Prairie Gardens & Family Farm
17673 French Prairie Road   503/633-8445
Seasonal   fpgardens.com
The Pohlschneider family has operated this gem since 1987. Through the years it has morphed from a self-service fruit and vegetable stand into a country experience on a working farm; the store was built in 1995. Fresh produce is sold in the farm market as are homemade fruit pies, muffins, cookies, scones and coffee cakes (March to mid-December) plus nursery products in the spring and summer. Fun festivals herald the first crop of strawberries, the fall harvest and other family-oriented gatherings.

STAYTON

Gardner House Cafe and Bed & Breakfast
633 N 3rd Ave   503/769-5478
Cafe: Tue-Sat: 8-3   gardnerhousebnb.com
Inexpensive
You'll find Stayton a charming small town not far from Silver Falls State Park. Proprietors Loni and James Loftus operate this classic Queen Anne Victorian turned into a cozy spot for breakfast, lunch or tea. Breakfast, served until 11, has plenty of egg combination plates, scones, crumpets and French toast. Salads, sandwiches, homemade soups and seasonal specials such as mac and cheese, stuffed Portobello mushrooms and flatbread pizzas satisfy lunchers. Afternoon tea is served (11 to 3, reservations required) with a delightful array of teas, fresh fruit, savory tarts, assorted finger sandwiches, scones and desserts. Talented Loni has won over 100 awards at the Oregon State Fair for her baked items. Some of those pies, cakes, cheesecakes and cookies are also served at the cafe. An overnight stay in the private cottage won't break the bank; breakfast is delivered to your room or you may opt to eat in the cafe.

COSTCO

Costco Wholesale (costco.com) has certainly changed the way the world shops. For many families, weekends begin with a trip to a Costco warehouse to stock up for the week and to nibble their way through the store grazing on ample samples. Headquartered in Issaquah, Washington, and with its first warehouse store in Seattle, Costco has grown to 748 locations worldwide in eight countries; over 500 in the U.S. alone. These membership-only warehouses stock brand name and reliable private label appliances, sporting goods, automotive products, office needs, clothing, books and movies, home goods and furniture, electronics and computers, health and beauty products, beer, wine and groceries. Top quality meats are cut and packaged in stores, prepared foods (love the Costco rotisserie chicken) are abundant and produce is always fresh. Who can resist fresh-from-the-oven pies, cakes, cookies and pastries? Stores may also include pharmacies, optical and hearing aid departments, photo services, tire centers, fueling stations and food courts. Here are Oregon's 13 current stores:

Albany (3130 Killdeer Ave, 541/918-7040)
Aloha (15901 SW Jenkins Road, 503/644-7615)
Bend (2500 NE Hwy 20, 541/385-9640)
Clackamas (13131 SE 84th Ave, 503/794-5500)
Eugene (2828 Chad Dr, 541/285-2000)
Hillsboro (1255 NE 48th Ave, 503/681-2800)
Medford (3639 Crater Lake Hwy, 541/734-4227)
Portland (4849 NE 138th Ave, 503/258-3700)
Roseburg (4141 NE Stephens St, 541/378-0020)
Salem (1010 Hawthorne Ave SE, 503/371-1729)
Tigard (7850 SW Dartmouth St, 503/639-0811)
Warrenton (1804 SE Ensign Lane, 503/338-4101)
Wilsonville (25900 SW Heather Pl, 503/825-4003)

TURNER

Enchanted Forest

8462 Enchanted Way SE   503/371-4242
Spring-summer; hours vary   enchantedforest.com
Reasonable

Fairy tales, nursery rhymes and stories come to life in this wonderful amusement park for families with young children. Opened in 1971 by park creator Roger Tofte, Enchanted Forest has over 20 acres of rides, entertainment, shopping, dining and hands-on activities geared toward the young and young at heart. Rides include the Big Timber Log Ride, Ice Mountain Bobsled Roller Coaster, Speedway Bumper Cars, Frog Hopper and more. Visit Storybook Lane, Tofteville Western Town, Old European Village and more. There are three gift shops and several options for food such as hot dogs, burgers and fries, barbecue, salads, ice cream, popcorn and snacks. Open daily mid-May through Labor Day, plus March spring break and select weekends and days in April, May and September. Generally opens at 10 a.m.; see website for exact hours.

Turnaround Cafe

7760 3rd St   503/743-1285
Tue-Sun: 7-2   turnaroundcafe.com
Inexpensive

Proprietor Nancy Walsh acquired a loyal following with her theme dinners that she donated to charitable auctions; she always had visions of one day owning a restaurant. Her aspiration became a reality when she leased a former bank building in downtown Turner and renovated it to suit her fancy. The result is a breakfast and lunch spot with local fare, decorated with images of roosters and cows, country fabrics and furnishings, photos of historic Turner, antiques and an original Western Security Bank vault door—all with rustic charm. Breakfasts are hearty enough for a lumberman or lighter for small appetites. Muffins, coffee cakes, cinnamon rolls, biscuits, sandwich buns and pies are all homemade. Breakfast temptations include their signature oatmeal pancakes, omelets and chicken-fried steak. Biscuits and sausage gravy are also homemade. Quiches, hamburgers, garden or chicken club sandwiches, hot turkey sandwiches and macaroni and cheese topped with Andouille sausage are all favorites. Cold deli sandwiches, salads and milkshakes round out the menu.

Willamette Valley Vineyards

8800 Enchanted Way SE   503/588-9463, 800/344-9463
Tasting room, Kitchen: Daily: 11-6 (extended summer hours)   wvv.com

Entrepreneur, civic leader and outstanding citizen Jim Bernau not only put Oregon pinot noir on the map, but has built one of the most visible and elegant wineries in the country; he is a legend in the wine business. The Estate Tasting Room is spectacular with warm woods, sofas surrounding an indoor fire pit and comfortable seating. Winery chef D.J. MacIntyre oversees the culinary domain and has developed menus for small plates and exquisite multi-course dinners. A separate tasting room for wine club members is beautifully appointed and features a fireplace and floor-to-ceiling windows that frame breathtaking views. The views continue on the outdoor terrace which is a superb place to enjoy wine and food. Complimentary winery tours open to the public at 2 p.m. daily and may include the underground wine library, if available. Two well-appointed hospitality suites are available for a unique overnight experience in wine country. Other tasting room locations are in McMinnville and Forest Grove.

VENETA

Our Daily Bread Restaurant
88170 Territorial Road   541/935-4921
Mon, Tue: 7-3; Wed-Fri: 7 a.m.-8 p.m.;
Sat, Sun: 8-8   ourdailybreadrestaurant.com
Inexpensive and up
Our Daily Bread is a suitable name for a restaurant and bakery in a renovated country church near Fern Ridge Reservoir. The dining area is especially cheery with sunlight streaming through the stained glass windows and front patio seating is perfect on a warm day. The extensive breakfast menu offers good ol' American standards: bacon, eggs, rustic red potatoes, hotcakes and more scrambles and omelet combinations than you can shake a stick at. Lunch lists a choice of soups, salads and sandwiches on housemade bread, plus wraps and specials. Weekly dinner specials, steaks, chops, pastas, seafood and chicken are filling dinner entrees. Sweet meal-enders include caramel or bourbon bread pudding and marionberry pie a la mode.

VIDA

Eagle Rock Lodge
49198 McKenzie Hwy   541/822-3630, 888/773-4333
Moderate and up   eaglerocklodge.com
Enjoy four acres of gardens and 400 feet of McKenzie River frontage. Fish from the backyard, take a raft trip, hike the Willamette National Forest, visit Koosah and Sahalie Falls—or just relax and enjoy the sounds of the river. Eagle Rock Lodge bed and breakfast consists of a main building with five rooms and suites and a cozy common room where guests can enjoy a good read and the wood-burning fireplace with a glass of wine and cookies. Three additional rooms are located a few steps away in the carriage house. Each unit has a small refrigerator, microwave and coffeemaker; en suite private bathrooms are supplied with fragrant toiletries. Morning breakfast is cooked to order in the main lodge, along with fresh fruit, freshly baked scones or muffins and homemade granola.

WILSONVILLE

Abella Italian Kitchen
8309 SW Main St   503/582-1201
Mon-Thu: 11:30-9; Fri, Sat: 11:30-10; Sun: 4-9   abellaitaliankitchen.com
Moderate
Start your Italian meal with a pleasant assortment of fresh soups, appetizers (gorgonzola cheesecake, bruschetta, broiled polenta) and salads (Caesar, Caprese and assorted greens). Pasta dishes prevail with tempting additions of prawns, Italian sausage, meatballs or chicken. Traditional choices
include chicken piccata, Marsala and parmesan; steaks; fish; seafood; pizzas and calzones. Most items are served for both lunch and dinner, including an extensive list of small plates. For dessert, the housemade double
chocolate torte is superb. Celebrate the first Thursday of each month with
a five-course dinner and wine pairings from a local vineyard.

Dar Essalam
29585 SW Park Pl, Suite A   503/682-3600
Mon-Thu: 11-8; Fri, Sat: 5-9   daressalam.org
Moderate
Fine North African spices and other exotic ingredients are featured at Dar
Essalam, which means "House of Tranquility." From the signature hummus
supreme with roasted red peppers, capers, feta and black olives served
with warm pita bread to a variety of kabobs or a gyro, you won't be disappointed. Dinner offers a choice of meat tajines combined with savory,
sweet or spicy options; gluten-free and vegetarian also. Interesting dessert options include the Casablanca dessert, buttery filo layers stuffed with
fruit, dusted with powdered sugar and toasted almonds and topped with
ice cream.

Oswego Grill at Wilsonville
30080 SW Boones Ferry Road   503/427-2152
Sun-Thu: 11-10; Fri, Sat; 11-11
Moderate
(See detailed listing with Oswego Grill at Kruse Way, Lake Oswego)

Slick's Big Time BBQ
9425 SW Commercial Circle, Suite 14   503/427-2414
Mon-Sat: 10:30-7 (Thu-Sat till 8 in summer)   slicksbigtimebbq.com
Inexpensive to moderate
Barbi and Dan Slick started with homemade sauces and rubs sold in
grocery stores and online, which then grew into a food truck and ca-

tering business. Now they have a full-service barbecue restaurant, too. Whether you choose ribs, brisket, pulled pork or chicken, you can't go wrong, because all feature flavorful, tender, hand trimmed meats. Try a bit of everything with the Pitmaster Plate (a slow smoked chicken thigh, a pulled pork and brisket slider and two ribs) served with two sides. The popular barbecue mac salad makes a great side, and the honey butter cornbread is not to be missed. Try salads that include meat and non-meat variations and a stuffed sweet potato with brisket for a fabulous gluten-free option.

World of Speed Motorsports Museum

27490 SW 95th Ave   503/563-6444
Tue-Sun: 10-5 (Sat open at 9)   worldofspeed.org
Nominal (under 5 and members free)

This is a cool place, not only for history buffs and motorsports enthusiasts, but also for just about anyone who wants to learn anything about the culture of American car racing. This nonprofit educational museum

WINE = TOURISM

The overall economic impact of the Oregon wine industry was valued at some $5.76 billion in 2016, more than double what it was in 2010 as the state began to emerge from the Great Recession. Perhaps even more illuminating, the value of Oregon wine tourism increased fivefold during that span, and now accounts for more revenue than winery sales itself: $787 million vs $529 million in 2016, according to statistics compiled for the Oregon Wine Board, which publicized them in late February.

These days an Oregon winery has to have a lot more going for it than a leggy red and an artfully designed label. In many cases it will need a business plan that understands and exploits not only winemaking, marketing and sales, but also tourism, lodging, fine dining and even musical entertainment, and it must do all this while remaining ethical stewards of the environment. This book is all about tourism, dining, lodging and entertainment, yet it would be impractical to include all the Oregon wineries in it (today there are close to 700, so it would take its own book). A relative few are mentioned, each for unique reasons. Oenophiles, fear not. There are many sources of information about Oregon wines and wineries, and one of the best is **Oregon Wine** (oregonwine.org). Here you'll find a calendar of special events at wineries,

includes roughly a dozen unique exhibits, some permanent, others rotating or temporary. With nearly 100 displayed cars, motorcycles and boats on loan and artifacts constantly being donated, loaned, or acquired by the museum, World of Speed makes each visit a fresh experience. You'll find open-wheeled racers, drag racers, cars from NASCAR, American muscle cars and classics in absolute cherry condition. Get in touch with some serious history In the Women in Racing exhibit, or get blown away in Wall of Sound, which explores how music influenced automobile design, and how automobiles forever changed how people listen to music. As adults wander through this family-friendly facility, youngsters stay entertained in their own educational play area. For those seeking out special interests, the museum offers workshops and clubs, and camps during summer and winter school breaks. Although generally closed Mondays, the museum is open on these holidays: Martin Luther King Jr. Day, Presidents Day, Memorial Day, 4th of July and Labor Day. It's also open Mondays that fall within Portland Public Schools' spring and winter breaks.

a free brochure on touring Oregon wineries and much more.

Most wineries, particularly in the Willamette Valley, pay special attention to two weekends during the year: Thanksgiving Weekend and Memorial Day weekend. During these times most wineries schedule open houses and special events in anticipation of literally thousands of people who set off on self-guided tours of their favorite vineyards and wineries.

Here are other websites where you can find good information about wine tourism in Oregon.

The Willamette Valley Visitors Association (oregonwinecountry. org): This project of six local visitors associations focuses on tourism and local winery events in the state's premier winegrowing region.

Oregon Wines (oregonwines.com): This educational site and search engine allows you to search for wineries by name, region or area nearest you. In some cases it allows for direct online wine sales or provides links to winery online sales. It, too, provides an events calendar.

Travel Oregon (traveloregon.com): This is the public face of the Oregon Tourism Commission, which provides a broader view of tourism in the state.

WOODBURN

Al's Garden Center

1220 N Pacific Hwy   503/981-1245
Mon-Fri: 10-6; Sat: 9-6; Sun: 10-5   als-gardencenter.com

A visit to one of the Al's Garden Center locations is a springtime ritual for folks far and wide. A dream of the Bigej family, Al's is a third generation family-owned and -operated nursery business. Nursery stock prevails, but plenty of other quality merchandise is attractively presented such as planters, patio furniture and grills, statuary, fountains, household decor and women's apparel. Al's experts are friendly and very informed and are easily spotted by their signature purple shirts. Al's has three additional re-tail stores including Sherwood (16920 SW Roy Rogers Road, 503/726-1162), Gresham (7505 SE Hogan Road, 503/491-0771) and Wilsonville (27755 SW Parkway Ave, 503/855-3527). Satisfied shoppers return for seasonal items like primroses, hanging baskets, pumpkins, Christmas trees and holiday gift items. Store hours vary slightly according to the season.

Woodburn Premium Outlets

1001 Arney Road   503/981-1900
Mon-Sat: 10-9; Sun: 10-7   premiumoutlets.com/woodburn

This attractive 110-store outlet mall is a wildly popular shopping desti-nation. Savings of up to 65% off retail draw huge crowds, especially on holiday weekends. Shoppers from the Northwest and Canada target Woodburn Premium Outlets for great deals and tax-free shopping at stores such as Adidas, Ann Taylor, Bose, Coach, Columbia Sportswear, Cole Haan, Fossil, Nike, Nine West, The North Face and dozens more. Twelve buildings are bursting with bargains in family clothing, footwear and accessories, housewares, luggage, fragrances, electronics, toys and fine jewelry. Boost your shopping energy with a break at Fresca's Mexican Grill, Jamba Juice, Starbucks, Subway and other assorted eateries. It's no wonder that this is one of Oregon's top tourist attractions.

Gerry's Exclusive List

BBQ
Adam's Rib Smoke House (1210 State St, Salem; 503/362-2194)
Ribslayer BBQ to Go (575 NE 2nd St, McMinnville; 503/472-1309)
Slick's Big Time BBQ (9425 SW Commercial Circle, Suite 14, Wilsonville; 503/427-2414)
Storrs Smokehouse (310 E 1st St, Newberg; 503/538-8080)

Bars and Pubs with Good Eats
Block 15 Restaurant & Brewery (300 SW Jefferson Ave, Corvallis; 541/758-2077)
Brewers Union Local 180 (48329 E 1st St, Oakridge; 541/782-2024)
Caves Bier & Kitchen (308 SW 3rd St, Corvallis; 541/286-4473)
Gilgamesh Brewing (2065 Madrona Ave SE, Salem; 503/584-1789)
Golden Valley Brewery & Restaurant (980 NE 4th St, McMinnville; 503/472-2739)
Seven Brides Brewing (990 N 1st St, Silverton; 503/874-4677)
Xicha Brewing (576 Patterson St NW, Suite 140, Salem; 503/990-8292)

Best Sleeps
The Allison Inn & Spa (2525 Allison Lane, Newberg; 503/554-2525)
The Grand Hotel (201 Liberty St SE, Salem; 503/540-7800)
Inn at the 5th (205 E 6th Ave, Eugene; 541/743-4099)

Breads and Bakery Goods
Blue Raeven Farmstand (20650 S Hwy 99W, Amity; 503/835-0740)
The Bread Board (404 N Main St, Falls City; 503/787-5000)
New Morning Bakery (219 SW 2nd St, Corvallis; 541/754-0181)
Red Fox Bakery (328 NE Evans St, McMinnville; 503/434-5098)

Breakfast/Brunch
Annette's Westgate (1311 Edgewater St NW, Salem; 503/362-9588)
The Broken Yolk Cafe (119 SW 3rd St, Corvallis; 541/738-9655)
Buster's Main Street Cafe (811 Main St, Cottage Grove; 541/942-8363)
Crescent Cafe (526 NE 3rd St, McMinnville; 503/435-2655): breakfast and brunch
JORY Restaurant (The Allison Inn and Spa, 2525 Allison Lane, Newberg; 503/554-2526): weekday breakfast, Sunday brunch
King Estate Winery (80854 Territorial Road, Eugene; 541/685-5189): weekend brunch

Off the Waffle (2540 Willamette St, Eugene, 541/515-6926; 840 Willamette St, Eugene, 541/632-4225)
The Original Pancake House (782 E Broadway Ave, Eugene, 541/343-7523; 4685 Portland Road NE, Salem, 503/393-9124; 4656 Commercial St SE, Salem, 503/378-0431)
The Pump Cafe (710 Main St, Springfield; 541/726-0622)
Word of Mouth Neighborhood Bistro (140 17th St NE, Salem; 503/930-4285)

Burgers
Bo & Vine Burger Bar (176 Liberty St NE, Salem; 971/301-2584)
Café 22 West (5152 Salem-Dallas Hwy, Salem; 503/363-4643)
Court Street Dairy Lunch (347 Court St NE, Salem; 503/363-6433)
First Burger (210 1st Ave W, Albany; 541/704-1128)
MarKum Inn (36903 S Hwy 213, Marquam; 503/829-6006)

Casual Dining/Casual Prices
Buster's Main Street Cafe (811 Main St, Cottage Grove; 541/942-8363)
Café 22 West (5152 Salem-Dallas Hwy, Salem; 503/363-4643)
Community Plate (315 NE Third St, McMinnville; 503/687-1902)
The Depot Cafe (822 SE Lyon St, Albany; 541/926-7326)
The Horse Radish (211 W Main St, Carlton; 503/852-6656)
MarKum Inn (36903 S Hwy 213, Marquam; 503/829-6006)
The Pump Cafe (710 Main St, Springfield; 541/726-0622)
Turnaround Cafe (7760 3rd St, Turner; 503/743-1285)

Coffee and Tea
Archive Coffee & Bar (120 Liberty St NE, Suite 120, Salem; 971/701-6266)
Gardner House Cafe and Bed & Breakfast (633 N 3rd Ave, Stayton; 503/769-5478): afternoon tea; reservations required

Confections
The Chocolate Box (301 E Main St, Silverton; 503/873-3225)
Euphoria Chocolate Company (946 Willamette, Eugene, 458/201-8750; Oakway Center, 21 Oakway Road, Eugene, 541/343-0407)
Honest Chocolates (217 E Main St, Carlton, 503/474-9042; 312 E 1st St, Newberg, 503/537-0754)

Desserts
Gerry Frank's Konditorei (310 Kearney St SE, Salem; 503/585-7070)
Sweet Life Patisserie (755 Monroe St and 1609 E 19th Ave, Eugene; 541/683-5676)
Sugar Sugar (335 State St, Salem; 503/385-1225): cupcakes

Doughnuts
Bauman's Farm & Garden (12989 Howell Prairie Road NE, Gervais; 503/792-3524)
E.Z. Orchards (5504 Hazel Green Road NE, Salem; 503/393-1506)
Voodoo Doughnut (20 E Broadway, Eugene; 541/868-8666)

Fish and Seafood
Fisherman's Market (830 W 7th St, Eugene; 541/484-2722)
Fitts Seafoods (1555 12th St, Salem; 503/364-6724): reliable source for all types of fresh seafood
Oregon Lox Company (4828 W 11th Ave, Eugene; 541/726-5699): smoked salmon, lox and trout
Newman's Fish Co. (1545 Willamette St, Eugene; 541/344-2371): outstanding selection; special orders; seafood salads, accompaniments and more

Foreign Flavors
CHINESE: Kwan's Original Cuisine (835 Commercial St SE, Salem, 503/362-7711); **Marco Polo Global Restaurant** (300 Liberty St SE, Salem, 503/364-4833)
FRENCH: Bistro Maison (729 NE 3rd St, McMinnville, 503/474-1888); **Cuvee** (214 W Main St, Carlton, 503/852-6555); **Marché** (296 E 5th Ave, Eugene, 541/342-3612)
GERMAN: Glockenspiel Restaurant & Pub (190 E Charles St, Mt. Angel, 503/845-6222); **Mt. Angel Sausage Co.** (105 S Garfield St, Mt. Angel, 503/845-2322)
HUNGARIAN: Novak's Hungarian Restaurant (208 2nd Ave SW, Albany; 541/967-9488)
ITALIAN: Abella Italian Kitchen (8309 SW Main St, Wilsonville, 503/582-1201); **Beppe & Gianni's Trattoria** (1646 E 19th Ave, Eugene, 541/683-6661); **DaVinci Ristorante** (180 High St SE, Salem, 503/399-1413); **Gamberetti's Italian Restaurant** (325 High St SE, Salem, 503/339-7446); **Mangiare Italian Restaurant** (114 S Main St, Independence, 503/838-0566), **Nick's Italian Cafe** (521 NE 3rd St, McMinnville, 503/434-4471)
LATIN: Del Alma Restaurant (136 SW Washington Ave, Corvallis; 541/753-2222)
MEDITERRANEAN: Café Soriah (384 W 13th Ave, Eugene; 541/342-4410)
MOROCCAN: Dar Essalam (29585 SW Park Pl, Suite A, Wilsonville; 503/682-3600)
SPANISH: La Rambla Restaurant & Bar (238 NE 3rd St, McMinnville; 503/435-2126)

Ice Cream and Other Frozen Treats
22 Below (4155 Rickey St SE, Salem; 503/602-7502)
Prince Pückler's Gourmet Ice Cream (1605 E 19th Ave, Eugene; 541/344-4418)
Serendipity Ice Cream (502 NE 3rd St, McMinnville; 503/474-9189)

Meats
Mt. Angel Sausage Co. (105 S Garfield St, Mt. Angel; 503/845-2322)

Personal Favorites
JORY Restaurant (The Allison Inn & Spa, 2525 Allison Lane, Newberg; 503/554-2525)
MarKum Inn (36903 S Hwy 213, Marquam; 503/829-6006)
The Painted Lady (201 S College St, Newberg; 503/538-3850)
Silver Grille (206 E Main St, Silverton; 503/873-8000)

Pie
Blue Raeven Farmstand (20650 S Hwy 99W, Amity; 503/835-0740)
Willamette Valley Pie Company (2994 82nd Ave NE, Salem; 503/362-8678)

Pizza
3rd Street Pizza Co. (433 NE 3rd St, McMinnville; 503/434-5800)
Giovanni's Mountain Pizza (146 NW Santiam Blvd, Mill City; 503/897-2614)
Padington's Pizza (5255 Commercial St SE, Salem, 503/370-7556; 410 Pine St NE, Salem, 503/378-0345)

Produce
Aspinwall's Nursery & Produce (5152 Salem-Dallas Hwy, Salem; 503/363-4643)
Bauman's Farm & Garden (12989 Howell Prairie Road NE, Gervais; 503/792-3524)
E.Z. Orchards (5504 Hazel Green Road NE, Salem; 503/393-1506)
French Prairie Gardens & Family Farm (17673 French Prairie Road, St. Paul; 503/633-8445)

Sandwiches
Court Street Dairy Lunch (347 Court St NE, Salem; 503/363-6433)
The Horse Radish (211 W Main St, Carlton; 503/852-6656)
The Pink House Cafe (242 D St, Independence; 503/837-0900)
Red Fox Bakery (328 NE Evans St, McMinnville; 503/434-5098)

Ritter's Housemade Foods (102 Liberty St NE, Suite 100, Salem; 503/339-7928)

Special Occasions
Bentley's Grill (The Grand Hotel, 291 Liberty St SE, Salem; 503/779-1660)
Bistro Maison (729 NE 3rd St, McMinnville; 503/474-1888)
Cuvee (214 W Main St, Carlton; 503/852-6555)
FairWay Restaurant & Bar (2025 Golf Course Road S, Salem; 503/385-8855)
JORY Restaurant (The Allison Inn and Spa, 2525 Allison Lane, Newberg; 503/554-2526)
King Estate Winery (80854 Territorial Road, Eugene; 541/685-5189)
Marché (296 E 5th Ave, Eugene; 541/342-3612)
Oregon Electric Station (27 E 5th Ave, Eugene; 541/485-4444)
The Painted Lady (201 S College St, Newberg; 503/538-3850)
Rudy's Steakhouse (350 Chemeketa St NE, Salem; 503/399-0449)
Tina's Restaurant (760 Hwy 99W, Dundee; 503/538-8880)

Steaks
Bentley's Grill (The Grand Hotel, 291 Liberty St SE, Salem; 503/779-1660)
JORY Restaurant (The Allison Inn and Spa, 2525 Allison Lane, Newberg; 503/554-2526)
Marché (296 E 5th Ave, Eugene; 541/342-3612)
Oregon Electric Station (27 E 5th Ave, Eugene; 541/485-4444)
Rudy's Steakhouse (350 Chemeketa St NE, Salem; 503/399-0449)

Vegan and Vegetarian Options
Marco Polo Global Restaurant (300 Liberty St SE, Salem; 503/364-4833)
Nearly Normal's (109 NW 15th St, Corvallis; 541/753-0791)
The Painted Lady (2015 College St, Newberg; 503/538-3850)
Tina's Restaurant (760 Hwy 99W, Dundee; 503/538-8880)
Vault 244 (244 1st Ave W, Albany; 541/791-9511)

Notes

Notes

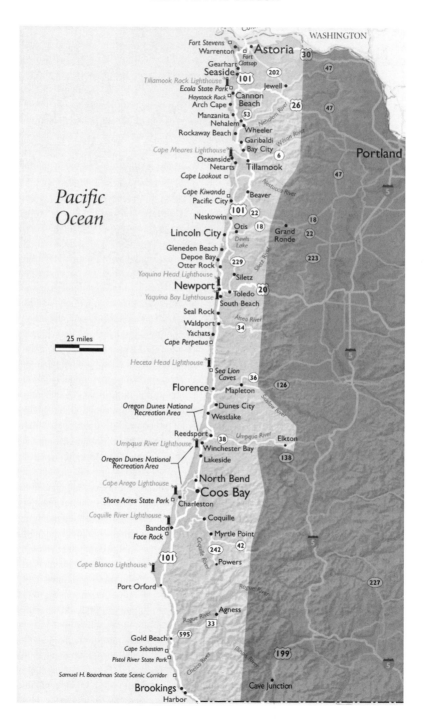

CHAPTER THREE

Oregon Coast

AGNESS

Cougar Lane Lodge

04219 Agness Road
Moderate

541/247-7233
thefirstburger.com

Some 32 miles inland from Gold Beach is an outdoor enthusiast's escape on the banks of the wild and scenic Rogue River. Arrive at Cougar Lane Lodge via jet boat, raft or automobile to enjoy delicious barbecue, relax in a full-service bar and then stay overnight or longer in six remodeled rooms (two with kitchenettes). The lodge is a hub of activity for anglers and rafters finishing their three-day whitewater float trips. It is also a lunch stop for jet boat excursions. The convenient general store, open year-round, offers food, snacks, propane and gas, and liquor, wine and beer. A log-cabin theme animates the bar and dining room, which serves excellent smoked, slow-cooked ribs, pulled pork, chicken and beef brisket, as well as homemade sides and local microbrews. Guests can enjoy scenic river views from the deck. Restaurant open May through October.

Singing Springs Resort

34501 Agness Illahe Road
Lodge: Seasonal
Inexpensive

541/247-6162, 877/330-3777
singingspringsresort.com

It is a given that the Rogue River is spectacular any time of the year. Consider Singing Springs Resort for a true Oregon getaway. You can drive (about an hour northeast of Gold Beach), but it's more fun to take a commercial jet boat from Gold Beach. Country cottages are clean and comfortable, accommodate two to four guests and are available throughout the year. The lodge is open from May through mid-October, and accommodations are available by the day, week or month. Continental breakfast is included with an overnight stay, and a lunch buffet and sandwiches are also available. The all-you-can-eat dinner buffet and salad bar (July and August) features Southern fried chicken, house-smoked ribs, turkey, brats, barbecued pork loin, freshly-baked biscuits, fresh fruits and vegetables from the garden and all the trimmings. Meals in the off-season are optional with prior arrangement. Fishing guides should be booked in advance.

ARCH CAPE

Arch Cape Inn & Retreat

31970 E Ocean Lane　　　　　　　　　　　503/436-2800, 800/436-2848
Moderate to expensive　　　　　　　　　　　　　　　archcapeinn.com

This romantic chateau, perfect for couples celebrating special occasions, is ranked among the top castle-like hotels in the United States by the website Travel + Leisure. It is sure to elicit plenty of oohs and aahs. The inn is well-appointed, service is extremely gracious and the experience is nearly magical. Nine rooms and one suite have private baths, European-style furnishings, soft pillows and Aveda bath products. Relaxing, oversized soaking or Jacuzzi tubs and gas fireplaces in most rooms enhance this getaway-from-it-all location with ocean and garden views. Overnight stays include a three-course gourmet breakfast with locally foraged ingredients and fresh-from-the-garden produce and herbs masterfully woven into an ever-changing menu. Other pleasant touches are afternoon wine and light appetizers and in-room refreshments. You'll want to plan a return visit even before you depart.

ASTORIA

Astoria Coffeehouse & Bistro

243 11th St　　　　　　　　　　　　　　　　　　503/325-1787
Daily: 7 a.m.-10 p.m. (Fri, Sat till 11; Sun till 9)
Moderate

The vintage decor at Astoria Coffeehouse & Bistro — high chairs, black vinyl booths and funky wall art — could convince some that they'd just walked into a Northwest Portland cafe. But make no mistake. This is the Northwest Oregon coast. The place serves fresh pastries, cakes and Caffé Vita brand java, like many cafes might, but it also offers full menus for breakfast (such as eggs Benedict or smoked salmon hash) and lunch (fish tacos with chipotle tomatillo salsa; classics like meatloaf), and there's buzz that it has the best breakfast, bar and chef in the area. Towards evening it becomes a true bistro offering "neo-regional" cuisine of direct-caught seafood, natural meats and wild produce foraged from the area (try the roasted lamb with red curry and butternut squash ravioli). Everything is made in-house, including the roasted turkey and corned beef — even the ketchup. Vintage cocktails, regional beers and wines complement the menu. If you catch yourself having a lazy Sunday, try the Sunday brunch from 7 a.m. to 5 p.m.

Astoria Column
2199 Coxcomb Dr   503/325-2963
Mon-Fri: 9-5:30; Sat, Sun: 9-5   astoriacolumn.org
Nominal (for parking)
Take a few deep breaths, put one foot in front of the other and before long you have climbed the 164-step spiral staircase to the observation deck of the Astoria Column, erected in 1926. The rewards are magnificent views of the Columbia River, the Pacific Ocean, forests and the community. Kids get a kick out of launching gliders (available in the gift shop) from the 125-foot-tall tower. Fourteen early Oregon events, such as Captain Robert Gray's discovery of the Columbia River and Lewis and Clark's wintering at Fort Clatsop, are depicted in murals that spiral the length of the column. The nonprofit Friends of Astoria Column look after its maintenance and were behind a major restoration in 1995, as well as more recent improvements.

Baked Alaska
1 12th St   503/325-7414
Daily: 11:30-9 (Fri, Sat till 10)   bakedak.com
Moderate
Jennifer and Chris Holen oversee this full-service restaurant overlooking the Columbia River. Opened in 2001 with an emphasis on soups, the restaurant has expanded its offerings as well as its dining environment. Enjoy the upscale dining room with its sweeping river view; reserve the Discovery Room for private groups; try the bar, which offers a dozen craft brews amid a modern industrial feel; or come to the family-friendly pizzeria. No matter when diners come or where they sit, the same menu is available to all. The menu emphasizes Northwest ingredients, exemplified by the fish and chips, salmon and scallop entrees, the pure seafood stew (the chef's favorite) and the always-available clam chowder. Hand-tossed pizza, steaks, burgers, daily soups and sandwiches served with housemade potato chips round out the menu. The newest addition to the property is the Baked Alaska Annex, which hosts events such as themed wine dinners

TRAVEL OREGON

When you plan to travel around Oregon, an exceptional planning source is **Travel Oregon** (800/547-7842, traveloregon.com). This official Oregon tourism agency is led by Chief Executive Officer, Todd Davidson, who knows Oregon inside and out. Special interest and visitor guides and maps are available through its website or at visitor centers throughout the state. The regional planning guides contain beautiful photography, lists and descriptions of places to stay, shop, eat, drink and much more.

and international guest chefs. And don't forget the Baked (or Half-Baked) Alaska for dessert.

Blue Scorcher Bakery & Cafe

1493 Duane St   503/338-7473
Daily: 7-2:30 for cafe; till 4 for bakery and beverages   bluescorcher.com
Inexpensive

Artisan breads, almond bear claws, scones, other pastries and handcrafted seasonal and organic foods are the bread and butter at this bakery. Fresh, quality ingredients make the difference; eggs, produce, honey, flowers and coffee are from local suppliers. Families come for healthy breakfasts (heartier choices on weekends) and lunches of seasonal soups, salads and sandwiches made on Scorcher bread, as well as pizza by the slice and occasional calzone specials. This worker-owned cooperative is fierce about creating top-shelf meals, breads and pastries in a relaxed setting with no white tablecloths in sight. A great spot for afternoon tea.

Buoy Beer Co.

1 8th St   503/325-4540
Daily: 11-9 (Fri, Sat till 10)   buoybeer.com
Moderate

At Buoy Beer Co. you can enjoy locally-sourced food, great beer and catch a glimpse of sea lions. This is the place for burgers made from Oregon beef, with trimmings and condiments made in-house or bought locally. Although the hamburgers are good, the clam chowder paired with fresh garlic bread, rockfish and chips and Willapa Bay oysters are classic. Other offerings include hearty sandwiches, salads, pasta specials, pan-fried petrale sole, ribeye steak and seasonal dishes. Complement your meal with one of nearly 20 handcrafted lagers and ales, all brewed on the Buoy Beer premises, an extensively remodeled former cannery on the great Columbia River. The place is also family friendly: There's a full kids menu and family dogs are allowed on the patio.

Bridgewater Bistro

20 Basin St   503/325-6777
Mon-Sat: 11:30-3 (lunch); Daily: 4-close (dinner);
Sun: 10:30-3 (brunch)   bridgewaterbistro.com
Moderate

Under the Astoria-Megler Bridge, this is a fabulous venue with stunning river views. You can feast upon small bites, salads and seafood dishes (wild local salmon, local steamer clams, seafood cakes of the day or pan-fried Willapa Bay oysters). If you're not in the mood for fish, the steaks, pork and fowl preparations may be more to your liking. Add a housemade soup or salad to make for a tasty dinner. Sunday brunch offers a bit of everything good such as eggs and oysters, hash, seafood cakes, smoked tomato mac and cheese, sandwiches and burgers (over 90% of the menu items are gluten-free).

Cannery Pier Hotel & Spa

10 Basin St   503/325-4996, 888/325-4996
Moderate to expensive   cannerypierhotel.com

Situated on 100-year-old pilings and jutting out into the mighty Columbia, this hotel was once the Union Fisherman's Cooperative Packing Company. The 38 rooms and eight suites have hardwood floors, private balconies, gas fireplaces and in-room mini-fridges, microwaves and dining tables. With a nod to the area's Scandinavian heritage and fishing industry, the complimentary continental breakfast features Finnish delicacies; Oregon wines, cheeses and smoked salmon are served each evening. If you need a lift around town, you may be chauffeured in a classic car or head out on your own to explore the area on one of the hotel's vintage loaner bikes. Other amenities include a hot tub, sauna, exercise room, day spa and library. For the ultimate experience, book the Pilot House penthouse (two bedrooms, jetted tub, guest bath, full kitchen, living and dining rooms and two decks). Pet packages include treats and necessities to care for your canine travel companion.

The Cellar on 10th

1004 Marine Dr   503/325-6600
Tue-Sat: 10-5:30   thecellaron10th.com

Over 4,500 bottles of local, domestic and imported fine wines and champagnes are in stock in this historic perfect-for-wine underground shop; more than 70% of the libations are from the Northwest. Proprietor Mike

Wallis will help pick just the wine you want. Also find wine-related linens and table pieces, international gourmet foods, spices, sea salts, stemware and accessories. Wine tastings, Saturdays between 1 and 4, feature a new winery, varietal or wine region each week. The shop remains open when cruise ships are in port.

Clemente's Cafe & Public House

175 14th St, Suite 180   503/325-1067
Seasonal hours   Facebook
Moderate
For fresh, local meats and seafood, one sure bet is Clemente's, now located in the historic Pilot Station Building. Owners Lisa and Gordon Clement change the menu seasonally, which includes fish and chips, cioppino, raw bar selections, organic beef steaks and burgers and handmade pasta dishes; all sauces and soups are housemade. See their Facebook page for current menus and hours.

Columbia River Maritime Museum

1792 Marine Dr   503/325-2323
Daily: 9:30-5   crmm.org
Reasonable
Land at this museum for fascinating exhibitions of Northwest maritime artifacts and collections that preserve the rich maritime heritage of the Columbia River region. View the Pilot Boat Peacock, the Lightship Columbia (kids especially enjoy roaming the officers' quarters, mess deck, radio room and galley), other vessels, nautical equipment, historical memorabilia and interactive displays spread among six galleries and the Great Hall. The Barbey Maritime Center is situated in the beautifully restored Astoria Railroad Depot at the east end of the property. The center focuses on maritime-related demonstrations, workshops and classes on wooden boat building, wood carving, bronze casting and tool making. The museum now features a 3D movie theater that shows two films rotated every 30 minutes (see the website for current titles). Allow plenty of time to meander among the exhibits. This is said to be the largest collection of Pacific Northwest maritime artifacts in the country.

Drina Daisy

915 Commercial St   503/338-2912
Wed-Sun: 11-3 (lunch); 5-8 (dinner)   drinadaisy.com
Moderate
Lovers of ethnic food will enjoy comfort food with an Old World twist at this Bosnian restaurant. The third-generation Bosnian chef presents flavors

that are very Euro-Mediterranean with cabbage rolls and goulash and the like. Many entrees are slow-cooked and braised to perfection and served with fresh pickled vegetables and tasty breads. Dishes are savory but not too spicy, traditional baklava is pleasingly sweet. Drina Daisy is derived from the name of a southern Bosnia river (the location of the chef's prior restaurant) and Daisy is the owner's mother.

Fort George Brewing & Public House

1483 Duane St
503/325-7468
Mon-Sat: 11-11; Sun: noon-11
fortgeorgebrewery.com
Moderate

Founded in 1811 as a principal fur trading post, Fort George (named after King George III) was Astoria's original settlement site. There's been a lot of water under the bridge since then, and today, dozens of craft beers from pale ales to stouts are produced in this renovated building. The beer complements the food. There is the Public House, serving fish and chips, burgers, tacos and other fare; there's Upstairs Pizza, offering pizzas, mac and cheese and more cooked in a wood-fired oven. Or step into the Lovell Taproom with 19 specialty taps and two cask engines, as well as good pub grub.

Frite & Scoop

175 14th St, Suite 150
503/468-0416
Hours vary
friteandscoop.com

Foodies of all stripes have long sought the perfect combination of salty and sweet (my favorite: a sprinkling of sea salt on fresh watermelon). At least it was until I tried Frite & Scoop, a shop that satisfies both cravings with its handcrafted ice cream and Belgian frites (fries that is, which by many accounts were invented in Belgium, not France). The ice cream, made twice a week in small batches, starts with a French-custard foundation to which local or housemade goodies are added (pecan brittle, caramel, coconut, seasonal fruits, toffee, chocolate, to name a few). The frites are tossed with your choice of sea salt or housemade rosemary salt, and served plain or with dipping sauces in classic paper cones. The flavors are ever-changing, so see their Facebook page for daily offerings and hours.

Fruffels

1296 Commercial St
503/436-4160, 503/468-0237
Daily: Seasonal hours
fruffels.com

Fruffels (formerly in Cannon Beach) is best described as a boutique department store. It is a store with quality gifts and home accessories plus complimentary gift wrapping and personal shopping services. No matter what your decorating taste, you're sure to find furniture, lighting, rugs and linens to furnish or accessorize one room or a whole house with unique tableware, tabletop items and glassware. Co-owners Tony Lawler and David Kiedrowski provide complete residential and corporate design services, room makeovers and landscape design. Luxurious bath and body products, scented candles and other tastefully selected items are thoughtful gifts.

A Gypsy's Whimsy Herbal Apothecary

1130 Commercial St   503/338-4871
Tue-Sat: 11-6   Facebook

A Gypsy's Whimsy started as a small herbal shop in 2001, but more recently it has flourished into a much larger store offering organic herbs, spices and teas, supplements, tinctures and fair-trade imports such as Buddhas, masks, Day of the Dead pieces and other eclectic items. Stop and chat with owner Vicky McAfee, a knowledgeable herbalist; she may have just the remedy for the utmost relaxing getaway.

Home Baking Co.

2845 Marine Dr   503/325-4631
Tue-Sat: 6-3   astoriacinnamontoast.com

The Tilander family has provided Astoria with authentic Finnish baked goods since 1910. Third generation Kathy and Jim Tilander continue to use traditional family recipes for breads, doughnuts, pastries, pies, cakes, apple fritters, prune tarts, cookies and more. Holiday spreads are extra special with their oh-so-good Scandinavian holiday breads. For a taste from the past, try their famous cinnamon toast. Its popularity dates back to Finland in the 1800s and also became a staple for Astorians and local fishing fleets because of the long shelf life. Sweet coffee bread is toasted, liberally sprinkled with cinnamon and sugar and packed in two-pound boxes. Enjoy any of these sweets and coffee at the bakery or to go. Order online, too.

Hotel Elliott

357 12th St   877/378-1924
Inexpensive and up   hotelelliott.com

Hotel Elliott is a boutique hotel with turn-of-the-century elegance but modern conveniences in the 32 rooms and suites. Designer bathrooms feature heated tile floors and plush terry robes. Signature beds are extra comfy and furnished with goose down pillows and custom duvet covers; up-to-date technologies are standard amenities. Additional luxuries await in the suites: custom-mantled gas fireplaces, cedar-lined closets, handcrafted cabinetry and Jacuzzi tubs (varies according to suite). The Presidential Suite is fit for a king: two stories with private access to the rooftop terrace, fully-furnished kitchen, living and dining rooms, two bedrooms and views of the city and river. Complimentary breakfast is offered in the expanded lobby and a wine bar is upstairs. Dining and shopping are steps away from the front door.

Josephson's Smokehouse & Specialty Seafood

106 Marine Dr   503/325-2190, 800/722-3474
Mon-Fri: 9-5:30; Sat: 9:30-5:30; Sun: 10-5   josephsons.com

For four generations and over 90 years, Josephson's has been specializing in seafood. Stop in for fish and seafood that has been smoked, canned or made into jerky. The deli offers lunch fare of chowders, salmon burgers and smoked seafood dishes; eat inside, on the deck or pack your choices into a basket or cooler for a picnic. The premium products are made from No. 1 grade seafood and natural ingredients and are free of preservatives, dyes and unhealthy additives. Likely you've encountered their products in leading retailers or read about them in numerous magazines and major newspapers. They do a whale of an online business and ship the best of the Northwest worldwide; catalogs available.

HISTORY ON THE CENTRAL COAST

The Lincoln County Historical Society (541/265-7509, oregoncoasthistory.org) brings the history of the central Oregon Coast alive. Collections of over 40,000 artifacts depicting life in the region are featured at these locations, both open Thursday through Sunday.

Burrows House Museum (545 SW 9th St, Newport) began as a Queen-Anne Victorian residence before functioning as both a boarding house and funeral parlor and was relocated a stone's throw from its original location to house the museum and historical society. Interesting exhibitions include handcrafted items, a Victorian parlor and coastal curiosities. Check out the representation of automobile trips along the coast in the early 1900s (donation).

Pacific Maritime and Heritage Center (333 SE Bay Blvd, Newport) was also a private residence as well as a restaurant. The museum and interactive center feature maritime-related exhibits and arts including history and innovations of the fishing industry over the last 150 years and tales and recovered objects from shipwrecks (nominal).

Oregon Film Museum

732 Duane St   503/325-2203
Daily: Hours vary   oregonfilmmuseum.com
Nominal

Oregon movie buffs will enjoy a visit to this museum in the old Clatsop County Jail (1914-1976). The museum celebrates the art and legacy of films and film-making in Oregon. A hallway of famous quotes, movie props and movie memorabilia from various movies with Oregon ties are displayed. You'll learn the ins and outs of making a major motion picture and create your own short film clip using green screens, lighting and cameras.

Pilot House

1 14th St   503/289-9926, 888/683-7987
Expensive   astoriapilothouse.com

An elegant three-bedroom vacation home is available on Pier 14 upstairs (no elevator) from the Columbia River Pilots station. This location gives a catbird seat to the pilots who masterfully guide ocean-bound or arriving ships right outside your windows all day long. Guests will appreciate the state-of-the-art electronic access and quality of the furnishings; many are maritime artifacts. Up to eight adults are accommodated in the spacious quarters that include three bedrooms, three bathrooms, a complete kitchen, living and dining areas and gas fireplaces in all bedrooms and the living area. Master bedroom guests enjoy a private balcony and bathroom Jacuzzi tub. Rates vary according to season and length of stay and are adjusted for couple-only occupancy. Operating seasonally, the Riverfront Trolley stop is right outside the front door.

Silver Salmon Grille

1105 Commercial St   503/338-6640
Daily: 11-4 (lunch); 4-10 (dinner, winter hours shorter)   silversalmongrille.com
Moderate

The Fisher Building has seen restaurants come and go since it was built in 1924. Today, salmon reigns at Laurie and Jeff Martin's restaurant. The lounge's antique bar (acquired in the 1950s) is a remnant of the Thiel Brothers restaurant operation at this location. The elaborate 130-year-old beauty is constructed of Scottish cherry wood that was shipped around Cape Horn in the 1880s. As the story goes, its first Astoria home was in Anna Bays Social Club, a house of ill repute in this fishing town. Now in a more refined setting, it is the lounge's centerpiece. Joining salmon dishes on the lunch menu are halibut fish and chips, Willapa Bay oyster stew, a variety of sandwiches (San Francisco melt: turkey, bacon, tomato, avocado, onions and cheese on sourdough bread, dipped in egg and grilled), soups and clam chowder. A number of salmon entrees headline the dinner selections plus halibut and other seafood, steaks, pastas and chicken. Lighter appetites will appreciate specialty salads (tropical prawn, seafood Caesar or Cobb, smoked salmon spinach) for lunch or dinner; also low-carb and vegetarian entrees. The fine dining is matched with an impressive selection of wines and cocktails from the saloon. An assortment of mouthwatering sweets is presented on the dessert tray.

Supple Rockers

1542 Grand Ave   503/791-8237
Mon-Fri: 8-5 by appointment   supplerockers.com

If you are passionate about baseball, a unique, handcrafted baseball-bat rocking chair from Supple Rockers may be a fine addition to your home, office or man cave. Made with six Marucci or Rawlings bats, each one-of-a-kind rocker has a laser-engraved backrest, or "ticket stub." Seats are upholstered with Italian leather and complemented with a hand-sewn baseball stitch detail. Patented, trademarked and serial numbered, these rocking chairs possess a baseball lore heartbeat. Kim and Dan Supple take great pride in their family-owned business (surely one reason the New York Yankees commissioned them to make one for the iconic relief pitcher Mariano Rivera when he retired).

T. Paul's Urban Cafe

1119 Commercial St   503/338-5133
Mon-Thu: 11-9; Fri, Sat: 11-10   tpaulsurbancafe.com

T. Paul's Supper Club

360 12th St   503/325-2545
Mon-Thu: 11-9; Fri, Sat: 11-10   tpaulssupperclub.com
Moderate

Two diverse menus distinguish the T. Paul venues. The Urban Cafe offers salads, sandwiches, quesadillas, pastas and beer and wine. Down the street and around the corner, the Supper Club serves seafood plus pastas, chicken, steaks and all-natural beef half-pound burgers. Creative salads make a meal on their own. A full bar with beer, wine and cocktails adds to the supper club ambience. Both restaurants feature live music every weekend. T. Paul's is also known for fabulous homemade desserts, many from grandma's tried-and-true recipes.

BANDON

Alloro Wine Bar & Restaurant
375 2nd St SE   541/347-1850
Seasonal days and hours   allorowinebar.com
Moderate to expensive
Alloro Wine Bar & Restaurant is a great dinner choice for those who fancy Italian-inspired fare but also crave fresh coastal cuisine. Offerings are made from local seafood and meats, fresh seasonal produce and imported specialties. Therefore the menu varies with availability and the season. Diners can expect to see housemade soups, oysters on the half shell, salads and antipasti on the starter menu. Entrees include fresh seafood pastas, vegetables and herbs, grilled ribeye steak, a hearty seafood salad and even a Tuscan-style seafood stew. The wine list includes Northwest and Italian wines with several available by the glass. Desserts carry on the Italian theme with choices of tiramisu, Italian custards infused with espresso and almond, sorbets and other seasonal offerings. Reservations are recommended at this small restaurant.

B Home Teak and Outdoor Living
49667 Hwy 101   541/347-4410
Mon, Tue, Fri: 8-6; Wed, Thu: 8-4:30; Sat: 10-6; Sun 10-5   bhome-bandon.com
Want to dress up your yard, deck or patio? Here you'll find well-made teak tables and chairs, bar stools, benches and loungers for your outdoor spaces. Give your bathroom a luxurious spa feel with teak shower stools and bathroom accessories as well as custom-made cushions. Teak wood is ideal for the wet and humid Oregon coast as it is low maintenance and becomes more beautiful as it weathers; the longevity of teak is 70-plus years.

Bandon Dunes Golf Resort
57744 Round Lake Dr   541/347-4380
Moderate to expensive   bandondunesgolf.com
Bandon Dunes Golf Resort offers a fantastic golfing experience. It might be the closest thing to the spirit of Scotland's ancient links that one can find on the West Coast. The resort features four 18-hole courses and one 13-hole, par-3 course, each offering great views and unique challenges. In addition, there is a 9-hole practice course and a practice center featuring two driving ranges, a short-game range and an 18-hole putting course. But that's just the beginning. Fine Northwest cuisine and exquisite wines are served in several unique restaurants, plus casual lounges, a Scottish-style pub and day-long casual dining (hours vary by season). Comfortable, luxurious lodge, inn and cottage accommodations are designed for singles,

couples and foursomes (rates vary). Resort amenities include shuttle service between lodging, courses, restaurants and lounges; a business center in the lodge; fitness center; well-stocked pro shops and daily golf clinics.

Devon's Boutique

92 2nd St SE   541/347-8092
Daily: 10:30-5   devonsboutlque.com

Look for unique investment pieces in beach casual, chic resort wear and special-occasion women's attire at this shop in Old Town. Owner Devon Matsuda hand knits scarves in luscious color combinations that are warm and stylish. Expect to find unusual pieces, new designers and updated lines of the highest quality.

The Loft

315 1st St SE   541/329-0535
Seasonal hours   theloftofbandon.com
Moderate

For stunning views and casual fine dining, head to the upper level of the High Dock building in Old Town. This coastal dinner house has been open since 2010 and features seafood, but not exclusively; all meals are built

---

WHALE SPOTTING

Whale watching occurs almost year round along the Oregon Coast. Peak season for the annual gray whale migration to warmer Pacific Ocean waters off Mexico occurs from mid-December through January. The spring watch begins near the end of March and ends in June with mothers and calves traveling north. Each migration brings some 18,000 whales close to the Oregon Coast. In summer, some 200 whales remain along the coast to feed from July to mid-November.Usually these huge mammals can be seen from almost any ocean view location. Watch for the off-shore whale spouts with your naked eye and then dial in with binoculars. For a closer view, take a charter boat whale-watching excursion or splurge for an airplane or helicopter adventure.

Oregon State Parks' Depoe Bay Whale Watching Center (126 N Hwy 101, 541/765-3304, oregonstateparks.org) is staffed year round by park rangers and volunteers who point out the parade of humpback whales, orcas, dolphins, porpoises and blue whales. The park's Whale Watching Spoken Here program also places volunteers at 24 great whale-watching sites during "watch weeks" (the last weeks in December and March) to help others spot the whales (free).

around fresh, seasonally available ingredients. Plates on the changing menu are beautifully presented and attractively garnished. Try the crab bruschetta appetizer and the sweet potato bread pudding if they are available. The 12-layer chocolate hazelnut praline dobos torte is made in-house like most of the offerings. Check the restaurant's Facebook page for up-to-date menus and hours.

Lord Bennett's

1695 Beach Loop Dr   541/347-3663
Daily: 5 p.m.-close (dinner); Sun: 10-2 (brunch)   lordbennetts.com
Expensive

Lord Bennett's has been owned and operated by Chef Rich Iverson since 1989. Locals and tourists keep coming back for wonderful steaks, chops and seafood, delicious pasta dishes, scallops and prawns. Appetizers are mainly of the ocean-going variety; soups and salads are fresh and made with healthy ingredients. Sunday brunch features items such as Dungeness crab Benedict, eggs Benedict, salmon hash, and ricotta soufflé pancakes, as well as more traditional lunch entrees including burgers, halibut tacos and chowder. The location affords magnificent views of Face Rock, sunsets and the crashing Pacific below the parking lot. (Facilities available for special events.)

Misty Meadows Jams

48053 Hwy 101   541/347-2575, 888/795-1719
Daily: 9-5   gotjam.com

Jam lovers will find just about any flavor to top their morning toast. At this family-owned and -operated farm, second generation Traci and Mike Keller offer marmalades, syrups, jellies, fruit butters, no-sugar-added items, seedless offerings, super honey, pepper jellies, barbecue sauces and salsas. Most all products are Oregon-grown and have been since they began business in 1970. Some of the interesting or hard-to-find products include tayberry, wild huckleberry, salal and chokecherry jams and local cranberry jams and syrups. Retail activity is in a large building next to the familiar roadside stand; phone, mail and Internet orders are also welcome.

Tony's Crab Shack

155 1st St   541/347-2875
Daily: 10:30-6   tonyscrabshack.com
Moderate

Owner Tony Roszkowski takes good care of customers at his restaurant and next-door Port O' Call bait and tackle shop. Crab is the main attraction on the menu — whole with drawn butter and in crab cakes, sandwiches, pastas, salads and cocktails. Shrimp and fish tacos are superb. Worth noting is the lack of a deep-fat fryer in this establishment. Salmon is smoked on-site and delicious in sandwiches and salads. Speaking of fresh — Tony rents crab rings for folks to catch their own (cleaning and cooking available) from Weber's Pier or other local hot crabbing spots. Port O' Call (daily 6-6) also carries fishing essentials — rods, licenses, tackle and bait. In case you get skunked, Tony always has fresh ocean fare on the menu.

BAY CITY

The Fish Peddler at Pacific Oyster

5150 Oyster Dr   503/377-2323
Daily: Hours vary   pacseafood.com
At this division of Pacific Seafood, nearly 10,000 pounds of oysters are processed weekdays. The oyster shucking is interesting to watch; it involves brute force, finesse and a certain twist of the wrist before triple washing and sorting. The retail counter and restaurant are open year-round. Nestled on Tillamook Bay, this picturesque setting has picnic tables available for outdoor dining. Inside, diners will find ocean-fresh dishes like cioppino, fish and chips, crab Louis salad, clam chowder (made in-house), shrimp, steamer clams, sandwiches and oyster shooters from the retail counter. If it swims nearby, you're likely to find it at this visitor-friendly operation.

Tillamook Country Smoker

8250 Warren Ave   503/377-2222, 800/325-2220
Daily: 9-5   tcsjerky.com
The county of Tillamook is famous for not only cheese and ice cream, but also for jerky and other smoked meats hot out of the Tillamook Country Smoker. From humble beginnings more than 50 years ago, Art Crossley started smoking and selling jerky and smoked meat sticks from his small meat market. Today, the business produces thousands of pounds of meat snacks that are sold nationwide. All of these items and gift packs, including a military care package, are available on the website and at the factory outlet.

BROOKINGS

Art Alley Grille

515 Chetco Ave   541/469-0800
Wed-Sat: 4:30-8:30   Facebook
Moderate
This is an unexpected find that brings together the coast, good food and

beautiful art. Dine in an intimate setting surrounded by art crafted by local artisans while enjoying wines from an extensive list and a variety of superb dinner entrees such as rack of lamb, steaks and surf and turf dishes. Other offerings include clam chowder (perfectly thick and creamy) and pasta and risotto entrees (seafood, meat and vegetarian). The live background music is a classy touch, and service is excellent.

Beachfront RV Park

16035 Boat Basin Road   541/469-5867
Inexpensive   beachfrontrvpark.com
If your family likes RV camping, this Port of Brookings-Harbor facility offers parking on the beach, a rarity on our state's coastline. Spaces are available year round, daily or weekly; reservations accepted. RVers have a choice of pull-through or back-in spots, ocean or river views and partial or full hook-ups; river view area is dry camping with no hookups. Tent sites are also available for those who wish to rough it.

Black Trumpet Bistro

625 Chetco Ave, Suite 200   541/887-0860
Lunch: Mon-Sat 11-3; Dinner: daily 3-9 (Fri till 10)   blacktrumpetbistro.net
Moderate
This colorful, cozy bistro and bar offers traditionally inspired international cuisine right in the heart of Brookings. For appetizers try steamed clams Italiano, wild mushroom crostini or chili-lime prawns, among several others. Entrees include chicken Marsala, ribeye steak topped with blue cheese, mustard crusted lamb chops with cranberry Chianti sauce and pan-seared sea scallops. There's also a variety of housemade pasta dishes and sandwiches to choose from; the lunch menu is geared toward soups, salads and sandwiches such as pork belly sliders. The chocolate flourless torte is a decadently divine dessert. The wine list is not only excellent, but extensive, and the bar features expertly mixed cocktails, both classic and those with a distinctive Black Trumpet twist.

Fat Irish Kitchen & Pub

16403 Lower Harbor Rd   530/520-8005
Daily: 11-9 (Fri, Sat till 10; Sun till 8)   fatirishpub.com
Inexpensive to moderate
For a great happy hour and wholesome pub grub, try Fat Irish Kitchen & Pub. This not your traditional Irish pub, although there are a few Irish-style additions such as toasted Dublin dunker and Irish lord sandwiches, a fully-loaded Irish farm salad and Fat Irish stew. Otherwise the menu reflects the fresh bounty of the Pacific Northwest with well-executed standards

ACROSS THE ASTORIA-MEGLER BRIDGE
Take it from your author, you will find great food and service to match at **The Depot Restaurant** (1208 38th Pl, Seaview, WA; 360/642-7880; depotrestaurantdining.com) where casual meets fine dining. Set in a century-plus-old train station, owner/chef Michael Lalewicz presents interesting small plates like Thai calamari and other delicacies from the international menu. Willapa Bay oysters, sea scallops, prawns, beef, pork and lamb are among the entrees; all are exceptionally well prepared. Wines and beers also share global origins. The Depot is a dinner only establishment. In the off season (mid-October to mid-June), Wednesdays are burger nights where customers create their burger with beef, buffalo or oysters and more than a dozen toppings.

like fish and chips; burgers, club, Reuben and steak sandwiches; chowders and fresh shucked Oregon oysters.

Oxenfrē Public House

631 Chetco Ave   541/813-1985
Dinner: Daily   oxenpub.com
Moderate to moderately expensive

Brookings has an excellent gastropub! It's not surprising that the warm and inviting Oxenfrē Public House is very busy; ownership is on the ball and the menu categories are outstanding (including inexpensive snacks). The best snacks are Bavarian pretzel bites with pub cheese, mustard and raw honey and a Rogue blue cheese walnut mousse served in a Mason jar. The fried chicken and Belgian waffle sandwich and braised short rib wraps were tempting, but I settled on the Ox-Pub Wagyu beef burger on ciabatta roll with seared pork belly, cheese and fries. To top it all off, Belgian waffle s'mores were good and gooey! A late night menu is available for those arriving after 9. There are no fewer than eight brews on tap along with a selection of wines, bottled beers and from-scratch cocktails. Live music is featured weekly and can be found on their events page or via Facebook.

Pancho's Restaurante Y Cantina

1136 Chetco Ave   541/469-6531
Lunch, Dinner: Daily   panchosalsa.com
Moderate

Pancho's is the place to go in this north-of-the-border town for south-of-the-border fare. Start with an ice-cold margarita (an excellent selection of tequilas), choose your favorite flavor (classic, strawberry or exotic) and munch on Pancho's Salsa Rubio and chips. Authentic dishes are home-made from family recipes using quality, fresh ingredients (no lard). A nice selection of chicken, seafood, vegetarian, beef and pork dishes and com-binations is offered.

Whaleshead Beach Resort

19921 Whaleshead Road 541/469-7446, 800/943-4325
Cabins: moderate whalesheadresort.com
Restaurant: Breakfast, Lunch, Dinner: Wed-Sun
Moderate

This is a unique stay. Cottages and cabins accommodate two to ten guests and have forest or ocean views; each unit is privately owned (amenities and furnishings vary). RVers enjoy terraced pads with concrete or cedar decks, restrooms, showers and utilities; a laundromat and market are with-in the confines of the resort. Whaleshead Beach is accessed through a 700-foot tunnel, and the Redwood National Park is just some 20 miles down the highway in California.

Wild River Brewing & Pizza Company

16279 Hwy 101 S 541/471-7487
Daily: 11-10 (Fri, Sat till 11) wildriverbrewing.com
Moderate

Cold beer pairs nicely with pizza. Add the cool, crisp air of Brookings to that combination and you get Wild River Brewing & Pizza. It's among Oregon's first microbreweries, and it just happens to serve top-notch food, too. Popular beer choices include Wild River IPA, Double Eagle Imperial Stout and Harbor Lights Kolsch. Or try any of their seasonal brews. Pizza variet-ies are extensive, and sandwiches come hot or cold and are topped on housemade breads. You'll also find a fresh salad bar and pressure-cooked chicken. Don't leave without a taste of their homemade desserts (there's a reason their brownies are "to die for"). An arcade room with pool tables keeps gamers entertained while sports fans watch their favorite teams on TV. Other locations include storefronts in Grants Pass, Medford and Cave Junction.

CANNON BEACH

Bistro Restaurant

263 N Hemlock St 503/436-2661
Dinner: Wed-Sun thebistrocannonbeach.com
Moderate

Located on the north end of Hemlock Street, the Bistro is a cozy, romantic, local hangout restaurant. The brick walkway and patio are utterly charming, especially during spring and summer when the garden is in bloom. The Bistro offers an amazing eclectic menu. Local Dungeness crab cakes, USDA certified Prime New York steaks, fresh local seafood, vegetarian and a few Asian inspirations The Bistro offers live music five nights a week by local well-known musicians and a happy hour from 4:30 to 6 in the lounge. For canine lovers, the Bistro also offers a dog menu on the patio during the summer months which is freshly made and served alongside your entrees. Reservations are recommended.

Bronze Coast Gallery
224 N Hemlock St, Suite 2   503/436-1055
Mon-Sat: 10-5, Sun: 11-5   bronzecoastgallery.com
This gallery is among the best in Cannon Beach, where art is big. Unique and limited-edition bronze sculptures, as well as original paintings, are exhibited by over 40 regional, national and international artists. Frequent citywide art events and festivals occur throughout the year.

Bruce's Candy Kitchen
256 N Hemlock St   503/436-2641
Daily: 10-5   brucescandy.com
Some four decades ago, Vicky Hawkins, an Englishwoman who was the editor of the Cannon Beach Gazette, asked the late Bruce Haskell whether he might be able to make the peppermint Bah Humbug candies she joyfully remembered from her childhood in England. Bruce's now mixes more than 200 pounds of this delicious seasonal (autumn and winter) treat. Family-owned and –operated since 1963, the fourth generation continues Cannon Beach's sweet tradition with salt water taffy (30 flavors, regular and sugar-free), hand-dipped chocolates (60 varieties) and assorted brittles, popcorns, caramels, hard candies and other favorites. Who can resist a purchase at this store with the distinctive clickity-clack of the taffy cutting and wrapping machine and aroma of homemade confections?

Cannon Beach Bakery
240 N Hemlock St   503/436-0399
Wed-Mon: 7-5   cannonbeachbakery.com
Begin your day at Cannon Beach Bakery, which has been in business for more than 50 years employing four generations of bakers. Choose hot coffee from the espresso bar and a traditional glazed doughnut, maple bar, fritter or bear claw, or go bold with a Swedish Tosca bar, a sailor jacks muffin or a savory quiche. Regardless of your choice, don't leave without taking home a loaf of the famous Haystack Bread (among several varieties).

Breakfast and deli sandwiches are also available, and diners can make their own creations. (Tip: build your haystack sandwiches with the family, grab a coffee and head down to the beach to enjoy them right near Haystack Rock.) Cakes for weddings, anniversaries or any special occasion can be custom-ordered.

Cannon Beach Book Company

130 N Hemlock St, Suite 2   503/436-1301
Daily: 10:30-6 (weekend and summer hours vary)   cannonbeachbooks.com
This is one of the better independent bookstores remaining in the state. If you like whodunits, there are plenty; latest New York Times best sellers, check here first; children's bedtime stories, a wonderful assortment and well-loved classics, you'll find them here, too. In essence, all types of books are in stock or can be specially ordered and quickly delivered. Other quality merchandise includes unique greeting cards, journals, sassy reading glasses, eco-friendly reusable bags, book lights and art supplies so you can release your inner artist at the beach.

Cannon Beach Hardware and Public House

1235 S Hemlock St   503/436-4086
Store: Thu-Tue: 10-10 (daily in summer)   cannonbeachhardware.com
Pub: Lunch, Dinner: Thu-Tue (daily in summer)
Moderate
This hardware store (aka the Screw & Brew) is the epitome of full service. Whether you need plumbing or electrical supplies, yard gear or most any do-it-yourself tools, you can find them here. And get this; they claim to be the singular hardware store to serve microbrews, wine and liquor! The sports bar side of the biz has fish and chips, burgers and other pub fare; they also smoke their own pork for pulled pork sandwiches and cure their own pastrami. (Be careful, you could be waylaid from those home projects.) Whether you need hardware or not, stop by for a casual pick-me-up when you're at the beach.

Cannon Beach Hotel

1116 S Hemlock St   503/436-1392
Inexpensive and up   cannonbeachhotellodgings.com
Since 1914, this hotel has offered lodging in midtown Cannon Beach. Now, a century later, the classically elegant New England-style hotel is totally refurbished. In addition, furniture is custom designed, linens and bedding are luxurious, and the artwork is original. This weathered beauty, one block from the ocean, has a cozy lobby with fireplace that sets the tone for a romantic getaway (no children under 16, pets or

smoking). Each of the ten guestrooms is impeccably furnished, has a private bathroom and may contain a fireplace, four-poster bed or claw-foot tub. An expanded continental breakfast includes frittatas, hash brown casserole and granola (all made in-house), pastries, yogurt and more (morning mimosas) and is included in the nightly rate. Inside the hotel, Cannon Beach Café is a Parisian-style eatery; open seasonally (March-November).

Cannon Beach Spa

232 N Spruce St   503/436-8772, 888/577-8772
Seasonal: Days and hours vary   cannonbeachspa.com

After a hike in Ecola or Oswald West state parks, book an appointment and pamper yourself at this luxurious spa or slip next door to the dec-adent **Chocolate Café** (503/436-4331, cannonbeachchocolatecafe. com). The spa has been in town for nearly 20 years and offers a variety of massage, hydrotherapy, skin-care and foot treatments. Total packages include seaweed, volcanic clay and aromatherapy applications to rejuve-nate the body and soul. Treat yourself at the Chocolate Café dedicated to exquisite Moonstruck Chocolate and other candies from France, Bel-gium, Switzerland and Ghana. An over-the-top shake is made from melt-ed chocolate — oh my! Desserts, hot chocolate and French press coffee are equally tempting; even the cafe's walls are painted a rich chocolate brown. Your body and your tastebuds will thank you for stopping by these indulgent shops.

Castaways

308 N Fir St   503/436-4444
Wed-Sun: 5-close   Facebook
Moderately expensive

This restaurant featuring international fusion cuisine remains highly pop-ular after five years in business. Dishes with Jamaican, Creole, Cajun and Thai influences are the focus of chef and co-owner Josh Tuckman and co-owner, manager Megan Miller. The place is relaxed and comfortable, the service is unpretentious and the platters are tasty. It's also small, so reservations are recommended. Popular entrees include the Jamaican jerk chicken, served with spicy and unusual sauces. The coconut prawns remain and crowd-pleasing appetizer. Ahi tuna, homemade seafood chowder and a variety of salads are popular for light eaters. Or try the bacon-bleu cheese pork Marsala, or a very different take on mac and cheese. You won't go wrong with the thirst-quenching cocktails.

Center Diamond

1065 S Hemlock St   503/436-0833
Daily: 10-5   centerdiamond.com

Another gem in this laid-back community is a store chock-full of fabrics, patterns, books and gifts especially for quilters and textile artists. The large selection of fabrics includes seashore, maritime and Asian designs, batiks and other colorful prints and solids. Beautiful ready-made wall hangings and quilts are a source of inspiration, and workshops will help you create your own keepsake.

Driftwood Restaurant & Lounge

179 N Hemlock St   503/436-2439
Lunch, Dinner: Daily   driftwoodcb.com
Moderate

For over 70 years, visitors have returned time and again to the Driftwood for dependable service and good food. Ward off a chilly day with home-made clam chowder served in a sourdough bread bowl or opt for entree salads, burgers and sandwiches. Steaks are hand-cut, tender and a complete dinner with a choice of sides. Smaller portioned entrees, appetizers and homemade marionberry pies are also offered. Claim a spot on the massive front patio for lunch or dinner; you never know who will stroll past while you enjoy libations and a tasty repast.

EVOO Cannon Beach

188 S Hemlock St   503/436-8555, 877/436-3866
Days and hours vary   evoo.biz

Guests gather around their table to wine, dine and watch the cooking show. Their goal has always been to inspire cooking at home with whole foods that are as fresh, seasonal, sustainable, local and organic as possible. Each new dinner show is prepared in front of guests while they learn a variety of cooking techniques as well as information about the ingredients. Special diet restrictions and food allergies are accommodated with advance notice.

Harding Trading Company

277 Beaver St   503/739-5777
Thu-Mon: 4-9   Facebook
Moderate to moderately expensive

Harding Trading Co. is well regarded for French-inspired cuisine served in a charming and cozy setting. I was particularly impressed by the house-made pastas (ravioli and orecchiette) and fresh seafood. The salmon was cured in house, baguettes were served with housemade cultured butter and salads were fresh and hearty. Other entrees included locally sourced braised lamb shank, Angus strip-loin, vegan cabbage rolls and more. Daily specials are written on a menu board, and if the seafood bisque is on the list, I recommend you try it. Pair dinner with the local beer on tap, one of their bottled beers (also local), a sweet French wine or opt to conclude with a port. Those looking for a healthier choice, the cheese plate served with bread, local honey, nuts and dried fruit pairs wonderfully with the port. Desserts include the lemon cardamom panna cotta with blueberry compote, lemon and vanilla bean cheesecake and the decadent chocolate tart with whipped cream and raspberry sauce.

The Irish Table
1235 S Hemlock St   503/436-0708
Dinner: Fri-Tue   theirishtable.com
Moderate

Come early to this casual restaurant where Crystal and Sean Corbin preside. Enter through Sleepy Monk Coffee Roasters for seating at a large convivial table in the center of the dining venue (the Irish table), at smaller tables around the room or in the coffeehouse. The menu changes frequently with a selection of soups, salads or cheeses for appetizers. Irish stew (lamb and vegetables) is offered, as well as a vegetarian shepherd's pie with wild mushrooms, a seafood dish and meat platter. My wintertime favorite is delicious corned beef with potatoes and cabbage accompanied by warm Irish soda bread. Trifles, scones with homemade lemon curd and Guinness ice cream sandwiches stand out on the dessert menu. Servers are attentive and the menu has unusual appeal.

Newmans at 988
988 S Hemlock St   503/436-1151
Dinner: Daily (Tue-Sun in winter)   newmansat988.com
Moderate to expensive

Many a return diner has made Newmans their go-to place for French-Italian fare. Husband-and-wife team Sandy and John Newman share restaurant duties; on most days John is in the kitchen and Sandy minds the front of the tiny house with room for about 30 diners. White table linens, fresh roses and classy dinner music set the tone for simple elegance. This gourmet eatery offers a three- or four-course chef's menu nightly, or order from exquisite a la carte selections (including vegan and gluten-free). With so many folks visiting this charming community, especially on weekends, it is a good idea to make reservations; also check for seasonal hours. A few of my favorites are lobster ravioli appetizers, marinated rack of lamb and an assortment of fine cheeses. John is a top-rated chef who works wonders in limited space!

The Ocean Lodge

2864 S Pacific St
Moderate to expensive
503/436-2241, 888/777-4047
theoceanlodge.com
The Ocean Lodge, a 1940s-style beach resort, is a fabulous destination for

LIGHTHOUSES

Eleven beautiful lighthouses dot Oregon's coast. Most have been restored and some are still functional navigation aids warning sailors of imminent dangers. All are a testament to Oregon's marine history. Each property offers unique opportunities, sights and activities.

BANDON

Coquille River Lighthouse (in Bullards Beach State Park, two miles north of Bandon on the north bank of the Coquille River, 541/347-2209): obsolete, restored as an interpretive center, open daily mid-May to September

BROOKINGS

The Port of Brookings Lighthouse (near the Port of Brookings Harbor at the mouth of Chetco River): privately owned and operated, attached to a residence; no public access

CANNON BEACH

Tillamook Rock Lighthouse (about a mile outside Ecola State Park between Seaside and Cannon Beach). Decommissioned in 1957 and replaced by a whistle buoy. Privately owned, no public access, visible from Ecola State Park.

CHARLESTON

Cape Arago Lighthouse, also known as Cape Gregory Light (12 miles southwest of North Bend and one mile north of Cape Arago): decommissioned in 2006, not accessible to the public

FLORENCE

Heceta Head Lighthouse (12 miles north of Florence, 541/547-3416). The strongest light on the Oregon Coast can be seen 21 miles from land. Lighthouse tours daily during May to September, and Friday to Monday during March, April and October; year-round group tours available. Bed and breakfast at the Heceta House, rentals and facilities for group events.

romantic getaways, family vacations or a small retreat. True to the name, this oceanfront property of 37 studios and suites in the lodge (plus eight more adjacent to the lodge) is just feet away from a long stretch of sandy beach and familiar Haystack Rock is directly off shore. The gorgeous lodge

NEWPORT

Yaquina Bay Lighthouse (Hwy 101 at the north end of Yaquina Bay, 541/265-5679). The Yaquina Bay Lighthouse was operational for only three years; the Yaquina Head Lighthouse made it obsolete in 1874. Self-guided tours allow visitors to view the living quarters. Open year round (free by suggested donation.)

Yaquina Head Lighthouse (off Hwy 101 three miles north of Newport, 541/574-3100). Ranger-led tours of the Oregon's tallest lighthouse, daily July to September and on a limited basis November to June. This is an outstanding natural area with views of seabird nesting areas.

PORT ORFORD

Cape Blanco Lighthouse (nine miles north of Port Orford off Hwy 101, 541/332-2973): visitor services and tours, spiral staircase to the lantern room; open April to October

REEDSPORT

Umpqua River Lighthouse (six miles south of Reedsport above the entrance to Winchester Bay): museum and tours of lighthouse with views of the light apparatus conducted May to October; by appointment in winter

TILLAMOOK

Cape Meares Lighthouse (ten miles west of Tillamook and Hwy 101, 503/842-2244): shortest lighthouse on the Oregon Coast, nice viewpoints for whale watching, Steller Sea Lions and nesting seabirds; open daily, April to October

YACHATS

Cleft of the Rock (about two miles south of Yachats): privately owned and closed to the public (catch a glimpse from the northwest of Cape Perpetua National Scenic Area)

is warm, welcoming and staffed by the friendliest, most helpful team on the north coast. A crackling fire in the lobby's river rock wood-burning fireplace warms up chilly days. Stacks of books are scattered throughout the lodge, in the library and around informal seating areas encouraging guests to enjoy a quiet respite. The delicious, complimentary breakfast buffet is upstairs; hot beverages and cookies are always available in the lobby. Oregon artist Andy Nichols' breakfast room chandelier depicting orange and blue tentacles and shells is spectacular. Other glass pieces and local artwork are displayed around the lodge. Bathrooms are luxurious; guest accommodations are tastefully furnished with gas fireplaces, balconies, microwaves and snack refrigerators. Family-friendly at The Ocean Lodge means a warm welcome for the four-pawed member, too.

The Oil & Vinegar Bar at Cannon Beach

139 W 2nd St, Suite 2   503/436-4148
Daily: 10-6 (June-Sep); 11-4 (off season)   getoliveoilnow.com

If you love olive oil the way I do chocolate, then The Oil & Vinegar Bar at Cannon Beach should be part of your next visit to town. Here you'll get to try as many premium infused olive oils and imported balsamic vinegars as you want. Bread cubes and toothpicks welcome you as you sample flavors ranging from fruity to spicy with stops at garlic and herbal along the way (chili garlic, Tuscan herb and rosemary are some favorites). The balsamic vinegars are infused with Pacific Northwest fruits and berries such as huckleberry and cucumber melon. I believe they have 15 flavors of each. Can't make it in? Shop their website or give them a call. Owners are informative, and the website is filled with recipes to enhance your shopping experience.

Pelican Brewing Company

1371 S Hemlock St   503/908-3377
Daily: 11-10 (Fri, Sat till 11)   pelicanbrewing.com
Moderate

With the long-time success of Pelican Brewing Company's first two ventures, (see entries for Pacific City and Tillamook), it should come as no surprise that the newest location, in Cannon Beach, sticks to the company's hop and barley roots. Oregon unquestionably is a national leader in the craft beer industry, and Pelican epitomizes the Oregon mystique (there are some others, too). The small brewing operation at the Cannon Beach brewpub is in full view as it churns out pale ales, pilsners and lagers, IPAs and more — keeping 20 taps flowing year-round, some with brews available nowhere else. But that's only part of the company's success. The other is pub grub, which Pelican Brewing raises to a unique level by incorporating many of their brew varieties into the recipes. The 14-hour slow smoked tri-tip with cheddar cheese smashed potatoes, cole slaw and Tsunami Stout barbecue sauce is just one example. There's fish and chips (of course), burgers, flatbreads and clam chowder; starters like the smoked oyster bruschetta and several salads including the Haystack with butter lettuce, roasted tomatoes, chopped pepper bacon, blue cheese and Oregon hazelnuts. For dessert, try the Oregon marionberry cobbler or chocolate stout float (yup, Tsunami Stout with a scoop of Tillamook vanilla bean ice cream).

Pizza a' fetta
231 N Hemlock St   503/436-0333
Lunch, Dinner: Daily   pizza-a-fetta.com
Inexpensive
Pizza a' fetta only uses the finest seasonal ingredients and offers Oregon and Italian wines, microbrews, pizzas, salads, appetizers and much more. Roma tomato sauce is cooked for three hours and fermented an additional 12; the pizza dough is made fresh daily, then hand tossed, just how owner James Faurentino's grandmother made it. The pizza ranks in the nation's top 50 for its original methods of preparation. Next door, **Bella Espresso** (503/436-2595, bella-espresso.com) offers air-roasted Arabica coffee, gourmet desserts, pastries, Panini sandwiches, fine wines, beer and fresh fruit smoothies. You will be transported back in time with its frescos, paintings and bronzes.

Sea Level Bakery + Coffee
3116 S Hemlock St   503/436-4254
Fri-Wed: 7:30-3   sealevelbakery.com
Enjoy some of the best coffee, breads and pastries on the coast at Sea Level Bakery + Coffee. Typically you can expect to find sticky buns, scones, banana bread, cookies, biscuits and pie. Baguettes, ciabatta and country loaves are available most days of the week; brioche (Fridays) and ten grain whole wheat (Mondays) a bit more selectively. For something a little more substantial, there's quiche, fresh soups, charcuterie and handful of sandwiches served on house baguettes, as well as acai bowls and granola/yogurt bowls topped with fresh fruit.

Sleepy Monk Coffee Roasters
1235 S Hemlock St   503/436-2796
Thu-Tue: 8-8 (Fri-Sun till 4)   sleepymonkcoffee.com
Inexpensive
Indulge in a superb cup of coffee at this organic coffeehouse or purchase beans by the bag (served at area restaurants and hotels, too). Come eve-

ning, the adjacent restaurant, The Irish Table, uses the Monk's space for additional seating.

Stephanie Inn

2740 S Pacific St   503/436-2221, 800/633-3466
Expensive   stephanie-inn.com

Not only does Stephanie Inn have all the elements necessary for a really "luxe" vacation, but it does it with a big smile. Guests enjoy a host of complimentary amenities including an afternoon wine and beer reception and the chef's breakfast buffet (Benedicts, homemade granola, morning-fresh baked goods and more). The guest rooms and suites, luxuriously appointed and designed with privacy and relaxation in mind, feature wet bars with refreshments and large bathrooms (including Jacuzzis and oversized towels). On-site massage services are available in two beautiful massage suites. A classy dining room serving excellent Northwest-inspired cuisine (moderate) is open nightly; reservations are required. The menu is irresistible; choose the multi-course prix-fixe option available with wine pairing or a la carte entrees such as filet mignon, Dungeness crab cakes, excellent appetizers and tempting desserts. Haystack Rock and sunset views from the hotel grounds are spectacular; Stephanie Inn is a first-class venue.

The Surfsand Resort

148 W Gower St   503/436-2274, 800/547-6100
Moderate   surfsand.com

Location, location, location! This full-service resort is steps away from Haystack Rock, adjacent to the Wayfarer Restaurant & Lounge and on the edge of Hemlock Street's eclectic, artsy shops, restaurants and galleries. Views are incomparable at the Surfsand Resort. Comfortable guest rooms are contemporary and appointed with deluxe bath amenities, gas fireplaces, luxe bathrobes and deep soaking tubs. Cabana service, a Sunday hot dog roast and a nightly community beach bonfire complete with s'mores, are included seasonally. Optional special packages are created with a host of extra goodies for beach bonfires, romance, celebrations and kids' birthday parties. Take a dip in the heated indoor swimming pool, play on the beach, relax, fly a kite or go for a bicycle or horseback ride (rentals nearby).

Tolovana Inn

3400 S Hemlock St   503/436-2211, 800/333-8890
Moderate   tolovanainn.com

The newly remodeled Tolovana Inn offers spacious accommodations and a winning combination of breathtaking views, friendly staff and affordability. Whether you are on a family vacation or a romantic getaway, the great beach location and amenities are sure to meet your needs. Beach fire pits, full kitchens, private balconies, fireplaces, fitness center, indoor saltwater pool, sauna and spa with on-site spa services make for a comfortable stay. While here, you can stroll miles of beach, explore tide pools and catch views of Haystack Rock. Rooms are reasonably priced, with special online offers.

Tom's Fish & Chips

240 N Hemlock St   503/436-4301
Lunch, Dinner: Daily   tomscannonbeach.com
Inexpensive to moderate

Family-friendly dining is a little brighter in Cannon Beach with the addition of Tom's Fish & Chips. Yes, there is a Tom; actually there's two! Tom Drumheller was a local hospitality impresario with the likes of The Ocean Lodge in his portfolio and his partner on this project is Tom Krueger. They make for a great team at this nautical themed restaurant. Fish baskets are prepared with arctic cod, prawns, clams, salmon or halibut; fresh fish is cut and breaded each morning. Other choices include Caesar salad (add shrimp or blackened salmon for a delicious option), New England clam chowder and shrimp cocktails; classic burgers, four draft beers and other thirst-quenchers round out the affordable menu. Large glass floats hang from the ceiling and a wall mural depicts pirates in search of plunder.

Wayfarer Restaurant & Lounge

1190 Pacific Dr   503/436-1108
Breakfast, Lunch, Dinner: Daily   wayfarer-restaurant.com
Moderate to expensive

Choose from an extensive breakfast menu featuring Dungeness crab cake Benedicts, waffles, biscuits and gravy, the perfect breakfast scramble and so much more. For lunch, try the Dungeness crab mac and cheese (with Beecher's Flagship cheddar), beer battered Alaskan halibut and chips or the half-pound chopped chuck burger. The full dinner menu offers clams, fresh fish and tender filet mignon. Starters (heavy on seafood options) make fine meals on the lighter side for lunch or dinner. Sit in the main dining room or bar and enjoy the view.

CHARLESTON

Portside Restaurant

63383 Kingfisher Dr   541/888-5544
Lunch, Dinner: Daily   portsidebythebay.com
Moderate

The selection is wide and varied at this fishing port dinner house: steak any way you please, fresh catch (broiled, fried, poached, grilled), chicken specialties, satisfying pastas and smaller portions for youngsters. There are plenty of appealing appetizers including salmon with capers and deep-fried bar bites plus homemade daily soups.

CLOVERDALE

Sandlake Country Inn

8505 Galloway Road   503/965-6745
Moderate   sandlakecountryinn.com

The "Old Allen Place" farmhouse near Pacific City was constructed of red fir bridge timbers around 1900. It is now on the Oregon Historic Registry and is also a green lodging facility. Choose from three very comfortable suites and a private brookside guest cottage. All rooms have whirlpool tubs, re-frigerators, fireplaces (wood, gas or electric) and private decks; each room is tastefully decorated in a different theme. Coffee, tea and a four-course breakfast are delivered to guest rooms each morning. The menu varies, but may include blackberry brûlée, baked or fresh fruit, hot egg dishes, crepes, roasted potatoes, meats and freshly-baked pastries and breads. This is a small, quiet, relaxing retreat (pets and children accommodated only in the cottage). All-inclusive small weddings and elopements are available.

COOS BAY

SharkBite's Seafood Cafe

240 S Broadway   541/269-7475
Lunch, Dinner: Mon-Sat   Facebook
Moderate

This is one shark bite you don't want to avoid. Fish tacos are the specialty of the house at SharkBite's Seafood Cafe. Two large corn tortillas are brimming with cod, shrimp or halibut and dressed with cabbage, onions, Jack cheese, avocados and housemade sauces. Baskets and sandwiches also feature ocean fare with house-cut French fries or beer-battered onion rings; land-lubbers may prefer grilled burgers or chicken sandwiches. Kids are welcome at the casual, surf-themed cafe. A full bar with signature mixed drinks, beers

COAST CASINOS

Casinos are operated by individual Native American tribal councils and have been successful in bringing additional revenues and jobs to Oregon. Here's a brief overview:

COOS BAY
Three Rivers Casino (1297 Ocean Blvd, 877/374-8377, threeriverscasino.com): 250 slots, cafe

FLORENCE
Three Rivers Casino Resort (5647 Hwy 126, 541/997-7529, threeriverscasino.com): 700 slots, table games, bingo, lodging, free RV sites, dining, concerts and entertainment

LINCOLN CITY
Chinook Winds Casino Resort (1777 NW 44th St, 541/996-5825, chinookwindscasino.com): 1,100 slots, table games, bingo, oceanfront lodging, golf course, dining, concerts and special events

NORTH BEND
The Mill Casino (3201 Tremont St, 541/756-8800, themillcasino. com): over 700 slots, table games, 200 guest rooms, over 100 RV sites, dining, entertainment and special events

and a nightly happy hour encourage conversations that center around the best surfing waters on the southern Oregon coast and shark sightings.

DEPOE BAY

The Channel House
35 Ellingson St   541/765-2140, 800/447-2140
Moderate to expensive   channelhouse.com
This prime location overlooks the ocean and Depoe Bay channel where boats continuously enter and leave the harbor. The intimate contemporary inn has 16 beautiful rooms and suites with Tempur-Pedic mattresses, gas fireplaces and Jacuzzis on the oceanfront decks. Select from wine, champagne or romantic packages (a bottle of wine or champagne, etched glasses); in-room massage service by appointment. Join fellow guests each morning in the dining room for a complimentary continental breakfast before exploring the central coast.

Gracie's Sea Hag Restaurant and Lounge

58 N Hwy 101   541/765-2734
Breakfast, Lunch, Dinner: Daily   theseahag.com
Moderate and up

Founded in 1963 by Gracie Strom, this is one of the central coast's favorite seafood restaurants and lounges. Current owners Clary and Jerome Grant continue Gracie's welcoming hospitality, and tunes are still being played on the liquor bottles. Hand-crafted recipes dominate the menu, even at break-fast with shrimp Neptune. The appetizers (seared ahi tuna) and mouthwatering seafood salads are well-presented and famous, award-winning clam chowder is creamy, thick and swimming with chunks of clam. Bouillabaisse, crab and shrimp au gratin, grilled or baked oysters, whole Dungeness crab, USDA Choice steaks and much more are available at dinner. There is live music year round in the lounge at this Depoe Bay classic.

Restaurant Beck

2345 S Hwy 101   541/765-3220
(See detailed listing with Whale Cove Inn)

Tidal Raves Seafood Grill

279 NW Hwy 101   541/765-2995
Lunch, Dinner: Daily   tidalraves.com
Moderate

Since its opening in 1990, the hallmarks of Tidal Raves have been consistently good seafood dishes and outstanding service. The menu features tasty starters, housemade soups (clam or smoked salmon chowder, spinach oyster bisque, black bean), classic seafood salads, Pacific cioppino, crab and shrimp mac, enticing entrees and more. A sampling of the menu includes a mixed platter of shrimp, Alaskan cod and oysters; pasta with seafood and choice of sauce; and red curry barbecued shrimp. The menu is beefed-up at lunch with sandwiches (snapper po' boy or hickory-smoked pulled pork) and grilled ribeye steak at dinner. Arrive early as the place is always packed.

Tradewinds Charters

118 Hwy 101   541/765-2345, 800/445-8730
Prices vary   tradewindscharters.com

Depoe Bay carries the title of Whale Watching Capital of the Oregon Coast with prime time viewing December through January and March through May during annual migrations. Whale watching excursions are informative and fun for the family (practice shouting "Thar she blows!" beforehand); one- and two-hour trips available. Tradewinds is the oldest charter company on the West Coast and offers a variety of fishing trips (bottom, salmon, tuna, halibut). Some excursions include setting crab pots along the way and vary between five hours and a full day.

Whale Cove Inn
2345 S Hwy 101   541/765-4300, 800/628-3409
Expensive   whalecoveinn.com
This is a very special, sumptuous bed and breakfast inn! Guests enjoy fantastic vistas of the Pacific Ocean from private balconies. This property includes seven signature suites, plus a three-bedroom premier suite and features walk-in showers, patios with hot tubs and continental breakfast. Classy in-house **Restaurant Beck** (541/765-3220, restaurantbeck.com) competes neck and neck with the amazing view. The evening's gourmet fare might be pork belly, halibut, pork brisket or some such local, in-season preparation. For a special occasion, splurge on the five- or seven-course tasting menu for your entire party.

ELSIE

Camp 18 Restaurant
42362 Hwy 26   503/755-1818, 800/874-1810
Breakfast, Lunch, Dinner: Daily   camp18restaurant.com
Moderate
If you're on the way to or from the north coast along Highway 26, you've probably spotted this roadside compound at milepost 18. The impressive log cabin restaurant is the dream of Gordon Smith who built the place in the early 1970s and still operates it with the help of next-generation family. The hand-carved double-door entry is made of 4½-inch thick old-growth fir; the massive fireplaces are fashioned from 50 tons of local rock and the 85-foot ridge pole in the central dining room weighs in at 25 tons and contains 5,600 board feet of lumber. The plates match in scale, piled high with comfort food for logger-type appetites for breakfast, lunch and dinner. You'll pick up some logging lingo from the menu headings; for example, choker setters, riggin' boss and hot deck. If your sweet tooth needs a fix, the gigantic homemade cinnamon rolls are just the thing!

FLORENCE

1285 Restobar
1285 Bay St   541/902-8338
Lunch, Dinner: Daily   1285restobar.com
Moderate
San Francisco-style Italian cuisine is served at this family-friendly trattoria

in Old Town. Select a table inside or on the relaxing outside patio (seasonal). Pizza and pasta are the mainstays, even better when made with San Marzano tomatoes or locally-made sweet Italian sausage. If you're not in the mood for Italian fare, grilled meats and seafood are an option. The selection of early dinner specials changes weekly and prime rib is served every Wednesday.

BJ's Ice Cream Parlor

1441 Bay St	541/902-7828
2930 Hwy 101	541/997-7286
Daily: hours vary	Facebook

Most communities have a local ice cream parlor; Florence has two. One location is in Old Town, a delightful stop for a dish or cone while you're wandering around the waterfront. Scoops are 14.2% butterfat, come in 36 hard-to-resist flavors (plus yogurt and sugar-free ice cream) and are also used in refreshing floats and malts. The second location (also the ice cream-making locale) is on the north end of town, an easy turn off Highway 101 for a quick pick-me-up when you're on the road. Forty eight flavors are offered at this shop.

Bridgewater Ocean Fresh Fish House and Zebra Bar

1297 Bay St	541/997-1133
Lunch, Dinner: Wed-Mon	bridgewaterfishhouse.com
Moderate	

The establishment's name is a mouthful and that's what you'll get at this Old Town eclectic dining house. Eclectic more in decor than menu, the African-themed bar with zebra-striped chairs is a fun setting. Seafood is definitely the order of the day, though "land" options are available, too. Choosing becomes a bit problematic with chowder, cioppino, crab cakes, mussels, clams, fish and chips, various fish entrees and seafood sides, red meat and fowl menu items; vegan and vegetarian options, too.

Driftwood Shores Resort & Conference Center

84416 First Ave	541/997-8263, 800/422-5091
Moderate to very expensive	driftwoodshores.com

Uninterrupted sandy beaches are the main attraction at this hotel — the only oceanfront hotel in the Florence area. All rooms have oceanfront views and a balcony, deck or patio. Most guest rooms contain a full kitchen; mini-refrigerators and microwaves are furnished in standard rooms. Surfside, the moderately priced on-site restaurant, is open daily for breakfast, lunch and dinner and offers Pacific Northwest cuisine. Event and banquet rooms with full-service catering are also available.

Edwin K Bed & Breakfast

1155 Bay St   541/997-8360, 800/833-9465
Moderate   edwink.com

Area pioneer William Kyle built this 1914 Sears Craftsman home. It is now a charming bed and breakfast accented with fine furnishings and antiques; there are six guest rooms with private bathrooms in the main building. A separate apartment with a full kitchen and living room accommodates up to four guests (breakfast on your own). Laurie and Marv VandeStreek prepare and serve a five-course gourmet breakfast to house guests in the dining room.

Kitchen Klutter

1258 Bay St   541/997-6060
Daily: 9:30-5:30   Facebook

This well-arranged shop features kitchen gadgets, tableware and items to turn your home kitchen into a gourmet showplace. Bath products, gifts and other fun and unique items round out the appealing merchandise.

La Pomodori Ristorante

1415 7th St   541/902-2525
Lunch: Tue-Fri; Dinner: Tue-Sat   lapomodori.com
Moderate

You can't go wrong at this fine Italian restaurant. Start with the garlic onion cheese bread as you peruse the expansive menu. Pasta dishes include prawns, seafood, pork, chicken, sausage, Italian vegetables and rich cream or tomato sauces. Ribeye steaks are well-seasoned; other meats and seafood are grilled or prepared as picattas, scaloppinis, marsalas or with special sauces and ingredients. Appetizing sandwiches (baked pastrami), soups, hearty salads and specials are served at lunch. Reservations accepted.

Little Brown Hen Cafe

435 Hwy 101   541/902-2449
Breakfast, Lunch: Daily   Facebook
Inexpensive

Voted by locals as serving the best breakfasts for miles around, the Little Brown Hen continues to do a bang-up job. Pop in for breakfast anytime. There's no skimping on biscuits and gravy, many egg incarnations, pancakes, Belgian waffles and French toast of several varieties. Lunchtime brings clam chowder, chili and other soups, salads, seafood dishes, burgers and moist pressure-fried (broasted) chicken. Tasty hand-sliced potatoes, covered with a secret seasoned-flour mixture and then deep fried, are referred to as "chirps." Look for locally inspired unique eats in Old Town at their sister property, **Nosh Eatery** (1269 Bay St, 541/997-5899) for small plates, wine, beer and spirits with a view.

Lovejoy's Restaurant & Tea Room

195 Nopal St   541/902-0502
Tue-Fri: 11-2; Sat: 8-2 (till 3 in summer)   lovejoysrestaurant.com
Inexpensive to moderate

If it's an English-style meal that you desire, try Lovejoy's. For lunch, they offer English pub food like bangers and mash, Cornish pasties, savory sausage rolls, stuffed Dover sole, homemade soups, salads (pear, walnut and blue cheese is excellent), sandwiches and specials. The Royal Tea is a four-course affair with salads, a choice of delectable tea sandwiches (cucumber and cream cheese, bay shrimp and more), scones with Double Devon clotted cream, a petite dessert and your choice of tea. The gift shop is the source for tea (30 kinds), unique tea pots and tea accessories. Hannah and Heather are the amiable mother/daughter team tending to customers; reservations are suggested.

Sand Master Park

5351 Hwy 101   541/997-6006
Seasonal hours   sandmasterpark.com

For a super memorable ride on the famous Florence dunes, grab a sandboard. If need be, instruction, equipment rental and sales are offered. The

---

GO FLY A KITE

If flying a kite is on your beach activity list, check out these shops. They offer a full selection of colorful traditional, box, sport, trick and soft kites, and almost every imaginable design of spinner, banner, flag and streamer.

CANNON BEACH
Once Upon a Breeze (240 N Spruce St, 503/436-1112)

LINCOLN CITY
Northwest Winds Kites & Toys (130 SE Hwy 101, 541/994-1004)
Winddriven (1529 NW Hwy 101, 541/996-5483)

NEWPORT
The Kite Company (407 SW Hwy 101, 541/265-2004)

only requirements for the thrill of a glide down the hill or hitting the jump ramps are your feet and the desire for fun. The park offers more activities (March through December): sand sculpting, dune buggy tours, games and RV parking; surfboard and wet suit rental, too.

The Waterfront Depot Restaurant
1252 Bay St   541/902-9100
Dinner: Daily   waterfrontdepot.com
Moderate

In a picturesque building that once housed the Mapleton train depot, this unpretentious restaurant has delicious offerings. The informal blackboard menu is appealing and the well-worn wood floors and cozy bar enhance the ambience. Seafood dishes shine, especially oyster Madrid and crab-encrusted halibut. You won't pay a fortune, and you will be treated to freshly-baked garlic French bread. Located on the Siuslaw River — delightful! Check out their newest venture in Florence, **Le Bouchon Wine Bar and Kitchen** (1277 Bay St, 541/902-1391), just across the street.

GARIBALDI

Garibaldi House Inn & Suites
502 Garibaldi Ave   503/322-3338, 877/322-6489
Inexpensive to moderate   garibaldihouse.com

When you're fishing, crabbing, clamming, whale watching, kayaking and such in the area, Garibaldi House can serve as a great place to drop anchor. The 50 rooms and suites are professionally run as a B&B rather than a motel, and offer hearty breakfasts and personal attention to customers' whims. An indoor heated pool and sauna will add "ahhhh" to your coastal home away from home. Cookies and coffee, local cheeses and meats, popcorn and other snacks are available 24/7. This is a hidden gem on the north coast!

Pirate's Cove Restaurant
14170 Hwy 101 N   503/322-2092
Breakfast: Wed-Sun; Lunch, Dinner: Daily
Moderate to expensive

The restaurant is situated to view fishing boats on Tillamook Bay, many laden with fresh catch. Perhaps your seafood dinner was on this morning's boat. Pirate's Cove is known for superb oyster stew; dinners and sandwiches are served with a choice of the stew, creamy clam chowder or salad. Steaks are excellent with the option of adding crab, seafood or other toppers. Lunch includes specials from the sea, burgers, sandwiches and salads, with plenty of appetizer choices for lunch or dinner. Breakfast Benedicts and omelets are utterly delightful when made with crab, lobster or prawns. Dressed up pancakes, waffles, egg dishes and hearty biscuits and gravy should keep your motor running for several hours; take time to enjoy a second cup of coffee by the beautiful bay.

GEARHART

Gearhart Crossing Pub and Deli
599 Pacific Way   503/738-7312
Daily: 9-8 (till 9 in summer)   gearhartcrossing.com
For more than half of a century, this building has been a community fixture in one form or another. The current pub, deli and convenience store have evolved in one local space where the family-friendly dine-in pub offers 16 craft beers on tap and daily lunch and dinner specials made to order. The selection includes homemade salads, sandwiches, fresh daily soup and clam chowder, homemade pies, fresh cut meats, fresh produce with convenient grocery items and a fine assortment of wines and other beverages. The catering side of the operation handles everything from a casual affair at the beach to an intimate wedding or family gathering; choices are many to meet customers' requirements.

Gearhart Ironwerks
1368 Pacific Way   503/738-5434
Mon-Fri: 9-5   gearhartironwerks.com
John Emmerling has been handcrafting metal into functional art since the early 1990s at his Gearhart shop. He transforms iron, stainless steel, copper, bronze and aluminum using modern techniques as well as old-fashioned hand blacksmithing. His one-of-a-kind creations include beds, fireplace screens, gates, lighting fixtures, garden art, sculptures and other home furnishings, all meant to last a lifetime. He also creates exquisite chef knives and other blades forged from high-carbon steel. He will work with your own design or desires, as well as that of your designer or architect. When visiting the north Oregon coast, don't hesitate to visit his shop and showroom, where three to five artisans work daily.

Gearhart Ocean Inn
67 N Cottage Ave   503/738-7373
Moderate   gearhartoceaninn.com
A former motor court is now a boutique lodging property with a dozen tastefully restored attached cottages converted into king and queen studio units and one- and two-bedroom suites. Rooms are light and charm-

ing and outfitted with gas Franklin stoves, well-equipped kitchenettes or kitchens, luxury linens, modern electronics and über comfortable furniture and beds. Locally-roasted coffee, herbal tea and use of books, DVDs, magazines, cruiser bikes, kites, clam-digging equipment and beach towels are complimentary to guests. The private backyard is designed for relaxation; lodgers may choose to sprawl on Adirondack chairs or warm themselves around the fire pit, and kids have plenty of room to romp. An outdoor gas grill and picnic tables are handy for cookouts. Don your walking shoes and stroll along the historic Ridge Path which offers up-front views of the dunes and Gearhart's historic homes. Well-mannered canines are also welcome; several rooms accommodate dogs and their masters.

Natural Nook Flower Shop

738 Pacific Way   503/738-5332
Seasonal days and hours   seasidenaturalnook.com
Irresistible specialty gifts are tucked here and there into eye-catching displays at this European-style flower shop brimming with plants, blooms and nifty accouterments to outfit any home or beach bungalow. Colorful seasonal flowers, vegetable plants, shrubs and decorative and useful garden art and accessories spill out onto the decks, raised beds and pathways. Each visually appealing vignette can be replicated in your yard or on your deck.

Pacific Crest Cottage

726 Pacific Way   503/738-6560
July-Sept: Daily; Oct-June: Wed-Mon (hours vary)   Facebook
This delightful bungalow is chock-full of large and small antiques, pillows, soaps and lotions, dishes and whatnots at all price points. Owner Joy Sigler is quick to welcome her customers and recommend uses for some of the more unusual items. On your way in, you can't miss the cast stone garden seating and decorative outdoor pieces. Authentic Japanese floats are available in sizes from two inches to 20 inches in diameter.

Pacific Way Bakery & Cafe

601 Pacific Way   503/738-0245
Bakery: 7 a.m.-1 p.m. (Thu-Mon)   pacificwaybakery-cafe.com
Cafe: Lunch: 11-3:30; Dinner: 5-close (Thu-Mon)
Moderate
When I was young, my family would spend summertime in Gearhart. We would leave our Portland environs for the low-key, charming, quaint coastal village and embark upon a summer filled with family, friends and activities. The season would start as soon as the school year was finished

and end on Labor Day. Gearhart has retained its charm and draws visitors year round. Lisa and John Allen's main street cafe/bakery is a favorite place to eat. Irresistible pizzas are built on handmade crusts. Traditional Italian pies are prepared on a tomato sauce base; Thai chicken, island ham and other varieties are made with specially flavored sauces. Homemade soups, sandwiches and entrees are served at lunch. Dinner starts with a basket of freshly-baked breads and features pizza and full meals from the seasonally-changing menu; ribeye steak, ravioli and lighter fare are a few examples. The cafe's desserts, of course, are fresh from the bakery where they also bake cookies, pastries, savories and assorted breads.

GLENEDEN BEACH

Cavalier Beachfront Condominiums

325 NW Lancer St   541/764-2352, 888/454-0880
Moderate   cavaliercondos.com

Families will love these spacious units with two bedrooms, two baths, fully-equipped kitchens, large living rooms with wood-burning fireplaces and open oceanfront decks. The 1,300-square-foot units are right on the coastline with easy beach access, covered parking, heated indoor swimming pool, two saunas and recreation room with pool and Ping-Pong tables. The large, exceptionally clean beach area gives families lots of room to run and build bonfires and sandcastles.

Salishan Spa & Golf Resort

7760 N Hwy 101   541/764-2371, 800/452-2300
Moderate to expensive   salishan.com

A new era is dawning at Salishan Spa & Golf Resort, once the destination gem of the Central Oregon Coast. A new ownership and management team says it is committed to restoring the luxury hotel and golf course to its former glory, while at the same time adding amenities that appeal to a new generation of travelers who demand expanded recreational experiences while placing great value on personal wellness and respect for the environment and local community. The new owner is Alpha Wave Investors, a California private equity firm led by CEO Ken Cruse, which also is heading up the restoration of the Redmond Hotel in downtown Redmond. In a nutshell, Alpha Wave plans to introduce new wellness programs, indoor and outdoor recreational opportunities such as tennis and other ball sports, nature lodging (called "glamping") and improve nature trails. Improved customer service in all areas is the first priority. In addition, food and beverage service will be revamped with a new restaurant concept. Arts education and enjoyment will be reemphasized, and the retail Salishan Marketplace will be reborn with new tenants. Meanwhile, there remains much to recommend about Salishan, which still has wonderful views of Siletz Bay, coastal forests and emerald fairways. Its 205 rooms and suites are spread among 21 buildings and are well appointed with modern technology, original artwork, fireplaces and timeless decor. Many overlook the golf course and forested areas from balconies and patios. Ocean beaches are accessible to all guests. Choose from four dining options to satisfy every appetite — four unique settings, four newly-renovated spaces, four fantastic views, four spots where, hopefully, you'll get impeccable service and downright delicious food embodying the cuisine of the Oregon Coast. Salishan also has one of the largest wine cellars in Oregon.

Side Door Café and Eden Hall

6675 Gleneden Beach Loop Road541/764-3825
Lunch, Dinner: Tue-Satsidedoorcafe.com
Moderate

Come with a big appetite; the portions are humongous! Brooke Price is a very hands-on person at her popular restaurant, working the floor, supervising the kitchen and making sure that her large facilities at the old Gleneden Brick and Tile Factory are kept in A-1 order. The evening menu features seafood salads and entrees (ribeye steak with oysters, fish, seafood, pork medallions) and also offers a great selection of pastas, quiches, steaks and several vegetarian items. Lunch soups, salads and quesadillas may also be ordered for dinner. Service is pleasant and informed. Adjacent to the cafe, Eden Hall is a 200-seat venue for live music and theater as well as private parties, exhibits and weddings (check website for schedule and prices).

GOLD BEACH

Ev's Hi-Tech Auto and Towing/Chevron

29719 Ellensburg Ave541/247-7525
Dailyevshitechautoandtowing.com

"May I clean your windshield? Check the tires and the oil?" All of this without a prompt? Seems unlikely these days, but when you're motoring through Curry County, fill 'er up at Ev's where courteous assistance is always provided. Additional work includes towing, recovery, lock-out, jumpstart, snow and beach recovery services for autos, RVs and motorcycles. This place is a model for all service stations.

Gold Beach Books

29707 Ellensburg Ave   541/247-2495
Daily: Seasonal hours   oregoncoastbooks.com

You never know what you'll find in a large book shop and this gem in Gold Beach is no exception. The inventory in the state's second largest bookstore encompasses well over 60,000 new and used books in every category. You're sure to find the latest tome from your favorite authors, classics, self-improvement and how-to books, travel guides and great reads. The Rare Book Collection features first edition works, autographed books and rare collectibles. Swing on by for specialty coffee and sweet treats baked right on site at Rachel's Coffeehouse.

Indian Creek Cafe

94682 Jerrys Flat Road   541/247-0680
Breakfast, Lunch: Daily   Facebook
Inexpensive

Located at the convergence of Indian Creek and the Rogue River, this small eatery just happens to serve great breakfasts and steaming hot coffee all day long. It's not fancy, but you'll find pancakes and waffles with fruits, berries or pecans and fluffy omelets with hash browns or fried grits. Burgers and sandwiches (served with fries and baked beans or potato salad), soups, salads and chili are satisfying lunch choices. Enjoy the outdoor deck as weather allows.

Jerry's Rogue Jets

29985 Harbor Way   541/247-4571, 800/451-3645
Seasonal   roguejets.com
Prices vary

Back in 1895, the only way to deliver mail and freight to communities up the Rogue River was by mail boat. Now, over a century later, a 64-mile trip follows the same route with your jet boat pilot delivering historical tidbits and lore along the way. Go a bit farther and take the exhilarating 80-mile whitewater round-trip excursion. Spend an unforgettable day when you travel 104 miles up and back to the wild section of the Rogue and Blossom Bar Rapids to experience the rugged wilderness and class II to III rapids. Trips include rest stops and lunch (separately priced). Take in abundant wildlife, lodges, breathtaking scenery and be wowed by your pilot's stories, skills and knowledge. Jerry's also transports guests to lodges along the river. Daily departures from May 1 to October 15; museum and gift shop open all year. This is another must-do Oregon adventure.

Nor'Wester Steak & Seafood

10 Harbor Way · 541/247-2333
Dinner: Daily · norwesterseafood.com
Moderate

Enjoy harbor sights from the upstairs dining room; there is always activity — boats, seagulls, occasional harbor seals, fishermen and romantic sunsets. This fine dining house serves fresh local catch (as available) in appetizers, chowder, salads and generously portioned entrees, combinations and pastas. Steaks, chops and chicken dishes are equally delicious; add prawns or oysters to a sirloin steak to create a land and sea platter. There is also a full bar, beer and wine selections and menu offerings for the younger set.

Rogue River Lodge at Snag Patch

94966 North Bank Rogue Road · 541/247-0101
Inexpensive to expensive · rogueriverlodge.com

Seasonal autumn leaves, ever-changing views of the Rogue River, osprey, falcons, wildlife, gardens and forests form a backdrop to the Rogue River Lodge at Snag Patch. The intimate lodge is perched above the river and is made up of eight units; six suites have river views and two rooms are secluded with views of the creek. A light breakfast is set out each morning in the main building. Suite retreats are cozy with gas parlor stoves, sitting rooms, kitchen facilities and private decks with a hot tub. The spacious Eagle House Suite has three bedrooms, two bathrooms, a full kitchen and outdoor gas grill.

Spinner's Seafood, Steak & Chophouse

29430 Ellensburg Ave · 541/247-5160
Dinner: Daily · spinnersrestaurant.com
Moderate

The large, often-full parking lot is your first clue; Gold Beach has a number of good dining spots and Spinner's falls into that category. Salads are fresh and entree salads are, indeed, a full meal, especially with the addition of chicken, prawns or oysters. Big burgers (including buffalo) and chicken main dishes are alternatives to seafood, steaks and chops. Seafood specialties may include scampi-style sea scallops, lobster, fresh salmon roasted in leeks or a seafood choice combined with pasta. The dessert menu lists several varieties of pies, cakes and pastries — all homemade and delicious. You won't go away hungry!

Tu Tu' Tun Lodge

96550 North Bank Rogue Road · 541/247-6664, 800/864-6357
Moderately expensive · tututun.com

Tu Tu' Tun Lodge has been one of my favorite R&R destinations for many

FESTIVALS & FAIRS AT THE COAST

FEBRUARY
Newport Seafood & Wine Festival (Newport, seafoodandwine.com)

MARCH
Savor Cannon Beach Wine and Culinary Festival (Cannon Beach, savorcannonbeach.com)

APRIL
Astoria Warrenton Crab, Seafood & Wine Festival (Astoria, oldoregon.com)
Crab Feed, Wooden Boat Show, and Ducky Derby (Depoe Bay, depoebaychamber.org)

MAY
Loyalty Days & Sea Fair Festival (Newport, facebook.com/newportloyaltydays)
Rhododendron Festival (Florence, florencechamber.com)

JUNE
Cannon Beach Sandcastle Contest (Cannon Beach, cannonbeach.org/events)

years. This resort is under the very capable management of owner Kyle Ringer whose friendly ease and hospitality acumen have made this an award-winning abode. When you go (and you should!), you'll be greeted as a friend as you enter this magical boutique river house, one of the best in the nation. The lodge's immaculate accommodations encompass two houses, two generous suites and 16 rooms, all gorgeously appointed and include top-notch creature comforts. Fabulous breakfasts, lunches and dinners are optional (availability varies by season). I wholeheartedly recommend you experience TTT's gourmet cuisine at least once during your stay (reservations necessary). Every season brings a different perspective of the river and forest from private decks and nicely landscaped outdoor spaces. Travel magazines have named this one of the best small resorts in the world!

Lincoln City Summer Kite Festival (Lincoln City, oregoncoast.org)
Waldport Beachcomber Days (Waldport, beachcomberdays.com)

JULY
Coos County Fair (Myrtle Point, co.coos.or.us)
Curry County Fair (Gold Beach, curryfair.com)
Lincoln County Fair (Newport, thelincolncountyfair.com)
Southern Oregon Kite Festival (Brookings, southernoregonkitefestival.com)

AUGUST
Charleston Seafood Festival (Charleston, charlestonseafoodfestival.com)
Clatsop County Fair (Astoria, clatsopfairgrounds.com)
Tillamook County Fair (tillamookfair.com)

SEPTEMBER
Gold Beach Brew & Art Festival (Gold Beach, goldbeachbrewfest. org)

OCTOBER
Lincoln City Fall Kite Festival (Lincoln City, oregoncoast.org)

HEMLOCK

Bear Creek Artichokes
19659 Hwy 101 S   503/398-5411
Daily: 9-close (seasonal variations)   bearcreekartichokes.com
You may not have heard of the small unincorporated community of Hemlock, but you may have stopped at or driven past this 20-acre farm about 11 miles south of Tillamook and 18 miles north of Neskowin. Fresh produce, a gift shop, farm kitchen (scrumptious strawberry shortcake all summer), greenhouse, display pond and the perennial crop of artichokes attract visitors. The market stocks preserves and gourmet goods prepared in the farm kitchen and smoked salmon artichoke dip, pesto, hummus, salsa and bruschettas. Customers know they will find fun and unusual fruits and vegetables and fresh, local crab (seasonal) and Netarts Bay oysters. The handmade hanging baskets and plants will perk up any yard from spring through autumn.

LANGLOIS

Langlois Market

48444 Hwy 101   541/348-2476
Mon-Sat: 8-6; Sun: 10-5   langloismarket.com
Midway between Bandon and Port Orford is a must-stop for world famous hot dogs (some are even named after your author: Gerry's Franks).
A secret mustard recipe makes these top dog among hot dog aficionados; sandwiches and burgers are also available. The market is tidy and
bright with various stuffed and mounted game animals hanging on the
walls and from the rafters, ostensibly keeping an eye on the merchandise.
Super-friendly second-generation owner Jake Pestana stocks the shelves
with staples, beer, local produce, snacks and local grass-fed beef from
his brother's ranch. Another must stop just down the road is The Greasy
Spoon (541/348-2514); this Pestana venture offers home-cooked breakfast
and lunch in a rustic, family atmosphere.

Wild Rivers Wool Factory

48443 Hwy 101   541/348-2033
Tue-Sat: 10-5   wildriverswool.com
Warm hats and scarves, socks, totes, toys and accessories are fashioned
in natural hues and a colorful array of bright and pastel shades by more
than 60 talented consignees. These quality goods are made with locally
produced fibers (sheep, alpaca, mohair and pygora goat, llama and angora
rabbit). Versatile wool and wool blend felt are sold by the yard and also
made into vests, handbags, bowls and wall art. Knowledgeable and novice
felters, spinners, weavers, knitters and crocheters shop here for supplies
and materials, including yarns sold in 101-yard skeins in bulky, worsted,
sport and lace weights. A unique process wraps aromatic bars of soap with
felt, which results in a long-lasting, gently exfoliating product. Sign up for
classes in spinning, felting and dying fibers.

LINCOLN CITY

Barnacle Bill's Seafood Market

2174 NE Hwy 101   541/994-3022
Daily: 9:30-5   barnaclebillsseafoodmarket.com
As you pass through town, look for a plume of steam billowing out of
massive crab cooking pots. The succulent crustaceans are sold whole, by
pieces or picked and ready to devour. Barnacle Bill's shrimp and crab cocktails are superb and so is the service. Owners Penny and Ron Edmunds
oversee the operation and son Sean Edmunds tends the smoker and turns

out some of the tastiest smoked salmon around. Other fresh catch makes its way to the counter; convenient Styrofoam coolers are available to tote your delights to the beach or home. No credit cards.

The Bay House

5911 SW Hwy 101   541/996-3222
Dinner: Wed-Sun   thebayhouse.org
Expensive

When Stephen Wilson took over the venerable Bay House in 2005, he knew he faced the challenge of keeping its excellent reputation intact. He rose to the test and also added a wine bar and cocktail lounge to the 1930s building which overlooks Siletz Bay. The gourmet menu is a standout on the Oregon Coast and includes seasonal items such as butternut squash ravioli, exquisitely prepared seafood, Piedmontese beef tenderloin and other Northwest tastes. If you'd like the chef to do the decision making, you won't be disappointed with the five-course tasting menu with recommended wine pairings from a superb wine collection (Oregon's largest, 2,100 selections). Sublime desserts include crème brûlée with housemade hazelnut biscotti and berry cobbler with a scoop of fresh vanilla ice cream. The adjoining lounge features small plates and a three-course, $30 locally-sourced Neighbors to Neighbors dinner menu. Periodic live music is a nice addition. The Bay House is one of only three restaurants in Oregon to earn AAA's Four Diamond award!

Christmas Cottage

3305 SW Hwy 101   541/996-2230
Daily: 10-5:30   christmascottage.net

If you're looking for the perfect holiday decoration or a personalized ornament for a special gift, then a visit here may be in order. The store was established in 1974 and is the oldest Christmas store in the state continuously operating under single ownership. Although the shop is open and celebrates Christmas year round, it is a beehive of activity in the weeks leading up to the holiday. In addition to the thousands of ornaments of every theme from around the globe, there are also nutcrackers, cards, figurines and a multitude of seasonal collectibles. Owner Barbe Jenkins-Gibson and her personable staff handle every customer service detail offering personalization and suggestions, answering questions, processing telephone orders.

The Coho Oceanfront Lodge

1635 NW Harbor Ave   541/994-3684
Inexpensive to very expensive   thecoholodge.com

Coho Oceanfront Lodge is a few blocks off busy Highway 101. This boutique-style hotel is a winning combination of ocean views, service, price and spacious accommodations; 65 spotlessly clean rooms and suites include decks overlooking the Pacific, jetted tubs, luxurious beds, flat-screen TVs and fireplaces. Kids are sure to enjoy the unique suite created with them in mind. One room is furnished with bunk beds, a kid-size table and Wii or Play Station. Other features of the property are a heated indoor pool, sauna, Jacuzzi, on-site spa, continental breakfast and outdoor fire pits. The service-oriented Lee family and staff go out of their way to make guests feel welcome.

The Culinary Center in Lincoln City
801 SW Hwy 101, 4th floor   541/557-1125
Tue-Sat: by reservation   oregoncoast.org/culinary
Culinary Center Manager, Donna Riani, manages the menu of cooking demonstrations, hands-on classes and wildly popular cook-offs. Joining her are chefs who share a penchant for working with fresh bounty from Oregon's fertile land and waters. Recreational cooking sessions (pasta, seafood) may last one to three hours or all day; multi-day courses may include canning, pickling or delve into one of many ethnic cuisines.

Lincoln City Glass Center
4821 SW Hwy 101   541/996-2569
Daily: 10-6   lincolncityglasscenter.com
Unleash your artistic bent and create a glass float, paperweight, heart, votive candle holder or bowl. Customers are paired with trained instructors to blow and twirl molten glass in a 2,300-degree "glory hole" until it takes shape. The creative process takes about 30 minutes, but cooling takes overnight. The artists display and sell stunning large and small glass pieces at the center and across the street at Volta Glass Gallery (4830 SE Hwy 101, 541/996-7600). Reservations are a must for glassblowing activities; hours vary by season and both operations are on hiatus the first two weeks of January.

Looking Glass Inn
861 SW 51st St   541/996-3996
Inexpensive to moderate   lookingglass-inn.com
Siletz Bay and a marvelous easily-accessible beach are in the historic Taft area with restaurants and shops close at hand. This inn is mere steps from the beach with incomparable bay and ocean views. Spacious studios and suites are nonsmoking and furnished with flat-screen TVs and kitchens; one suite is outfitted with a king bed, whirlpool tub and deck. Some one- and two-bedroom suites also include a gas fireplace and living area with sofa bed. Guests receive complimentary continental breakfast each morning. Several rooms are dog-friendly; Fido is sure to enjoy chasing sticks on the beach or playing in the waves.

Inn at Spanish Head

4009 SW Hwy 101 — 800/452-8127

Moderate — spanishhead.com

What sets the Inn at Spanish Head apart from other oceanfront resorts are two unique features. First, it's the only hotel in the state built right on the beach, according to management; thus, sand, tide pools and driftwood can all be explored starting with just a quick elevator ride. Second, all of the hotel's 120 oceanfront rooms, suites and studios are individually owned and decorated by their owners. All have floor-to-ceiling windows that face the ocean for unobstructed views. Most have balconies, and suites feature full kitchens. Studios and bedrooms offer kitchenettes or wet bars. Rooms feature free Wi-Fi and up-to-date entertainment technology, refrigerators, microwaves, coffee makers and other conveniences. The resort also has an oceanfront heated pool, enclosed spa, game and fitness rooms, men's and women's saunas and free parking, among many amenities. For breakfast, lunch and fine dining, don't overlook Fathoms Penthouse Restaurant & Bar.

Northwest Winds Kites & Toys

130 SE Hwy 101 — 541/994-1004

Daily: 10-6 (summer); 10-5 (winter) — nwwinds.biz

Plan on stopping at this D River Wayside business before you hit the beach. Northwest Winds offers a large selection of kites and kite accessories, garden decorations, beach accessories, flags, games, puzzles and toys.

MANZANITA

Awtrey House

38245 James Road — 503/368-5721

Very expensive — awtreyhouse.com

Warm and contemporary, this luxurious two-bedroom bed and breakfast is a Northwest architectural beauty. Situated between Manzanita and Neahkahnie cliffs, it was designed to showcase the capricious Pacific Ocean and seven miles of sandy beach. Private terraces, sumptuous king-sized beds and an inviting living room provide front-row access to the beach and ocean. In-room amenities include complimentary beverages, espresso/coffee makers, an oversized soaking tub, overhead rain shower and modern electronics. Hosts Peggy and Dennis Awtrey delight in preparing a full breakfast while Dennis, a former NBA player, captivates guests with stories of his experiences with the Blazers, Sonics and other basketball teams. There is no other inn like this on the Oregon coast.

Big Wave Cafe

822 Laneda Ave   503/368-9283
Lunch, Dinner: Daily   oregonsbigwavecafe.com
Moderate

Gourmet burgers, sandwiches, wonderful specialty salads and a handful of entrees are offered at lunch and dinner with steaks and seafood on the dinner menu. Be sure to check out the specials. Desserts like marionberry pie and chocolate cake are homemade and even better with a scoop of ice cream.

Bread and Ocean

154 Laneda Ave   503/368-5823
Breakfast, Lunch: Wed-Sun; Dinner: Fri, Sat   breadandocean.com
Inexpensive

This deli and bakery offers sit-down lunches serving up a variety of salads, sandwiches, deli items, baked goods, breads and desserts all while using local and organic products whenever possible. If it's before 11 a.m., energy-fueling breakfast items can be found in the deli cases with dishes like the frittata and polenta with layers of spongy grains, Tillamook cheddar cheese, scrambled eggs and smoked ham. Specialty bread schedules are found on their website listing all the week's specials. Organic grains and flours, European butter, free-range eggs, organic cinnamon and vanilla are used to create their unbelievably good breads and pastries. They also make organic multigrain, wild yeast sourdough and baguettes every day. The fun part about their deli menu is that you can make anything into a picnic lunch box for just $3.25 extra; this includes your choice of a side salad or soup and a cookie. On a nice day, enjoy patio seating or take your lunch to the beach, just steps away. The bakery fills up fast, especially in the morning when the regulars come for their hot coffee and morning pastry. Dinner is a full-service affair (Friday and Saturday 5-8) with favorites like pot roast, crab quiche or roast chicken. Whether you are a carnivore, vegetarian or going gluten-free, they have something to satisfy your craving.

Coast Cabins

635 Laneda Ave   503/368-7113
Moderate to very expensive   coastcabins.com

There are coastal cabins, and then there are the accommodations at Coast Cabins. Six private cabins, which provide perfect escapes for those "wanting to get away from it all," are as charming as Manzanita. Units are one or two levels of varying sizes plus a modern ranch cabin. Tranquil comfort is achieved at this Zen-like property through intimate gardens, relaxing courtyard, cozy fire pit and wooded surroundings. Amenities differ among the quarters, full or convenience kitchens, outdoor jet spas, dry sauna,

---

GLASS FLOATS ON THE BEACH

The **Lincoln City Visitor and Convention Bureau**'s popular **Finders Keepers** glass float project runs annually from mid-October to Memorial Day. Colorful, hand-crafted floats are signed, numbered and then placed along seven miles of public beach from the Roads End area south to Siletz Bay. The number of floats corresponds to the year; for example, 2,108 floats were placed in 2018. Floats are placed between the high tide line and beach embankments. Occasionally special pieces of glass art, such as sand dollars, crabs and starfish, are added to the hidden treasures. When you discover one of these pieces, notify the Visitor and Convention Bureau (541/996-1274, oregoncoast. org/glass-floats) to register your find and receive a certificate of authenticity and information about the artist who created your float.

---

steam shower and wood or gas barbecues. The spa and modern ranch cabin are the ultimate in relaxation and romance.

The Inn at Manzanita

67 Laneda Ave   503/368-6754
Moderate   innatmanzanita.com

At the end of Manzanita's main avenue of appealing shops is a delightful inn. Four buildings (two to four units per building) are nestled on beautifully landscaped grounds amid coastal pine and spruce trees. Main and cottage building amenities include queen beds, jetted spa tubs, gas fireplaces and wet bars with a refrigerator. The north building is similar, with a captain-style queen bed situated in a curtained nook. Larger units are located in the Manzanita building; some have kitchen facilities. The three-bedroom, two-bathroom penthouse is a home-away-from-home with full kitchen, partial ocean view and full amenities.

Left Coast Siesta

288 Laneda Ave   503/368-7997
Lunch, Dinner: Wed-Sun   leftcoastsiesta.com
Inexpensive

For great Mexican food with a healthy twist, check out Jeff Kyriss' establishment. Serving hungry customers since 1994, Left Coast has become a traditional "first stop" for visitors returning to the area. Burritos and tacos are assembled with a choice of tortilla, chicken, pork or beef, organic refried or black beans and organic rice, plus veggies and freshly-made salsa available in three heat levels. Enchiladas are prepared with white or blue corn tortillas, one filling and topped with red or green sauce. Portions are large and tasty; kids' menu, too. Left Coast has a unique bar of 100 to 200 hot sauces (hot, hotter, hottest and grab the fire extinguisher!) to sample or purchase.

MacGregor's

387 Laneda Ave   503/368-2447
Daily: 4-10   macgregorswhiskeybar.com
Moderate to expensive

MacGregor's offers much to recommend in food and drink, but for the truly hungry or thirsty, this is not the place to go. This is a whiskey bar, where a visit is like an international tour as experienced by the senses through the expert pairings of distilled brown liquor. Whiskeys of Ireland; peaty and smoky single malts from the highlands, lowlands and other distilling regions of Scotland; Japanese and Canadian whiskey (or whisky, if one prefers) and the bourbons, ryes and other variations of the craft from the U.S. (including a handful made in Oregon) — more than 150 brands in all — are available for pourings. Take the tour with a flight of whiskeys (three one-ounce pourings in glasses served on a whiskey barrel stave) as chosen by you or with the expert guidance of owner Chip MacGregor and his staff. MacGregor, also a literary agent, opened his namesake at the site of the Vino wine bar, which was damaged in the tornado that struck Manzanita in October 2016 and never reopened. The summer of 2018 will mark MacGregor's first anniversary in business. The bar also offers fine specialty beers and wines and expertly mixed cocktails. Its food selection includes small plates, hearty bowls (lobster bisque, MacGregor and cheese) and several boards of cheese and crackers, charcuterie, and pâtés — all fine companions on the whiskey tour. Top your evening off with a liqueur or port paired with flourless chocolate cake, Scottish shortbread or other desserts. New to the pleasures of whiskey but eager to learn? Then check out some of the weekly evening educational events. This is an intimate place, but reservations are not necessary.

NEHALEM

Buttercup Homemade Ice Creams and Chowders

35915 N Hwy 101   503/368-2469
Wed-Sun: 11:30-6 (winter till 5)   Facebook
Moderate

Like the name says, this place focuses on two things. But what owner Julie Barker has done is reimagine what chowder and ice cream can be. Buttercup rotates numerous styles of chowder; the menu changes monthly and could include traditional, Caribbean seafood, potato and artichoke, smoked salmon and Thai veggie, as well as vegan and gluten-free options. Not every chowder house uses local clams, but at Buttercup they not only use Northwest razor clams and other local ingredients, but they make their chowder to order — important for those with dietary restrictions or fussy eaters. Ice cream flavors are equally creative, diverse and changing: blood orange basil sorbet, blueberry lemon balm cheesecake, lemon poppy seed, pineapple mint, Chile sorbet — and even smoked salmon — are some examples. Of course, I went straight for the most decadent: triple chocolate mascarpone mousse.

Wanda's Cafe
12870 Hwy 101 N   503/368-8100
Breakfast, Lunch: Fri-Tue (Thu-Tue in summer)   wandascafe.com
Inexpensive
When you see a waiting line spilling onto the porch of a Nehalem establishment, you know you've arrived at Wanda's! Once you're seated, the quick, personal service is impressive. Wanda's specialties are big breakfasts (served all day), satisfying lunches, daily specials and a fine array of homemade pastries. Outdoor patio seating is great when Oregon's beach weather cooperates. You'll be tempted by glass cases filled with fresh and tasty goodies to take out.

NESKOWIN

Breakers Beach Houses
48060 Breakers Blvd   800/224-7660
Moderate and up   meredithlodging.com
You can't get much closer to the beach than in one of these privately-owned and -decorated townhouses. The location affords unobstructed views of glorious sunsets with long stretches of beach just yards away. Each of the ten homes is tastefully furnished and has three bedrooms and two bathrooms, a wood-burning fireplace, an ocean-facing deck and a completely outfitted kitchen. Check out the seasonal senior discounts for a really good deal.

The Cafe on Hawk Creek
4505 Salem Ave   503/392-4400
Breakfast, Lunch, Dinner: Daily   cafeonhawkcreek.com
Inexpensive to moderate
This perfectly charming cafe is located in the perfectly charming village of Neskowin. Cafe on Hawk Creek is no secret on the Oregon Coast. On any given evening, people are lined up out the door and down the sidewalk of this gourmet bistro. Owners Genie and Frank Ulrich have remodeled the 1982 building to make the cozy atmosphere even better. The outdoor deck is a fabulous place to gather with friends on a warm evening. The

menu offers many rustic pizzas, all cooked in the wood-fired oven. Other scrumptious offerings are steaks, seafood, pastas, crisp entree salads and homemade soups. There is also a wide selection of Northwest wines and brews and cocktails as well.

Neskowin Trading Company and Beach Club Bistro

48880 Hwy 101 S   503/392-3035
Daily: 8-8 (Fri, Sat till 9)   neskowintradingcompany.com

This attractive gourmet market has become a cornerstone of the Neskowin community. Owners Kim and Mike Herbel turned a 1984 building into a welcoming village market offering necessities and gourmet delights to vacationers and local patrons. You can make your selection from the tasty sandwiches, salads, quiches, fresh-baked pastries, deli treats and espresso bar. Ask Mike for help in selecting a great bottle of wine; seasonal wine tastings. The latest addition to the market is the Beach Club Bistro. Choose from a delicious menu of foods with an international flair. Popular choices are calamari with sweet and hot Thai sauce, handmade pot stickers and fresh local fish. The Bistro has received a "Best of the Coast" award for clam chowder. Also of note, Kim runs the Beach Club Bistro and her art is shown in the restaurant.

NETARTS

The Schooner

2065 Netarts Bay Blvd   503/815-9900
Lunch, Dinner: Daily   theschooner.net
Moderate

The Schooner has been a Netarts fixture for over 60 years. The dining room is inviting and glass windbreaks shield the outdoor deck from coastal breezes without spoiling the view. The menu leans toward local ocean and farm products and wood-fired gourmet pizzas (available in the winter months). Schooner cioppino is made with rockfish, wild prawns, clams, calamari and Netarts Bay oysters in a savory broth served with a baguette. The lounge serves classic and contemporary cocktails and area microbrews; live music on special occasions.

NEWPORT

Bridie's Irish Faire

715 NW 3rd St   541/574-9366
Daily: 11-6   bridiesirishfaire.com

All things Ireland! Bridie's is a treasure trove of Irish and handmade jewelry, apparel and gifts. Popular additions include Irish tweed hats for men and women, men's vests and the nostalgic collarless "grandfather shirt." The shop is owner Susan Jeanne Spencer's celebration of Irish traditions. She also organizes and accompanies small group pilgrimages to Ireland, Scotland and elsewhere in the world; check the website for tour dates.

Cafe Stephanie

411 NW Coast St   541/265-8082
Breakfast, Lunch: Daily   Facebook
Moderate

Hearty breakfasts are served in an unpretentious building. Quiches, waffles, burritos and delicious homemade buttermilk pancakes are on the breakfast menu and priced right. Lunch choices include soups, chowder, salads, sandwiches (whole or half) and fish tacos. Outdoor tables expand the limited inside seating capacity; it's always a good sign when locals fill the seats.

Canyon Way Restaurant

1216 SW Canyon Way   541/265-8319
Lunch: Mon-Fri; Dinner: Fri   canyonway.com
Moderately expensive

Dozens of places along the coast offer crab cakes with a variety of ingredients and presentations, but none better than those served by Roguey and Ed Doyle at their bookstore/restaurant. These Dungeness delicacies are just the right size and consistency, containing a great deal of crab meat. Homemade soups are another customer favorite; choices may include chicken curry, mushroom, cream of roasted garlic, New England-style clam chowder. Oyster or shrimp po' boys, Szechuan chicken pasta or fresh spinach salad are also good. Custardy bread pudding is made with homemade bread and topped with warm caramel rum sauce; rich and unforgettable!

Captain's Reel Deep Sea Fishing

343 SW Bay Blvd   541/265-7441, 800/865-7441
Year round   captainsreel.com

Grab your fishing license, sack lunch, rain gear and sunscreen, and head to Newport's waterfront to board one of Captain's fleet (six to 20 passengers). Tackle and hot coffee are provided onboard. Depending on season and luck, you might pull in a prize halibut, albacore tuna, salmon or lingcod; squid and bottom fishing are options. Most trips offer a crab combo opportunity. Excursions range from five to 12 hours with prices varying accordingly; fish filleting is available on the dock.

Elizabeth Oceanfront Suites

232 SW Elizabeth St   541/265-9400, 877/265-9400
Moderate to expensive   elizabethoceanfrontsuites.com
Expect to be pampered: cozy fireplaces, comfortable robes, hot breakfast buffet, private balconies and an indoor saltwater swimming pool. All rooms face the beach and some have an extra window facing north toward Yaquina Head Lighthouse. Choose from several accommodation types: queen, king or king Jacuzzi rooms and a spacious family suite; a limited number of pet-friendly rooms are also available. In addition to the complimentary breakfast, fresh cookies are set out in the lobby each evening and smoked salmon chowder is an afternoon treat.

Fishtails Cafe

3101 Ferry Slip Road   541/867-6002
Breakfast, Lunch: Daily   fishtailscafe.com
Inexpensive to moderate
Plenty of fish tales are surely told at Fishtails, a local hangout that dishes up fishermen-size meals for breakfast and lunch. The house is not fancy, but you'll be welcomed warmly and the food is good; prices are easy on the wallet, too. As expected, seafood is often a feature with various egg dishes or choose pancakes, biscuits and gravy or homemade cinnamon rolls. The sautéed Marionberry French toast, though, takes the prize with lightly sweetened cream cheese stuffed between two pieces of homemade bread and topped with homemade berry sauce. Lunch also turns to seafood options, burgers, sandwiches and slumgullion (original recipe clam chowder).

Georgie's Beachside Grill

744 SW Elizabeth St   541/265-9800
Breakfast, Lunch, Dinner: Daily   georgiesbeachsidegrill.com
Inexpensive to moderately expensive
On the same property as Newport's Hallmark Resort (hallmarkinns.com/Newport) is Georgie's Beachside Grill, a favorite. Georgie's combines a casual feel with a sophisticated look for an ambience to suit any mood. Like the hotel, the grill is also very family-friendly, treating your little ones with "Georgie's Money" to pick something out of the treasure chest upon leaving. The panoramic ocean views from the restaurant are a treasure in themselves. This beachside grill offers authentic northwest coastal cuisine. Menu options include dishes in their simplest form such as traditional bacon and eggs, fresh salmon and halibut, juicy steaks and burgers to more spiced up entrees like the Diablo seafood pasta. The kids' menu is one of the most expansive found in Newport. Georgie's not only offers great food, but a full bar as well, and has been voted for the best oceanfront dining in Newport.

Inn at Nye Beach

729 NW Coast St 541/265-2477, 800/480-2477

Moderate innatnyebeach.com

Nestled into a cozy bluff, the Inn at Nye Beach offers the only oceanfront infinity spa in Oregon. The nearby fire pits create another distinguished vantage point to enjoy the view. This is just the beginning of what makes the Inn at Nye Beach special. The 20 guest rooms and suites include gas fireplaces, balconies and hand-selected, luxury amenities. The hotel features complimentary weekly wine socials, outdoor gas fireplaces overlooking the ocean, private direct beach access, and maintains sustainable practices and eco-friendly design.

La Maison Bakery & Cafe

315 SW 9th St 541/265-8812

Breakfast, Lunch: Tue-Sun lamaisoncafe.com

The attractive green cottage sets the stage for what's inside. Fare is distinctly French: eggs Sardou, Chambord crepes, Provence omelets, croissant sandwiches and more. Tres délicieux gourmet desserts are presented on fused-glass plates; local, organically-grown produce and eggs are used in all dishes.

Local Ocean Seafoods

213 SE Bay Blvd 541/574-7959

Daily localocean.net

Moderate

Seafood is always best fresh — and it's really fresh at this place. Products in the cases are tagged with specific information about the catch, the name of the boat and how and where it was caught. Only high-grade products are purchased, and the flavors show this advantage. Fish tacos, tuna kabobs, tuna wraps, plus salmon, halibut and crab are popular choices. (Only the French fries are deep-fried here.) Owner Laura Anderson runs a spotless restaurant with an open kitchen; as weather allows, roll-up glass doors are opened to bring the fresh ocean air into the dining area. The menu emphasizes a fine selection of seafood (as seasonably availabale), including oyster shooters, steamer clams, Thai-style mussels, Dungeness crab and fishwives' stew (in a garlic and herb broth). A half-pound burger, kids' selections, homemade ice cream and a full bar are also available.

Made in Oregon

342 SW Bay Blvd 541/574-9020

(See detailed listing with Made in Oregon, Portland)

Nana's Irish Pub

613 NW 3rd St
Lunch, Dinner: Daily
Moderate

541/574-8787
nanasirishpub.com

Traditional Irish fare here! Shepherd's pie, corned beef and cabbage, Irish beer-battered fish and chips and bread pudding made with Irish whiskey

FAMILY ACTIVITIES

ASTORIA

Astoria Column (2199 Coxcomb Dr, 503/325-2963, astoriacolumn.org): 164-step spiral staircase, magnificent views

Columbia River Maritime Museum (1792 Marine Dr, 503/325-2323, crmm.org): interactive displays, historical memorabilia, demonstrations, workshops, classes (reasonable)

Lewis and Clark National Historical Park (92343 Fort Clatsop Road, 503/861-2471, nps.gov): replica of Fort Clatsop, ranger-led programs, interpretive center (nominal)

BANDON

West Coast Game Park Safari (46914 Hwy 101, 541/347-3106, westcoastgameparksafari.com): hands on experience with 450 exotic and unusual animals (reasonable)

FLORENCE

Sea Lion Caves (91560 Hwy 101, 541/547-3111, sealioncaves. com): America's largest sea cave, wildlife preserve and bird sanctuary (reasonable)

GARIBALDI

Garibaldi Maritime Museum (112 Garibaldi Ave, 503/322-8411, garibaldimuseum.org): features Captain Robert Gray and his sailing boats; mid-March to November (nominal)

Oregon Coast Scenic Railroad (Port of Garibaldi Depot, 503/842-7972, oregoncoastscenic.org): round trip between Garibaldi and Rockaway or special occasion excursions (expensive)

GOLD BEACH

Jerry's Rogue Jets (29985 Harbor Way, 800/451-3645, roguejets.com): Rogue River whitewater excursions; May to mid-October (prices vary)

are the order of the day at this family friendly stop. You won't go wrong with a Bunratty Reuben or Cu Chulainn chicken sandwich, and for good measure, a few American favorites are offered, too. The outdoor patio is pleasant on warm summer days (and pet-friendly) and weekend entertainment draws a crowd. Of course, it wouldn't be a pub without stouts, lagers and ales; Nana's has imported beers on tap, wine and a full bar.

NEWPORT
OSU Hatfield Marine Science Center (2030 SE Marine Science Dr, 541/867-0226, hmsc.oregonstate.edu): animals, exhibits, hands-on activities in visitors center (free, suggested donation)
Oregon Coast Aquarium (2820 SE Ferry Slip Road, 541/867-3474, aquarium.org): 39 acres of indoor and outdoor exhibits (reasonable)

PORT ORFORD
Prehistoric Gardens (36848 Hwy 101 S, 541/332-4463, prehistoricgardens.com): 23 life-size dinos set in a temperate zone rainforest (reasonable)

REEDSPORT
Oregon Dunes National Recreation Area (541/271- 3611, fs.usda. gov): miles of mountainous sand dunes, lakes, trails

SEASIDE
Seaside Aquarium (200 N Prom, 503/738-6211, seasideaquarium. com): seals, touch tank, underwater exhibits (nominal)

TILLAMOOK
Tillamook Creamery (4175 Hwy 101 N, 503/815-1300, tillamook.com): new visitors center, interactive features, cafe
Tillamook Forest Center (45500 Wilson River Hwy, 503/815-6800, tillamookforestcenter.org): interpretive center, pedestrian suspension bridge, trails; seasonal (free)

WARRENTON
High Life Adventures (92111 High Life Road, 503/861-9875, highlife-adventures.com): one mile, eight zip lines; reservations recommended (expensive)

Ocean House Bed and Breakfast

4920 NW Woody Way   541/265-3888
Moderate   oceanhouse.com

Your getaway to an oceanfront setting should include the Ocean House Bed and Breakfast, which offers a private path to miles of sandy beach and tide pools. This inn has seven spacious rooms, each with a view of crashing waves (opt for the Sandcastle Room with private balcony). All rooms have a private bath, free Wi-Fi, docks for mobile devices, and luxury bedding and bath linens, among many amenities. Select rooms come with a double Jacuzzi tub and a separate shower. Innkeepers Dawn and Craig take care of all of your desired comforts, such as complimentary Oregon and Washington wines, soft drinks, freshly baked cookies and a full, plated breakfast that includes freshly squeezed orange juice and coffee. A comfortably sized and designed living room has ocean views and a fireplace to curl up next to while reading or playing a game of chess. Or get cozy next to a wood-burning fire pit on the outdoor deck. This hidden gem is just minutes from the Nye Beach area.

Oregon Coast Aquarium

2820 SE Ferry Slip Road   541/867-3474
Daily: 10-5 (till 6 in summer)   aquarium.org
Reasonable

The Oregon Coast Aquarium is a world-class center of excellence for ocean literacy and plays an active role in conservation, education and marine animal rehabilitation efforts. The 39-acre facility features indoor and outdoor exhibits that earn the aquarium consistent recognition as one of the top ten aquariums in the country. International notoriety was earned when it hosted Keiko, the orca whale that starred in the movie Free Willy during his rehabilitation from 1996 to 1998. After Keiko departed for Iceland the aquarium was transformed into the iconic Passages of the Deep gallery, which features three immersed tunnels. Visitors have 360-degree views of the three marine habitats found off Oregon's shores, complete with thousands of fish and over 100 sharks. Fun and educational opportunities include seal, sea lion and giant octopus encounters, overnight stays to Sleep in the Deep, private parties and more. Over 250 species call the facility home as well as various exhibits (sandy and rocky environs, sea otters, seals and sea lions, sea nettle jellies and a seabird aviary); many are hands-on. A full-service cafe offers food and beverages for visitors. Before you depart, browse the aquarium's gift shop; books, colorful posters and DVDs about the marine life, plus art, toys, clothing and ocean-themed gifts are displayed.

OSU Hatfield Marine Science Center

2030 SE Marine Science Dr   541/867-0226
Daily: 10-5 (Thu-Mon: 10-4 in winter)   hmsc.oregonstate.edu/visitor
Admission by donation

An ocean-related educational experience awaits you and your children. The visitor center (a Coastal Ecosystem Learning Center) is the public wing of Oregon State University's Mark O. Hatfield Marine Science Center and is managed by Oregon Sea Grant. This fascinating operation is part aquarium and part ocean laboratory. Learn about "habitat snatchers," aquatic invasive species (such as Asian clams and zebra mussels) that are an environmental threat to native wildlife, earthquakes, tsunamis and more. Engaging exhibits include getting up close and personal with an octopus and other live marine animals, interactive wave tanks, plus games and puzzles that demonstrate marine science concepts. Request a film to view in the auditorium and visit the well-stocked gift shop with ocean and natural science-related books, videos and the like. Check the website for feeding and event schedules.

Saffron Salmon

859 SW Bay Blvd   541/265-8921
Lunch: 11:30-2:30 (Fri-Sun); Dinner: 5-close (Thu-Tue)   saffronsalmon.com
Moderate

Exceptional "from-scratch" cooking lends itself to exceptional entrees and desserts. Wild salmon takes a starring role in salads and entrees and in a sandwich with saffron aioli on the lunch menu. Local farms provide lamb, beef and chicken; produce is purchased at the seasonal farmers market and local fishermen supply the restaurant with in-season crab and seafood. Warm marionberry cobbler with ice cream is the signature dessert. Reservations suggested; seasonal hours in November.

Sylvia Beach Hotel

267 NW Cliff St   541/265-5428, 888/795-8422
Moderate   sylviabeachhotel.com

Sylvia Beach Hotel is the most unusual bed and breakfast. Built a century ago, it opened as the New Cliff House and later became Hotel Gilmore before current owners Sally Ford and Goody Cable and friends turned it into a novel beachside 21-room B&B with rooms furnished and named after renowned authors (Agatha Christie, Dr. Seuss, J.K. Rowling, F. Scott Fitzgerald). Room types are categorized as classic, bestseller or novel (all have private baths) and are designed for relaxation, reading and writing. No TVs, Wi-Fi, telephones or other tech conveniences here. Guests and non-guests are in for an informal and relaxed treat at Tables of Content where the Northwest cuisine dinner menu changes daily. When dinner reservations are made, diners are asked which of four entrees they prefer (seafood, poultry, meat or vegetable). Seating is family-style with six or eight at a table; diners may play a fun dinner ice-breaker game called Two Truths and One Lie to get acquainted with their tablemates. There is one seating each evening (6 p.m. during the winter and 7 p.m. on weekends, during the summer and holidays). Meals include tasty appetizers, a fresh salad, vegetable and starch with the main course, dessert and coffee or tea (beer and wine are available). Group luncheons and special occasions are accommodated.

The Whaler

155 SW Elizabeth St   541/265-9261, 800/433-9444
Moderate   whalernewport.com

The 73-room Whaler has great Pacific views from guest room balconies. Various units are equipped with fireplaces, wet bars and microwaves; all rooms offer Internet access and refrigerators. A continental breakfast is complimentary to guests with hot beverages and fresh popcorn available throughout the day. Walk along the beach, visit Nye Beach or Old Town's excellent restaurants and shops or enjoy the indoor pool, spa and exercise facility. Five comfortable three- and four-bedroom homes with ocean views are also available. Owner/host John Clark operates a first-class establishment and is also one of the strongest supporters of good causes on the Coast.

OCEANSIDE

Roseanna's Cafe

1490 Pacific Ave   503/842-7351
Lunch, Dinner: Thu-Mon (11-8; Sat, Sun 10-8)   roseannascafe.com
Moderate

Roseanna's Cafe is nestled in a distinctive 1900s building with siding weathered gray by the elements. Large windows frame evening sunsets, tidal activity and Three Arch Rocks. A bowl of steaming clam chowder and homemade marionberry cobbler are lunch favorites, or choose from lunch and dinner menus and daily specials like spicy seafood pasta.

OTIS

Otis Cafe

1259 Salmon River Hwy   541/994-2813
Breakfast, Lunch, Dinner: Daily   otiscafe.com
Inexpensive

This, my friends, is a quintessential stop about five miles northeast of Lincoln City. The tiny, funky roadside diner is a must-visit for down-home cooking, especially breakfast. Toast is a big deal here; it is made from homemade black molasses bread. Loaves of black molasses, sourdough and pumpkin bread are available for purchase. Eggs and such are served with or without meats and with homemade hash browns (shredded baked russet potatoes). Sourdough or buttermilk pancakes and waffles are also popular; the kids' pancake version is made in the shape of a teddy bear face. With only a half-dozen small tables, be ready to wait in line; outside seating available in warmer months. Hot and cold sandwiches, burgers, soups, salads and creamy clam chowder welcome a new wave of midday diners. Soup or salad, starch, vegetables and, of course, homemade bread accompany the comfort food dinners.

PACIFIC CITY

Ben and Jeff's Burgers and Tacos
33260 Cape Kiwanda Dr   503/483-1026
Breakfast: Sat, Sun; Lunch, Dinner: Daily   benandjeffs.com
Inexpensive
The name of this business aptly describes the menu. Burgers are juicy and tacos and burritos are filled with pork, chicken, halibut or prawns (deep fried or grilled); if you prefer fish and chips, they are also available. Other selections include delicious breakfast burritos, homemade clam chowder and carne asada tacos and burritos. In the liquid department, there are sodas, beers and margaritas. Ben Johnson and Jeff Mollencop also operate **Moment Surf Company** (503/483-1025, momentsurfco.com), a small surf shop where they rent and sell surfing and water-related beach activity gear and the latest surf inspired clothing and accessories.

Grateful Bread Bakery
34805 Brooten Road   503/965-7337
Thu-Mon: 8-3   gratefulbreadbakery.com
Robyn Barcroft, owner of Grateful Bread Bakery, says her business' name was just a play on words, but fans of the legendary band started to flock to the place; now the entire staff wear tie-dyed uniforms. That sense of community is reflected throughout this restaurant, which has created a friendly atmosphere to enjoy fresh baked breads, pastries such as fruit and savory scones, coffee and espresso and full breakfast and lunch menus (both served all business hours). Breakfast features a variety of pancakes, or try the French toast, made with housemade challah bread and served with marionberry-apple compote. Other choices include egg scrambles and omelets. For lunch there are meat, seafood and vegetarian sandwich-

es served on fresh-baked bread and with your choice of cole slaw or potato chips, burgers, fish tacos, soups, salads and rice bowls. While you're here, pick up a tie-dyed T-shirt.

Headlands Coastal Lodge & Spa

33000 Cape Kiwanda Dr   503/965-5037
Moderate to expensive   headlandslodge.com
With an unbeatable location near Cape Kiwanda and Haystack Rock, the brand new Headlands Coastal Lodge & Spa will delight visitors. Its 33 new lodge rooms have private oceanfront balconies. In addition, 18 pre-existing cottages (formerly the Cottages at Cape Kiwanda), are now part of the Headlands brand and also feature great views and amenities. One walk through the lodge and guests will know that great care and regard for that "Oregon flair" went into its design and construction. The new lodge is the creation of Mary Jones and Jeff Schons, the royal couple of Pacific City, whose other business endeavors include Pelican Brewing Company (see write-ups this chapter), the Inn at Cape Kiwanda (ditto) and the remodeled Stimulus Coffee & Bakery. Guest rooms offer comfort and luxury with fancy soaps and linens, modern TV technology and iPads. Tidepools, the on-site spa and wellness center, features massage and treatment rooms, steam rooms and a fitness studio, as well as a fireplace and hot tub. And it offers complimentary group classes in beach yoga, meditation and Pilates. Also on-site is the restaurant Meridian, serving up ocean-to-table cuisine. Led by Executive Chef Andrew Garrison, the dinner menu is ever changing based on the season's best offerings, but expect house favorites like black cod with Oregon black truffles, parsnip mash, escarole and truffle jus. Breakfast and lunch are equally exciting, featuring sweet and savory dishes and classics like eggs Benedicts, soups, salads and sandwiches. There is a vegan/vegetarian menu, and the full bar creates coastal-themed cocktails while also serving Pelican Brewing beers and Northwest wines. And there's a Pelican Brewing Company pub right next door. While all these amenities are a plus, what makes Headlands truly memorable is its hospitality. Staff are anxious to help and will tailor your stay with everything from the fill of your pillows to connecting you with an on-site adventure coach, who can customize a recreational or sightseeing itinerary based on your interests.

Inn at Cape Kiwanda

33105 Cape Kiwanda Dr   503/965-7001, 888/965-7001
Moderate to expensive   yourlittlebeachtown.com/inn
Each of the 35 rooms has a private balcony overlooking the ocean at this friendly and attractive family-oriented property. Nice touches include complimentary newspapers, cozy gas fireplaces, pillow top mattresses

and feather pillows, complimentary chocolates on arrival and free Wi-Fi. The Haystack Suite includes a living room, large bedroom and Jacuzzi tub with ocean view. Take a spin on one of the inn's courtesy cruiser bikes to explore this delightful coastal community.

The Oar House Bar and Grill

34455 Brooten Road   503/965-2000
Mon-Thu: 11-9 (Fri till 11); Sat: 9-midnight;
Sun: 9-9   theoarhousebarandgrill.com

This is a great choice for fresh seafood, burgers with all the trimmings, juicy steaks, pastas and more. Start with calamari fries, steamer clams, salmon cakes or creamy clam chowder. More than a dozen varieties of sandwiches and burgers are accompanied by your choice of fries or tots. Vegetarians will find delight in chipotle black bean or portobello burgers. You'll also find hearty salads, hand battered fish and fries, steaks and pasta dishes (seafood, meat and vegetarian). If you've really worked up an appetite, opt for the captain's platter, which includes fried Coho salmon, surf clams, coconut prawns, calamari, house slaw and fries. Reasonable prices get even better during daily happy hour (3-6 and 9-close), and there's even a breakfast menu on Saturday and Sunday from 9 to 11. Families are welcome with their kiddos until 9 p.m.

Pelican Brewing Company

33180 Cape Kiwanda Dr   503/965-7007
Daily: 10:30-10 (Fri, Sat till 11)   pelicanbrewing.com
Moderate

The first Pelican brewpub was launched here in 1996 as Oregon's first oceanfront brewery (there are now two more locations; see listings for Cannon Beach and Tillamook). Like the others, the original is a beehive of activity for intimate brewery tours, suds and beer cuisine. The menu gives diners choices of everyone's favorites plus malt-crusted salmon, cioppino, salads, gourmet flatbreads, burgers and fish and chips. The restaurant offers more than a dozen varieties of ales, lagers and stouts, and these brews complement meals and are used in the preparation of numerous dishes like pale malt-crusted salmon. Beer pairings are a specialty and so noted on the menu.

PORT ORFORD

Hawthorne Gallery

517 Jefferson St   541/366-2266
Daily: 11-5 (closed Tue in winter)   hawthornegallery.com

Redfish

541/366-2266
Restaurant: Lunch, Dinner: Daily; Brunch: Sun   redfishportorford.com
Moderately expensive to expensive (restaurant); Expensive (lodging)
Opening in 2010, the gallery has become a destination for art lovers and collectors around the world. With over 30 artists, ten being from the Hawthorne family, expect to view an amazing, eclectic mix of glass, sculpture, paintings, furniture and more. Walk through the sculpture garden and into Redfish, the Hawthorne's upscale restaurant, where coastal cuisine is offered for brunch, lunch and dinner. WindDownWednesdays have become a favorite event (every Wednesday from 5:30-8:30) for an evening of wine, great food and local musical talent. Above the restaurant is a unique guest suite, Redfish Loft (541/366-2266, redfishloft.com), where you can take in the view, soak in the huge tub or sit by the fireplace.

WildSpring Guest Habitat

92978 Cemetery Loop   866/333-9453
Expensive   wildspring.com
From its hilltop location, this overnight gem is akin to staying in a private estate. Five beautiful cabin suites and the ocean view Guest Hall are nestled on five forested acres. Amble over to the Guest Hall for a tasty morning breakfast buffet; enjoy beverages, fruit, popcorn and chocolates anytime during the day; gaze at the Pacific while soaking in the open-air, slate jetted hot tub; or arrange for spa treatments, guest bikes, hiking guides and other services. Luxurious appointments vary among the cabins; sliding doors separate the cozy living rooms from bedrooms. Cabins are appointed with artwork, down comforters, antique and vintage pieces, oversize walk-in slate showers, massage tables, refrigerators and a flat-screen TV/DVD for movies (over 600 titles available in the Guest Hall library). No telephones, in-room cooking facilities or TV reception; however, guests are free to use a fully-equipped kitchen in the Hall. This small, eco-friendly property is a year-round destination for relaxation, picnics in the forest and walking the labyrinth.

REEDSPORT

Sugar Shack Bakery

145 N 3rd St   541/271-3514
Daily: 3 a.m. to 7 p.m. (seasonal variations)   sugarshackbakery.biz
When you're in or passing through Reedsport, stop in for coffee and a doughnut, other sugary treats or a dish of ice cream to keep you going. The Bigfoot doughnut (chocolate and maple icings with whipped cream

filling) is large enough to tame Sasquatch-size cravings! All delicious cookies, scones, cakes and candies are made from scratch. More substantial offerings include breakfast sandwiches and biscuits and gravy; soups and sandwiches are served midday until closing.

Umpqua Discovery Center

409 Riverfront Way 541/271-4816
Seasonal hours umpquadiscoverycenter.com
Reasonable

This interesting educational and cultural center with interactive, multi-sensory exhibits and programs geared to families is situated along the tidewater of the Umpqua River. The displays will take you back in time to experience life in a 1900s tidewater town, loggers' camp and salmon cannery; meet the early explorers such as Jedediah Smith and learn the culture of coastal Indian tribes. "Pathways to Discovery" exhibit takes visitors on a simulated outdoor hike through the four seasons where they learn about the plants and animals of the area. There's much to entertain and inform kids, including a 35-foot periscope in the community room for capturing 360-degree views of the surrounding area.

ROCKAWAY BEACH

Surfside Oceanfront Resort

101 NW 11th Ave 503/355-2312, 800/243-7786
Inexpensive to moderate surfsideocean.com

Surfside Oceanfront Resort is family-friendly to kids and pets. The sprawling, two-story resort has rooms with one or two beds, ocean-facing decks and gas fireplaces. The expansive beach is conducive to kite-flying, beachcombing, walking, bird and whale watching and building sandcastles. If you prefer other activities, there is a heated indoor swimming pool; most rooms have kitchens equipped to prepare and serve a family meal. Fishermen take note! The large parking area offers plenty of space to park your car and boat!

Twin Rocks Motel

7925 Minnehaha St 877/355-2391
Moderate twinrocksmotel.net

Folks have been coming to Rockaway Beach since it was incorporated as a beach resort in the early 1900s. There are seven miles of sandy beaches accessible from the motel and waysides. This property has five updated homey cottages, each containing a living room and two bedrooms and equipped with full kitchens, fireplaces and large outdoor decks. Three oceanfront units are directly ashore from the namesake Twin Rocks, and the other two units offer ocean views. Modern amenities include Wi-Fi and flat-screen TVs with cable. The property's location allows for hours of walking the beach, building sand castles, flying kites or playing fetch with your canine.

SEAL ROCK

Brian McEneny Woodcarving Gallery
10727 Hwy 101　　　　　　　　　　　　　　　　541/563-2452
Daily: 10-4 (closed Mon in winter)　　　　　　woodcarvinggallery.com
Ultra-talented artist and owner Brian McEneny creates incredible artwork using driftwood, Port Orford cedar, Manzanita roots, cypress, myrtlewood and other coastal woods. The fluidity of ocean life makes up the bulk of his menagerie, but you'll also find other animals, abstracts and Native American works. Pieces are finished to enhance distinctive wood grains. The two floors of the gallery are chock-full of Brian's small decorative pieces, driftwood tables with glass tops as well as impressive large carvings; works by other Northwest carvers and master carvers are interspersed throughout. The gallery is closed for six weeks during the winter, so best to call ahead.

SEASIDE

Bell Buoy of Seaside
1800 S Roosevelt Dr　　　　　　　　　　　　　800/529-2722
Daily　　　　　　　　　　　　　　　　　　bellbuoyofseaside.com
A landmark neon bell buoy sign tops this family-owned specialty seafood store on the south end of town. Fish is purchased right off the local fishing boats and sold fresh; look for fresh Oregon Dungeness crab (whole or crabmeat only); salmon, albacore tuna, sturgeon and oysters are smoked and canned on-site. Gift boxes contain smoked and canned Oregon ocean delicacies. Enjoy clam chowder and fish and chips at their next-door restaurant (503/738-6348).

Bigfoot's Steakhouse
2427 S Roosevelt Dr　　　　　　　　　　　　　503/738-7009
Lunch, Dinner: Daily (closed Mon from
Labor Day to Memorial Day)　　　　　　　bigfootssteakhouse.com
Moderate and up
Every so often there are reported sightings of the elusive and mysterious Sasquatch. There is nothing mysterious about Bigfoot's in Seaside! The home cooking appeals to Yeti-size appetites and consists of big steaks, ra-

zor clams, halibut fish and chips, burgers, from-scratch soups, pub-style eats and housemade potato chips. Food and drink choices are abundant. This is a fun, family-friendly, casual spot where the Bigfoot theme prevails.

Bruce's Candy Kitchen

Seaside Factory Outlet Center
1111 N Roosevelt Dr   503/738-7828
(See detailed listing with Bruce's Candy Kitchen, Cannon Beach)

Nonni's Italian Bistro

831 Broadway   503/738-4264
Dinner: Daily   nonnisitalianbistro.com
Inexpensive to moderately expensive

Conveniently located east of the promenade, Nonni's is the best place to enjoy a quality Italian dinner in a comfortable setting. This family-owned and -operated restaurant strives to create food just like their nonni (the Italian name for grandma) used to make, always using the freshest ingredients. Desserts such as panna cotta with fresh berries and tiramisu are also homemade. Their spaghetti and meatballs entree is enormous; the meatballs are stuffed with fontina cheese for a more flavorful bite. The chicken piccata is another house favorite; pair it with a glass of red wine or amaretto from their full-service bar and you have yourself a topnotch Italian dinner. A nightly happy hour (3-5:30) features smaller portions of their most popular dishes as well as drink specials. For a mom-and-pop style breakfast and lunch spot, visit their next door restaurant, Firehouse Grill (503/717-5502, Facebook).

Norma's Seafood & Steak

20 N Columbia St   503/738-4331
Lunch, Dinner: Daily   normasseaside.com
Moderate to moderately expensive

Award-winning clam chowder and accommodating service draw folks to Norma's, located a stone's throw off Broadway in downtown Seaside. There are a dozen or so seafood appetizers; oysters, crab, shrimp, clams are prepared raw, fried, steamed, in crab cakes and as tangy shrimp or crab cocktails. Fish and seafood entrees dominate the early-bird lunch specials accompanied by fresh-baked bread and choice of green salad with bay shrimp, French fries or chowder. Dinner portions and more are available all day; the captain's platter contains salmon, prawns, halibut, calamari, scallops, oysters and a razor clam. Create your favorite surf and turf platter by adding a choice of seafood to natural Angus beef steaks or porterhouse-cut pork chops. Pasta dishes, seafood salads, burgers and assorted sandwiches are tasty alternatives. Satisfy your sweet tooth with mocha mud pie, chocolate nut torta, chocolate layer cake, brownie sundae, housemade marionberry cobbler or apple crisp.

Osprey Café

2281 Beach Dr   503/739-7054
Breakfast, Lunch: Daily   Facebook
Inexpensive to moderate
To fuel your family before the next round of beach activities, try Osprey

---

BEST FOR CLAM CHOWDER

ASTORIA
Baked Alaska (1 12th St, 503/325-7414)
Mo's (101 15th St, 971/704-1750)

BANDON
Tony's Crab Shack (155 1st St SE, 541/347-2875)

BAY CITY
The Fish Peddler at Pacific Oyster (5150 Oyster Dr, 503/377-2323)

CANNON BEACH
Driftwood Restaurant & Lounge (179 N Hemlock St, 503/436-2439)
Mo's (195 Warren Way, 503/436-1111)
Pelican Brewing Company (1371 S Hemlock St, 503/908-3377,)
Tom's Fish & Chips (240 N Hemlock St, 503/436-4301)

DEPOE BAY
Gracie's Sea Hag Restaurant and Lounge (58 N Hwy 101,
541/765-2734)
Tidal Raves Seafood Grill (279 NW Hwy 101, 541/765-2995)

FLORENCE
Bridgewater Ocean Fresh Fish House and Zebra Bar (1297 Bay
St, 541/997-1133): ocean food chowder
Mo's (1436 Bay St, 541/997-2185)

LINCOLN CITY
The Bay House (5911 SW Hwy 101, 541/996-3222)
Mo's (860 SW 51st St, 541/996-2535)

Café for breakfast or lunch where the food is fresh. Meals are homemade with South and Latin American influences in addition to everyone's favorites of pancakes, omelets, sandwiches, salads, cinnamon rolls and such. Huevos rancheros and arepas (South American corn and cheese dumplings) are tasty and nicely presented. There is both inside and outside seating in this corner eatery located amidst hotels and vacation rentals.

NEHALEM
Buttercup Homemade Ice Creams and Chowders (35915 Hwy 101 N, 503/368-2469)

NESKOWIN
The Cafe on Hawk Creek (4505 Salem Ave, 503/392-4400)

NEWPORT
Canyon Way Restaurant (1216 SW Canyon Way, 541/265-8319)
Chowder Bowl (728 NW Beach Dr, 541/265-7477)
Fishtails Cafe (3101 Ferry Slip Road, 541/867-6002)
Mo's (622 SW Bay Blvd, 541/265-2979 and 657 SW Bay, 541/265-7512)

OTTER ROCK
Mo's (122 1st St, 541/765-2442): open March to September

PACIFIC CITY
Pelican Brewing Company (33180 Cape Kiwanda Dr, 503/965-7007)

SEASIDE
Bell Buoy of Seaside (1800 S Roosevelt Dr, 503/738-6357)
Firehouse Grill (841 Broadway St, 503/717-5502)
Norma's Seafood & Steak (20 N Columbia, 503/738-4331)
Tom's Fish & Chips (1 Holladay, 503/739-7386)

YACHATS
Luna Sea Fish House and Village Fishmonger (153 NW Hwy 101, 541/547-4794): Manhattan or New England style
Ona Restaurant and Lounge (131 Hwy 101 N, 541/547-6627)

Relief Pitcher

2795 S Roosevelt Dr   503/738-9801
Lunch, Dinner: Daily   Facebook
Inexpensive to moderate

The exterior doesn't have much curb-appeal and the funky interior isn't anything to write home about, but superb burgers are served here. The Grand Slam burger, a half-pound juicy beauty topped with ham, egg, Tillamook and provolone cheese, along with cole slaw or fries make up for the environs. Albacore tuna tacos, sandwiches and Reubens are also popular. Brews are available by the pitcher, glass or pint; full bar and wine offerings also. Check out the three horseshoe pits for fun!

Seaside Aquarium

200 N Prom   503/738-6211
Daily: 9-5 (seasonal closing hours)   seasideaquarium.com
Nominal

The Seaside Aquarium is privately owned and is one of the oldest aquariums on the West Coast. The 1924 building was originally a salt water bath house and pool; after major renovations, it reopened in 1937 as this quaint aquarium. As you enter, visitors are delighted by the barking of seals anticipating their fish treats; underwater and touch tanks are home to some 100 species of marine life. It is said that the first program to breed harbor seals in captivity was started here. Marine-related mementos await discovery in the small gift shop.

Seaside Mostly Hats

300 Broadway, Suite 20   503/738-4370
Daily: Hours vary   seasidemostlyhats.com

This shop is one of the most complete hat stores in the state. Located in the Carousel Mall, you'll find fun and dress hats for men, women and kids at reasonable prices in a variety of fabrics, styles and sizes. Depending on the weather, pop in to buy a rain hat or a straw hat. Some of the whimsical lids are made to look like fish or embellished with characters and attention-grabbing adornments; others come with synthetic hair attached.

Tipton's

319 Broadway   503/738-5864
Hours vary   tiptonsdecor.com

Shopping for classy home decor and holiday items? Visit George Tipton's attractive 2,500-square-foot shop; George has a discerning eye for warm Tuscan and French Country tabletop items, lamps, canisters, pictures, candles and soft goods. Don't overlook the case of delicious gourmet chocolates (once the mainstay of the business). Delightful smells, nice background music (George is also a talented musician) and appealing merchandise blend harmoniously to create a pleasant ambience.

TILLAMOOK

Blue Heron French Cheese Company
2001 Blue Heron Dr   503/842-8281, 800/275-0639
Daily: 8-8 (till 6 in winter)   blueheronoregon.com
Housed in a 1930s Dutch Colonial barn, this marvelous retail business includes a deli and tasting room with fantastic cheeses, gourmet foods and wines. Products, tasty samples and gift items are arranged throughout the store suggesting attractive entertaining possibilities. The pièce de résistance is the cheese counter featuring the famous Blue Heron Brie with a selection of other fine cheeses; free samples provided. Another popular attraction is the wine tasting bar. For a nominal fee, sample five Northwest wines from four flights. The deli features homemade soups, chowder, salads and sandwiches on freshly-baked bread. Outside, kids can get up close and pet farm animals or engage in other activities geared to the pint-size set.

Latimer Quilt & Textile Center
2105 Wilson River Loop   503/842-8622
Daily: April-Oct (closed Sun, Mon in winter)   latimerquiltandtextile.com
Nominal
The former Maple Leaf Schoolhouse building is home to a changing gallery, a research library and a fine gift shop where you'll find handmade items by local craftspeople, books, vintage fabrics, quilt patterns and other vintage and contemporary pieces. The nonprofit working museum opened in 1991 and showcases textiles from the mid-19th century to the present. Watch the interesting weaving and spinning demonstrations or arrange for weaving, spinning, knitting, quilting and rug-hooking instruction.

Pelican Brewing Company
1708 1st St   503/842-7007
Daily: 11-9   pelicanbrewing.com
Moderate
This was the second Pelican brewpub to open, and it now is home to a 50,000-barrel-per-year production facility, which is viewable from the taproom (tours are available). Like the other locations (see entries for Pacific City and Cannon Beach), the taproom offers a full complement of pilsners and lagers, pale ales, porters, stouts and more. The menu is scaled back

somewhat compared with the other brewpubs, but diner favorites (fish and chips, chowder, burgers, fish tacos) are still available, and there are a few items not found at the other locations (try the Tillamook Taproom Poutine, or an elk burger). And the quality and dedication to excellence remain at Pelican Brewing's high standards.

Rodeo Steak House & Grill

2015 1st St   503/842-8288
Lunch, Dinner: Daily   rodeosteakhousegrill.com
Moderate

Rodeo Steak House stakes its claim on good steaks, in particular, ba-con-wrapped filets. First thing you'll notice when you enter is the fun, fam-ily-friendly, casual ambience and peanut shells strewn on the floor. The peanuts are free and the selection from the full bar is sure to wet your whistle. Many of the appetizers and entrees are prepared with a Texas in-fluence: rodeo egg rolls are served with jalapeno jelly for dipping, grilled steak tips are listed as "road kill" and crispy critters (chicken or fish) are offered on the kids menu. There are plenty more choices including pasta dishes, generously-portioned salads and really good homemade chili. A second location is in Coos Bay (1001 N Bayshore Dr, 541/808-0644).

Tillamook County Pioneer Museum

2106 2nd St   503/842-4553
Tue-Sun: 10-4   tcpm.org
Nominal

This small museum has a large collection of over 56,000 artifacts and 20,000 photographs depicting the rich history of the north Oregon coast. Exhibits pertain to pioneers, Native Americans, the military, natural histo-ry and musical instruments, plus the area's industries (logging, beaches, dairy). Take note of the late Senator Mark Hatfield's superb Abraham Lin-coln collection, which once graced the walls of his Washington, D.C. office.

Tillamook Creamery

4175 Hwy 101 N   503/815-1300, 800/542-7290
Daily: 8-6 (Labor Day–Mid-June),
8-8 (Mid-June–Labor Day)   tillamook.com

Founded more than 100 years ago as a farmer-owned co-op, the Tillamook County Creamery Association continues to create high-quality Tillamook dairy products, including its outstanding naturally aged cheddar cheese from the original recipe. A brand new visitor facility opened at the Tillamook Cream-ery in summer 2018, where fans of the brand can peer through large viewing windows on a free self-guided tour to see how Tillamook makes and packages its famous cheese and also explore fun and educational exhibits about Tillamook's products, history and dairy farming heritage. Tillamook produces hundreds of varieties of cheese, ice cream, yogurt, sour cream and butter, which are all sold at the on-site retail area at the Creamery and in grocery stores across the country. Every flavor of Tillamook ice cream (more than 30 in all) is scooped into cones and dishes or used in milkshakes and sundaes at the Creamery's brand new indoor/outdoor ice cream counter; the enticing aroma of hot-off-the-griddle waffle cones permeates the retail and eating areas. Other Tillamook dairy products are featured at the newly expanded café, with menu items such as macaroni and cheese, grilled cheese sandwiches, burgers, salads and pizzas from the new wood-fired oven. For those stopping in for a short visit, a new coffee counter and yogurt parfait bar are perfect for a quick snack or breakfast. Before you leave, make a stop at the gift shop for Tillamook souvenirs, gourmet food items and Northwest goods.

Tillamook Forest Center

45500 Wilson River Hwy   503/815-6800, 866/930-4646
Seasonal days and hours   tillamookforestcenter.org
Free

Longtime Oregonians will remember the devastating fire in 1933 that ravaged nearly 240,000 acres of prime forest land, mostly in Tillamook County. (Smaller fires in 1939, 1945 and 1951 burned an additional 120,000 acres and are also considered part of the Tillamook Burn.) A massive reforestation effort resulted in more than 72 million Douglas fir seedlings planted in the area. An interpretive center owned and operated by the Oregon Department of Forestry is located near Jones Creek, 22 miles east of Tillamook on Highway 6. It offers fascinating, interactive exhibits along with a 40-foot tall replica of a fire lookout tower and a dramatic 250-foot-long pedestrian suspension bridge that leads to the Wilson River Trail and onto the nearby Jones Creek. A classroom, theater and interpretive trails provide educational opportunities; this is an exceptional destination for exploration, outdoor learning and free family fun.

WHEELER

Rising Star Cafe

92 Rorvik St   503/368-3990
Wed-Sat: 5 p.m.-close (dinner); Sun: 10 a.m.-close (brunch)   risingstarcafe.net
Moderate

This charming blue house is a bright spot in Wheeler. At this time Rising Star is primarily a dinner house (except for a lovely brunch on Sunday). Amply appointed choices might include several fresh fish-of-the-day entrees, cioppino, sandwiches, and pasta options using as many local and organic vegetables as possible. Dinner menus change daily based upon current sourcing and consist of fresh seafood, pasta and at least one meat item for carnivores (vegetarians and special diets accommodated where possible, please request ahead of time). The menu is generally posted on their Facebook page. Entrees are accompanied by crisp organic salads and great desserts that are made daily. Rising Star has a full wine list and also serves premium liquors. Reservations are recommended except Thursdays, which are first come; no credit cards at the Star (cash or check only).

WINCHESTER BAY

Sportsmen's Cannery & Smokehouse
182 Bayfront Loop   541/271-3293, 800/457-8048
Mon-Fri: 10-5 (closed Wed); Sat: 10-4
(daily 10-5 in summer)   sportsmanscannery.com
At Brian Reeves' store, the business is catching and packaging some of the best quality seafood available. Fresh fish and seafood are caught, smoked, canned and packaged right here in summer. The catch may include salmon, tuna, ling cod, oysters, prawns and crab; pollock roe is a special treat. Pick something up at the store or arrange for overnight shipping anywhere in the country. Gift boxes also include local and gourmet seasonings, jams and preserves; the price is right.

Umpqua Oysters
723 Ork Rock Road   541/271-5684
Daily: 9-6 (Wed-Mon: 9-5:30 in winter)
Fresh oysters are a delicacy, especially those cultivated at the confluence of the Umpqua River and Pacific Ocean. Cindy and Vern Simmons operate their aquaculture farm using innovative oyster "curtains" that keep the shellfish suspended in the water, free of air and mud exposure. This method produces a cut-above quality of tasty morsels, shucked or in the shell. When you are at the retail shop, pick up perfect condiments and sauces, observe shuckers and inspectors as they process the catch and watch an informative video depicting the long-line growing system.

YACHATS

The Adobe Resort
155 Hwy 101   541/547-3141, 800/522-3623
Inexpensive and up   adoberesort.com
The Adobe has been a popular respite on this stretch of the Pacific for

COASTAL STATE PARKS

There's much to explore up and down the coast, especially outdoors. Oregon State Parks (800/551-6949, oregonstateparks.org) has the coast covered with campgrounds and other recreational spots, scenic viewpoints and heritage sites. Here are a few of the area's gems:

NORTH COAST

Cape Kiwanda State Natural Area (Pacific City): along the Three Capes Scenic Route, spectacular waves, home of the Pacific Dory Fleet
Ecola State Park (84318 Ecola Park Road, Cannon Beach): stunning scenery, hiking, Indian Beach, Tillamook Head; eight miles of the Oregon Coast Trail
Fort Stevens State Park (100 Peter Iredale Road, Hammond): year round camping, bike and hiking trails, wreck of the Peter Iredale, Coffenbury Lake, wildlife and scenic observation platforms, historic military site

CENTRAL COAST

Jessie M. Honeyman Memorial State Park (84505 Hwy 101 S, Florence): camping, yurts, sand dunes, Cleawox and Woahink lakes

SOUTH COAST

Shore Acres State Park (89039 Cape Arago Hwy, Coos Bay): former estate of timber baron Louis Simpson, gardens, ponds, observation building; annual holiday lights show and programs in December
Umpqua Lighthouse State Park (460 Lighthouse Road, Winchester Bay): year round camping, yurts, log cabin, Lake Marie, Umpqua River Lighthouse

several decades. All guest rooms are furnished with refrigerators, microwaves and other conveniences and have views of the ocean or mountains. Suites are outfitted with king beds, Jacuzzi tubs with ocean views, electric fireplaces and other amenities. Appealing features include an indoor pool, children's pool, expansive lawn, accessible beach and tide pools, convenient pathway into town, pleasant lounge and meeting and banquet space (ideal for weddings). Seasonal hotel packages include breakfast or dinner in the award-winning ocean-view restaurant. Dinner entrees are moderately priced and deliciously prepared; same goes for early-bird dinner specials. There is a nice variety of beef, pork, fish and poultry offerings served by a friendly and efficient wait staff. This family-owned resort also welcomes canine buddies.

Earthworks Gallery

2222 Hwy 101 N   541/547-4300
Daily: 10-5   gocybervision.com/earthwork
For more than 20 years, Earthworks Gallery has been featuring some 150 Northwest artists at this same location. Talented artists represent all art mediums; fine-art pieces, sculptures, glass, baskets, clay, watercolors, jewelry and other selections, all attractively arranged.

Green Salmon Coffee and Tea House

220 Hwy 101 N   541/547-3077
Daily: 7:30-2:30   thegreensalmon.com
Next time you're in Yachats, indulge in a cup of wonderful custom-roasted coffee. If coffee is not your cup of tea, then opt for a pot of tea from the selection of teas and infusions. Fair trade and organic beans (eight seasonal selections) and teas (over 30 varieties) are sold in the retail store. Add a bit of sustenance with homemade breakfast pastries, scones and savories, hearty and delicious panini sandwiches or a smoothie, espresso or mocha drink.

Heceta Head Lighthouse Bed & Breakfast

92072 Hwy 101 S   866/547-3696
Moderate to expensive   hecetalighthouse.com
Another unique Oregon experience awaits at one of the last remaining lighthouse keeper's cottages on the Pacific Coast. This year-round bed and breakfast has a capacity for 15; four rooms have private bathrooms and two rooms share a bathroom. The cottage has been restored to its original look and appointed with warm down comforters, antique furnishings and a fully-equipped guest kitchen. A nighttime view of the lighthouse is memorable, as is the seven-course gourmet breakfast. Built around 1894, the lighthouse is one of the historic highlights of our state and one of the best-preserved beacons anywhere; a full renovation was completed in 2013.

Luna Sea Fish House and Village Fishmonger

153 Hwy 101   541/547-4794
Daily: 8 a.m. - 10 p.m. (10:30-9 in winter)   lunaseafishhouse.com
Inexpensive
Luna Sea is owned and operated by a local fisherman who also knows a thing or two about preparing the fruits of his labor. The menu is predominantly fish and seafood, but also includes meat and veggie burgers, fish tacos, bean burritos and salads. Fish and chips come in several varieties or

combinations including cod, halibut, salmon, tuna, scallops, oysters and clams. There's Manhattan and New England clam chowders and slumgullion (a chowder with added white cheese and bay shrimp that is then baked and served with garlic bread — do not be fooled by the name!). The breakfast menu includes pancakes and traditional dishes as well as seafood versions of omelets, hash and Benedicts. Seating is limited. Call for orders to go.

Ona Restaurant and Lounge

131 Hwy 101 N   541/547-6627
Dinner: Fri-Tue: 4-8:30 (Lunch, Dinner: daily in summer)   onarestaurant.com
Moderate to expensive
The warm ambience and sophisticated menu at this casual restaurant and lounge combine nicely with views of the mouth of the Yachats River and Pacific Ocean. For starters, Manila clams are steamed with garlic, butter, dry vermouth and grape tomatoes and come with warm crusty bread to soak up the broth; remoulade sauce with capers adds a dimension to Dungeness crab cakes (as a starter or entrée). Menu standouts include the mixed grill of Oregon seafood; meatloaf made with ground beef, lamb and pork; and cedar plank skirt steak with roasted shitakes. The beet salad with chévre, pickled fennel and roasted shallot vinaigrette comes in two sizes and with optional seafood or chicken add-ons that can make this choice a meal in itself. And there's always clam chowder and halibut fish and chips. The wine list is extensive, and chosen mostly from Oregon producers. An array of house-grown herbs and flowers go into cocktail mixers for their craft cocktails.

Overleaf Lodge & Spa

280 Overleaf Lodge Lane   800/338-0507
Moderate and up   overleaflodge.com
All 54 lodge rooms and suites (with optional adjoining rooms) have unobstructed ocean views. Accommodations in seven room-types may include patios (standard for first floor units), balconies or window seats, fireplaces, full kitchens and whirlpool tubs. The complimentary breakfast includes freshly-baked scones or muffins, a delicious main entree and homemade granola in addition to the usual fruit, cereal and beverage spread. The spa, showers, steam rooms, saunas and therapy tubs are located on the third floor; refreshing spa treatments include massages, therapeutic body care treatments and facials. Not coincidentally, seaweed is used in many of the treatments to moisturize the skin and limit the effects of aging. The neighboring sister property, Overleaf Village, consists of charming privately-owned cottages situated along a nature path to the ocean. These view and non-view homes are fully furnished and designed for six to 12 guests.

Gerry's Exclusive List

Bars and Pubs with Good Eats
Cannon Beach Hardware and Public House (1235 5 Hemlock St, Cannon Beach; 503/436-4086)
Fort George Brewing & Public House (1483 Duane St, Astoria; 503/325-7468)
Harding Trading Company (277 Beaver St, Cannon Beach; 503/739-5777)
Oxenfre Public House (631 Chetco Ave, Brookings; 541/813-1985)
Pelican Brewing Company (33105 Cape Kiwanda Dr, Pacific City, 503/965-7007; 1371 S Hemlock St, Cannon Beach, 503/908-3377; 1708 1st St, Tillamook, 503/842-7007)

Best Sleeps
Arch Cape Inn & Retreat (31970 E Ocean Lane, Arch Cape; 503/436-2800)
Awtrey House (38245 James Road, Manzanita; 503/368-5721)
Cannery Pier Hotel & Spa (10 Basin St, Astoria; 503/325-4996)
Cavalier Beachfront Condominiums (325 NW Lancer St, Gleneden Beach; 541/764-2352)
Gearhart Ocean Inn (67 N Cottage Ave, Gearhart; 503/738-7373)
Headlands Coastal Lodge & Spa (33000 Cape Kiwanda Dr, Pacific City; 503/965-5037)
Inn at Nye Beach (729 NW Coast St, Newport; 541/265-2477)
The Ocean Lodge (2864 S Pacific St, Cannon Beach; 503/436-2241)
Salishan Spa & Golf Resort (7760 Hwy 101 N, Gleneden Beach; 541/764-2371)
Stephanie Inn (2740 S Pacific St, Cannon Beach; 503/436-2221)
Tu Tu' Tun Lodge (96550 North Bank Rogue, Gold Beach; 541/247-6664)
Whale Cove Inn (2345 S Hwy 101, Depoe Bay; 541/765-4300)
The Whaler (155 SW Elizabeth St, Newport; 541/265-9261)

Breads and Bakery Goods
Bread and Ocean (154 Laneda Ave, Manzanita; 503/368-5823)
Cannon Beach Bakery (240 N Hemlock St, Cannon Beach; 503/436-0399)
Grateful Bread Bakery (34805 Brooten Road, Pacific City; 503/965-7337)
Home Baking Co. (2845 Marine Dr, Astoria; 503/325-4631): Finnish
Pacific Way Bakery & Cafe (601 Pacific Way, Gearhart; 503/738-0245)
Sea Level Bakery + Coffee (3116 S Hemlock St, Cannon Beach; 503/436-4254): crusty bread

Breakfast/Brunch
Astoria Coffeehouse & Bistro (243 11th St, Astoria; 503/325-1787)

Bridgewater Bistro (20 Basin 5t, Astoria; 503/325-6777): brunch
Cafe Stephanie (411 NW Coast St, Newport; 541/265-8082)
Camp 18 (42362 Hwy 26, Elsie; 503/755-1818)
Fishtails Cafe (3101 Ferry Slip Road, Newport; 541/867-6002)
Lord Bennett's (1695 Beach Loop Dr, Bandon; 541/347-3663)
Otis Cafe (1259 Salmon River Hwy, Otis; 541/994-2813)
Redfish (517 Jefferson St, Port Orford; 541/366-2200): brunch
Wanda's Cafe (12870 Hwy 101 N, Nehalem; 503/368-8100)

Burgers
The Oar House Bar and Grill (3445 Brooten Road, Pacific City; 503/965-2000)
Relief Pitcher (2795 S Roosevelt Dr, Seaside; 503/738-9801)
Tom's Fish & Chips (240 N Hemlock St, Cannon Beach; 503/436-4301)

Casual Dining/Casual Prices
Indian Creek Cafe (94682 Jerry's Flat Road, Gold Beach; 541/247-0680)
Little Brown Hen Cafe (435 Hwy 101, Florence; 541/902-2449)

Cheese
Blue Heron French Cheese Company (2001 Blue Heron Dr, Tillamook; 503/842-8281)
Face Rock Creamery (680 2nd St SE, Bandon; 541/347-3223)
Tillamook Creamery (4175 Hwy 101 N, Tillamook; 503/815-1300)

Coffee and Tea
Green Salmon Coffee and Tea House (220 Hwy 101 N, Yachats; 541/547-3077)
Lovejoy's Restaurant & Tea Room (195 Nopal St, Florence; 541/902-0502)
River Roasters (1240 Bay St, Florence; 541/997-3443)
Sleepy Monk Coffee Roasters (1235 S Hemlock St, Cannon Beach; 503/436-2796)

Comfort Food
Camp 18 (42362 Hwy 26, Elsie; 503/755-1818)
Harding Trading Company (277 Beaver St, Cannon Beach; 503/739-5777)
Otis Cafe (1259 Salmon River Hwy, Otis; 541/994-2813)
Side Door Café and Eden Hall (6675 Gleneden Beach Loop Road, Gleneden Beach; 541/764-3825)
T. Paul's Urban Cafe (1119 Commercial St, Astoria; 503/338-5133)
Wanda's Cafe (12870 Hwy 101 N, Nehalem; 503/368-8100)

Confections
Bruce's Candy Kitchen (256 N Hemlock St, Cannon Beach, 503/436-2641; Seaside Factory Outlet Center, 1111 N Roosevelt Dr, Seaside, 503/738-7828)
Chocolate Café (232 N Spruce St, Cannon Beach; 503/436-4331)
Indulge Sweets (10645 Pacific Coast Hwy, Seal Rock; 541/563-2766)

Deli
Bread and Ocean (154 Laneda Ave, Manzanita; 503/368-5823)
Josephson's Smokehouse & Specialty Seafood (106 Marine Dr, Astoria; 503/325-2190)

Fireside Dining
Morris' Fireside Restaurant (100 E 2nd St, Cannon Beach; 503/436-2917)

Fish and Seafood
Baked Alaska (112th St, Astoria; 503/325-7414)
Barnacle Bill's Seafood Market (2174 NE Hwy 101, Lincoln City; 541/994-3022)
The Bay House (5911 SW Hwy 101, Lincoln City; 541/996-3222)
Bell Buoy of Seaside (1800 S Roosevelt Dr, Seaside; 800/529-2722)
Bowpicker Fish & Chips (1634 Duane St, Astoria; 503/791-2942): battered Albacore tuna and steak fries
Bridgewater Ocean Fresh Fish House and Zebra Bar (1297 Bay St, Florence; 541/997-1133)
The Fish Peddler at Pacific Oyster (5150 Oyster Dr, Bay City; 503/377-2323)
Gracie's Sea Hag Restaurant and Lounge (58 N Hwy 101, Depoe Bay; 541/765-2734)
Local Ocean Seafoods (213 SE Bay Blvd, Newport; 541/574-7959)
Lord Bennett's (1695 Beach Loop Dr, Bandon; 541/347-3663)
Luna Sea Fish House and Village Fishmonger (153 NW Hwy 101, Yachats; 541/547-4794)
Norma's Seafood & Steak (20 N Columbia St, Seaside; 503/738-4331)
Portside Restaurant (63383 Kingfisher Dr, Charleston; 541/888-5544)
Redfish (517 Jefferson St, Port Orford; 541/366-2200)
Saffron Salmon (859 SW Bay Blvd, Newport; 541/265-8921)
Silver Salmon Grille (1105 Commercial St, Astoria; 503/338-6640)
Spinner's Seafood, Steak & Chophouse (29430 Ellensburg Ave, Gold Beach; 541/247-5160)
Tidal Raves Seafood Grill (279 NW Hwy 101, Depoe Bay; 541/765-2995)
Tom's Fish & Chips (240 N Hemlock St, Cannon Beach; 503/436-4301)

Tony's Crab Shack (155 1st St, Bandon; 541/347-2875)
Umpqua Oysters (723 Ork Rock Road, Winchester Bay; 541/271-5684)

Foreign Flavors
BOSNIAN: Drina Daisy (915 Commercial St, Astoria; 503/338-2912)
FRENCH: La Maison Bakery & Cafe (315 SW 9th St, Newport; 541/265-8812)
INTERNATIONAL: Castaways (308 N Fir St, Cannon Beach; 503/436-4444)
IRISH: The Irish Table (1235 5 Hemlock St, Cannon Beach, 503/436-0708); **Nana's Irish Pub** (613 NW 3rd St, Newport, 541/574-8787)
ITALIAN: La Pomodori Ristorante (1415 7th St, Florence, 541/902-2525); **Nonni's Italian Bistro** (831 Broadway St, Seaside, 503/738-4264)
MEXICAN: Left Coast Siesta (288 Laneda Ave, Manzanita, 503/368-7997); **Pancho's Restaurante Y Cantina** (1136 Chetco Ave, Brookings, 541/469-6531)

Hot Dogs
Langlois Market (48444 Hwy 101, Langlois; 541/348-2476)

Ice Cream and Other Frozen Treats
BJ's Ice Cream Parlor (1441 Bay St, Florence, 541/902-7828; 2930 Hwy 101, Florence, 541/997-7286)
Buttercup Homemade Ice Creams and Chowders (35915 N Hwy 101, Nehalem; 503/368-2469)
Frite & Scoop (175 14th St, Suite 150, Astoria; 503/468-0416)

Liquid Libations
MacGregor's (387 Laneda Ave, Manzanita; 503/368-2447): whiskey bar

Meats
Langlois Market (48444 Hwy 101, Langlois; 541/348-2476)
Tillamook Country Smoker (8250 Warren Ave, Tillamook; 503/377-2222)

Outdoor Dining
The Cafe on Hawk Creek (4505 Salem Ave, Neskowin; 503/392-4400)
Driftwood Restaurant & Lounge (179 N Hemlock St, Cannon Beach; 503/436-2439)
The Schooner (2065 Netarts Bay Blvd, Netarts; 503/815-9900)
Wanda's Cafe (12870 Hwy 101 N, Nehalem; 503/368-8100)

Personal Favorites
The Bay House (5911 SW Hwy 101, Lincoln City; 541/996-3222)
The Irish Table (1235 S Hemlock St, Cannon Beach; 503/436-0708)
Newmans at 988 (988 S Hemlock St, Cannon Beach; 503/436-1151)
The Spa at Salishan Resort (7760 Hwy 101 N, Gleneden Beach; 503/764-4300)
Tu Tu' Tun Lodge (96550 North Bank Rogue, Gold Beach; 541/247-6664)

Picnic Fixings
Bread and Ocean (154 Laneda Ave, Manzanita; 503/368-5823)

Pizza
Baked Alaska (112th St, Astoria; 503/325-7414)
The Cafe on Hawk Creek (4505 Salem Ave, Neskowin; 503/392-4400)
Pacific Way Bakery & Cafe (601 Pacific Way, Gearhart; 503/738-0245)
Pizza a'fetta (231 N Hemlock St, Cannon Beach; 503/436-0333)
Wild River Brewing & Pizza Company (16279 Hwy 101 S, Brookings; 541/471-7487)

Produce
Bear Creek Artichokes (19659 Hwy 101, Hemlock; 503/398-5411)

Sandwiches
Blue Scorcher Bakery & Cafe (1493 Duane St, Astoria; 503/338-7473)
Bread and Ocean (154 Laneda Ave, Manzanita; 503/368-5823)
Fat Irish Kitchen & Pub (16403 Lower Harbor Rd, Brookings; 530/520-8005)
Fishtails Cafe (3101 Ferry Slip Road, Newport; 541/867-6002)
Neskowin Trading Company and Beach Club Bistro (48880 Hwy 101 S, Neskowin; 503/392- 3035)
Otis Cafe (1259 Salmon River Hwy, Otis; 541/994-2813)
Pelican Brewing Company (33105 Cape Kiwanda Dr, Pacific City, 503/965-7007; 1371 S Hemlock St, Cannon Beach, 503/908-3377; 1708 1st St, Tillamook, 503/842-7007)

Soups
Canyon Way Restaurant (1216 SW Canyon Way, Newport; 541/265-8319)
Fishtails Cafe (3101 Ferry Slip Road, Newport; 541/867-6002)

Special Occasions
The Bay House (5911 SW Hwy 101, Lincoln City; 541/996-3222)
Bistro Restaurant (263 N Hemlock St, Cannon Beach; 503/436-2661)
The Depot Restaurant (1208 38th Pl, Seaview, WA; 360/642-7880)

Georgie's Beachside Grill (744 SW Elizabeth St, Newport; 541/265-9800)
Newmans at 988 (988 S Hemlock St, Cannon Beach; 503/436-1151)
Restaurant Beck (Whale Cove Inn, 2345 S Hwy 101, Depoe Bay; 541/765- 3220)
Stephanie Inn (2740 S Pacific St, Cannon Beach; 503/436-2221)
Tidal Raves Seafood Grill (279 NW Hwy 101, Depoe Bay; 541/765-2995)

Steaks
Bigfoot's Steakhouse (2427 S Roosevelt Dr, Seaside; 503/738-7009)
Bistro Restaurant (263 N Hemlock St, Cannon Beach; 503/436-2661)
Driftwood Restaurant & Lounge (179 N Hemlock St, Cannon Beach; 503/436-2439)
Nor'Wester Steak & Seafood (10 Harbor Way, Gold Beach; 541/247-2333)
Norma's Seafood & Steak (20 N Columbia St, Seaside; 503/738-4331)
Pirate's Cove Restaurant (14170 Hwy 101 N; Garibaldi; 503/322-2092)
Rodeo Steak House & Grill (2015 1st St, Tillamook; 503/842-8288)
Spinner's Seafood, Steak & Chophouse (29430 Ellensburg Ave, Gold Beach; 541/247-5160)

Vegan and Vegetarian Options
Side Door Café and Eden Hall (6675 Gleneden Beach Loop Road, Gleneden Beach; 541/764- 3825)

View Restaurants
The Adobe Resort (155 Hwy 101, Yachats; 541/547-3141)
Baked Alaska (112th St, Astoria; 503/325-7414)
The Bay House (5911 SW Hwy 101, Lincoln City; 541/996-3222)
The Loft (315 1st St SE, Bandon; 541/329-0535)
Meridian Restaurant & Bar (Headlands Lodge, 33000 Cape Kiwanda Dr, Pacific City; 503/483-3000)
Nor'Wester Steak & Seafood (10 Harbor Way, Gold Beach; 541/247-2333)
Ona Restaurant and Lounge (131 Hwy 101 N, Yachats; 541/547-6627)
Pelican Brewing Company (33105 Cape Kiwanda Dr, Pacific City; 503/965-7007)
Redfish (517 Jefferson St, Port Orford; 541/366-2200)
Restaurant Beck (Whale Cove Inn, 2345 S Hwy 101, Depoe Bay; 541/765- 3220)
Roseanna's Cafe (1490 Pacific Ave, Oceanside; 503/842-7351)
Tidal Raves Seafood Grill (279 NW Hwy 101, Depoe Bay; 541/765-2995)
The Waterfront Depot Restaurant (1252 Bay St, Florence; 541/902-9100)
Wayfarer Restaurant & Lounge (1190 Pacific Dr, Cannon Beach; 503/436-1108)

Notes

Notes

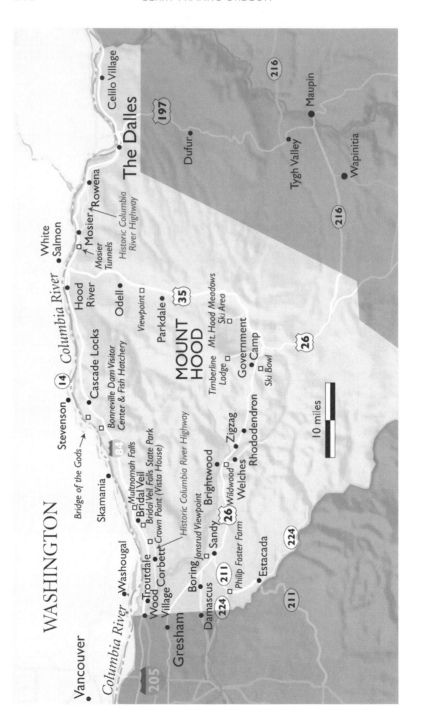

CHAPTER FOUR

Columbia Gorge and Mount Hood

BRIDAL VEIL

Multnomah Falls

50000 Historic Columbia River Hwy   503/695-2372
Visitors Center: Daily: 9-5   multnomahfallslodge.com
Restaurant: Mon-Thu: 9-6; Fri-Sun: 8-8   503/692-2376, ext. 200
Moderate to moderately expensive

Update: Multnomah Falls and Multnomah Falls Lodge (including the restaurant, gift shop, restrooms and U.S. Forest Service information center) have reopened following the now infamous Eagle Creek Fire, which broke out in early September 2017. But as of spring 2018 the trail to the upper falls and other adjacent trails remain closed. The lower viewing platform will remain closed until the next round of repairs is completed. The trails will remain closed until Shady Creek Bridge can be replaced and a complete trail condition assessment can inform repair needs. For the latest on closures, go to www.fs.usda.gov/crgnsa or call the Multnomah Falls Lodge Information Center at 503/695-2372.

A stunning site at any time of the year, this is the Pacific Northwest's most visited natural attraction. Multnomah Falls is Oregon's tallest waterfall and the second-tallest year-round waterfall in the nation. Simon Benson donated the land and money that led to the construction of the famed Benson Bridge; his magnanimous gesture influenced other private and public entities to join the project. The park was dedicated in 1915, and the lodge was completed in 1925. Albert E. Doyle (architect for the Meier & Frank Co. building in downtown Portland) designed the impressive stone and timber building, now home to a visitor center, snack and gift shops and a wonderful restaurant, serving breakfast, lunch and Sunday brunch and dinner. The cuisine at Multnomah Falls is Northwest-inspired with fresh local ingredients.

CASCADE LOCKS

Bonneville Fish Hatchery
70543 NE Herman Loop   541/374-8393
Daily: 7 a.m.-8 p.m. (Mar-Oct); 7-5 (Nov-Feb)
Free   dfw.state.or.us/resources/visitors/bonneville_hatchery.asp
Not surprisingly, the main attraction at this Columbia River hatchery, at the mouth of Tanner Creek, is Herman the Sturgeon. Herman is approaching his 80th birthday and packs almost 500 pounds onto his 11-foot boneless frame. The sturgeon interpretive center offers informational displays and sturgeon viewing. Guests may also walk to the rainbow trout ponds where they will see trophy-size trout, a visitor center for the spawning room and the historic Hatchery Incubation Building. The hatchery rears steelhead, Chinook and Coho salmon. Keep your binoculars handy as birds of prey, songbirds, wading birds and waterfowl are prevalent in this area.

Columbia Gorge Sternwheeler
355 Wanapa St   503/224-3900, 800/224-3901
Seasonal: May-Oct   portlandspirit.com
Expensive
Board this authentic triple-decker paddle wheeler from Marine Park for a memorable sightseeing excursion on the Columbia. There are a number of cruise options (one hour to a half-day, brunch and dinner cruises) to appreciate the natural beauty and historic points of interest along this section of the Columbia Gorge. Northwest cuisine is served on brunch and dinner cruises; snacks and beverages are available at the full-service bar.

East Wind Drive-In
395 NW Wanapa St   541/374-8380
Daily: 7-7 (Fri-Sun till 7:30)   Facebook
Inexpensive
This quaint drive-in got its 15 minutes of fame with a cameo at the end of "Wild," the movie starring Reese Witherspoon who portrayed writer Cheryl Strayed as she hiked the Pacific Crest Trail. So you might have to wait in line a bit longer for its go-to menu item: insanely large ice cream cones. The small soft-serve vanilla, chocolate or twist combination cone is a somewhat manageable six inches. The large version, which is a whopping foot tall and weighs about a pound and a half, is so precarious it's immediate-

ly plopped into a 32-ounce cup. The diner also serves breakfast, burgers, fries, shakes and other drive-in fare.

CORBETT

Vista House
Crown Point, 40700 E Historic Columbia River Hwy 503/695-2240
Daily: 9-6 (summer; other seasonal hours) vistahouse.com
If you drive the Historic Columbia River Highway, it takes you right to the doorstep of the Vista House. Completed in 1917, this octagonal, cliff-top structure was built as a comfort station and viewpoint. These facilities, however, are far from typical. The restrooms are outfitted in elegant marble and mahogany with circular marble stairways leading to the lower level. An extensive restoration completed in 2006 brought this gem back to grandeur. It houses interpretive displays of the region's rich history, a gift shop and an espresso cafe. This is one of the windiest spots in Oregon, so hang on to your hat.

GOVERNMENT CAMP

Collins Lake Resort
88149 E Creek Ridge Road 800/234-6288
Moderate and up collinslakeresort.com
Open all year and geared for the outdoors, this resort is touted as providing luxury Chalets (four to ten people) and Grand Lodges (two or three bedrooms). Mt. Hood Skibowl owner Kirk Hanna is behind the master plan for this 28-acre parcel surrounded by the Mt. Hood National Forest. Snowmobiling, snowshoeing, cross-country skiing, sleigh rides, tubing and sledding are at your winter doorstep. Depart your basecamp via local shuttle buses to Skibowl, Summit Ski Area and Timberline or via car to Mt. Hood Meadows. On your return, enjoy the hot tub, heated pool or sauna or simply stretch out by the fireplace. When the snow melts, you may opt to explore the network of interpretive trails eventually leading to the village. Guests receive VIP discounts for outdoor recreation including three major ski areas and the Mt. Hood Adventure Park (mthoodadventure.com) at Skibowl.

The Glacier Haus Bistro
8817 E Government Camp Loop Road 503/272-3471
Seasonal hours glacierhaus.com
Inexpensive to moderate
This family-owned and -operated restaurant serves authentic Europe-

an comfort food made from fresh ingredients. Classic European dishes include wiener schnitzel, Hungarian beef goulash and sauerbraten. Other notables are homemade pizzas, sandwiches, salads, cakes and pies. These folks have a full-service bar and accept reservations as well as catering requests. The best part is, it's just down the street from Mt. Hood.

Huckleberry Inn

88611 E Government Camp Loop   503/272-3325
Daily: 24 hours   huckleberry-inn.com
Cafe: Inexpensive to moderate
Lodging: Moderate
Huckleberry hotcakes for dinner or at midnight? No problem, Huckleberry Inn is open 24/7. Since 1967 this family restaurant has been a welcoming stop for folks looking for friendly dining in Government Camp. During ski season and holiday weekends, the Huckleberry Inn offers a steak and seafood menu in its cozy, candlelit steakhouse. Fuel up for outdoor activities with a giant maple bar or fresh doughnut; better yet, treat yourself to a refreshing huckleberry milkshake or a slice of delicious homemade huckleberry pie, a la mode, of course. On-premises lodging includes 17 standard and deluxe rooms and a two-bedroom suite with a kitchen and bunk room (sleeps 10).

Mt. Hood Cultural Center & Museum

88900 Government Camp Loop   503/272-3301
Daily: 9-5   mthoodmuseum.org
Free (donations accepted)
Did you know that Government Camp was an encampment in 1849 for a detachment of the U.S. Mounted Rifles on their way to Fort Vancouver from Fort Leavenworth, Kansas? The descriptive name has stayed with this community as it grew first into a summer resort followed by a year-round destination. Today the multi-faceted Mt. Hood Cultural Center & Museum is a repository for Mt. Hood-related collections. Exhibits include natural history, the U.S. Forest Service and management of the Mt. Hood National Forest (including a 1920s ranger's office), artifacts from the Barlow Road section of the Oregon Trail and history of the exploration and development of the area. There is also a fascinating assortment of winter and mountain sports equipment and clothing used since the introduction of winter sports on Mt. Hood in the early 1900s. A gallery features fine arts and artworks by local artists. An interesting sidebar: my cousin, the late Jack Meier of the Mt. Hood Development Association, was a guiding force behind the construction of Timberline Lodge in the 1930s.

Mt. Hood Skibowl

87000 E Hwy 26   503/272-3206
Seasonal   skibowl.com
Fees vary by activity
Good family fun can be found on a visit to one of Oregon's best year-round
resorts. Almost 1,000 acres of snow-covered topography affords alpine skiing (including the largest night-skiing terrain in the country), snowboarding, snowshoeing, cross-country skiing, sleigh rides, snowmobiling, day
and cosmic tubing plus much more. Return in the summer to experience
the Mt. Hood Adventure Park (mthoodadventure.com) when it comes to
life with over 20 mild to extreme attractions for all ages, including the
alpine slide, scenic sky chair, bungee tower, zip line, Indy carts, batting cages, rock climbing wall, miniature and disc golf and mountain biking. The
casual eateries offer welcome and satisfying breathers. This destination is
awesome any time of the year.

Ratskeller Alpine Bar & Pizzeria

88335 E Government Camp Loop   503/272-3635
Sun-Thu: 11-10 (Fri, Sat till midnight)   ratskellerpizzeria.com
Moderate
Here's another winning combination on the mountain: a historic mountain town restaurant/pub with giant high-definition screens showing the
big games, huge beer selection and super pizzas. Highly recommended
dishes include The Rat combo pizza (pepperoni, sausage, salami, mushrooms, onions and black olives); fresh, local grass-fed beef burgers (gigantic) and build-your-own pizzas and calzones. Satisfying food and beverages are served fireside in winter and outdoors in good weather. Closing
time may be later than posted. General manager Jeff DeMerchant leads his
fun-loving, ski-town staff in providing superior service.

HOOD RIVER

Apple Valley Country Store

2363 Tucker Road   541/386-1971
Seasonal   applevaleystore.com
Make a trip to the Hood River Valley for a taste of Oregon's world-famous
fruit featured at Apple Valley Country Store and Bakery. Start with a thick
milkshake and wander the country store to choose among jams, jellies,
butters, syrups, sauces and pie fillings; all made on-site. Mustards, mixes
and sugar-free options are also available. Their scratch pies are a local
favorite, and don't forget to add Tillamook ice cream on top. Further up the
road in Parkdale, the same family operates **Apple Valley BBQ Restau-**

rant and Catering (4956 Baseline Dr, 541/352-3554). It specializes in modestly- priced smoked pork ribs, pulled pork and prime rib dinners on Friday and Saturday. Hours are 11 to 8, Wednesday through Sunday. The meats are smoked with local fruit woods, complemented by side dishes of pear cole slaw and apple-cider baked beans.

Bigfoot Lodge B&B

3747 Pinemont Drive   541/399-4222
Moderate   bigfoot-lodge.com
Views of Mt. Hood, the Hood River Valley and wildlife are just part of the incomparable setting of this 5,000-square-foot custom-built, hand-hewn log lodge. Each of the four guest rooms is warm and inviting and outfitted with quality furnishings and private baths. The Eagle's Nest features a California King bed, private deck, vaulted ceiling and steam shower. The Timberline Room features two queen beds, a jetted tub and covered patio.

ON THE WASHINGTON SIDE OF THE GORGE

Visitors take note: There are many "don't miss" attractions on the Washington side of the Columbia River within minutes of Oregon. Some of these sights are along the historic Lewis and Clark Trail (lewisandclarktrail.com).

GOLDENDALE

Maryhill Museum of Art (35 Maryhill Museum Dr, 509/773-3733, maryhillmuseum.org) was originally built by Samuel Hill as his grand home. Works by Rodin, unique chess sets and European and American paintings are featured. Nearby is the Stonehenge Memorial, a full-scale replica built by Hill. Open mid-March to mid-November.
Maryhill Winery (9774 Hwy 14, 877/627-9445, maryhillwinery.com), established in 2001, is a destination for fine wines and world-class summertime concerts in the 4,000-seat amphitheater. While there, take in spectacular panoramic views, tasting rooms, picnicking, a tour or game of bocce ball.

PASCO

Sacajawea State Park (2503 Sacajawea Park Road, 509/545-2361, parks.state.wa.us/575/sacajawea) is a 284-acre park located at the confluence of the Snake and Columbia rivers. The park's Sacajawea Interpretive Center (seasonal) features exhibits about Sacajawea and the Lewis and Clark Expedition. Park activities include hiking, boating, fishing,

The John Wayne Cowboy Room is rustic with Pendleton decor, and the Mt. Hood Room has Native American accents and can accommodate up to four guests. The lodge is situated on 44 private acres on the edge of the Mt. Hood Wilderness (directions provided with reservation), so there's plenty of room to hike, bike, trail ride, snowshoe or cross-country ski. Five major ski resorts are a short drive away, or you can stay put and simply enjoy the hosts' hospitality. A hearty four-course organic breakfast is prepared each morning.

Boda's Kitchen
404 Oak St   541/386-9876
Daily: 11-7   bodaskitchen.com
Moderate
Sandwiches from gourmet delis are innovative, often inspired by fresh, local ingredients and more often than not, more than a mouthful. Such is

---

swimming, waterskiing, birdwatching, wildlife viewing and horseshoe pits.

SKAMANIA
Beacon Rock State Park (34841 SR 14, 509/427-8265, parks.state. wa.us/474/beacon-rock) offers camping and a full range of day-use outdoor recreation activities such as hiking, mountain biking, rock climbing, paddling, fishing and boating on the Columbia River.

STEVENSON
Columbia Gorge Interpretive Center Museum (990 SW Rock Creek Dr, 509/427-8211, columbiagorge.org) features human and natural history of the Gorge. Exhibits and artifacts illuminate ancient and traditional Native American life in the area and include pictographs, stone tools and baskets. The huge fish wheel, logging equipment and railroad machinery provide a fascinating look at the region's early history.

Skamania Lodge (1131 SW Skamania Lodge Way, 509/427-7700, skamania.com) is across the Bridge of the Gods from Cascade Locks. There are 254 guest rooms with river and mountain views, tree houses, a golf course, outdoor zip lines and aerial park, amphitheater, spa and restaurants.

the case with creations from Boda's Kitchen. A tasty sampling includes a Cubano panini on local rustic wheat bread, stuffed with Cuban seasoned roast pork loin, ham and cheese. Local favorites include Oregon-caught albacore tuna salad wrapped in a spinach tortilla and a turkey masterpiece featuring roasted turkey breast, house-made cranberry chutney, greens and cheese on local rustic wheat. Pickles made in-house accompany each sandwich; daily specials and wholesome soups and salads are also available. Boxed lunches are a specialty and include a sandwich, chips and jumbo cookie.

Celilo Restaurant and Bar

16 Oak St   541/386-5710
Daily: 5-close (dinner); Fri-Sun: 11:30-3 (lunch)   celilorestaurant.com
Moderate

Local, organic and sustainable are the by-words at contemporary Celilo where great healthy foods are crafted. From the ever-changing menu, a bowl of housemade soup or hazelnut and blue cheese salad are tasty starters for lunch or dinner. A varied selection of lunchtime sandwiches is accompanied by organic mixed greens or fries. For dinner, beef, fish, pasta, poultry and pork options are expertly and creatively prepared to showcase the regional bounty; occasional wine dinners masterfully pair outstanding Northwest wines with Celilo's best menus. Dessert showcases local fruits that are superb in delicious sorbets, tarts and cakes, or you may prefer a cheese course with regional touches. Busy chef Ben Stenn also conducts popular cooking classes.

Chemistry Jewelry

310 Oak St   541/386-7069
Daily: 10-6 (Sun till 5)   chemistryjewelry.com

This inviting gallery shows handcrafted jewelry curated from outstanding local talent as well some of the most famous and sought-after artists in the world. Designs are traditional and contemporary, casual and elegant and are made using gems, jewels, pearls and turquoise. It's a great place to buy a gift or indulge yourself.

Columbia Cliff Villas

3880 Westcliff Dr   866/912-8366
Moderate and up   columbiacliffvillas.com

This fabulous setting and layout are ideal for retreats, romantic getaways and family gatherings. A stay here yields ultra-comfortable digs and magnificent river and mountain views. Thirty-seven luxury rooms and suites rest above a 208-foot waterfall. Accommodations in this condominium hotel incorporate everything from European-style hotel rooms up to one- and three-bedroom adjoining villa and penthouse suites. Amenities vary by room and may include private decks (some look straight down the cliffs to the Columbia River), gas fireplaces, marble and tile walk-in showers, soaking tubs and gourmet kitchens.

Columbia Gorge Hotel

4000 Westcliff Dr — 541/386-5566, 800/345-1921

Moderate to expensive — columbiagorgehotel.com

The Columbia Gorge Hotel opened in 1921 as a haven for guests traveling by steamboat. Highway promoter Simon Benson purchased the hotel in 1920 with dreams of grandeur to reward motorists journeying along the Columbia Gorge Scenic Highway. The hotel was home away from home to such distinguished guests as Presidents Franklin Roosevelt and Calvin Coolidge and film legends Myrna Loy, Jane Powell and Rudolph Valentino. Through the years it fell in and out of prosperity, at one time functioning as a retirement home. Fortunately, a major restoration project propelled the now legendary hotel back to its stately beauty. There are 40 cozy and charming guest rooms furnished with either wood-carved or canopy beds, all with views of the Gorge or vibrant manicured gardens and lawns and the hotel's own 208-foot Wah Gwin Gwin Falls. It is truly a romantic, restful destination. Diners at **Simon's Cliff House** have much to enjoy, starting with the magnificent view. There are plenty of breakfast choices. Soups, salads and hot or cold specialty sandwiches make a fine lunch, especially when served with the unique Simon's fries or sweet potato fries. Dinner starts with housemade herb garlic bread, followed by appetizers and gourmet entrees fit for screen legends. The Pièce de Résistance is the Sunday brunch: seven courses beginning with champagne and progressing through the pastry chef's special scones, a granola and yogurt parfait, seasonal fruit, an assortment of cheeses, a choice of chef's entrees and culminating with coffee, pastries and petits-desserts.

Full Sail Brewing

506 Columbia St — 541/386-2247

Daily: 11-9 (brew pub) — fullsailbrewing.com

Moderate

Full Sail Brewing operates a brewery and brew pub in a building that formerly housed the Diamond Fruit Co. The cannery is gone, but the site is still bustling with dozens of skilled brewery specialists working full speed ahead at this independent enterprise crafting award-winning beers. Free brewery tours are conducted daily from 1 to 4 p.m. during the summer months and Friday through Sunday during the winter (see website for more info). Brewery products are often used in the bill of fare: Session Lager-battered wild Alaskan salmon with fries and slaw, salads and Sesíon Cerveza mac and cheese featuring Cavatappi pasta are served all day. Sweet-tooth tamers include Imperial Stout brownies and Bourbon Beer Tillamook ice cream floats. The panorama of the Columbia River from the rooftop deck is awesome, making this a great stop to unwind and savor brews and views.

G. Williker's Toy Shoppe
202 Oak St   541/387-2229
Mon-Sat: 10-6; Sun: 10-5   gwtoyshoppe.com
I recall spending many hours as a youngster wandering the toy department in my family's department store, eyeing the newest colorful toys and games. To this day, I check out toy stores on my travels. Every inch of this delightful shop is stocked with toys of every kind. There are plush animals, puzzles and games, small items for stocking stuffers, an entire wall of Lego products, chemistry sets, doll houses (and dolls), books and a bit of everything else. The merchandise mix includes the latest finds, nostalgic favorites and an irresistible candy counter.

The Gorge White House
2265 Hwy 35   541/386-2828
Daily: 10-7 (Jun-Sep); Fri-Mon: 10-6 (Apr, May, Oct)
Other seasonal hours   thegorgewhitehouse.com
This attraction is truly an event as it offers so many things to do. Once a private residence and still surrounded by orchards, this Dutch Colonial Revival landmark offers five acres of cut flower fields and u-pick fruit, local wine, hard cider and beer tasting, local fruit sales, a farm fresh gourmet food cart, local artwork, gifts and more. Taste wine and cider in the converted old farm shop while taking in stellar double mountain and east hill views.

Hood River Inn
1108 E Marina Way   541/386-2200, 800/828-7873
Moderate to expensive   hoodriverinn.com
This Best Western Plus-branded inn features 194 guest rooms, many with small, private balconies and scenic views of the Columbia River and the Hood River Bridge that connects to White Salmon, Washington. With several room types, suite types and Deluxe Suites available, there are accommodations for every budget. Rooms and suites are well-appointed with cable television, refrigerators, free Wi-Fi, microwave ovens and coffeemak-

ers, among many features. Site amenities include a fitness center, outdoor heated pool, spa and sauna. For dining and nightlife there is the popular Riverside restaurant and Cebu Lounge (see separate write-up in this section).

Hood River Lavender Farms

3801 Straight Hill Road 541/490-5657
Seasonal hoodriverlavender.com

Finding calm in your busy everyday life can be difficult. Here's a suggestion: surrounded yourself with fragrant lavender fields on the volcanic slopes with mountain views. In July Hood River Lavender Farms holds the Lavender Daze Festival (hoodriverlavender.com), which features arts, crafts, food and wine, face painting and live music. Whether you visit at festival time or pass through at another time, pick up some high quality organic lavender essential oil to ease physical and emotional stress. The retail farm not only grows 75 varieties of lavender available for picking seasonally, but it also uses lavender in crafts and products that are offered for sale at the farm and online.

Hood River Vineyards and Winery

4693 Westwood Dr 541/386-3772
Daily: 11-5 (Jun-Oct);
Thu-Mon: 11-5 (Nov-May) hoodrivervineyardsandwinery.com

Wineries and craft breweries are more than plentiful. It would take more than a weekend to take in the vast variety, but tasting rooms, brew pubs and most restaurants include these local beverages on their menus. Founded in 1981, this winery is the Gorge's oldest and specializes mainly in estate grown red, white and fruit wines; ports and sherry, too.

Mount Hood Railroad

110 Railroad St 541/386-3556, 800/872-4661
Seasonal mthoodrr.com
Expensive

For more than 100 years, this train has chugged through the picturesque Hood River Valley. Depending on the season, rail excursions depart from the Mount Hood Railroad depot for Parkdale near the base of Mt. Hood. Murder mystery dinners and re-enacted train robberies are popular special events. Kids anxiously await the Polar Express excursion to the North Pole in November and December. The round-trip journey re-creates the Polar Express storyline and includes hot cocoa, treats and a visit from Santa Claus. Food and beverages are available on all trips; call for information about Sunday champagne brunch.

FOREST SERVICE FIRE LOOKOUTS
For a unique getaway experience, U.S. Forest Service fire lookouts and cabins (firelookout.org/lookout-rentals) are available for seasonal (and economical) campouts. Amenities (bathrooms, cooking facilities, running water) vary by location, so be sure to read descriptions carefully before renting; most are remote and require packing in your gear. Availability varies seasonally and whether the lookouts are used by the Forest Service for active fire detection. Here's a sampling of locations:

Mt. Hood National Forest
Clear Lake Cabin Lookout
Fivemile Butte Lookout
Flag Point Lookout

Oak Street Hotel

610 Oak St   541/386-3845
Moderate   oakstreethotel.com

The Oak Street Hotel is a nine-room boutique hotel, centrally located and within walking distance to fine dining and shopping. The comfortable 1909 home has been adapted to include modern amenities in each of the unique guest rooms. Rooms may have views of the Columbia River, courtyard or Oak Street. The hotel offers a wheelchair-accessible room and dog-friendly rooms. The farm-to-table breakfast includes housemade sweet or savory pie, fruits, eggs, vegetables and herbs from the family farm. Oak Street Hotel also offers vacation home rentals of varying sizes; check the website for mention of Gorge Escape Vacation Homes.

pFriem Family Brewers

707 Portway Ave, Suite 101   541/321-0490
Daily: 11:30-9   pfriembeer.com
Inexpensive to moderate

How does one decide on the best burger? Personally, I like to keep it simple — great tasting, high quality beef without too many toppings that overpower the flavor of the patty. Others require their burger to be served with a refreshing, ice cold beer on the side; pFriem Family Brewers couldn't agree more. Their popular Mt. Shadow burger is made up of housemade pimento cheese, bread and butter pickles, tomato, lettuce, onion and garlic aioli. Pair it with the award-winning Pilsner, IPA or Winter Ale while soaking up views of the Columbia River inside or around the outdoor fire pit; you may have just become a regular. Vegetarian? No problem — their menu includes a tasty veggie burger along with a small selection of pub grub, samplers as well as some healthier alternatives; ingredients are seasonal and locally sourced.

The Pines Tasting Room
202 Cascade Ave, Suite B   541/993-8301
Daily: Hours vary   thepinesvineyard.com
Lonnie Wright, owner of The Pines 1852 in The Dalles, has been working and expanding the century-old vine zinfandel since 1982. Originally planted by an Italian immigrant, the vineyard has consistently yielded high-quality wine grapes. The tasting room offers boutique wines in a comfortable space with a large cherry wood bar, bistro seating and living room area. A giant garage door rolls up in fair weather for indoor/outdoor tasting. Guests needing overnight accommodations can rent The Pines Cottage (5450 Mill Creek Road, The Dalles, 541/993-8300) in the peaceful surroundings of the vineyard estate just up the highway in The Dalles. Rent the entire cottage (three bedrooms and a shared bath, kitchen and living areas) or individual bedrooms through Airbnb.

Riverside
1108 E Marina Dr   541/386-4410
Breakfast, Lunch, Dinner: Daily   riversidehoodriver.com
Moderate to expensive
Hungry travelers dining at Riverside are practically guaranteed a great view of the Columbia River, whether from the dining room, lounge or outdoor deck. But Hood River's only riverfront restaurant has more to offer — namely some of the best food in town. Chef Mark DeResta cooks up locally-sourced Northwest cuisine and serves it with an Italian flair. Signature breakfast items include a housemade cinnamon roll (a Sunday special), corned beef hash browns and a popular veggie bowl. The lunch menu includes a variety of handmade soups, salads, sandwiches and entrees such as fish and chips, liver and onions, and baked pasta. A similar mix is offered for dinner. Braised short ribs, unique pasta creations, locally sourced Chinook salmon, sea scallops and lamb chops are a few of the featured dinner specialties that change seasonally. Cebu Lounge, known throughout the Gorge for its great happy hour specials, offers the complete restaurant menu and its award-winning wine list that includes around 200 selections, many local. All of this is found at the Best Western Plus branded Hood River Inn (hoodriverinn.com). No other hotel in the area offers such a complete combination of amenities. For guests at the inn, Riverside's full-service sit down breakfast is included with most rate plans.

Romuls West

315 Oak St   541/436-4444
Daily: 4-close   romuls.com
Moderate

Romul and Lillie Grivov are experienced restaurateurs; they operated another restaurant by the same name for a dozen years before opening a new location in Hood River. Tantalizing aromas from slow-cooked Pomodoro and Bolognese sauces permeate the restaurant and hint at the Italian/Mediterranean cuisine. Cooked-to-order dishes such as eggplant parmigiana, veal piccata and lemon caper chicken may take a while to prepare, but are worth the wait. Chef Romul turns out homemade meatballs, pastas, gelato, desserts and the best robust lasagna. People travel to this house specifically for the scrumptious layers of sausage, mushrooms, olives and roasted red pepper sauce; daily specials feature seasonal ingredients from the land and sea. Patio seating is available in warmer months.

The Ruddy Duck

504 Oak St   541/386-5050
Mon-Sat: 9-6; Sun: 10-6   ruddyduckstore.com

This 1893 two-story house hosts a family-run mini-department store. You'll find high quality, trendsetting casual attire; men's, women's and kids' clothing and shoes. Just-right accessories finish the look; sunglasses, scarves, headwear, bags and jewelry. Many items are acquired from the proprietor's trips around the globe. Merchandise reflects the Gorge lifestyle and is sold at affordable prices. After shopping, or just because, relax on the lawn with a cone or fresh huckleberry shake from next-door enterprise, Mike's Ice Cream (541/386-6260, mikesicecream.com). This sister operation is open seasonally and serves Prince Pückler's gourmet ice cream.

Sakura Ridge

5601 York Hill Dr   541/386-2636
Moderate and up   sakuraridge.com

Deanna and John Joyer operate this secluded bed and breakfast at the end of a short gravel road six miles outside of Hood River. They also operate an 83-acre organic farm where they grow pears, berries, vegetables and flowers and raise chickens, sheep and honey bees. Guests can participate in the farm experience or just settle into an Adirondack chair to admire the fruits of someone else's labor. Three of the five guest rooms offer spectacular views of Mt. Hood from private patios; other rooms provide views of the valley or orchard. The Northwest-style accommodations are well-appointed, comfortable and peaceful. Sakura Ridge specializes in preparing the farm's organic abundance for breakfast and will accommodate special diet requirements upon prior request. Other options include ploughman's platter, picnic basket, cooking classes or an opportunity in the summer to work the bees with John; advance arrangement and additional costs apply. A minimum two-night stay is required April through October.

Simon's Cliff House

4000 Westcliff Dr   541/386-5566
Daily: 7 a.m.-9 p.m.   columbiagorgehotel.com
Moderate to moderately expensive
(See details with Columbia Gorge Hotel, in Hood River)

Solstice Wood Fire Cafe & Bar

501 Portway Ave   541/436-0800
Daily: 11-8:30 (Fri, Sat till 9; closed Tue in winter)   solsticewoodfirecafe.com
Moderate

Talk about inventive pizza! Solstice has garnered a lot of attention with its Country Girl Cherry pizza — a unique combination of cherries from the Columbia River Gorge paired with chorizo sausage and goat cheese, topped off with a dash of rosemary and thyme. Not inventive enough? There are many others, or build your own from the menu's long list of meat, cheese and veggie toppings. Owners Suzanne and Aaron Baumhackl believe in sourcing food from local farmers, ranchers and purveyors to bring customers good organic food (with many gluten-free and vegan options) at a fair price. Although pizza baked in a wood-fired Italian oven is their specialty, they have lunch (served 11-4) and dinner menus that also feature small plates, salads (try the Siragusa pear salad), seasonal soups and pastas/entrees such as their house-made spaghetti with Dungeness crab. It doesn't end there. They have a full bar with culinary-inspired cocktails, rotating local microbrews, hard cider and a house wine to enjoy in the cafe or on the patio. They also offer a menu and play area for kids.

Stonehedge Gardens

3405 Wine Country Ave   541/386-3940
Daily: 5-close   stonehedgeweddings.com
Moderate and up

This charming dinner house is situated on seven acres of spectacular gardens and terraces. Indoors, a fireplace, cozy tables and wood-paneled walls create a romantic setting. The alfresco site is a popular wedding venue; the ceremonial area is cleverly framed with heart-shaped shrubbery. Shawna and Mike Caldwell's gourmet menu features delicious specials such as authentic French onion soup, halibut and rack of lamb.

Regular menu offerings include such tempting plates as a garlic mushroom dish, Thai-style crab cakes, spicy peanut chicken, steak Diane, wild salmon and pork scaloppini. Gluten-free gourmet entrees, housemade dinner rolls, stocks and sauces are also specialties. For dessert, try the flaming bread pudding topped with crème brûlée.

Western Antique Aeroplane & Automobile Museum

1600 Air Museum Road   541/308-1600
Daily: 9-5   waaamuseum.org
Reasonable

This fascinating museum houses one of the largest collections of flying antique airplanes and operating antique automobiles in the country. It showcases over 300 working planes, cars, motorcycles, military jeeps and tractors. Volunteers are always tinkering on engines, polishing chrome and ensuring that the collection is in functioning order. For added enjoyment, plan a visit on the second Saturday of the month when proud drivers take the antique cars out for a spin (weather permitting) offering rides between 10:30 a.m. and 2 p.m. Allow plenty of time to partake in the monthly cookout and view the demonstrations.

MOSIER

Three Sleeps Vineyard B&B

1600 Carroll Road   541/478-0143, 541/490-5404
Moderate   threesleepsvineyardbandb.com

Enjoy a welcoming evening taste of Dominio IV wine (dominiowines.com) with owners Liz and Glenn Bartholomew at their manicured environs. The accommodation overlooks the Dominio Estate Vineyard and Mt. Adams in the distance; take a vineyard tour if you'd like. Choose from either a king or queen room, each with a private entrance and bath and a patio where world-class views are yours; arrangements for in-room massages are gladly made. The business name originates from the Lewis and Clark expedition when explorers asked how far it was to the ocean. Native Americans replied "three sleeps."

MT. HOOD

Mt. Hood Meadows

14040 Hwy 35   503/337-2222
Seasonal   skihood.com

Locals call it "Meadows;" the premier ski area on the mountain, with 2,150 skiable acres, 11 lifts and the widest variety of skiing for all abilities. When conditions cooperate, powder hounds will appreciate Heather Canyon, which is like its own separate ski area - endlessly steep pitches of powder into the spectacular Canyon. There's an additional 1,700 vertical feet for hikers who want to drop into the double blacks of Super Bowl above Heather, bringing the total vertical available in just one run to almost 4,500 feet. The location on the southeast flank of the mountain is sunnier and more wind-protected than the south-facing slope, resulting in broader and more diverse downhill opportunities. As a day area so close to Portland (90 driving minutes away), weekends and school vacations can bring huge crowds; consider a mid-week visit. Energizing and delicious dining options in the South and North lodges include sit-down service at the Alpenstube Restaurant and Vertical Restaurant and Sports Bar and two quick, casual eateries. On the slopes, Mazot serves bistro fare at 6,000 feet, where the view is awesome. Additional services incorporate ski and snowboard schools and Nordic and demo centers.

Mt. Hood Organic Farms

7130 Smullin Dr   541/352-7492, 541/352-7123
Seasonal   mthoodorganicfarms.com

Apples and pears fresh from the orchard are the specialty of Mt. Hood Organic Farms, where crops are biodynamically grown. This was the first farm in the Hood River Valley to receive full organic certification and is the largest certified biodynamic orchard in the country. Brady and John Jacobson raise over a million pounds of apples and pears each year. All told, there are nearly 100 varieties; the selection varies as orchards mature

HYDROPOWER

An interesting and educational stop is one of the visitor centers at **Bonneville Lock and Dam**. On the Oregon side, the Bradford Island Visitor Center (Cascade Locks, 541/374-8820, nwp.usace. army.mil/bonneville) has four floors open to visitors and includes interpretive displays about hydropower, salmon migration, local history and geology. The rooftop view of the spillway is impressive. Inside, visitors can view a hydroelectric powerhouse and observe salmon and sturgeon underwater as they swim past windows in the fish ladder. The Navigation Lock Visitor Center (541/374-8344) tells the story of inland commercial navigation and offers views of a working lock. If you are on the Washington shore, check out the Washington Shore Visitor Center (509/427-4281) for another opportunity to see inside a working powerhouse and fish ladder on Cascades Island.

and they are replaced with new stock. Only fruits from their 200-acre farm are sold at the farm stand. Ask about their champagne-style hard cider. The farm is also a popular destination for a picturesque wedding, with farm-to-table wedding dinners. The gardens, architecture and incredible views are worth the drive.

PARKDALE

Apple Valley BBQ Restaurant and Catering

4956 Baseline Dr   541/352-3554
Wed-Sun:11-8   applevaleybbq.com
Moderate
(See details with Apple Valley Country Store, Hood River)

Old Parkdale Inn Bed & Breakfast

4932 Baseline Dr   541/352-5551
Moderate   hoodriverlodging.com
Three guest rooms reflect Oregon's state symbols: Meadowlark, Douglas fir and Chinook; the latter two are suites with separate living rooms. All are furnished with queen beds and private baths, flat-screen televisions, microwaves, refrigerators and Internet access. Breakfasts feature famous Hood River fruits and produce, served in the dining room or delivered to your room. The deck or picturesque gardens are tranquil morning coffee venues. The innkeepers have created several packages ranging from romantic seclusion to outdoor adventures.

RHODODENDRON

Mt. Hood Roasters

73451 E Hwy 26   503/622-6574
Daily: 8-5   mthoodroasters.com
As you enter Mt. Hood Roasters you are sure to be energized by the aroma of their air-roasted coffee. The business is passionate about quality over quantity, always using 100% Arabica coffee beans. Coffee is handcrafted on site and each ten-pound batch of coffee is guaranteed to be rich in flavor and smooth in taste. Mt. Hood Roasters is a quaint shop with a table or two outdoors to enjoy a pastry with your afternoon coffee. Call ahead for a possible staff tour of the facility. Their great reputation has allowed them to distribute gourmet coffee to restaurants, professional offices and other retail operations; remember them when searching for a gift for the coffee lover in your life. Coffee is available for purchase in-store and online; customize your purchase with a private label, picture or logo.

Zigzag Mountain Cafe

70171 E Hwy 26   503/622-7681
Mon-Fri: 7-2 (Sat, Sun till 6)   Facebook
Inexpensive
Many travelers making a trek to Mt. Hood stop regularly at the rustic Zigzag Mountain Cafe. The cafe cooks up feel-good favorites at breakfast and
lunch such as housemade biscuits and jam, chicken noodle soup, stew and
chili. Enjoy hot cocoa on the mezzanine, the tables overlooking Bear Creek
or near the large stone fireplace.

SANDY

Calamity Jane's Hamburger Parlor

42015 SE Hwy 26   503/668-7817
Daily: 11-9 (Fri, Sat till 10)   Facebook
Moderate
The Western façade is appropriate for this calorie-laden emporium named
for the famous 19th century frontierswoman. Many a hungry skier and
hiker have eaten here on their way to and from the Mt. Hood area. The
restaurant's burgers (over 50 variations) are claimed to be award-winning
and world renowned. Other comfort foods on the menu include pot roast,
chicken dishes, fish and chips, sandwiches and pizza burgers — all in large
portions.

The Hidden Woods Bed & Breakfast

19380 E Summertime Dr   503/622-5754
Moderate   thehiddenwoods.com
Guests here will spend a memorable night (or longer) in a private two-bedroom log cabin with rustic charm and modern conveniences. The relaxed
setting (ten miles east of Sandy) includes beautiful gardens, a trail to the
nearby Sandy River, a contemplative trout pond and a deck with a hot tub
and fire pit. Come evening, unwind in front of the living room's rock fireplace and prepare your favorite dinner in the well-appointed kitchen. A
splendid breakfast is served in the hosts' log home just a short walk from
the guest cabin. (Cash or checks only; no pets or children under 8)

Joe's Donut Shop

39230 Pioneer Blvd   503/668-7215
Mon-Fri: 4 a.m.-5 p.m.; Sat, Sun: 5-5   joes-donuts.com
On your way to the mountain, stop in at this local landmark for a brac-
ing cup of coffee to accompany the freshest pastries around. You'll want
apple fritters, maple bars and scrumptious doughnuts (made with the

same doughnut production technology since 1974). Weekend customers often find themselves choosing among baked pastries like strudels, filled croissants, Danish and turnovers. Look for the recognizable red and white block front building.

Rainbow Trout Farm

52560 E Sylvan Dr   503/622-5223
Daily: 9-5 (Apr, May); 8-6 (Jun-Oct)   rainbowtroutfarm.com
Inexpensive and up

Visit this Sandy trout farm for a fishing excursion that requires no fishing license. Bring your own rod and reel or use theirs. There are four ponds open, and the fish range in size from small to lunkers. The charge is based on the size of the fish caught. Their staff will gladly clean your fish. This is a great site for group outings, so call for group reservations. The farm is wheelchair accessible.

Sandy Salmon Bed & Breakfast Lodge

61661 E Hwy 26   503/622-6699
Expensive   sandysalmon.com

This 6,000-square-foot log building sits on a bluff some 60 feet above the confluence of the Sandy and Salmon rivers. Choose from four guest rooms with private bathrooms, including two with a Jacuzzi tub that could serve as a romantic bridal suite; other suites have outdoor decks and all feature native Oregon woods. The beautiful lodge hideaway also offers hearty breakfasts and plenty of recreation, including games around the comfortable stone fireplace, a theater room with a 73-inch TV screen and a handcrafted pool table. Artistic wood carvings, a koi pond, waterfall and massive antler chandelier enhance the interior of the lodge's ambience. The vistas around this five-acre setting are breathtaking and enjoyed from the relaxing decks or while fishing, rafting, hiking, mountain biking and skiing — all nearby.

Tollgate Inn Restaurant & Bakery

38100 Hwy 26   visittollgate.com
Restaurant: Daily: 6 a.m.-10 p.m.   503/668-8456
Bakery: Daily: hours vary   503/826-1009
Moderate

The menu is large and portions are satisfying at this destination stop for travelers in the Mt. Hood corridor. Breakfast classics are built around three eggs and sided with hash browns, home fries, toast, pancakes or fruit; omelets are prepared with meats, cheese, vegetables and all the trimmings. Breakfast is served till 11:30 Monday to Friday; till 12:30 Saturday and Sunday. The sandwich choices include burgers (nine variations) and a tasty assortment of BLTs, tuna and turkey melts, clubs, Reubens and an eight-ounce New York steak fully-loaded on a homemade hoagie roll. Specialties like pot roast, chicken-fried steak, liver and onions and favorites such as chicken pot pie, roasted turkey dinner and grilled pork chops are on the dinner menu, as well as char-broiled steaks and prime rib (Thursday through Saturday). This is home-style cooking in a homey atmosphere complete with a big stone fireplace to warm your bones after a trek through the snow. Also here is Two Mike's Saloon, serving great cocktails, beer and wine. The Tollgate Bakery is next-door, where it turns out breads, pastries, cakes, pies, muffins and cookies to go along with freshly-made soups, sandwiches and espresso drinks; the irresistible baked goods are also served in the restaurant. The bakery is open Monday to Thursday 6 a.m.-9 p.m. (till 10 Friday); 7 a.m.-10 p.m. Saturday and 7 a.m.-9 p.m. Sunday.

THE DALLES

Baldwin Saloon

205 Court St   541/296-5666
Mon-Thu: 11-9 (Fri, Sat till 10)   baldwinsaloon.com
Moderate

Originally opened in 1876, the business at this saloon was primarily provided by railroad and Columbia River activity. The building has morphed through many entrepreneurial uses, and in 1991 Tracy and Mark Linebarger purchased and restored it, adding a pleasant outdoor patio. Now it's a great place to browse the acquired antiques and artwork while enjoying lunch or dinner. The large and varied menu of soups, salads, sandwiches, burgers, seafood, steaks and pasta dishes is fresh and homemade. Standouts are the French onion soup topped with Gruyere cheese and old-fashioned bread pudding with blueberries and whipped cream.

Big Jim's Drive-In

2938 E 2nd St   541/298-5051
Daily: 10-9 (till 10 in summer)   bigjimsdrivein.com
Inexpensive

Big Jim's has been the spot in The Dalles since 1966 for great tasting burgers, fresh fruit milkshakes, fish and chips, chicken strips and huge salads made fresh daily. Hungry burger lovers have lots of flavors and sizes from which to choose as well as other sandwiches and dozens of hard ice cream concoctions to quell hunger pangs. This local landmark offers inside dining, an enjoyable fresh-air patio and drive-through service; call-in orders are welcome.

Celilo Inn

3550 E 2nd St541/769-0001

Inexpensive and upceliloinn.com

From its hillside perch, this updated circa-1950 motel provides wondrous views. Accommodations include free Wi-Fi in all rooms, which range from a deluxe family suite (with both queen- and king-size beds), king suites, junior king rooms and queen rooms (non-view rooms). Ease into your stay with a complimentary glass of local wine at check in. Pastries, granola and fruit are presented early mornings and a 24-hour coffee bar satisfies caf-

---

FAMILY ACTIVITIES IN THE GORGE/MT. HOOD AREA

BRIDAL VEIL
Multnomah Falls (503/695-2372, fs.fed.us/visit/destination/multnomah-falls): Iconic lodge; spectacular hiking and scenery, however some of the trails and viewing areas may be inaccessible due to the Eagle Creek Fire. Check the website for updated information.

CASCADE LOCKS
Bonneville Lock and Dam (541/374-8820, nwp.usace.army.mil/bonneville): visitor centers explaining hydropower, salmon migration, local history, navigational locks and more
Columbia Gorge Sternwheeler (Marine Park, 503/224-3900, portlandspirit.com): sightseeing excursions; brunch and dinner options (seasonal)

CORBETT
Vista House (Crown Point, 40700 E Historic Columbia River Hwy; 503/695-2240; vistahouse.com): one of the windiest spots in Oregon, interpretive historical displays; stunning Gorge views

GOVERNMENT CAMP
Mt. Hood Cultural Center & Museum (88900 Government Camp Loop, 503/272-3301): Mt. Hood related items
Mt. Hood Skibowl (87000 E Hwy 26, 503/272-3206, skibowl.com): skiing, snowboarding, snowshoeing, night skiing, tubing; summer alpine slide, sky chair, bungee tower, miniature and disc golf and more

feine cravings. An outdoor patio with fire pit, fitness facility with a view, seasonal outdoor pool and wine tasting packages are nice additions to this property.

The Columbia Gorge Discovery Center & Museum

5000 Discovery Dr   541/296-8600
Daily: 9-5   gorgediscovery.org
Nominal

Have you ever wondered how the Gorge was formed? Check out the Ice Age exhibit when you begin your journey through this beautiful museum adjacent to the Columbia River. Interactive displays depict the past; live birds of prey are featured in the center's raptor program. Learn how this

---

HOOD RIVER

Hood River WaterPlay (1108 E Marina Way, 541/386-9463, hoodriverwaterplay.com): lessons and rentals; windsurfing, Hobie sailing, stand up paddleboarding, kayaking, jet ski rentals

Mount Hood Railroad (110 Railroad Ave, 541/386-3556, mthoodrr. com): sightseeing excursions, murder mystery dinners, Western train robbery, holiday Polar Express trips

MT. HOOD

Mt. Hood Meadows Ski Resort (14040 Hwy 35, 503/337-2222, skihood.com): 11 lifts, 85 runs, seasonal

SANDY

Rainbow Trout Farm (52560 E Sylvan Dr, 503/622-5223): no fishing license required; four trout ponds

THE DALLES

The Columbia Gorge Discovery Center & Museum (5000 Discovery Dr, 541/296-8600, gorgediscovery.org): interactive interpretive center for the Columbia Gorge National Scenic Area and Wasco County

TIMBERLINE

Timberline Lodge & Ski Area (27500 E Timberline Road, 503/272-3311, timberlinelodge.com): world-class skiing, iconic lodge

area was shaped and influenced by early inhabitants, the Lewis and Clark expedition and settlers along the Oregon Trail. Catch a glimpse of Wasco County in a re-created setting. The award-winning building and location are magnificent, surrounded by phenomenal vistas, trails, a pond and overlooks; don't miss the nature walk.

Cousins Country Inn
2114 W 6th St   541/298-5161, 800/848-9378
Inexpensive to moderate   cousinscountryinn.com
One look at this welcoming complex beckons travelers to stop in for a meal or overnight respite. All of the rooms are outfitted with a refrigerator, microwave, DVD player and coffeemaker; a seasonal outdoor pool and hot tub are on-site. In addition to 97 deluxe accommodations, eight rooms are enhanced with large showers (three showerheads), fireplaces, patios, balconies and sundecks. Feel free to dip into the large jar of homemade cookies at the front desk where you can request a complimentary pass to The Dalles Fitness Club. An expansive menu of wonderful comfort food is a few steps away all day, every day at **Cousins Restaurant & Saloon** (cousinsthedalles.com). Generous portions of homemade chicken pot pie, loaded chicken salad, old-fashioned meatloaf, pot roast sandwiches and fresh, gigantic cinnamon rolls are sure to please anyone. Breakfast is served all day, and a fun saloon menu of appetizers and libations satisfies the of-age group. As the name implies, this is a family-friendly place. The proprietor is Escape Lodging.

Fairfield Inn and Suites, The Dalles
2014 W 7th St   541/769-0753
Moderate   marriott.com
Offering amenities for both leisure and business travelers, this Marriott branded hotel's location is prime for touring wineries and other attractions and participating in outdoor activities such as wind surfing and Deschutes River fishing. It's also near the Google Data Center, the Bonneville Power Administration, Insitu and Columbia Gorge Community College. Thoughtfully designed rooms and suites are complemented with amenities like an indoor pool, exercise room and free Wi-Fi throughout the hotel. A free breakfast is offered daily and includes choices of eggs, sausage, oatmeal, fresh fruit and yogurt.

Fort Dalles Museum
500 W 15th St   541/296-4547
Daily: 10-5 (Mar-Nov); by appointment (Dec-Feb)   fortdallesmuseum.org
Nominal (6 and under free)
This is one of Oregon's oldest history museums, housed in the former

Surgeon's Quarters of Fort Dalles, a U.S. Army outpost from 1850 to 1860. The museum was founded in 1905 with collections dating back to that time, as well as new additions on display. Early furniture, Native American artifacts, clothing, kitchen items, cookware, books and photographs of the area's people and places are spread throughout the two-story building. Saddles and guns are displayed in an upstairs bedroom. Over 30 antique wagons and vehicles are housed in two buildings on the property; a stage coach, mail wagon, horse-drawn hearses, surreys, buses, road-building equipment and early automobiles are among the collection of items with local connections. The Anderson Homestead was relocated from nearby Pleasant Ridge to property across the street from the main museum; the log home, granary and two-story barn were restored to original condition. Admission includes a welcome and orientation to the complex; peruse the museum and grounds at your own pace.

Momma Jane's Pancake House
900 W 6th St   541/296-6611
Daily: 6-2   Facebook
Inexpensive
This pancake house serves breakfasts sure to please the heartiest of eaters. Omelets and scrambles are filled with delicious cheese combinations, breakfast meats and vegetables and are served with a choice of hash browns, home fries or fruit and toast, biscuits and gravy or all-you-can-eat pancakes. Specialty pancakes are filled with fruits, berries, nuts and other good things; squirrel pancakes feature sliced almonds and homemade honey-cream cheese topping. Other options include fruit crepes, cinnamon roll French toast (made with housemade cinnamon rolls), Benedicts and waffles. At lunch, burgers and favorite hot and cold sandwiches are just as tasty and are accompanied by fries, cottage cheese, soup, salad or homemade potato salad. Filling hot roast beef or turkey sandwiches are served with mashed potatoes and gravy plus soup or salad. Hot lunches include meatloaf, chicken strips, beer-battered fish filets and country-fried steak with all the trimmings, including homemade cornbread.

Nichols Art Glass
912 W 6th St   541/296-2143
Wed-Sun: 10-6   nicholsartglass.com
Artist and entrepreneur Andy Nichols found his dream niche in hot glass work and opened his gallery in 2007. You've likely seen his signature salmon, pumpkin and cherry pieces and other glasswork in galleries and installations throughout the Northwest. He produces unique pieces in his 2,700-square-foot studio, incorporating a wine barrel, barge or other

unexpected element (custom orders are welcome). The comfortable gallery contains colorful and interesting displays; an open viewing area gives browsers the opportunity to see Andy and associates in action. Classes in glass blowing and art glass are offered throughout the year.

Petite Provence of the Gorge

408 E 2nd St   541/506-0037
Daily: 7-3   provencepdx.com
(See detailed listing with Petite Provence, Portland)

The Pines Cottage

5450 Mill Creek Road   541/993-8300
Listed through Airbnb
(See details with The Pines Tasting Room, Hood River)

Sunshine Mill Artisan Plaza and Winery

901 E 2nd St   541/298-8900
Daily: noon-6   sunshinemill.com
The Sunshine Mill has been a towering landmark in The Dalles for over a century and previously milled wheat for the Sunshine Biscuit Co. That industry is just a memory, but the setting is alive with mechanisms, artifacts and contrivances from that business. The new name describes the campus' newest use. Quenett and Copa Di Vino wines are produced on-site by local vintners Molli and James Martin and are featured in the tasting room; specialty appetizers are available. Good use is made of the property's boiler house, warehouse and open spaces. An outdoor amphitheater is a delightful place to sip wine in the sunshine at the Sunshine Mill. Check the events schedule for occasional closures for private functions, otherwise, the venue is open year round.

TIMBERLINE

Timberline Lodge

27500 E Timberline Road   503/272-3311, 800/547-1406
Moderate and up   timberlinelodge.com
Timberline Lodge sits at 6,000 feet on the shoulder of Mt. Hood, Oregon's tallest mountain and one of America's most iconic. Whether you ski, bike or hike, or come to eat, spend the night or take a day trip to this National Historic Landmark, you won't be disappointed. The lodge was dedicated in 1937, a project of the Depression-era Works Progress Administration, and is appointed with incredible handmade furniture and artwork, all centered around a massive stone fireplace. The **Cascade Dining Room** (503/272-

OUTLET SHOPPING
Quality merchandise at impressive discounts is available at the
Columbia Gorge Outlets (450 NW 257th Way, Troutdale; 503/669-
8060, shopcolumbiagorgeoutlets.com) where you can find frequent
sales and events at more than 30 big name retailers.

3104) continues to serve first-class alpine cuisine. Tantalizing buffet offerings can be enjoyed for breakfast and lunch. Dinner offers a full service
menu (reservations required). Oregon produce and products are highlighted with entrees such as alder-smoked and grilled ribeye with black truffle
butter, braised lamb shank, chicken and Northwest cheeses. Lighter fare is
served at the lodge's other lounges and eateries. Overnighters will find cozy
lodge rooms outfitted with handmade furnishings, modern necessities
and wood-burning fireplaces in some rooms. Chalet rooms (outfitted with
bunks to accommodate two, six or eight guests; shared bathrooms) are
an option for groups and families. A larger chalet room, with private bath,
sleeps ten. Silcox Hut, a hand-crafted stone and timber cabin, is situated
farther up the mountain at 7,000 feet and offers groups of 12 to 24 unique
lodging, dinner, breakfast and round-trip transportation from the lodge. An
extra special indulgence at this restored rustic beauty is the winemaker's
dinner series featuring Oregon wines, a six-course gourmet meal and unforgettable snowmobile transportation between the lodge and hut. The ski
area and lift network appeal to beginning and intermediate skiers. Palmer
Snowfield offers summer skiing above the tree line, although much of the
hill is reserved for summer racing camps; mountain biking and hiking.

TROUTDALE

Caswell Sculpture
Studio: 903 E Historic Columbia River Hwy
Gallery: 253 E Historic Columbia River Hwy   503/492-2473
Tue-Sat: 10-5; Sun, Mon: by appointment
Foundry: 803 NE Harlow Rd   503/912-0400
Foundry tours by appointment   caswellsculptures.com
Rip Caswell's path to full-time sculpting has been an interesting one. Caswell
studied animal anatomy in detail and was named best taxidermist in the
nation in 1991. He went on to study human anatomy, and the rest is his-
tory. His bronze pieces include the National Monument of Admiral Chester
Nimitz at Pearl Harbor, the magnificent larger-than-life-size former Governor
Tom McCall in Salem's Riverfront Park, two life-size elk at the High Desert

Museum near Bend, an Iraq war memorial in Madras, an entryway monument in Tualatin and other installations around the country. The artist's studio and gallery are also featured in Troutdale's monthly First Friday Art Walk.

McMenamins Edgefield

2126 SW Halsey St   503/669-8610
Moderately expensive   mcmenamins.com
This 74-acre complex features a historic hotel, several restaurants, a movie theater, a brewery, winery and distillery, among many attractions. There's lots of live entertainment.
(For a detailed description of the McMenamins brand, see Page 12)

Ristorante Di Pompello

177 E Historic Columbia River Hwy   503/667-2480
Daily: 8 a.m.-10 p.m. (Mon open at 11 a.m.)   dipompello.com
Moderate
Ristorante Di Pompello is a delightful Italian family restaurant serving breakfast, lunch and dinner under the direction of Ruby and Saul Pompeyo. Classic pasta dishes such as ravioli marinara, garlicky fettuccini alfredo and layered lasagna are delicious dinner options, or choose from chicken basil tortellini, gnocchi alle bistecca, chicken parmesan and other robust dinners. Tiger prawns alle lobster sauce, Tuscan salmon and more scampi entrees are also enticing. The lunch menu has a full array of salads, sandwiches, Italian entrees, pasta, fish and seafood choices. Roman pan-fried lamb stewed in red wine, Milanese pork with a light mushroom sauce and seafood risotto are standouts. Breakfast is available most mornings with the usual items: bacon, eggs, potatoes, pancakes, French toast, chicken-fried steak and such. Local sculptor Rip Caswell's bronze trout statues flank the signage, which reads "Troutdale, Gateway to the Gorge." Just down the street is Troutdale's illuminated Centennial Arch.

Riverview Restaurant

29311 SE Stark St   503/661-3663
Tue-Sun: 4:30-8 (Fri, Sat till 9)   riverviewportland.com
Moderate
Linda and Junki Yoshida's romantic dinner house along the Sandy River was meticulously designed to capture the area's natural beauty; inside, original artwork from their private collection is displayed. The Northwest cuisine showcases game dishes (seasonally available), fresh seafood, steaks and chicken punctuated with Asian influences. The lounge has daily happy hour specials and plenty of good eats including Mr. Yoshida's Teriyaki Bowl, sandwiches, salads and bar favorites. Diners are often enter-

tained with local musical talent. In winter, the restaurant is only available for private events Monday through Wednesday.

Shirley's Tippy Canoe

28242 E Columbia River Hwy 503/492-2220
Daily: 8 a.m.-10 p.m. Facebook
Moderate to moderately expensive

This enjoyable restaurant offers plentiful portions from a large menu, and absolutely everything is made in house. Breakfast consists of egg dishes with, among the usual offerings, Italian or Polish sausage; corned beef hash; omelets with everything imaginable and freshly-squeezed juices. Sandwiches prevail on the lunch menu and are especially filling with freshly-cut French fries. Hungry beef lovers may opt for the 60-ounce ribeye or New York steak. Other choices include fresh seafood, meat and pasta entrees. Jams, soups, salad dressings, sauces and desserts are homemade from old-fashioned recipes; try the Sloppy Sally cake (named for the process, not the lady). Most every Friday and Saturday night, the Tippy has live music, or cozy up to the outside fire pits where blues and jazz liven up summer Sundays. There's also a Sunday barbecue from 1 to 5 p.m.

Tad's Chicken 'n Dumplins

1325 E Historic Columbia River Hwy 503/666-5337
Mon-Fri: 5-10; Sat: 4-10; Sun: 4-9 tadschicdump.com
Moderate

Every time I dine on chicken and dumplings, I am reminded of family dinners long ago. While Tad's is known for this stick-to-your-ribs dish, it also entices diners with crispy fried chicken and chicken liver dinners, and has done so for many years. You may also choose seafood, beef (liver and onions, too) and pasta entrees plus hearty salads. Dinners include a relish tray, soup or salad, bread and home-style green beans. A trip to Tad's merits a Sunday drive on this scenic highway along the Sandy River.

Troutdale General Store

289 E Historic Columbia River Hwy 503/492-7912
Tue-Fri: 8-5; Sat, Sun: 9-5 Facebook

You'll be taken back to a simpler time when you visit this store in the heart of town. Browse through 8,500 square feet of nostalgic toys, decor and souvenirs. You can also enjoy an inexpensive breakfast or lunch of gluten-free cheesy ham and egg casserole or roasted turkey sandwich, or splurge at the ice cream counter. Weekends offer piping-hot smoked salmon chowder, a meal in itself, or pair it with a great sandwich. Watch their Facebook page for possible closures due to market shows or other circumstances.

WELCHES

Barlow Trail Roadhouse

69580 E Hwy 26   503/622-1662
Mon-Thu: 8 a.m.-9 p.m.; Fri, Sat: 7 a.m-9 p.m.;
Sun: 7 a.m.-8 p.m.   barlowtrailroadhouse.com
Inexpensive to moderate

Home-style cooking is the signature of this historic 1926 log cabin, which originally served as a general store and later became an inn. The name is derived from the famous Oregon Trail namesake toll road (circa 1846), constructed by Sam Barlow. For breakfast (served until 2 p.m.), try omelets or classic combos centered on two eggs; for a sweet alternative, dig into mountain toast (Texas toast dipped in pancake batter, oats and frosted flakes, then deep fried). Lunch offerings include about a dozen burger variations, halibut fish and chips, plus soups and classic sandwiches. Dinner entrees (served after 4 p.m.), include chicken-fried steak with all the accompaniments, dinner salads, meatloaf and fried chicken.

The Rendezvous Grill and Tap Room

67149 E Hwy 26   503/622-6837
Daily: 11:30-8 (Fri, Sat till 9)   thevousgrill.com
Moderate to moderately expensive

"Vous Grill" as it is affectionately called by regulars, has been a casual yet inviting mainstay in Welches since 1995. Owners Susie and Tom Anderson offer fresh, innovative dishes and daily specials masterminded by Executive Chef Mathias Engblom. Menu selections are made to order with good options of hearty soups, salads and interesting sandwiches such as the Vous Grill Reuben (with gruyere and Russian dressing) for lunch (served until 5). Well-prepared seafood, beef, pork and fowl entrees, such as the apricot and soy glazed duck breast, are served for dinner beginning at 5.

The Resort at the Mountain

68010 E Fairway Ave   503/622-3101
Moderate to expensive   mthood-resort.com

Located on what was Oregon's first golf resort in 1928, The Resort at the Mountain is an outstanding northwest destination. Golf courses Foxglove, Pinecone and Thistle, collectively known as the Three Nines, offer a distinct golfing challenge in 27 holes. There are 157 spacious guest rooms, suites and villas appointed with rich, warm woods and bright, welcoming colors and free Wi-Fi. Dine on fresh, farm-to-table cuisine at the year-round Altitude Restaurant & Lounge. Room service and additional casual eating venues are open in the spring and summer. On-site features include a business center, fitness center, spa, putting course, playground and more. This is a great getaway with family-oriented leisure activities including an outdoor swimming pool (enclosed and heated seasonally), mountain bike rentals, sand volleyball and badminton courts and croquet and lawn bowling courts. Mountain sports and other activities are close by.

Gerry's Exclusive List

BBQ
Apple Valley BBQ Restaurant and Catering (4956 Baseline Dr, Parkdale; 541/352-3554)

Bars and Pubs with Good Eats
Full Sail Brewing (506 Columbia St, Hood River; 541/386-2247)
pFriem Family Brewers (707 Portway Ave, Suite 101, Hood River; 541/321-0490): Mt. Shadow cheeseburger

Best Sleeps
Columbia Gorge Hotel (4000 Westcliff Dr, Hood River; 541/386-5566)
The Resort at the Mountain (68010 E Fairway Ave, Welches; 503/622-3101)

Breads and Bakery Goods
Petite Provence of the Gorge (408 E 2nd St, The Dalles; 541/506-0037)
Tollgate Inn Restaurant & Bakery (38100 Hwy 26, Sandy; 503/668-8456)

Breakfast/Brunch
Cousins Restaurant & Saloon (2114 W 6th St, The Dalles; 541/298-2771)
Egg River Cafe (1313 Oak St, Hood River; 541/386-1127)
Momma Jane's Pancake House (900 W 6th St, The Dalles; 541/296-6611)
Simon's Cliff House (Columbia Gorge Hotel, 4000 Westcliff Dr, Hood River; 541/386-5566): brunch

Burgers
Big Jim's Drive-In (2938 E 2nd St, The Dalles; 541/298-5051)
Calamity Jane's Hamburger Parlor (42015 SE Hwy 26, Sandy; 503/668-7817)
pFriem Family Brewers (707 Portway Ave, Suite 101, Hood River; 541/321-0490): Mt. Shadow cheeseburger

Casual Dining/Casual Prices
Baldwin Saloon (205 Court St, The Dalles; 541/296-5666)
Barlow Trail Roadhouse (69580 E Hwy 26, Welches; 503/622-1662)
Calamity Jane's Hamburger Parlor (42015 SE Hwy 26, Sandy; 503/668-7817)

HISTORIC COLUMBIA RIVER HIGHWAY
Travel on the **Historic Columbia River Highway**
(columbiariverhighway.com) has been restricted due to the Eagle
Creek fire in September 2017. The scenic waterfall corridor and most
trails along the route are closed. Before heading out to this area,
check the latest on closures at www.fs.usda.gov/crgnsa.

Cousins Restaurant & Saloon (2114 W 6th St, The Dalles; 541/298-2771)

Huckleberry Inn (88611 E Government Camp Loop, Government Camp; 503/272-3325)

Tad's Chicken 'n Dumplins (1325 E Historic Columbia River Hwy, Troutdale; 503/666-5337)

Tollgate Inn Restaurant & Bakery (38100 Hwy 26, Sandy; 503/668-8456)

Zigzag Mountain Cafe (70171 E Hwy 26, Rhododendron; 503/622-7684)

Coffee and Tea
Mt. Hood Roasters (73451 E Hwy 26, Rhododendron; 503/622-6574)

Doughnuts
Huckleberry Inn (88611 E Government Camp Loop, Government Camp; 503/272-3325)

Joe's Donut Shop (39230 Pioneer Blvd, Sandy; 503/668-7215)

Fireside
Stonehedge Gardens (3405 Wine Country Ave, Hood River; 541/386-3940)

Tollgate Inn Restaurant & Bakery (38100 Hwy 26, Sandy; 503/668-8456)

Foreign Flavors
EUROPEAN: The Glacier Haus Bistro (8817 E Government Camp Loop Road, Government Camp; 503/272-3471)

ITALIAN: Ristorante Di Pompello (177 E Historic Columbia River Hwy, Troutdale; 503/667-2480)

MEDITERRANEAN: Romuls West (315 Oak St, Hood River; 541/436-4444)

Ice Cream and Other Frozen Treats
East Wind Drive-In (395 NW Wanapa St, Cascade Locks; 541/374-8380): insanely large ice cream cones

Outdoor Dining
Full Sail Brewing (506 Columbia St, Hood River; 541/386-2247)
Romuls West (315 Oak St, Hood River; 541/436-4444)
Shirley's Tippy Canoe (28242 E Columbia River Hwy, Troutdale; 503/492-2220)

Personal Favorites
Columbia Gorge Hotel (4000 Westcliff Dr, Hood River; 541/386-5566)
Stonehedge Gardens (3405 Wine Country Ave, Hood River; 541/386-3940)
Timberline Lodge (27500 E Timberline Road, Timberline; 503/272-3311)

Pizza
Ratskeller Alpine Bar & Pizzeria (88335 E Government Camp Loop, Government Camp; 503/272- 3635)
Solstice Wood Fire Cafe & Bar (501 Portway Ave, Hood River; 541/436-0800)

Produce
Mt. Hood Organic Farms (7130 Smullin Dr, Mt. Hood; 541/352-7492)

Sandwiches
Boda's Kitchen (404 Oak St, Hood River; 541/386-9876)

Special Occasions
Riverview Restaurant (29311 SE Stark St, Troutdale; 503/661-3663)
Columbia Gorge Hotel (4000 Westcliff Dr, Hood River; 541/386-5566): Simon's Cliff House, too
Stonehedge Gardens (3405 Wine Country Ave, Hood River; 541/386-3940)
Timberline Lodge (27500 E Timberline Road, Timberline; 503/272-3311): Cascade Dining Room, too

Steaks
Shirley's Tippy Canoe (28242 E Columbia River Hwy, Troutdale; 503/492-2220)

Simon's Cliff House (Columbia Gorge Hotel, 4000 Westcliff Dr, Hood River; 541/386-5566)
Stonehedge Gardens (3405 Wine Country Ave, Hood River; 541/386-3940)

View Restaurants
Cascade Dining Room (Timberline Lodge, 27500 E Timberline Road, Timberline; 503/272-3311)
Full Sail Brewing (506 Columbia St, Hood River; 541/386-2247)
Riverside (1108 E Marina Dr, Hood River; 541/386-4410)
Simon's Cliff House (Columbia Gorge Hotel, 4000 Westcliff Dr, Hood River; 541/386-5566)

Notes

Notes

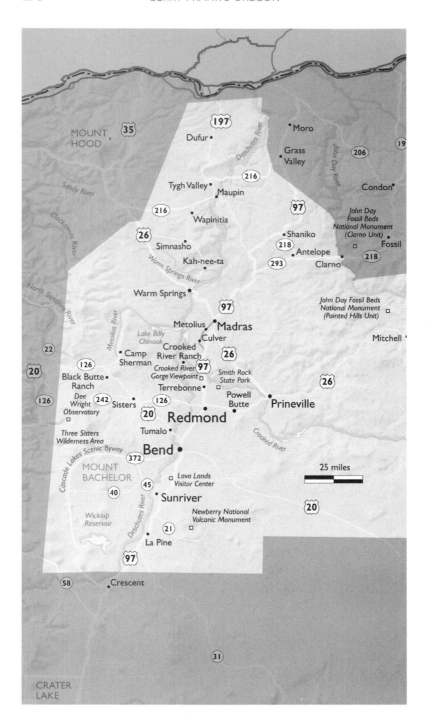

CHAPTER FIVE

Central Oregon

BEND

10 Barrel Brewing Co.

62950 NE 18th St (East pub and headquarters	541/241-7733
1135 NW Galveston Ave (West pub)	541/678-5228
Daily: 11-11 (till midnight Fri, Sat)	10barrel.com

Moderate

When 10 Barrel Brewing was sold to Anheuser-Busch InBev, some worried that it would lose its authenticity and its local flavor. That did not happen. The craft brewery is still a local favorite and still serving award-winning craft beers and grub — now at a new Eastside pub next to its headquarters and a newly remodeled Westside pub as well. Continued popularity means these pubs can be busy, especially in summer as they open up outdoor space and get the fire pit going. Whether you are craving an IPA, cider or a sour, you're covered. The food is just as good and includes a variety of starters (roasted Anaheim chili hummus, anyone?), pizzas, salads and pub grub like fish and chips, burgers and sandwiches (try the roasted pork with ginger balsamic glaze). Brewery tours are available from 3 to 4 p.m. on Fridays at the 18th Street location. Visit their Portland location (and Boise and Denver and San Diego), too.

900 Wall

900 NW Wall St	541/323-6295
Daily: 3-9 (Fri, Sat till 10)	900wall.com

Moderately expensive

A great dinner choice is the restaurant 900 Wall, in a two-story brick building built in 1920 in the heart of downtown. Here Chef Cliff Eslinger serves up Pacific Northwest cuisine with French and Italian influences. The restaurant space was recently renovated and can accommodate private events. Fresh, local ingredients are evident in every dish, cocktails are expertly mixed, and the place boasts among the best wine and whiskey selections in Bend. You'll find an assortment of small plates like fresh oysters, shrimp (or my favorites: the kale salad and roasted beets). Entrees include flatiron steak, risotto, roasted chicken, the signature 900 Wall burger and more. There's also a gluten-free menu. Desserts include the chocolate-hazelnut bombe and housemade ice creams and sorbets. Reservations are recommended as this spot gets quite busy.

Ariana

1304 NW Galveston Ave   541/330-5539
Tue-Sat: 5-close   arianarestaurantbend.com
Expensive
Exceptional food and professional service combine nicely with the relaxed atmosphere of this Craftsman bungalow. The changing bistro menu has an international flair with appetizers such as a spicy calamari, roasted beet salad and an assortment of meat, vegetarian and seafood entrees like braised rabbit, roasted carrots with cilantro salsa verde and seared jumbo scallops with crab risotto. I recommend the chocolate cake for dessert; other choices include the smoked almond cake, crème brûlée and banana cream pie. The outdoor patio is the perfect place to appreciate Bend's warm summer evenings.

The Blacksmith Restaurant

211 NW Greenwood Ave   541/318-0588
Mon-Thu: 4-10; Fri, Sat: 4-11; Sun: 4-9   bendblacksmith.com
Expensive
This steakhouse, bar and lounge under the culinary direction of Bryan Chang features distinctive, bold cuisine, and it will not disappoint. Stone and brick walls, a copper bar top, subtle lighting and leather upholstery create a casual yet elegant ambience in the historic Pierson's Blacksmith Shop. The sophisticated comfort food is attractively plated with delicious accompaniments. The Tomahawk, a 24-ounce bone-in ribeye steak is a customer favorite. Other not-to-be-missed dishes are cider-brined pork chops, decadent mac and cheese sides, shrimp and grits and crab corn dogs. Local, natural, dry-aged steaks are prepared in exquisite sauces or served simply. Desserts include the show-stopping Fostered bananas split, prepared tableside.

Bontà Natural Artisan Gelato

920 NW Bond St, Suite 108   541/306-6606
Daily: noon-9   bontagelato.com

Bontà is the all-natural gelato handcraft of Juli and Jeff Labhart. Inspired in part by a year-long world trip, and wanting to showcase local products, their ice cream is a denser, more flavorful creation. Nearly 20 rich and creamy offerings include salted chocolate, pistachio, roasted strawberry, Theo dark chocolate, vanilla bourbon pecan and peanut butter with chocolate fudge and dairy-free northwest berry sorbetto. The Scoop Shop is actually on Minnesota Avenue, just west of the Oxford Hotel.

Brickhouse

5 NW Minnesota Ave   541/728-0334
(See detailed listing with Brickhouse, Redmond)

Cascade Culinary Institute

2555 NW Campus Village Way   541/318-3780
Thu, Fri (lunch); Wed-Fri (dinner)   cascadeculinary.com, elevationbend.com
Moderate

Students learn how to run a fine-dining restaurant at this state-of-the-art training facility on the campus of Central Oregon Community College. At Elevation, the institute's student-operated restaurant, seatings are available for lunch and dinner during the various academic terms, thus reservations are highly recommended (groups of ten or more should call ahead). Ingredients include locally sourced bounty and other quality components in preparations rivaling the area's better restaurants. Menus change with the season and academic term, but a typical lunch may feature a winter greens salad, a lamb tagine simmered in Middle Eastern spices; chicken cutlet with chipotle mayo, pico de gallo and avocado; or salmon fish and chips with dark ale batter. Dinner options are equally intriguing and may include soup, salad and appetizers, and entrees such as Dungeness crab saffron risotto or pan roasted duck breast.

Chi Chinese & Sushi Bar

70 NW Newport Ave   541/323-3931
Tue-Sun: 4-9   bendchi.com
Moderate

This contemporary Chinese restaurant with views of the Deschutes River finally brings good Chinese fare to Central Oregon. Everything at Chi, whether it be the decor and menu or the food preparation and display, is much classier than your typical Chinese restaurant and all with a modern twist — the tables are even preset with formal chopsticks. With crab being one of my favorite foods, I'd recommend starting with the golden crab purses, also recognized as crab puffs. The ginger beef is particularly good; other entrees include chicken, beef and pork; there are plenty of noodle and rice dishes, too, and a handful of vegetarian and seafood options. You will also find traditional and specialty sushi rolls, all creatively and beautifully plated. This restaurant's fresh and flavorful dishes, good service and cleanliness stand out.

Deschutes Brewery & Public House

1044 NW Bond St   541/382-9242
Lunch, Dinner: Daily   deschutesbrewery.com
Moderate to moderately expensive
This is a great place to unwind after a day in the outdoors in Deschutes County. There are plenty of food choices including Central Oregon's best soft pretzel with white Tillamook cheddar cheese and Black Butte Porter stone-ground mustard and a unique salt and pepper calamari. The Power Salad with rainbow quinoa and steak salad are hearty enough for a meal. Wings, bar snacks, sandwiches (like the Nashville chicken sandwich), burgers and satisfying entrees (think rigatoni bolognese) are easily washed down with one of the dozen and a half year-round and seasonal beers brewed on site (also liberally used in house recipes). While at the brewery, purchase a keg to go or fill a growler.

Desperado

330 SW Powerhouse Dr, Suite 120   541/749-9980
Mon-Sat: 10-8; Sun: 11-6   desperadoboutique.com
Desperado and its shoes and accessories boutique, side by side in Bend's Old Mill District, offer topnotch Western clothing with a mix of bohemian charm. In addition to clothing and boots, Desperado also features jewelry, gifts and home decor from top designers like Ryan Michael, Johnny Was, Double D Ranchwear, Tasha Polizzi, Minnetonka and bootmaker Old Gringo and Liberty Black. Owner Joanne Sunnarborg has created an eclectic array of American, Native American and Western fashions appropriate for special occasions and every day.

Dudley's Bookshop Cafe

135 NW Minnesota Ave   541/749-2010
Daily: Hours vary   dudleysbookshopcafe.com
Dudley's Bookshop Cafe is a locally-owned bookstore and cafe featuring a curated, in-depth selection of new and used literary fiction, western history, outdoor guides, and the best collection of adventure and exploration titles in Central Oregon. Dudley's is the downtown spot for meetings,

BEND ALE TRAIL

For a city of its size, Bend has more beer breweries than just about any other in the nation (it's fourth nationally per capita, according to Forbes). That poses a dilemma for the true brew connoisseur: Should your pub crawl try to find them all, or just the best (and who decides that, anyway)? **The Bend Visitor Center** (750 NW Lava Road, Suite 106, 541/382-8048, visitbend.com; Mon-Fri: 9-5; Sat, Sun: 10-4) can help with its **Bend Ale Trail**, which features 16 craft breweries along the way. Pick up a "passport" and map at the center (during office hours), a participating brewery or print one from the website (or download the app). Leave the driving to a tour operator, ride a trolley or take the Bend Brew Bus (or walk to many of them in the downtown area).This is a great way to explore Bend while tasting some of the best beer available anywhere. On the tour you'll find, to name a few:

10 Barrel Brewing: (see our write-up)

Bend Brewing Co. (bendbrewingco.com): great location overlooking the Deschutes River

Boneyard Beer (boneyardbeer.com): an auto shop turned brewery with less focus on food and more focus on brews

Crux Fermentation Project (cruxfermentation.com): neat atmosphere with some of the friendliest service and an outdoor fire pit

Deschutes Brewery (deschutesbrewery.com): the brewery that started it all (see our write-up)

The trail also includes **GoodLife, McMenamins Old St. Francis School, Rat Hole Brewing, Riverbend Brewing Co., Silver Moon Brewing** and **Sunriver Brewing Co.**, all nearby. **Three Creeks Brewery, Wild Ride Brew Co.** and **Worthy Brewing** are found off trail, but still deserving of a visit.

both formal and informal. The cafe uses Bonsai Beans, one of the best local micro-roasters for beans with a nice, chocolaty, dark roast Guatemalan. In addition to coffee, they also serve a variety of specialty baked goods from local Too Sweet Cakes and Farmhouse Pies to complement that perfect espresso. Stop by for live music every first Friday.

Elk Lake Resort

60000 Century Dr   541/480-7378
Inexpensive to expensive   elklakeresort.net

Central Oregon offers some of Oregon's finest skiing, winter hiking and mountain relaxation. For a wintertime family treat, park your vehicle at Dutchman Flats and ski, snowmobile or take the Sno-Cat to the resort. Cabins and homes are most appealing; they are outfitted with kitchens, bathrooms and other necessities and accommodate up to ten guests. Three heated camping cabins are rustic with no power, bathrooms, water or amenities. The year-round lodge functions as the activity hub with a store, equipment rentals (summer and winter sports) and dining room.

Five Fusion & Sushi Bar

821 NW Wall St   541/323-2328
Daily: 4-close   5fusion.com
Moderately expensive

Joe Kim became the executive chef at the Five Fusion & Sushi Bar in 2012. Since then the restaurant has positioned itself as one of Bend's most important and garnered some national acclaim as well. And the chef himself has been named a semi-finalist for the James Beard Foundation's Best Chef in the Northwest — three times. OK, so the food quality is a given, but what exactly is "Asian Fusion" cuisine? In a sense all cooking could be thought of as fusion, but specifically here we're talking about combining the traditions and techniques of Chinese and Japanese and Korean cooking with the ingredients and flavors of the Pacific Northwest. Thus, the Wagyu beef burger (locally sourced Wagyu beef with kimchi slaw, provolone and wasabi aioli); or the citrus glazed scallops (on any other menu as "pan seared;" here the emphasis is on the kaffir lime, lemongrass and pomegranate). Happy hour (Monday-Friday, 4-6) in this narrow but inviting space is equally adventurous, with a dozen or so specialty cocktails (Angry Mango, Asian Pear) and an equal number of aged Japanese whiskeys to sample. And there's plenty of starters and separate sushi and tasting menus.

Greg's Grill

395 SW Powerhouse Dr   541/382-2200
Sun-Thu: 11-10; Fri, Sat: 11-11 (open at 8 Sat, Sun for breakfast)   gregsgrill.com
Moderately expensive

This Northwest lodge-themed restaurant in the Old Mill District offers relaxing views of the Deschutes River framed by floor-to-ceiling windows and a magnificent, soaring wood ceiling. The restaurant features a mesquite and apple wood-fired rotisserie grill and menus offering steaks, prime rib, burgers, sandwiches, chicken, seafood, salads and soups for lunch and dinner. The bar features cocktails, hard ciders, liqueurs, and bottled and draft beers. Desserts include locally-made ice cream and gelato, housemade cobbler and the indisputably decadent Chocolate Indulgence.

High Desert Museum

59800 S Hwy 97   541/382-4754
Daily: 9-5 (summer); 10-4 (winter)   highdesertmuseum.org
Reasonable

Located five miles south of Bend, this museum highlights the natural and cultural resources of the High Desert. Meet raptors, porcupines, bobcat, otters and more live animals in natural habitat settings and in fun, educational programs. Kids love to explore the nature trails on 135 forested acres and learn through hands-on activities. Indoor and outdoor exhibitions feature historical characters portrayed live at a re-created 1880s town, working a homestead ranch and a 100-year-old sawmill. Collections of High Desert historic artifacts and Western art are outstanding. Additional features include changing exhibitions throughout the year, guided tours, play spaces for young kids, a cafe and Silver Sage Trading (the museum store). Parking is plentiful and convenient for tour buses, RVs and autos; the complex is ADA accessible. Picnic areas are provided, but beware, chipmunks and squirrels may be brazen in their quest for your picnic goods!

The Hillside Inn

1744 NW 12th St   541/389-9660
Moderate   bendhillsideinn.com

This unique lodging offers an urban setting with a location convenient to bustling downtown. Proprietor Annie Goldner's inn features a pond, waterfall and a nearby hot tub, perfect for unwinding after a busy day. Breakfasts are especially nice, healthy and flexible to address special dietary issues. Newly constructed in 1999, this is not an antique-filled country inn; it is light and bright with contemporary furnishings and modern conveniences. The balcony suite overlooks the patio and pond while the ground-floor studio suite is complete with a fully-equipped kitchen and dining area, ideal for longer stays. Comforting amenities include silky robes, Turkish towels and luxury soaps and lotions. Shops, a park, bike trails and downtown are easily accessible within a mile.

Ida's Cupcake Cafe

1314 NW Galveston Ave   541/383-2345
Daily: 10-5 (Sun till 4)
1155 SW Division St, A-7   541/678-5057
Mon-Sat: 10-6   idascupcakecafe.com

Thank you for appealing to my insatiable sweet tooth. I could be here all day contemplating the perfect combination of cake and frosting flavors, about 80 in all, not counting the seasonal or rotating flavors. Request your favorite pairing or choose from pre-frosted regular size "kidcakes" or twice-the-size gourmet cupcakes. Special occasions are more distinct with these beautiful uniquely decorated treats. Other party-worthy options are personalized Bundt cakes, small layer cakes and mini-cupcakes — just about bite size. There are a few gluten-free cupcake flavors — and one gluten-, egg- and dairy-free version. Visitors to Redmond can taste their treats at a third location (738 SW Highland, 541/548-8164).

Jackson's Corner

845 NW Delaware Ave	541/647-2198
1500 NE Cushing Dr	541/382-1751
Breakfast, Lunch, Dinner: Daily	jacksonscornerbend.com
Moderate	

If you're away from home and have a hankering for home cooking, you'll want to make note of Jackson's Corner. Basics include breakfast eggs and go-with dishes, housemade biscuits with gravy and brioche French toast. Pizzas, sandwiches and salads are offered at lunch and dinner; seasonally available ingredients determine the menu particulars. Pasta is made in-house for dinner and paired with tasty sauces and other ingredients. Burgers, formerly featured only one night a week, are now a permanent addition to the offerings and are presented on a brioche bun topped with corner sauce and just-right trimmings and fixings.

Joolz

916 NW Wall St	541/388-5094
Mon-Sat: 4:30-9	joolzbend.com
Moderate	

Joolz has found success blending Eastern Mediterranean cuisine with the American West. Unique small plates include vegetarian stuffed grape leaves, pan-seared unripened cheese with a tart pomegranate reduction, sauce-laden elk served over hummus, and salads. Entrees include steak kabobs, chili made with braised organic elk, chicken kabobs with garlic sauce, seasonal fish and seafood, plus beef, elk or lamb burgers. For something different, try a warm sandwich made with ground falafel. Wines are as eclectic as the menu, with labels from around the world. Cocktails may contain sagebrush-infused spirits. Overall, this is great choice for all things Mediterranean (Oregon style).

Kanpai

990 NW Newport Ave	541/388-4636
Mon-Sat: 4-9	kanpaibend.com
Moderate	

Look to this Westside restaurant for satisfying sushi and Pan-Asian cuisine prepared with French techniques. Guests are assured that only local-ly-sourced, fresh, natural, hormone- and antibiotic-free meats and produce are used whenever possible; and a good-size takeout list includes Nigiri and seared filet mignon. Talented instructors show diners how delicious Kanpai dishes are created and assist neophytes in selecting items from the ample menu including the area's largest selection of imported Japanese saké and beer (a full bar and wine, too). Kanpai!

Lone Crow Bungalow
937 NW Wall St   541/383-2992
Mon-Sat: 10-6; Sun: 11-5   lonecrowbungalow.com
Don't miss Lone Crow Bungalow for a wonderful selection of quality hand-crafted home goods made in America and from around the world. Fea-tured items for your nest include pottery, clocks, dinnerware, artisan can-dles, garden accents, textiles and rugs, jewelry, lighting and much more. The staff at this beautiful shop is talented, helpful and creative.

McKay Cottage Restaurant
62910 O.B. Riley Road, Suite 340   541/383-2697
Breakfast, Lunch: Daily   themckaycottage.com
Inexpensive to moderate
Enjoy award-winning comfort food breakfasts and lunches with a cre-ative twist: Baja chicken hash stack, stuffed croissant French toast, Smith Rock "Benny" (a change-up on the usual eggs Benedict), Mahi fish tacos, homemade soups, salads and sandwiches. Cinnamon rolls, pecan sticky buns, plump muffins, scones and a variety of desserts are made daily from scratch. Depending upon the weather, choose indoor seating next to the warm fireplace or pleasant outdoor seating on the lawn.

Mt. Bachelor
13000 SW Century Dr   800/829-2442
Seasonal   mtbachelor.com
Mt. Bachelor is the tallest (elevation 9,065 feet) resort peak in the Cascade Range covering 3,365 feet of vertical drop from summit to base. It is one of the few peaks in the world that affords skiing the entire mountain 360 degrees off the top. Grab a trail map before you venture out; there is a network of 12 lifts (quads, triples and tubing) and 88 runs. Guests of all ages and levels of experience will find their Eden on the mountain, from Dilly-Dally Alley for youngsters to the double black diamond extreme terri-tory on the backside. Four lodges are conveniently located to refresh snow enthusiasts with food and drink. Other services include lessons; retail, rental and tuning shops; a demo center; child care; guide service; sled dog

rides; cross country skiing and snowshoe tours. Just in case, Bend Memorial Clinic Urgent Care has an outpost in the ski patrol building. For an entirely different perspective, head to the mountain in summer for activities including the newly-introduced mountain bike park, disc golf, spectacular vistas from scenic lift rides and sunset gourmet dinners at mid-mountain Pine Marten Lodge.

Next Level Burger

70 SW Century Dr, Suite 120   541/306-6778
Lunch, Dinner: Daily; Breakfast: Sun   nextlevelburger.com
Inexpensive

Husband-and-wife owners, Cierra and Matt de Gruyter, have reinvented the all-American burger. They have created a 100% plant-based burger, and it's delicious. Being true health advocates, they simply wanted a place where they could have a healthy burger with a side of fries and a shake, so they created it. Much of the menu is housemade, organic and non-GMO produce bought locally. Their heart-healthy, cholesterol-free menu is sure to please anyone dieting or just trying to live a healthier life. Besides burgers, menu options include salads, hot dogs and sandwiches. Don't live in town? Visit their newest location in Portland (4121 SE Hawthorne Blvd, 503/719-7058).

The Original Pancake House

1025 SW Donovan Ave   541/317-0380
Daily: 6-2   originalpancakehouse.com
Moderate
(See detailed listing in Salem, Chapter 2.)

The Oxford Hotel

10 NW Minnesota Ave   541/382-8436, 877/440-8436
Moderate   oxfordhotelbend.com

This 59-suite, four-diamond boutique hotel is dedicated to sustainable hospitality. The Oxford Hotel has all the amenities of a top-drawer hotel, combined with "green" bedding, selections from a pillow menu, plush bathrobes, premium organic toiletries, in-room French press coffee service, room service and a state-of-the-art fitness center. Cruiser bicycles (summer only) are complimentary to guests. Airport shuttle and pet-friendly rooms are available; a nominal fee includes a size-appropriate bed for your canine, housemade treats and more. Three squares a day of "urban-organic" cuisine are available on the lower level at **10 Below Restaurant and Lounge**. Offerings change to capture the essence of the seasons. Sophisticated, contemporary luxury is a stunning addition to historic downtown.

Pilot Butte Drive-In

917 NE Greenwood Ave   541/382-2972
Daily: 7-7   pilotbuttedrivein.com
Inexpensive

A local and visitor favorite since 1983, Pilot Butte Drive-In has earned a reputation for quality food and big portions. Burgers are just the way I like them: flavorful, juicy and requiring several napkins. Variations to the basic burger are created with the addition of bacon, cheese, mushrooms, jalapenos, ham, guacamole, roasted garlic or a combo of fixings. The Pilot Butte burger is 18 ounces of beef — quite a mouthful. Plain or seasoned fries or onion rings and a float, freeze, shake or malt complete the meal. Breakfast orders are also generously portioned.

Pine Ridge Inn

1200 SW Mt. Bachelor Dr   541/389-6137
Moderate to expensive   pineridgeinn.com

Perched above the Deschutes River Canyon is a boutique hotel overlooking the river, Farewell Bend Park and the Old Mill District. The location and superb views can't be beat! All 20 suites are furnished with gas fireplaces, private patios, plush king beds and mini-fridges. Overnight stays include

---

OLD MILL DISTRICT

The **Old Mill District** (450 SW Powerhouse Dr, 541/312-0131, oldmilldistrict.com) is Bend's premier shopping location featuring over 40 local, regional and national shops. The property formerly housed two competing lumber mills (Shevlin-Hixon Lumber and Brooks-Scanlon Lumber). At their peak the mills were two of the largest pine sawmills in the world, employing more than 2,000 workers each. Now this 270-acre parcel along the Deschutes River is a mixed-use area known for its shops, galleries and restaurants. Elements of some of the original buildings, including the area's three signature smokestacks, have been maintained. Refuel at one of over a dozen restaurants and food shops or indulge in wine tasting at Naked Winery. Other features of the Mill include canoe, kayak, bike and paddle board rentals; a fly-casting course; sand volleyball courts; an off-leash dog park; and a network of trails maintained by Bend Parks and Recreation, complete with historical and memorial plaques. The Les Schwab Amphitheater hosts numerous concerts and events, including Bend Brew Fest. Regal Cinemas, IMAX and several topnotch hotels are conveniently located within the district.

complimentary breakfast, an afternoon glass of wine or locally-made beer upon arrival. The well-tended property is beautiful; suites are spacious and relaxing, perfect for an R&R getaway.

Pine Tavern

967 NW Brooks St   541/382-5581
Lunch, Dinner: Daily   pinetavern.com
Moderate

Founded in 1936, the Pine Tavern has faithfully served Bend and its timber industry workers and their families, soldiers from Camp Abbot and tourists. The building overlooks picturesque Mirror Pond and has morphed through the years to accommodate additional customers and modern facilities. Two gigantic Ponderosa pine trees are enclosed in the Garden Room, and the patio and garden remain an important part of the ambience. The menu features classic and eclectic choices prepared with Northwest ingredients, daily lunch specials, pastas and steak dinners. Signature scones with honey butter are like manna from heaven; this is a traditional Central Oregon dining excursion.

Pronghorn

65600 Pronghorn Club Dr   866/320-5024
Expensive   pronghornresort.com

Pronghorn is a superior getaway for golfers and non-golfers. Exquisite lodging includes 48 lodge units situated on the 18th hole of the Jack Nicklaus Signature Course. Junior suites consist of one bedroom and bathroom. Spacious two-, three- and four-bedroom units are furnished with gourmet kitchens, a home theater system and other technology, private patios and original art work. Personal concierge services (pre-stocked groceries, local activities, dining) are also available. All guests have access to the clubhouse, restaurants, fitness facility, sports courts and pools; shuttle service is available to Roberts Field-Redmond Municipal Airport. The Jack Nicklaus golf course is open to the public while the Tom Fazio Championship Course is restricted to club members. While at the resort, pamper yourself in the newly renovated Spa at Pronghorn; amazing treatments for everyone. As for dining, there are multiple outlets with varying fare. This property is ideal for weddings, corporate retreats, special events and, of course, golf tournaments.

Riverhouse on the Deschutes

3075 N Business Hwy 97   541/389-3111, 866/453-4480
Moderate to moderately expensive   riverhouse.com

Book your stay at the newly renovated Riverhouse on the Deschutes, located right on the banks of the Deschutes River. Indoor and outdoor heated pools and spas, as well as the adjacent 18-hole River's Edge Golf Course, keep the whole family busy. With direct access right from the resort, outdoor enthusiasts enjoy dog walking, hiking and running on the Deschutes River Trail. The redesigned guest rooms include modern technology and free Wi-Fi, and many feature stone fireplaces and personal balconies overlooking the river. Accommodations are now more quest-focused, featuring modernized entryways for those who ski, snowboard or bike, and improved workspaces for business travelers. **Currents** (currentsbend.com), the new and improved restaurant and lounge that has replaced Crossings, serves breakfast, lunch and dinner and features regionally-sourced Pacific Northwest cuisine. The outdoor patio overlooks the river and has a fireplace and heaters to keep you warm. The lounge is open until 10 p.m. With 16 handcrafted beers on tap, an innovative cocktail list and carefully selected Northwest wines, you are sure to end your evening in comfort.

The Sparrow Bakery

50 SE Scott St	541/330-6321
Daily: 7-2	
2748 NW Crossing Dr, #110	541/647-2323
Mon-Fri: 7-5; Sat, Sun: 7-3	thesparrowbakery.net
Inexpensive	

Owners Whitney Keatman and Jessica Keatman specialize in rich French pastries and bountiful fresh salads. Their Ocean Roll (hand-rolled croissant dough filled with sugar, vanilla and cardamom) is a popular treat; c'est magnifique! Ask any repeat customer and they will heap accolades on other croissants, tarts, breads, cookies and breakfast sandwiches. Chicken Waldorf, croque monsieur or Monte Cristo sandwiches and savory quiches are very satisfying. These bakeries, with super lattes, are warm, cozy and friendly, just as a bakery should be.

Spork

937 NW Newport Ave	541/390-0946
Lunch, Dinner: Daily	sporkbend.com
Inexpensive to moderate	

This 50-seat restaurant began as an Airstream chow cart. Its continuing success stems from the globally-inspired healthy menu which incorporates flavors of Asia, Mexico and elsewhere. Beef, pork, chicken, catfish and tofu are the main ingredients in rice bowls, tacos, salads, sandwiches, small plates and more. If you prefer gluten-free or vegan choices, there are plenty of those options, too. Your mouth will go wild when you eat the grilled vegetable coconut green curry dish or one of the daily chalkboard specials.

Tetherow Lodges

61240 Skyline Ranch Road   541/388-2582, 877/298-2582
Moderate to expensive   tetherow.com

After a full day of fun, whether it includes tours of the local breweries, biking the 300 miles of available trails or exploring the great outdoors, nothing beats a comfortable bed. Tetherow Lodges is Bend's newest world-class resort. This 50-room boutique hotel brings you the best of both worlds: the most spectacular views in the area with the feeling of being secluded, plus the convenience of being seven minutes from shops, restaurants and entertainment. Opening in 2014, all rooms feature gas fireplaces, flat-screen TVs and terraces with views that make it hard to leave your room. Luxurious finishes fill the rooms as well as locally crafted coffee, tea and chocolate — they had me at chocolate. For golf enthusiasts, it's off with your coat and out with the clubs at the resort's award-winning golf course, voted number 54 on *Golf Digest*'s "Top 100 Greatest Courses" of 2015 and created by the same course architect who designed Bandon Dunes. Aside from the golf course, the development also includes two restaurants and well-appointed vacation homes. Light fare is served in The Row (open daily at 7 a.m., closing hours vary), a family-friendly pub where American and Scottish-inspired items such as bangers and mash, braised elk shepherd's pie, fish and chips, sandwiches, salads and mini-corndogs (which are actually bangers) are on the menu. Fine-dining Solomon's highlights vibrant offerings from the Pacific Northwest where pheasant, elk and seafood are thoughtfully prepared alongside vegetarian creations and decadent dessert (Wednesday-Sunday, 5 p.m. to close; reservations are encouraged).

Tim Garling's Jackalope Grill

750 NW Lava Road, Suite 139   541/318-8435
Dinner: Daily   jackalopegrill.com
Moderately expensive

French/Northwest cuisine is featured at this upscale, fine-dining establishment where local art accents the walls. Ease into dinner with an order of escargot a la bourguignonne served in a delectable garlic and shallot broth or Dungeness crab-stuffed mushroom caps. The menu includes game entrees (medallions of elk are superb), schnitzels, fish, charbroiled ribeye steak, osso bucco prepared with pork and other delicious items from local ingredients. A variety of luscious desserts, such as crème brûlée, are fresh from the kitchen. Outside dining is available in the summer. Chef Tim Garling's award-winning restaurant is the result of culinary training in Paris and a successful restaurant venture in Utah. He teaches culinary classes at Central Oregon Community College.

Trattoria Sbandati

1444 NW College Way 541/306-6825
Dinner: Mon-Sat trattoriasbandati.com
Moderately expensive
Upscale Italian cuisine in Bend translates into a visit to Trattoria Sbandati. Chef Juri Sbandati is from Tuscany and has earned a much-deserved reputation for authentic, cooked-to-order dishes that are superb. For instance, meatballs are made from Juri's family recipe, served with delightful tomato sauce and a side of sautéed spinach. Handmade tagliatelle will surely melt in your mouth. Other entrees are made with pork, beef, veal or fish. This dinner house is warm and inviting and service is professional.

The Victorian Cafe

1404 NW Galveston Ave 541/382-6411
Breakfast, Lunch: Daily victoriancafebend.com
Moderate
For locals, see you at "The Vic" means The Victorian Cafe, a Central Oregon institution for great breakfasts in a fun environment with commendable service. Traditional breakfast fare morphed into gourmet cuisine with the arrival of proprietor John Nolan in 2002. His reinvented menu offers about 20 descriptively-named omelets (the Green Hornet includes spinach, asparagus, jalapenos, scallions and avocados), eggs Benedict (Cuban ham, mango and black beans make up the Caribbean version) and potato specialties like the Apollonius (linguica sausage, artichoke hearts, spinach, Kalamata olives, red peppers and feta cheese). Legendary Bloody Marys and "ManMosas" (crafted with The Vic's private label champagne) put this full-service bar on the radar. About a dozen sandwiches (as a wrap or on bread), burgers and fresh salads entice the lunch crowd. The Vic is so popular, you may find yourself settling into an outside bench as you wait for your table.

Wanderlust Tours

61535 S Hwy 97 541/389-8359, 800/962-2862
Prices vary wanderlusttours.com
For a really cool experience in the Bend area, how about a visit to a high desert lava cave? Half-day tours take visitors beneath the area's desert floor. In winter, this outfit does a series of extraordinary experiences including snowshoeing by the light of a full moon and bonfires on the snow. Professional naturalist guides accompany groups; delicious desserts and warm drinks are added treats. For the 21 and older generation, hop on Wanderlust's Bend Brew Bus for a rollicking tour of four local craft breweries. The Local Pour jaunt includes beer, cider, wine and spirit stops; samples are a part of the package.

CENTRAL OREGON CASINO

There's plenty of gaming in Oregon for folks who want a chance at Lady Luck. Casinos are operated by individual Native American tribal councils and have been successful in bringing additional revenues and jobs to Oregon. Here's an overview of Central Oregon's:

WARM SPRINGS
Indian Head Casino (3236 Hwy 26, 541/460-7777, indianheadcasino.com): slots, blackjack, casual dining, lodging at nearby Kah-Nee-Ta Resort and Spa (6823 Hwy 8, 541/553-1112, 800/554-4786)

Warmer weather tours involve canoeing, kayaking, GPS Eco-challenge, volcano sightseeing. Morning, afternoon and evening tours depart daily and guides, transportation and appropriate equipment are furnished. Bring the wee ones and grandma; certain activities can be modified for the whole family and specialized tours are available for groups of ten or more people.

Wild Rose

150 NW Oregon Ave   541/382-0441
Daily: 11-9 (till 10 Fri, Sat)   wildrosethai.com
Moderate

Don't be intimidated by the lines that sometimes form outside this small Thai restaurant. Service moves quickly, and the wait is well worth it in any case. The place features a rural cuisine based on family recipes that originated in the mountainous province of Chiang Mai in northern Thailand. You'll find a menu organized around dishes to be shared by the whole table, and with unfamiliar names that will require you to move out of your comfort zone just a bit. Nonetheless, the menu items are well described, as in Som Tum: shredded papaya salad in a spicy tri-flavored dressing with carrots, peanuts, green beans, tomato, lime, dried shrimp powder and fresh chili. Got that? What you won't find is Pad Thai or other dishes commonly found at "mainstream" Thai restaurants (and sometimes smothered in peanut sauce). Co-owner and head chef Paul Itti, who with his family also founded a Thai restaurant in Port Townsend, Washington, says his dishes are what you'd actually find in Chiang Mai, but cooked the way his family likes it ("more lemongrass, less coconut milk" as he puts it). Reservations are required and accepted only for groups of six or more, and they must be made over the phone or in person at least one day in advance. For smaller parties, just drop on by.

Zydeco Kitchen & Cocktails

919 NW Bond St   541/312-2899
Daily: 5-close (dinner); Mon-Fri: 11:30-2:30 (lunch)   zydecokitchen.com
Moderately expensive

The hands-down favorite at this classy Cajun place is barbecue shrimp served with a Southern grits cake. The Southwest Louisiana-inspired fare features étouffée; shrimp po' boy; artichoke and corn fritters and shrimp, Andouille and crawfish jambalaya. Other standouts are Acadian flat-bread (you choose the toppings), Mama G's steak salad (avocado, tomato, chopped egg and blue cheese), sandwiches, pot pie and seasonal prepara-tions made from scratch using fresh, quality ingredients. The Creole food is super and the atmosphere loads of fun; your toes will be a tappin'.

CAMP SHERMAN

Cold Springs Resort

25615 Cold Springs Resort Lane   541/595-6271
Moderate (seasonal rates)   coldspringsresort.com

Cold Springs Resort features fully equipped cabins, cottages and RV sites with full hook-ups just steps from the famed Metolius River. Their private bridge across the river allows quick access to Camp Sherman's general store. There's also easy access to hiking and biking trails and the river's world class fly-fishing opportunities. Each of the five riverfront cabins has a large outdoor deck and offers a full view of the Metolius and the rolling lawn that slopes toward its banks. Log benches and fire pits dot the lawn area, creating the perfect setting for picnics. Cabins can sleep up to six. Cottages are set farther back, offering a filtered river view, and can sleep four to six, depending on size. They, too, are fully equipped and finished on the interior with striking tongue-and-groove pine that brings out the true log cabin feel. The entire resort is nestled beneath a canopy of pine trees, which is part of the resort's true appeal: a peaceful, outdoor setting far from urban cares.

House on Metolius

National Forest Road 980   541/595-6620
Expensive   metolius.com

Retreat. Relax. Rewind. Renew. This privately owned 200-acre estate on the Metolius River dates back over a century, looks to the Mt. Jefferson and Three Finger Jack mountain peaks and is surrounded on all sides by the Deschutes National Forest which offers impressive hiking, fishing, bird-watching, biking and skiing. Choose from the rustic, upscale Main House (eight guest rooms); Reidun's Cabin (one or two units); or one of the other four cabins (Eleanor's, Ponderosa, Gorge, Power House) for a special recreational weekend, wedding, business conference or other occasion. Accommodations are available year-round. This is a gated locale; specific directions will be given upon reservation. Fishermen, take note: there is private and exclusive fly-fishing access on both banks of the Metolius River.

DIAMOND LAKE

Diamond Lake Resort
350 Resort Dr   541/793-3333
Inexpensive and up   diamondlake.net
Seven miles north of Crater Lake National Park's north entrance is a resort with a variety of lodging choices: motel rooms, studio units, cabins (modern or rustic) and a Jacuzzi suite. Rates vary by season, lodging type and features. The resort's restaurant is open to guests and the public throughout the year for breakfast, lunch and dinner; herb-crusted prime rib is featured on Friday and Saturday nights. There is always a full slate of seasonal activities. The store and marina are the rental centers for fishing, patio, paddle and bumper boats; kayaks; canoes and other recreational equipment. By the way, access roads are kept clear when the snow falls for snow tubing, snowboarding, Sno-Cat skiing, cross country skiing, snowshoeing and snowmobiling at Mt. Bailey located ten miles west of Diamond Lake.

DUFUR

Balch Hotel
40 S Heimrich St   541/467-2277
Inexpensive to moderate   balchhotel.com
Grace, ease and simplicity await at the boutique Balch Hotel which was recently named #1 Fan-Favorite Travel Destination in the Columbia Gorge, and #7 in Oregon (according to Trip Advisor, Yelp and Google). Three hundred days of sunshine, on-site dining and spa services, sunny patio, garden grounds and majestic Mt. Hood views inspire getaways for rejuvenation and re-connection. Centrally located where the Columbia River Gorge meets the high desert, after a short drive, you'll feel like you're a world away. Each of the 19 cozy rooms is uniquely styled with antiques, original art and comfy beds. The casual vintage elegance of this historic country inn, surrounded by the golden expanse of wide open meadows and big sky, invites a clarity of mind and heart that settles the soul. This is an exceptional venue for weddings, wellness retreats, family reunions, business meetings and auto or bike touring.

LA PINE

Paulina Lake Lodge

22440 Paulina Lake Road   541/536-2240
Moderate to expensive   paulinalakelodge.com
Adventurous Oregon travelers shouldn't miss this rustic lodge on the
shores of Paulina Lake (23 miles south of Bend on Highway 97, then 12
miles east on Road 21) deep in the Deschutes National Forest. Depending
on the season, enjoy fishing, boating, swimming, snowmobiling, hiking
and more. There are 200 miles of groomed snowmobile trails. Vintage cabins are equipped with bathrooms, linens, firewood and kitchenware. Moderately priced, hearty full lunches and dinners are served in the 1929 log
lodge restaurant (call to verify hours); the famous prime rib dinner is a Saturday night staple on the home cooking menu. A general store (summer
only) is convenient for fishing licenses, food, clothing, equipment rentals,
gas and oil (for boats in summer and snowmobiles in winter), beer and
groceries. This area's history is an interesting read.

Paulina Plunge

53750 Hwy 97   541/389-0562, 800/296-0562
Daily: May 1-Sep 15   paulinaplunge.com
Take the plunge, the Paulina Plunge, for an all-downhill mountain biking
adventure from Central Oregon's Newberry National Volcanic Monument.
You'll drop more than 2,500 vertical feet on four, 1½-mile segments and
stop at up to six pristine waterfalls (two are natural waterslides where you
can cool down and play). A couple of lively hikes are required to reach the
falls, but they're easily achievable for tots to seniors. Experienced guides
lead the charge and along the way impart insight into the local history,
geology and archeology. A few details: catch a shuttle at Sunriver Resort
for a 25-minute ride to the gathering spot. Bike, helmet and day pack are
included in the price. There's plenty of fine print; call or check the website
for the minutiae and pricing.

MADRAS

Richardson's Rock Ranch

6683 NE Hay Creek Road   800/433-2680
Rock shop daily: 7-5 (Mar-Oct); 9-4 (Nov-Feb)
Digging is seasonal   richardsonrockranch.com
Most rock hounds know that the thunderegg is the state rock of Oregon.
What they may not know about is Richardson's Rock Ranch, a prime place
to dig for them in Central Oregon. The ranch's goal is to make the rock

hounding hobby as easy and enjoyable as possible, for families and experts alike. There's no trick to finding a nice thunderegg, they claim. Just follow their simple rules and dig where they recommend, and you'll be safe and successful. The ranch is also a working cattle ranch, and the digging beds range from easy to expert-only. The ranch also has a grand rock shop full of agates, thundereggs, geodes, fossils, polished spheres and other rough and polished stones available for purchase, as well as rough stone suitable for outdoor landscaping. The ranch will loan digging equipment such as picks and buckets, and your finds will cost you $1.25 per pound with a $12.50 minimum. Rock digging is highly dependent on weather, and the rock beds are generally closed from Nov. 1 to sometime after March 1, but Richardson's Rock Shop has not been closed for a single day since it opened 44 years ago. (Please note that the rock beds are not accessible to recreational vehicles, and there is no overnight camping at the ranch, although Richardson's can direct you to abundant camping facilities in the area.) This is a unique place, 11 miles north of Madras off Highway 97.

MAUPIN

Deschutes Canyon Fly Shop

599 S Hwy 197   541/395-2565
Mon-Sat: 8-5 (Sun till 1)   flyfishingdeschutes.com

John Smeraglio, fisherman and owner of this fly shop and guide service, shares his love of angling and the outdoors with others. John and his team teach the finer art of fly-casting, offer customized guided float and non-float tours and stock high-quality brand name gear. They also share information on river conditions, fishing reports and fish counts. Throughout the year, look for seasonal product demos, clinics, lessons and more. Their customer-friendly motto is: "We guide; you fish!"

Imperial River Co.

304 Bakeoven Road   541/395-2404, 800/395-3903
Lodging: Inexpensive to moderate   deschutesriver.com
Restaurant (seasonal hours): Moderate

When hardworking entrepreneurs Susie and Rob Miles purchased this whitewater rafting and lodging operation in 2001 they added a full-service restaurant, quiet bar, 45-seat conference room, courtyard with fire pit, sand volleyball court, additional guest rooms and a photo shop to take digital pictures of everyone rafting this stretch of the Deschutes River. All 25 guest rooms have names and Oregon themes appropriate to the area, are well-appointed and include wader dryers. Try to plan your stay to coincide with restaurant hours (open daily in the summer). Angus beef and lamb are sourced from nearby Imperial Stock Ranch; chicken, fish, sandwiches and desserts are also good. Well-trained personnel, guided whitewater rafting, great photo ops, and superb fishing are available.

POWELL BUTTE

Brasada Ranch
16986 SW Brasada Ranch Road   541/526-6865, 888/322-6592
Moderate to very expensive   brasada.com
Just east of Bend, this high desert getaway offers all the beauty of the Oregon Trail, but with modern luxuries you might expect from an award-winning resort. Brasada Ranch was named *Condé Nast Traveler*'s "Best Resort in the Pacific Northwest" in 2014 and 2015. Stay in an intimate Ranch House Suite ideal for couples or a one- to four-bedroom Sage Canyon Cabin for families. In addition to lodging, the welcoming Ranch House (541/526-6870) restaurant offers full-service, family-friendly dining for breakfast, lunch and dinner year-round; plus outside seating on the wrap-around deck. The 17,000-square-foot athletic center has an indoor lap pool, two outdoor pools and a waterslide. Take advantage of the full workout facility and complimentary fitness classes while children stay entertained in The Hideout. The semi-private Peter Jacobsen-designed 18-hole Brasada Canyons Golf Course (541/504-4421) is limited to members and resort guests. The full-service spa is open to the public and affords clients (and one additional guest) entrance into the athletic club pools. Biking and hiking trails, horseback riding, whitewater rafting and fishing are easily accessible on the 1,800-acre property. Fine dining at the Range Restaurant and Bar (541/426-6862) opens to a panoramic view of the Cascades and is a perfect vantage point for a stunning sunset show. The changing menu is innovative, yet down-to-earth; most importantly, fresh, local ingredients are used to a large extent for this farm-to-fork experience.

PRINEVILLE

Bellavista Bed & Breakfast
5070 SE Paulina Hwy   541/416-2400
Inexpensive   bellavistab-b.com
For fabulous 180-degree views of the Three Sisters and the Cascades, try this hilltop bed and breakfast accented with furnishings from Fulvia and Ben Guyger's Tuscan home. They will make you feel at ease with two comfy bedrooms with bathrooms. The signature gourmet breakfast served on the sun deck or upper gazebo consists of orange-glazed sausage and apricot kabobs, eggs and fruit. The gracious hosts, unbeatable scenery and

European elegance produce a memorable stay anytime of the year. (Credit cards not accepted.)

REDMOND

Brickhouse

412 SW 6th St   541/526-1782
Dinner: Daily   brickhouseco.com
Moderate

One of Redmond's best restaurants is the casual fine dining Brickhouse. In addition to natural, hormone-free steaks you'll find crab, lobster, ahi tuna, fresh Alaskan salmon and halibut, white prawns and bivalves. Chops, chicken and pasta dishes, soups and nice meal-size salads are equally tasty choices. Cobbler a la mode is housemade as are other desserts and savory sauces. A sister Brickhouse has moved to the Firehall Building in Bend (5 NW Minnesota Ave, 541/728-0334) and is open nightly for dinner.

Diego's Spirited Kitchen

447 SW 6th St   541/316-2002
Lunch, Dinner: Daily   diegosspiritedkitchen.com
Moderate

Diego's is crowded, lively and serves up great Mexican cuisine. Start with guacamole made tableside; it doesn't get any fresher! Although you may be tempted to make a meal of guacamole, chips and a margarita or two, pace yourself. Excellent dinner choices include pork osso buco, pork fajitas, carne asada and gulf shrimp dishes. Service is friendly, portions are generous and there are plenty of menu options to satisfy south-of-the-border cravings.

Eagle Crest Resort

1522 Cline Falls Road   541/923-2453, 855/682-4786
Lodge: Inexpensive to moderate   eagle-crest.com
Vacation rentals: Moderate to expensive

Nestled against the magnificent Cascade Mountains with Deschutes River frontage, the fully renovated Eagle Crest Resort is truly an all-season oasis. Summer months invite you to venture out and experience the best recreation in the region. The Stables at Eagle Crest Resort provide everything from pony rides to multi-hour trail rides. Located on 1,700 acres in high desert, this is the ultimate golfer's paradise with two championship golf courses, including a putting course and a challenge course. At the Ridge Sports Center, one of three on-site sports centers, adults can choose to be lulled into bliss by professional spa therapists at The Spa at Eagle Crest with a variety of pampering options or take a fitness class while kids play at the outdoor Splash Park. This family-fun resort also features indoor and outdoor pools, bike rentals to explore over 11 miles of trails and they even welcome your four-legged friends. Winter months bring a new experience to your stay with the colorful holiday lights celebration known as Starfest, running from Thanksgiving to New Years with a mile long exhibit. If marveling at the lights doesn't get you in the spirit, the holiday carolers, weekend horse-drawn wagon rides and cowboy Santa will! As far as dining goes, enjoy breakfast at Aerie Cafe where kids under 12 eat free; lunch at Greenside Cafe or Silverleaf Cafe where you can enjoy fresh sandwiches, wraps, burgers and a variety of snacks; and dinner and drinks at Niblick and Greene's serving an array of entrees including seafood, chicken, beef and pasta. Enjoy all of these amenities for yourself with a stay at one of their spacious 100 guestrooms or choose to stay at the two-, three- or four-bedroom vacation rentals.

Ida's Cupcake Cafe
738 SW Highland Ave   541/548-8164
(See detailed listing in Bend)

Madaline's Grill
2414 S Hwy 97   541/548-9964
Mon-Fri: 6 a.m.-10 p.m.; Sat, Sun: 7 a.m.-10 p.m.   madalinesgrill.com
Moderate
Known for its tacos, Madaline's is so much more. Serving breakfast, lunch and dinner, the restaurant offers a variety of dishes such as omelets, Benedicts, crepes and waffles; salads, sandwiches, burgers and pasta; and various entrees (seafood, beef, pork and chicken). The crab mac and cheese is a house favorite (although, it's often the fresh tableside guacamole, Pablo's famous shrimp ceviche, the sizzling signature fajitas or Mexican jambalaya that have the locals coming back). Pair dinner with a delicious margarita, a glass of wine or a beer from the full-service bar. Portions are large, but if you manage to save room for dessert, indulge in cheesecake, a gooey double fudge chocolate cake, homemade flan, a cheesecake chimi or deep fried ice cream.

The Original Pancake House
3030 SW 6th St   541/316-2515
Daily: 6-2   originalpanckagehouse.com
Moderate
(See detailed listing in Salem, Chapter 2.)

FAMILY ACTIVITIES

BEND

Cascade Indoor Sports (20775 High Desert Lane, 541/330-1183, cascadeindoorsports.com): roller hockey, soccer, volleyball, pickleball, large indoor play structure, birthday parties, leagues and sports camps

Deschutes Historical Museum (129 NW Idaho Ave, 541/389-1813, deschuteshistory.org): exhibits and artifacts depicting early Bend, pioneers, Native Americans and forests; Bend Heritage Walk Mobile Tour

High Desert Museum (59800 S Hwy 97, 541/382-4754, highdesertmuseum.org): natural and cultural resources of the High Desert

Mt. Bachelor Ski Resort (13000 SW Century Dr, 800/829-2442, mtbachelor.com): skiing, 12 lifts, lessons, equipment rental in winter; mountain bike park, disc golf, lift rides in summer

Newberry National Volcanic Monument (58201 S Hwy 97, 541/593-2421, fs.fed.us): Lava River Cave, Lava Cast Forest, hiking trails, lava flows (seasonal)

Sun Mountain Fun Center (300 NE River Mall Ave, 541/382-6161, sunmountainfun.com): indoor and outdoor activities: bowling, billiards, arcade, bumper cars, water war park, mini golf, go karts

Wanderlust Tours (61535 S Hwy 97, 541/389-8359, wanderlusttours.com): small groups, half-day guided outdoor tours and activities for all seasons and ages

MADRAS

Erickson Aircraft Collection (2408 NW Berg Dr, 541/460-5065, ericksoncollection.com): Erickson Aircraft Collection of rare, vintage fighter planes; ride in a warbird with experienced pilot

Richardson's Rock Ranch (6683 NE Hay Creek Road, 800/433-2680, richardsonrockranch.com): dig for thundereggs (seasonal)

Pig & Pound Public House

427 SW 8th St
Lunch: Sat, Sun; Dinner: Mon-Sat
Inexpensive and up

541/526-1697
Facebook

What do you get when a native Brit moves to Central Oregon? An English pub, of course. This cozy corner establishment is bent on preparing food from scratch with local products and serving a changing selection of local beers and hard ciders. Be sure to order the beer-battered onion rings; they are superb. I took a liking to bangers and mash while I was a

SISTERS
Black Butte (Hwy 20 to Forest Service Road 11): hike to the summit for panorama of the Cascades and two historic fire lookouts (seasonal)
Hoodoo Ski Area (Santiam Pass, Hwy 20, 541/822-3799, skihoodoo. com): 32 groomed runs, lessons, equipment rentals
Sisters Rodeo (Rodeo Grounds, Hwy 20, 541/549-0121, sistersrodeo. com): PRCA Rodeo second weekend in June, parade, fun activities

SUNRIVER
Oregon Observatory (57245 River Road, 541/598-4406, oregonobservatory.org): largest collection of telescopes for public use in the country; solar and night sky viewing
Sunriver Nature Center (57245 River Road, 541/593-4394, sunrivernaturecenter.org): hands-on activities, native animal exhibits, botanical garden, cave

TERREBONNE
Central Oregon Bungee Adventures (PS Ogden State Park, 541/668-5867, oregonbungee.com): jump from 300 feet above the Crooked River; May to October wind/lightning permitting
Smith Rock State Park (22 miles north of Bend, 541/548-7501, oregonstateparks.org; 541/516-0054, smithrock.com): hiking and mountain biking trails, guide services

WARM SPRINGS
The Museum at Warm Springs (2189 Hwy 26, 541/553-3331, museumatwarmsprings.org): permanent and changing exhibits of Pacific Northwest Native Americans; interpretive trail

student in England and owner Paul Mercer does an admirable job with his version of housemade sausage spiced with fennel and apple. Other common pub fare includes fish and chips, steak and ale pot pie and a half pork/half beef burger named the Oink and Boink. The menu is seasonal with hearty dishes in winter and lighter choices in summer. Chocolate Pig is the featured dessert; think of it as the classic Ding Dong treat on steroids.

Tate and Tate Catering

1205 SW Indian Ave	541/548-2512

Mon-Fri: 9-5:30; Sat: 9-4

2755 NW Crossing Dr, Suite 109, Bend	541/706-9317
Mon-Fri: 10-6	tateandtatecatering.com

Stop in at either location for a grab-and-go (not your typical fast food) lunch or dinner; order in (nominal delivery fee) or place your phone or e-order the day prior (before 5 p.m.). Choose from multiple soups, salads, land and sea entrees and desserts. "Special value packages" with such items as casseroles (cabbage rolls, spaghetti and meatballs or three cheese pasta, to name a few) are ideal for now or to stow in the freezer. Tate and Tate Catering is available to cater any event, from office lunches to full-service affairs; voted Best Caterer in Central Oregon for five years running.

SISTERS

Angeline's Bakery & Cafe

121 W Main St	541/549-9122
Daily: 6:30-6 (winter till 4)	angelinesbakery.com

Start your morning coffee routine with muffins, scones, cinnamon rolls, coffee cakes and bagels. All of these temptations, breads, cookies, brownies and more are handcrafted each day. Creative salads, homemade soups, wraps, polenta pizza and specials make tasty lunchtime choices. Many of the items are vegan, gluten-free, agave-sweetened and/or dairy-free in response to the dietary demands of health-conscious people; a strong emphasis is placed on raw foods and green smoothies. You can also find these flavorful baked products at small health food stores and coffee shops in Central Oregon. Angeline's white rice bread makes super sandwiches.

Aspen Lakes Golf Course

16900 Aspen Lakes Dr	541/549-4653
Golf Shop: Daily: 6:30 a.m.-dusk (summer)	aspenlakes.com

Aspen Lakes Golf Course began as an ongoing Cyrus family project in 1987 with the first nine holes completed in 1996 and the second in 2000. Natural elements were incorporated into the design and red cinders from the Cyrus property were crushed to fill the sand traps creating signature red sand bunkers. Restaurants operate seasonally; Brand 33 (541/549-3663) features Northwest cuisine, a mix of land and sea platters with fresh fruits and vegetables. Sandwiches, burgers, appetizers, pizza and entrees are offered at The Frog Pond (541/549-3663), the casual bar and lunch option. It is clear why Aspen Lakes is on many golfers "must play" list when visiting

Central Oregon. Golf boards are a fun alternative to riding in a cart; they feel similar to boarding or surfing.

Black Butte Ranch

13899 Bishops Cap   541/595-1252, 866/901-2961
Moderate and up   blackbutteranch.com

With magnificent views of Central Oregon meadows and mountains, the Black Butte Ranch setting is one of the most dramatic in the state. All manner of activities are available, including horseback riding, canoeing, fishing, snowshoeing and cross country skiing, and nearby winter skiing at Hoodoo Ski Area. Recreational facilities include two 18-hole golf courses, tennis courts, swimming pools and 18 miles of bike paths. In the early 1900s the area was the home of the Black Butte Land and Livestock Co. It later became the summer home of Howard Morgan and his family, members of the pioneer Portland Corbett dynasty. The 1,280 acres were then sold to Brooks-Scanlon Lumber firm. Now homeowners own and oversee the property's management. The Lodge Restaurant is popular with residents, vacationers and those who simply come to enjoy dining in a rustic but upscale atmosphere.

Clearwater Gallery and Framing & The Open Door

303 W Hood Ave   541/549-4994
Gallery: Mon-Sat   theclearwatergallery.com
Bistro: Lunch, Dinner: Mon-Sat   541/549-6076

Food, wine, art and music are all under one roof at this social and cultural gathering spot. When owners Julia and Dan Rickards remodeled the building for the gallery and framing business they created a cozy space for a bistro, cocktails and a wine bar. The inventory of fine arts, sculptures, pottery, woodworks and Dan's wildlife and landscape paintings is ever-changing. Works by over a dozen artists, mainly from the Northwest, are also displayed throughout the pine-paneled rooms. Daily specials at The Open Door bistro include satisfying homemade soups and pasta entrees. One of the best features is the outdoor courtyard; bask in the sunshine and enjoy food and drink with regular live entertainment and other fun weekly events.

The Cottonwood Café

403 Hood Ave   541/549-2699
Thu-Tue: 8-3   cottonwoodinsisters.com
Moderate

Restaurants sometimes evolve beyond the original intentions of their owners. That may be the story with Jen's Garden, which made its home in a circa-1930s cottage and was known for its southern French-inspired fare. At the time of its opening, the town of Sisters was in need of fine dining options, and Jen's Garden provided. Today the vision of owners Jennifer and T.R. McCrystal is no longer to be the renowned restaurant that was saved for special occasions, but instead to be the every-day special regular place, with the same dedication to quality and in the same cottage. Thus, Jen's is now The Cottonwood Cafe. Don't worry, the freshness, flavors and service remain the same as it serves breakfast (all day) and lunch (starting at 11), but now the name is more in tune with the updated offerings and ambiance. And there's a new dog-friendly backyard with a fire pit, heaters and bicycle parking. Don't miss the parmesan biscuits served with organic gravy for breakfast or for something a little more decadent indulge in the French toast bread pudding or a housemade cinnamon roll. Lunch offerings include a soup special, a variety of salads, sandwiches, wraps, burgers and a handful of signature dishes like the meatloaf burger and Brad's beer-braised brat (a family recipe).

Depot Cafe

250 W Cascade Ave   541/549-2572
Mon-Fri: 11-4 (seasonally till 6); Sat, Sun: 8-4   sistersdepot.com
Inexpensive to moderate

No matter the time of year, the town of Sisters sees a steady flow of traffic. It's long been a popular break for folks driving over the mountains on Highway 20 to walk the Western-style main street and peruse the shops, restaurants and boutiques. This rustic cafe makes everything from scratch with an emphasis on local ingredients. With that in mind, breakfasts (weekends only) are large and inexpensive; so are the excellent lunch-time turkey club and other sandwiches. Bread is homemade and you will want to save room for a delicious piece of pie (also homemade). Be sure to look up when you're inside to catch a glimpse of an electric train that continually chugs along an overhead track. The beautiful outdoor patio is restful in summer.

FivePine Lodge and Conference Center

1021 Desperado Trail   541/549-5900, 866/974-5900
Moderate to expensive   fivepinelodge.com

In addition to being a sought after romantic getaway location, FivePine Lodge caters to business groups who want five-star facilities in a small community. The state-of-the-art meeting facility also doubles as an intimate wedding, party and family reunion scene. Forget the briefcases and laptops and the luxurious accommodations become attractive for romantic stays; distractions are at a minimum. There are 32 cabins and eight lodge rooms outfitted with Amish-built hardwood furniture, oversized soaking tubs, gas fireplaces and large-screen TVs. Bookings include complimentary deluxe coffee and tea service in the morning and hosted wine and craft beer reception in the evening. Borrow a free cruiser bicycle (seasonal) or play in the outdoor heated pool (seasonal). The campus encompasses Sisters Athletic Club (541/549-6878, sistersathleticclub.com), where guests can take advantage of pursuing personal health and wellness; Shibui Spa (541/549-6164, shibuispa.com) for pampering treatments; and other food and entertainment venues. One could only hope to be snowed in over a long weekend.

Hoodoo Ski Area

Santiam Pass, Hwy 20   541/822-3799
Seasonal   skihoodoo.com

At the summit of Santiam Pass is Central Oregon's original ski area. Skiers, sledders, boarders, tubers and snow bikers are all accommodated on beginning and expert runs at this family-friendly butte. First-timers to Hoodoo will find convenient lessons and equipment rentals. Part of Hoodoo's appeal is its affordability and proximity to the Mid-Willamette Valley compared to the larger ski areas. There are 32 groomed runs, night skiing, over 800 acres of terrain, five lifts, a full-service lodge and the Autobahn Tubing Park with multiple runs (free tubes and cable tube tow with ticket purchase).

Hop in the Spa

371 W Cascade Ave   844/588-6818
Wed-Sat: 10-6; Sun: 11-5   hopinthespa.com

With an abundance of breweries in Bend, Sisters tends to be overlooked when travelers search for beer-themed activities. At least that was the case until the opening of Hop in the Spa, a beer-centric spa that invites you to get some real R & R with one of their hop-infused spa treatments. Learning about the operation was like listening to scientists describe their work. A first timer may think they just pour the microbrew right into the cedar soaking tubs, but it's much more of a process than that; one that involves extracting hop oils and other essential oils from Deschutes Brewery's microbrews, creating a blend of beer-inspired ingredients with other proprietary additives that will help your body in the healing process. The process for the client is as easy as setting up an appointment, starting out with a nice cold pint to unwind, followed by a microbrew soak (with the addition of another pint, if you please) and if that's not enough, a massage after your soak. Single 45 minute soaks start at $79 per person or $150 for couples. A variety of spa packages are available.

Long Hollow Ranch

71105 Holmes Road   541/923-1901
Seasonal: March-Oct   lhranch.com
Moderate

If you're looking for a guest ranch experience you'll find it at this historic Oregon ranch. With a history as a working ranch that goes back over a century, Long Hollow offers guest activities associated with producing hay, running cattle and operating a large ranch. Choose from five guest rooms, two cabins, one a former stage stop and one the original homestead house, each offering different themes and daily or weekly stays. The ranch operates on the American plan, which includes home-cooked meals, lodging and many other things you might want to do, including horseback riding, fishing, whitewater rafting, cookouts, games, reading, playing the piano or mingling with other guests and ranch hands. History comes alive in the redesigned ranch that was once headquarters of the Black Butte Land and Livestock Company; remnants of the old ways are still evident. Check the website for pricing, restrictions and additional information.

Sisters Bakery

251 E Cascade Ave   541/549-0361
Daily: 5-5   sistersbakery.com

Sisters Bakery is a great place to discover! The glass case is chock-full of decadent pastries and eclairs, brownies, cookies, muffins, scones, breads, pies and cobblers all made from scratch and baked fresh daily. You will also find cheese sticks and marionberry biscuits (made with whole berries), artisan and sandwich breads, as well as soups and coffee drinks. Beautifully decorated cakes are created from a menu of several cake, filling and icing flavors. Handmade, all-butter croissants are out of the oven by 7 every morning and filled with sweet or savory ingredients for breakfast-on-the-run. The list of tempting delights is mighty long and everything is delish!

Sno Cap Drive In

380 W Cascade Ave   541/549-6151
Lunch, Dinner: Daily   Facebook
Inexpensive

A Central Oregon tradition is a treat at this tiny burger and ice cream joint that showcases the fast food of yesteryear: thick ice cream shakes and tasty burgers and fries. There are over 25 flavors of homemade hard ice cream, delicious in shakes and sundaes. If you can't decide on just one, combine flavors to make your favorite combination. The menu lists several burgers, corn dogs and assorted basket options. No wonder there always seems to be a line at the window.

LES SCHWAB IS NO. 1

If there is one Oregon institution that symbolizes the very best in customer service, it is **Les Schwab Tires** (lesschwab.com) with over 480 stores throughout the Western United States. Founded in Prineville in 1952 by a gentleman who understood the value of efficient, competent customer attention and good products, Les Schwab brought the same level of customer care to all outlets, largely through employee opportunity and empowerment. (Example: Phil Wick began changing tires in the vehicle bays in 1965. By the time he retired in 2008, he was the company's chairman.) Personnel run, not walk, to greet customers; they are clean cut and well trained; free flat repairs is routine policy; prices are competitive. Quite simply, Les Schwab is the best.

Stitchin' Post

311/331 W Cascade Ave   541/549-6061
Mon-Sat: 9-6 (till 5 in winter); Sun: 10-4 stitchinpost.com

The mix of commerce in Sisters would not be complete without Stitchin' Post, a store dedicated to the bold use of color and modern techniques in sewing, quilting and knitting. Offering a wide assortment of materials, yarns, patterns, gadgets and notions, Stitchin' Post offers a fresh take on a traditional art form. Stitchin' Post recognizes that sewing, especially quilting, is a social activity, so the store (and its website) provides information on workshops and classes and information for experts and beginners alike.

Suttle Lodge & Boathouse

13300 US Hwy 20   541/638-7001
Moderate   thesuttlelodge.com

There's new ownership and renovations at Suttle Lodge & Boathouse in the beautiful Deschutes National Forest. This rustic timber lodge offers the comforts of an urban hotel and the excitement of the open wilderness. Each of the 11 lodge rooms includes a gas fireplace. Some have hot tubs and all offer excellent views of the lake or adjacent forest. Suttle's personalized "SL" Pendleton blankets are a nice touch. The outdoor concierge and Boathouse have you covered, whether you choose to rent a boat, kayak, canoe or paddle board; or get lost in adventure on a hike to the nearby lava lands. The small but welcoming in-lodge cocktail lounge, called Skip, will be there for an evening nightcap. The Boathouse includes a provisions shop and beer garden and serves casual breakfast, lunch and dinner from a selection of hot and cold sandwiches, chowder, salads and sides. The lodge menu includes more offerings such as small plates and snacks, pizzas and other soups, salads and sandwiches. For more privacy, opt for a fully-equipped lakeside cabin or one of the camp cabins when booking.

SUNRIVER

Garrison's Fishing Guide Services

Prices vary

541/593-8394, 541/410-8374
garrisonguide.com

This is Central Oregon's only year-round guide service for both fly and spin fishing. John Garrison and his expert guides provide the knowledge and gear to reel in the big ones from the best lakes and rivers in Central Oregon. Fish for kokanee, mackinaw or rainbow, brook, lake and bull trout; you can either keep or release your catch. Fishing trips are suitable for families (imagine the excitement of your youngster landing their first fish) as well as serious anglers and are competitively priced. Garrison uses 24-foot pontoon boats with space for kids to roam about; only one fishing party of up to six guests is booked on a boat.

Oregon Observatory

57245 River Road
Seasonal days and hours
Fees vary

541/598-4406
oregonobservatory.org

With its elevation, pitch-dark surroundings and crystal clear air, Sunriver is perfect for star-gazing (weather permitting). At the Oregon Observatory, there are many telescopes, from Tele Vue refractors to a 30-inch Newtonian to focus on outer space. View planets, faraway galaxies, nebulae and deep space binary stars. Daytime activities include solar viewing, classes and an extensive schedule of programs; solar viewing is included with on-property Sunriver Nature Center admission.

Sunriver Nature Center & Observatory

57245 River Road
Seasonal days and hours
Inexpensive

541/593-4394
sunrivernaturecenter.org

Whether or not you have kids in tow, stop in at the Sunriver Nature Center and Oregon Observatory for hands-on activities, native animal exhibits, a beautiful botanical garden and a creature cave where you can get up close to snakes, frogs, lizards and more. The Oregon Observatory offers daytime solar viewing and night sky viewing seasonally.

Sunriver Resort

17600 Center Dr 541/593-1000, 866/930-2687
Prices vary sunriver-resort.com

In 1965, Portland developers John D. Gray and Donald V. McCallum embarked on building this planned resort and residential community on property that once served as Camp Abbot, a World War II Army Corps of Engineers training facility. Through the following years, the natural environment has remained protected while attaining the reputation as a casual yet luxurious destination for families, conferences and special events. River Lodge and Lodge Village guestrooms and suites are within walking distance to the main lodge, Great Hall and other meeting spaces. Accommodations include free Wi-Fi, stone gas fireplace, a private deck and access to the Sage Springs Club and Spa (541/593-7890). Homes and condos are also available for rent. Resort amenities and activities are scattered throughout the enclave: equipment rentals, bike paths, 11 restaurants (varying fare, seasonal operating hours), retail shops, horse stables, four golf courses and a putting course, private airport and marina. The lodge restaurant is open year-round for breakfast and lunch (seasonal dinner service) and the cozy pub is open from 11 a.m. until closing. The Cove features a giant zero-entry pool and hot tub, private cabanas, a waterslide, nature walk and discovery area. This is a family-friendly resort with something for everyone.

WARM SPRINGS

Kah-Nee-Ta Resort and Spa

6823 Hwy 8 541/553-1112, 800/554-4786
Moderate to expensive kahneeta.com

This resort along the Warm Springs River offers a fun destination for the entire family. The Olympic-size pool is fed by mineral hot springs and features water slides. Revive the body at Spa Wanapine (spa by the river), test your putting skills at the miniature golf course, or find other recreational opportunities on the basketball and volleyball courts and horse stables. Lodging options range from village suites, RV parking spaces and tipis. Additional rooms are in the lodge (a half mile away, complimentary shuttle service), which also contains the convention center, restaurants and another pool. Indian Head Casino (indianheadgaming.com) is located 13 miles down the road. The area boasts 300 days of sunshine a year.

The Museum at Warm Springs

2189 Hwy 26 541/553-3331
Daily: Seasonal hours museumatwarmsprings.org
Nominal

Collections and exhibitions of Pacific Northwest Native American ceremonial clothing and ritual implements as well as baskets, beadwork, paintings, photographs and sculptures are featured at this beautiful museum
on the Warm Springs Indian Reservation. Artifacts are displayed in permanent and changing exhibits; interactive exhibits come alive with colorful
visuals and authentic audio recordings; a small amphitheater is outside.
The museum, built in 1993 (Oregon's first tribal museum), is dedicated to
preserving, advancing and sharing the cultural, traditional and artistic heritage of the Confederated Tribes of Warm Springs. The interpretive Twanat
Trail is a quarter-mile trail with educational displays about the area's animals, birds, plants and water creatures.

Gerry's Exclusive List

BBQ
Baldy's BBQ (2670 NE Hwy 20, Bend, 541/388-4227; 235 SW Century Dr, Bend, 541/385-7427; 343 NW 6th St, Redmond, 541/923-2271)

Bars and Pubs with Good Eats
Deschutes Brewery & Public House (1044 NW Bond St, Bend; 541/382-9242)
Pig & Pound Public House (427 SW 8th St, Redmond; 541/526-1697)

Best Sleeps
Black Butte Ranch (13800 Bishops Cap, Sisters; 541/595-1252)
Brasada Ranch (16986 SW Brasada Ranch Road, Powell Butte; 541/526-6865)
Eagle Crest Resort (1522 Cline Falls Road, Redmond; 541/923-2453)
Five Pine Lodge (1021 Desperado Trail, Sisters; 541/549-5900)
The Oxford Hotel (10 NW Minnesota Ave, Bend; 541/382-8436)
Pronghorn (65600 Pronghorn Club Dr, Bend; 866/320-5024)
Riverhouse on the Deschutes (3075 N Business Hwy 97, Bend; 541/389-3111)
Sunriver (17600 Center Dr, Sunriver; 541/593-1000)
Tetherow Lodges (61240 Skyline Ranch Road, Bend; 541/388-2582)

Breads and Bakery Goods
Angeline's Bakery & Cafe (121 W Main St, Sisters; 541/549-9122)
Nancy P's Cafe & Bakery (1054 NW Milwaukee Ave, Bend; 541/322-8778)
Sisters Bakery (251 E Cascade Ave, Sisters; 541/549-0361)
The Sparrow Bakery (950 SE Scott St, Bend, 541/330-6321; 2748 NW Crossing Dr, #110, Bend, 541/647-2323)

Breakfast/Brunch
The Cottonwood Café (403 Hood Ave, Sisters; 541/549-2699)
Currents (Riverhouse on the Deschutes, 3075 N Business Hwy 97, Bend; 541/389-3111): brunch
Jackson's Corner (845 NW Delaware Ave, Bend, 541/647-2198; 1500 NE Cushing Dr, Bend, 541/382-1751)
Depot Cafe (250 W Cascade Ave, Sisters; 541/549-2572)
McKay Cottage Restaurant (62910 O.B. Riley Road, Suite 340, Bend; 541/383-2697)

The Sparrow Bakery (950 SE Scott St, Bend, 541/330-6321; 2748 NW Crossing Dr, #110, Bend, 541/647-2323)
The Victorian Cafe (1404 NW Galveston Ave, Bend; 541/382-6411)

Burgers
Bogey's Burgers (2115 NE Hwy 20, Bend, 541/241-2890; 655 NW Greenwood Ave, Redmond, 541/316-1786)
Dawg House II (507 SW 8th St, Redmond; 541/526-5989)
Pilot Butte Drive-In (917 NE Greenwood Ave, Bend; 541/382-2972): bacon cheeseburger

Casual Dining/Casual Prices
The Cottonwood Café (403 Hood Ave, Sisters; 541/549-2699)
Depot Cafe (250 W Cascade Ave, Sisters; 541/549-2572)
McKay Cottage Restaurant (62910 O.B. Riley Road, Suite 340, Bend; 541/383-2697)
One Street Down Cafe (124 SW 7th St, Redmond; 541/647-2341)
Sno Cap Drive In (380 W Cascade Ave, Sisters; 541/549-6151)
The Sparrow Bakery (50 SE Scott St, Bend, 541/330-6321; 2748 NW Crossing Dr, #110, Bend, 541/647-2323)
Spork (937 NW Newport Ave, Bend; 541/390-0946)

Coffee and Tea
AK's Tea Room (525 6th St, Redmond; 541/526-5522)
Coho Coffee Co. (306 NW 7th St, Redmond; 541/526-0368)
Dudley's Bookshop Cafe (135 NW Minnesota Ave, Bend; 541/749-2010)
Lone Pine Coffee Roasters (845 Tin Pan Alley, Bend; 541/306-1010)
Sisters Coffee Company (273 W Hood Ave, Sisters; 541/549-0527)
Suttle Tea (450 E Cascade Ave, Sisters; 541/549-8077)
Thump Coffee (25 NW Minnesota Ave, Bend; 541/388-0226)

Confections
Goody's (1111 SE Division St, Bend, 541/385-7085; 957 NW Wall St, Bend, 541/389-5185; 57100 Beaver Dr, Sunriver, 541/593-2155)

Deli
Newport Avenue Market (1121 NW Newport Ave, Bend; 541/382-3940)

Desserts
Ariana (1304 NW Galveston Ave, Bend; 541/330-5539)

The Blacksmith Restaurant (211 NW Greenwood Ave, Bend; 541/318-0588)
Brickhouse (5 NW Minnesota Ave, Bend, 541/728-0334; 412 SW 6th St, Redmond, 541/526-1782)
Greg's Grill (395 SW Powerhouse Dr, Bend; 541/382-2200)
Ida's Cupcake Cafe (1314 NW Galveston Ave, Bend, 541/383-2345; 1155 SW Division St, A-7, Bend, 541/678-5057; 738 SW Highland, Redmond, 541/548-8164)
Madaline's Grill (2414 S Hwy 97, Redmond; 541/548-9964)
Tim Garling's Jackalope Grill (750 NW Lava Road, Suite 139, Bend; 541/318-8435)

Doughnuts
The Dough Nut (1227 NW Galveston Ave, Bend; 755 NE Greenwood Ave, Bend, 541/241-8788)
Richard's Donuts and Pastries (61419 S Hwy 97, Suite T, Bend; 541/385-3310)
Sisters Bakery (251 E Cascade Ave, Sisters; 541/549-0361)
Sweetheart Donuts (210 SE 3rd St, Bend; 541/323-3788)

Fireside
McKay Cottage Restaurant (62910 O.B. Riley Road, #340, Bend; 541/383-2697)

Fish and Seafood
Anthony's at the Old Mill District (475 SW Powerhouse Dr, Bend; 541/389-8998)
Kayo's Dinner House and Lounge (415 NE 3rd St, Bend; 541/323-2520)

Foreign Flavors
BRITISH: Pig & Pound Public House (427 SW 8th St, Redmond; 541/526-1697)
CHINESE: Chi Chinese & Sushi Bar (70 NW Newport Ave, Bend; 541/323-3931); **Five Fusion & Sushi Bar** (821 NW Wall St, Bend; 541/323-2328)
EASTERN MEDITERRANEAN: Joolz (916 NW Wall St, Bend; 541/388-5094)
ITALIAN: Trattoria Sbandati (1444 NW College Way, Bend; 541/306-6825)
JAPANESE: Kanpai Sushi & Sake Bar (990 NW Newport Ave, Bend; 541/388-4636)

MEXICAN: **Diego's Spirited Kitchen** (447 SW 6th St, Redmond; 541/316-2002); **Madaline's Grill** (2414 S Hwy 97, Redmond; 541/548-9964)

Game

Tim Garling's Jackalope Grill (750 NW Lava Road, Bend; 541/318-8435)

Hot Dogs and Sausage

Dawg House II (507 SW 8th St, Redmond; 541/526-5989)
Primal Cuts Meat Market (1244 NW Galveston Ave, Bend; 541/706-9308)

Ice Cream and Other Frozen Treats

Bontà Natural Artisan Gelato (920 NW Bond St, Suite 108, Bend; 541/306-6606)

Liquid Libations

The Stihl Whiskey Bar (550 NW Franklin Ave, Suite 118, Bend; 541/383-8182): 300 whiskeys; steaks, chops, appetizers

Personal Favorites

Ariana (1304 NW Galveston Ave, Bend; 541/330-5539)
Pine Tavern (967 NW Brooks St, Bend; 541/382-5581)

Pie

Depot Cafe (250 W Cascade Ave, Sisters; 541/549-2572)
Nancy P's Cafe & Bakery (1054 NW Milwaukee Ave, Bend; 541/322-8778)
Sisters Bakery (251 E Cascade Ave, Sisters; 541/549-0361)

Pizza

Blondie's Pizza (57195 Beaver Dr, Sunriver; 541/593-1019)

Sandwiches

Planker Sandwiches (824 NW Wall St, Bend; 541/317-5717)
Primal Cuts Meat Market (1244 NW Galveston Ave, Bend; 541/706-9308)
Sisters Meat and Smokehouse (110 S Spruce St, Sisters; 541/719-1186)

Soups
McKay Cottage Restaurant (62910 O.B. Riley Road, #340, Bend; 541/383-2697)

Southern
Zydeco Kitchen & Cocktails (919 NW Bond St, Bend; 541/312-2899)

Steaks
The Blacksmith Restaurant (211 NW Greenwood Ave, Bend; 541/318-0588)
Brickhouse (412 SW 6th St, Redmond, 541/526-1782; 5 NW Minnesota Ave, Bend, 541/728-0334)

Sushi
Chi Chinese & Sushi Bar (70 NW Newport Ave, Bend; 541/323-3931)
Five Fusion & Sushi Bar (821 NW Wall St, Bend; 541/323-2328)
Kanpai Sushi & Sake Bar (990 NW Newport Ave, Bend; 541/388-4636)

View Restaurants
Greg's Grill (395 SW Powerhouse Dr, Bend; 541/382-2200)

Notes

Notes

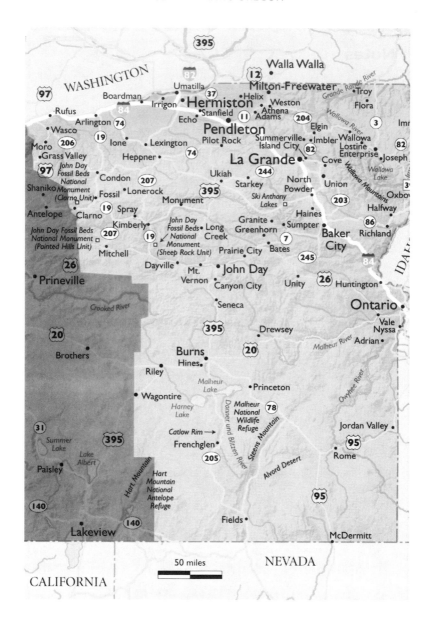

CHAPTER SIX

Eastern Oregon

BAKER CITY

Baker Heritage Museum

2480 Grove St
Seasonal: March-Oct
Nominal

541/523-0308
bakerheritagemuseum.com

Baker City was once the third-largest city in Oregon and fastest-growing community in the West. Housed in the city's former natatorium, this building helps preserve the area's eclectic chronicles. Along with many artifacts, the Cavin-Warfel Collection of rocks, fossils and minerals, begun in the 1930s as a hobby of two Baker City sisters who continued their passion for 45 years, is housed here; the Wyatt Family Collection is an assemblage of some 2,000 agates, jasper and other rocks and gems. The Adler House Museum (2305 Main St, 541/523-9308) is also managed by the Baker Heritage Museum. Mr. Adler, a low-key gent, was very successful in the magazine distribution business and became a major benefactor to nearly every local cause. A lifelong bachelor, Leo died in 1993 at the age of 98 and left his $20 million fortune to his beloved community. His Italianate home (circa 1889) has been restored to its glory days with period wallpaper, original furniture, artwork and light fixtures.

Barley Brown's Beer

2190 Main St
Mon-Sat: 4-10
Moderate

541/523-4266
barleybrowns.com

The aim of this tap house and restaurant is to provide "small batch handcrafted beer, good food, good company, good times" according to owner Tyler Brown. Here you'll find plenty of comfort food along with award-winning beer to wash it down. Standout dinners include a one-pound rack of baby back ribs, shrimp and alligator pasta, steaks, salads and pub grub; a few menu items are available at the tap house. A production brewery and tap house are across the street and feature 44 of Barley Brown's beers. Not unlike the iconic Cheers television show, everyone is likely to know your name; or get to know it should you venture in more than a time or two.

BELLA Main Street Market

2023 Main St   541/523-7490
Daily: 9-6 (Sun till 5)   bigmerlot.com

Check out the impressive selection of groceries plus gourmet foods, fine wines, kitchenware, gifts and good java drinks from the unique espresso bar (a massive 18-foot long, two-inch thick slab of slate). The shelves hold local and organic staples and an extensive selection of cheese and salami and handmade pastries from Sweet Wife Baking (541/403-6628, sweetwifebaking.com). Many of the gourmet foodstuffs are Baker City exclusives; gather up an assortment to include in a personalized gift (choose a basket, beautiful platter or whatever strikes your fancy) appropriate for any occasion. Kitchen necessities, gadgets and accessories of all sizes and prices will spiff up your kitchen, dining room and pantry. Check out their store in La Grande, too.

Charley's Deli & Ice Cream

2101 Main St, Suite 101   541/524-9307
Mon-Fri: 9-6; Sun: 11-5   charleysdeli.com
Inexpensive

"Eat well. Laugh often. Love Charley's." That's the motto for this family delicatessen at Main and Broadway. Premium meats are sliced fresh for each sandwich made here, every time. It might be the best sandwich in town. Enjoy many flavors of hand scooped ice cream plus housemade soups and salads, shakes, espresso and more.

Geiser Grand Hotel

1996 Main St   541/523-1889, 888/434-7374
Moderate to expensive   geisergrand.com

Barbara and Dwight Sidway undertook an unbelievable project in 1993 to bring this historic landmark back to life, a restoration that has garnered prestigious awards. First opened in 1889, the Geiser Grand is an architectural jewel with ornate mahogany, gleaming brass, crystal chandeliers in every room and leaded stained glass. Spend a memorable night in the grand Cupola Suite, where you will enjoy impressive mountain views and luxuriate in the large, well-appointed bathroom. Other accommodations are also tastefully decorated and outfitted. Belly up to the mahogany bar in the 1889 Cafe for sundown libations or dinner and enjoy local musicians and other entertainment. The classy Palm Court restaurant is surrounded by a mahogany balcony and basks under a stained glass ceiling. Fine dining entrees include meats, fish and seafood, in-house smoked meats and decadent homemade desserts. In 2018 the hotel will expand into an 1889 building next door, adding 18 rooms and suites and a rooftop terrace bar with hot tub and fire pits.

Inland Cafe
2715 10th St   541/523-9041
Mon-Sat: 6 a.m.-8 p.m.; Sun: 7-2   Facebook
Inexpensive to moderate

Inland Cafe is endorsed by ranchers and loggers for stick-to-your-ribs meals for breakfast, lunch and dinner. The menu features a dozen versions of one-third-pound Angus beef burgers, salads, appetizers and other popular entrees like traditional roast beef, roasted turkey, steaks, liver and onions and a one-pound chicken-fried steak; prime rib is offered on Friday and Saturday evenings. You're likely to find folks queued up for breakfast, especially giant homemade cinnamon rolls, and substantial lunches. Not to worry though if you have a small appetite; there are senior meals, as well as lighter menu options.

The Sycamore Tree
2108 Main St   541/523-4840
Mon-Sat: 10-6   sycamoregifts.com

You will easily wrap up your gift list and please any recipient with fudge, elegant gifts, home decor, religious items or a piece from the art gallery featuring local artists. Attractive vignettes showcase the merchandise and suggest eye-appealing arrangements. If you have a sweet tooth, make a beeline to the fudge counter for morsels of chocolate sensations or other interesting flavor variations, all made in the store by hand with quality ingredients.

BATES

Boulder Creek Ranch
72585 Middle Fork Lane   541/421-3031
Moderate   bouldercreekranch.net

Journey to Blue Mountain country for the rare opportunity to stay in an authentic Basque sheepherder's wagon. Sheepherders and their camps were a common sight in the 1800s, and now this ranch brings the Old West back to the forefront with this unique idea. The canvas-covered wagon has a full-size bed and offers a table with bench seating. Amenities? No power, no running water, no phone, no television — that's the point. Coupled with the authentic wagon is a one-bedroom guest cabin immediately next door. With the cabin's modern-day facilities (bath, kitchen, woodstove), perhaps mom and dad will stay there and let the kids have a private adventure in the wagon (available only in summer months). Provisions are supplied to prepare a full ranch breakfast before you head out to explore the property or help with ranch chores.

BOARDMAN

River Lodge and Grill

6 Marine Dr   541/481-6800, 888/988-2009
Mon-Thu: 6 a.m.-10 p.m.; Fri: 6 a.m.-9 p.m.
Sat, Sun: 7 a.m.-9 p.m.   riverlodgeandgrill.com
Moderate (restaurant); Inexpensive (lodge)
Don't make the mistake of missing Boardman; it is definitely worth the detour from I-84. River Lodge and Grill offers affordable lodging along the Columbia River in a log and river-stone complex in rooms that are tidy, clean and well-appointed. The riverside rooms and restaurant overlook the private rocky beach. You'll get good, quality comfort food at the family-friendly, lodge-style restaurant where the menu changes seasonally.

BURNS

Crystal Crane Hot Springs

59315 Hwy 78   541/493-2312
Inexpensive to moderate
Resting your head in the middle of nowhere is fun and a great way to better understand our diverse state. This is just such a quaint, atypical place where more adventurous travelers can spend the night in their tent, use the available RV hookups or the 26-foot tipi (seasonally) with soaking tub. Newly added are five hotel-like rooms with amenities such as modern TVs, private bathrooms and private soaking tubs. Other comfortable digs include one of the establishment's four rustic cabins or a room in Sage Inn (mostly shared bathrooms), a three-bedroom apartment and a three-bedroom home. Enjoy the great outdoors from the warm geothermal spring-fed pond or private soaking tubs in The Bathhouse, which also offers showers and restrooms; a nominal fee is charged for day use. The Commons Room is the social center and has kitchen facilities.

RJ's Restaurant

920 W Tyler St   541/573-6346

Daily: 7-2

Inexpensive

Proclaiming "anything you want, any time of the day," new owners Mark and Maria Webb continue this quality operation just like patrons have known it for four decades. The menu includes many flavors of malts, shakes and sundaes, salads, hamburgers, fish and chips, baked potatoes and a kids' menu. Burgers are accompanied with a hearty portion of fries (don't miss the super Swiss cheese and mushroom burger); breakfast from an extensive menu is available throughout the day.

CANYON CITY

Oxbow Wagons & Coaches

303 S Canyon City Blvd   541/575-2911

Call for appointment   oxbowwagonsandcoaches.com

In this high-tech day and age, horse-drawn vehicles are an anomaly. However, owners Mary and Jim Jensen buy and restore these wonderful antique vehicles for aficionados like themselves. They sell high quality carriages, coaches, wagons, chuck wagons, sleighs, carts and an occasional hearse at fair prices. They also carry Amish-made harnesses, parts and accessories such as sleigh bells, cast iron horse heads, gears, lamps, western decor items, antiques and necessary accessories. Visitors are welcome, but call ahead to make sure someone is minding the shop. Frequent auctions and shows pull the proprietors away, but it's necessary so they can add to their stock and locate hard-to-find pieces for customers.

CONDON

Country Flowers

201 S Main St   541/384-4120

Mon-Sat: 9-6; Sun: noon-5   countryflowerscondon.com

This family-owned shop offers expert floral arrangements in contemporary and traditional styles, suitable for weddings, funerals or any special occasion, and all backed by prompt, friendly service. In addition to a large inventory of fresh flowers, the shop also features plants, European/dish gardens, unique gifts and clothing. Outside the shop there's a very inviting façade with potted plants on the sidewalk and an awning for shade. Inside there's an old-fashioned soda fountain serving espresso, ice cream and food. Oh, and one more thing: Piggybacking inside is a small branch of Powell's Books. Yes, of the same Powell's City of Books that is world famous in Portland. (The Web address goes to their Teleflora page; find more information on Facebook.)

Hotel Condon

202 S Main St   541/384-4624
Moderate   hotelcondon.com

Although this historic hotel was built in 1920, it has all of the amenities you would expect in a 21st century hotel, while retaining its original charm. The 18 guest rooms and private bathrooms are individually decorated. A complimentary wine and cheese reception is served every afternoon and a continental breakfast is served each morning. There are winter rates available Nov. 1 to Feb. 28, and the dining room and Sage Lounge are available to rent for special occasions (catering options are available). The hotel is conveniently situated for day trips to the John Day Fossil Beds and Paleontology Center and the new Cottonwood Canyon State Park on the John Day River. Condon hosts special events throughout the year including Robert Burns Festival; the Tumbleweed Basketball Tournament; the fabulous 4th of July celebration featuring a classic small town parade, Soap Box Derby and Tricycle Races; and a Fall Festival. The region offers year-round fishing, biking, hiking and seasonal hunting. Condon also has a seasonal farmer's market, golf course, movie theater and community swimming pool.

DAYVILLE

Thomas Condon Paleontology Center
John Day Fossil Beds National Monument

Hwy 19, 8 miles north of Dayville   541/987-2333
Hours vary   nps.gov/joda
Free

The Thomas Condon Paleontology Center serves as a visitor center for the Sheep Rock Unit of the John Day Fossil Beds National Monument. See over 500 fossils in the museum and marvel at the giant murals depicting life in Eastern Oregon before it became a sagebrush desert. There are an additional 50,000 fossils stored in the collection room where cutting-edge research goes on year-round. All fossils on display were found in the John Day Fossil Beds; look for rhino, giraffe-deer, camels, horses, bear-dogs, oreodonts and entelodonts, but no dinosaurs. The park's headquarters are in the James Cant 1917 homestead dwelling; its history is an interesting story. Venture a bit farther to see two other components of this national monument: Painted Hills Unit (Hwy 26, nine miles northwest of Mitchell) and Clarno Unit (Hwy 218, 20 miles west of Fossil); the colorful formations attract visitors from around the world. Don't even think about digging for fossils on these properties; instead, head to the town of Fossil where collecting is available to the public behind the high school (wheelercounty-oregon.com/fossils.html).

DIAMOND

Hotel Diamond
49130 Main St   541/493-1898
Seasonal: April-Oct   historichoteldiamond.com
Inexpensive
With Steens Mountain, the Malheur National Wildlife Refuge, Kiger Gorge and the Alvord Desert as backdrops, the great Oregon Outback beckons to a certain variety of traveler. The Hotel Diamond, billed as the oldest hotel in the area, may be just the rustic place for them. Built in 1898, the hotel offers eight rooms, some with shared baths, others with private baths, and the easy price includes breakfast. There's also a cottage and a three-bedroom ranch house that require a two-night minimum stay. Breakfasts, lunches and family-style dinners are available daily, and you'll enjoy comfortable digs with tasteful antique furnishings that make you feel at home. The screened porch is a favorite place for guests.

ENTERPRISE

Arrowhead Ranch Cabins
64745 Pine Tree Road   541/426-6420
Seasonal: May-Oct   arrowheadranchcabins.com
Moderate
Whether you are staying a few days or longer, this updated ranch with modern conveniences could provide just the right retreat. You can bicycle the local country roads, meander the walking paths and observe the abundant flora and fauna. Each cabin has a private outdoor sitting space with picnic table, Adirondack chairs and charcoal grill. The one-bedroom Ruby Peak cabin provides 800 square feet of living, bed and bath space that accommodates up to four people. The white clapboard Wagon House cabin is slightly larger. Both vintage knotty-pine paneled cabins have full-service kitchens, leather recliners, first-rate bed linens and down comforters making "camping" here first-class. The stately white peg-constructed barn (circa 1888) has been a favorite feature of the Wallowa County Barn Tour. Board your horse for $10 a day; you provide feed unless pasture is available (no other pets or smoking). A secluded open-air fire pit is the perfect setting for star-gazing. Guests are treated to a box of handcrafted truffles from their **Arrowhead Chocolates** (100 N Main St, 541/432-2871) operation in Joseph.

FAMILY ACTIVITIES

BAKER CITY
Baker Heritage Museum (2480 Grove St, 541/523-9308, bakerheritagemuseum.com): permanent and changing exhibits
National Historic Oregon Trail Interpretive Center (22267 Hwy 86, 541/523-1843, oregontrail.blm.gov): exhibits, hiking trails, Oregon Trail ruts

BOARDMAN
SAGE Center (101 Olson Road, 541/481-7243, visitsage.com): interactive experience of region's sustainable agriculture

DAYVILLE
Thomas Condon Paleontology Center (John Day Fossil Beds National Monument, Hwy 19, 8 miles north of Dayville, 541/987-2333, nps.gov/joda): museum, murals, history in visitor center

ELGIN
Eagle Cap Excursion Train (300 Depot St, 800/323-7330, eaglecaptrainrides.com): May through October; about 20 themed excursions

JOSEPH
Wallowa Lake State Park (72214 Marina Lane, 541/432-4185, oregonstateparks.org): outdoor recreation
Wallowa Lake Tramway (541/432-5331 in summer, 503/781-4321 in winter, wallowalaketramway.com): 3,700 feet vertical ascent to the

Barking Mad Farm Bed & Breakfast

65156 Powers Road   541/886-0171
Moderate   barkingmadfarm.com

If you'd like time away from the kids, you'll love a stay with Emily and Rob Klavins in their restored farmhouse. The working farm setting couldn't be more idyllic; grazing buffalo, alpine vistas, tranquil grounds and a short drive to Joseph and Wallowa Lake and local brew pubs. Guest rooms are spacious, well-appointed and afford glorious views. You're in for a treat each morning with gourmet breakfasts featuring local farm-fresh ingredients served on the wrap-around porch with an uninterrupted view of the Eagle Cap. Whether you spend your day shopping in Joseph, exploring the backcountry or just reading a book, unwind each night watching the sun

summit of Mt. Howard; seasonal

NORTH POWDER
Anthony Lakes Mountain Resort (47500 Anthony Lakes Hwy, 541/856-3277, anthonylakes.com): seasonal skiing

ONTARIO
Four Rivers Cultural Center and Museum (676 SW 5th Ave, 541/889-8191, 4rcc.com): performing arts theater, museum, Japanese garden, gallery

PENDLETON
Pendleton Underground Tours (37 SW Emigrant Ave, 541/276-0730): walking tour of the real Old West highlighting legal and illegal pursuits
Tamástslikt Cultural Institute (47106 Wildhorse Blvd, 541/966-9748; tamastslikt.org): interactive exhibits, Living Culture Village

PRINCETON
Malheur National Wildlife Refuge (36391 Sodhouse Lane, 541/493-2612, fws.gov/malheur): birding, wetlands

SUMPTER
Sumpter Valley Railroad (211 Austin St, 541/894-2268, sumptervalleyrailroad.org): seasonal weekend and holiday excursions

set with a glass of wine around a crackling campfire. With backgrounds in outdoor education and sustainability, the Klavins are living their dream to share the natural beauty of an oft-overlooked, world-class corner of the state with visitors from around the world.

Enterprise House Bed & Breakfast
508 1st South St   541/426-4238
Moderate   enterprisehousebnb.com
This circa-1910 Colonial Revival mansion is minutes from Joseph and Wallowa Lake. Relaxation beckons as guests approach the beautifully restored home, resplendent with white picket fence, a porch swing, stained glass, ornate woodwork and nostalgic wood-frame screen doors. Choose from

three guest rooms and two suites with private baths. Proprietors Judy and Jack Burgoyne start each day with an impressive breakfast buffet of organic and locally grown products.

RimRock Inn

83471 Lewiston Hwy   541/828-7769
Summer season   rimrockinnor.com
Inexpensive to moderate

The RimRock Inn is 34 miles north of Enterprise. The summer season opens Memorial Day weekend and runs through September. Lodging includes two vintage trailers and four tipis, which sleep one to six people. Both options are fully outfitted with luxury bedding. Fire pits with complimentary firewood and battery-powered lighting are provided. Water, restrooms and showers are nearby. One indoor suite is available. Accommodations include a full country breakfast at the inn. The full-service restaurant offers breakfast, lunch and dinner, and a view that overlooks the beautiful canyon. Reservations are required for dinner. Fresh, local, organic fare is served and almost everything is made from scratch. This experience is also described as "glamping on the edge" (glamorous camping on the edge of Joseph Creek Canyon in Wallowa County).

Terminal Gravity Brewing and Public House

803 SE School St   541/426-3000
Sun, Mon: 11-9; Wed-Sat: 11-10 (seasonal)   terminalgravitybrewing.com
Inexpensive to moderate

Pub grub reigns supreme at this home of extensive beer-making. Order a pale ale, ESG (extra special golden), IPA, porter, stout or other brewed delight (also sold in many supermarkets) to go along with family dining favorites. A sample of menu items includes nachos and other starters, beer mac and cheese, salads, burgers (buffalo and locally-raised grass-fed beef), sandwiches and pastas. Picnic tables, shaded by aspens, are liberally spread around the grounds; a refreshing stop all the way around.

FIELDS

The Fields Station

22276 Fields Dr   541/495-2275
Mon-Sat: 8-6; Sun: 9-5   Facebook
Inexpensive

Fields is a small, unincorporated community deep in the Oregon Outback — 112 miles south of Burns on Highway 205 (also known as Catlow Valley Road in the area). The Fields Station store is at the center of the community and stocks groceries, toiletries, auto supplies, beer, beverages and snacks, and it features Oregon's smallest liquor store (with a full range of "snake bite medicine"). The cafe (closes daily at 4 p.m.) is famous for its burgers such as the half-pounder with chili and the double bacon cheeseburger. Breakfasts are equally satisfying and large. Nothing is more refreshing on a hot summer day than a huge milkshake or malt, made by hand the old-fashioned way and served in a frosty steel cup. A most welcome sight for motorists running on fumes is one of the few gas pumps in the area (diesel and propane available, too). If you're looking for a place to call it a night, there are guest rooms, or you may prefer to stay in the Old Hotel which rents as a single unit; RVs are accommodated in the adjacent facility.

FOSSIL

Fossil Mercantile Company
555 Main St   541/763-4617
Mon-Sat: 8-7 (till 6 in winter); Sun: 8-5
Locally known as "The Merc," this true general store has been reincarnated several times since its 1883 opening, yet still retains the feel of yesteryear. It's at the heart of this small community, and to those who live, work and play miles from city shopping opportunities, it's a godsend for fabrics, clothing, groceries, dry goods and more.

Wilson Ranches Retreat Bed & Breakfast
15809 Butte Creek Road   541/763-2227, 866/763-2227
Year round   wilsonranchesretreat.com
Inexpensive to moderate
The pioneer ancestors of fifth-generation Nancy and Phil Wilson settled in Wheeler and Gilliam counties, choosing one of the most picturesque areas in Eastern Oregon for their homestead. For an authentic Western retreat, book accommodations at this 9,000-acre working cattle and dude ranch. Up to 20 guests are housed in the 1910 Sears Roebuck Ranch House; each of the six pristine ranch-style guest rooms, some with private baths and fireplaces, is uniquely decorated. There is plenty to do with multiple scenic horseback riding trails, fishing, birding, hiking, mountain biking and, of course, the John Day Fossil Beds National Monument. While Nancy and Phil regale visitors with tales of family history, a hearty full-course ranch-style breakfast is served in preparation for a memorable day in the beautiful Butte Creek Valley. Guests are invited to grill their own steaks and burgers for dinner. Rooms are outfitted with amenities befitting a nice hotel and guests have access to a movie library, books, games, TV/DVD and cowboy gear (boots, hats and saddle

bags). Turn your stay into an occasion with optional activities, flowers, chocolates or other thoughtful touches.

FRENCHGLEN

Frenchglen Hotel
39184 Hwy 205   541/493-2825
Mid-March to Nov   frenchglenhotel.com
Inexpensive to moderate
When you want to go to Oregon's outback but camping isn't your cup of tea, make a reservation at this historic State Heritage Site at the base of Steens Mountain. Guest rooms are rustic and restrooms are down the hall. Breakfast, lunch and dinner are served in the dining room; dinners by reservation. The name stems from Peter French's 1800s cattle operation financed by Californian Dr. Hugh Glenn; thus, the French-Glenn Livestock Co. Commonly referred to as the P Ranch, it was once the largest spread for miles around, if not statewide (30,000 to 45,000 cattle, 3,000 horses and mules on 140,000 acres). French, unfortunately, met his demise in 1897 during a squatter's squabble when an illegal settler shot him.

HAINES

Haines Steak House
910 Front St   541/856-3639
Dinner: Wed-Mon   hainessteakhouse.com
Moderate
For Old West-style dinners, set your sights on the building with a chuck wagon above the entrance. This family-owned, Western-themed steak-house has long been known for large portions of prime rib, steaks and extensive seafood offerings; there are also options for petite appetites or young buckaroos. Start with the chuck wagon salad bar of fresh fixings, chili, baked beans and cowboy bread. Folks from all over the world venture off the beaten track for dinner here; opening hours vary.

HALFWAY

Cornucopia Lodge
Queen Mine Road   541/742-4500, 800/742-6115
Inexpensive to moderate   cornucopialodge.com
Miners working the gold strike in the northeastern Oregon town of Cornu-copia in the 1800s would have wished for accommodations like Cornucopia Lodge, adjacent to the Eagle Cap Wilderness. The lodge's guest room and

common areas are tastefully appointed with comfortable furniture, and the five cabins (four to six people) are just as appealing. There are plenty of activities for every season: Horseback riding, hiking, fishing, hunting and snowmobiling. Take a guided trail ride in spectacular country on one of their experienced horses (no riding experience necessary), or trailer your own horses to the property. Hearty home-cooked dinners of roast pork loin, steak, chicken and more are served family style in the classy dining room (breakfast is family style, too). Schedule a lunch in the lodge, or request a sack lunch to take outdoors. The lodge is accessible spring, summer and fall by paved and gravel road. In winter the area is a destination for skiers, snowshoers and snowmobilers who park at the bottom of the hill and either sled in or schedule transportation in the lodge's tracked vehicles.

Inn at Clear Creek Farm

Clear Creek Road   541/742-2238
Moderate   clearcreekinn.com

When you want a place to really get away from it all, head to the northeast corner of our diverse state. This renovated farmhouse offers unique quarters near the Oregon Trail, halfway to the top of Eagle Cap. Five rooms and one family suite (all with private baths) are decorated a la turn-of-the-century. The full country breakfast is a relaxing affair, even more so watching deer and wild turkeys graze outside the dining room window. Seasonal fresh-from-the-orchard apples and pears are a special treat and the hosts are mindful of dietary needs (prior notification, please). You're smack dab in the middle of a working cattle ranch, surrounded by wildlife, trails, orchards and other delights. If fishing is on the agenda, there are bass- and trout-filled ponds, not to mention the Snake River running through nearby Hells Canyon and Brownlee Reservoir. Horseback riding, waterskiing, canoeing, bicycle tours, llama pack trips, day hikes and ranch chores are great activities during nice weather. With four feet of snow during the winter months, cross-country skiers and snowmobilers will think they're in seventh heaven (snowmobile rental available in-house). This gorgeous home is ideal for family getaways.

JOHN DAY

Kam Wah Chung State Heritage Site

125 NW Canton St   541/575-2800
Daily: 9-5 (May-Oct)   oregonstateparks.org/park_8.php
Free

This unusual museum has roots that date to the late 1800s when it became a social and religious center for the area's Chinese immigrants working the gold strikes. After a century of little notice, the building was deteriorating, and the collections begged for preservation. A successful state fundraising campaign in 2002 resulted in an interpretive center and museum exhibitions that now chronicle Chinese culture in Grant County. Today it is a National Historic Landmark that highlights the living quarters for Doc Hay and Lung On as well as their places of business. Hay was a practitioner of herbal medicine, and On was a merchant, labor contractor and immigration assistant. Hundreds of interesting items from On's general store, Hay's medical supplies and furnishings are on display. Entrance to the historic Kam Wah Chung building departs from the interpretive center, by guided tour only.

The Snaffle Bit Dinner House

830 S Canyon Blvd   541/575-2426
Tue-Sat: 4:45-10   Facebook
Moderate

The Snaffle Bit Dinner House, serving dinner only, declares "where there's smoke there's fire, and where there's fire, there's usually steak." Yes, there certainly are steaks at the Snaffle Bit, along with ribs, seafood and chicken. Try the Copper Cricket, an eight-ounce top sirloin laden with bay shrimp, scallops, asparagus and mushrooms. Try a quarter rack of barbecue ribs or a tenderloin, ribeye or New York steak. Burgers are served with soup, salad or fries. The menu includes baked spuds and salads — each loaded with lots of extras — several pasta dishes, appetizers and great desserts such as Oregon berry cobbler. This is a dining gem in John Day (reservations suggested).

JOSEPH

Arrowhead Chocolates

100 N Main St   541/432-2871
Daily: 7-5   arrowheadchocolates.com

Arrowhead has you covered — with the aroma of fresh chocolate melting right before your eyes. Not enough, you say? Then try their signature drink — a mocha made with fresh Stumptown espresso and chocolate. The award winning huckleberry and espresso truffles are a must try, as are the sea salt-chocolate covered caramels. This little shop makes everything in house, using local and organic ingredients when possible. If you're craving something more substantial, opt for a biscuit, scone or even a petite quiche.

Beecrowbee

1 S Main St   541/432-0158
Daily: 10:30-5   beecrowbee.com

Beecrowbee handcrafts bath and body items that promote beautiful, healthy skin. Scented mild soaps, lotion bars with shea butter and various oils, bath soaks blended with natural salts, and essential oils for bath and body. The product line is complemented with five varieties of high-quality teas, soy wax candles and home decor. All these items and more are sold in their retail shop and online.

Bronze Antler Bed & Breakfast

309 S Main St   541/432-0230
Inexpensive to expensive   bronzeantler.com

Look to the Bronze Antler B&B as your home away from home when visiting scenic Wallowa County. Hosts Heather Tyreman and Bill Finney provide attentive service so you can go about exploring the area. Full breakfasts feature fresh fruits and savory or sweet entrees with accommodations for those on special diets. Coffee and tea are brewing early each morning for before-breakfast walkers. Amenity-loaded bathrooms adjoin the three second-floor guest rooms. The ground floor suite features modern Asian styling, private entrance and a bathroom more akin to a private spa. Three outdoor garden spaces expand the gathering areas on the property with a bocce ball court, water features and perennial gardens.

Embers Brew House

206 N Main St   541/432-2739
Mon-Sat: 11-9; Sun: noon-8   embersbrewhouse.com

Embers Brew House is especially fun during summer with live outdoor music that even your furry companion can enjoy (as long as it's on a leash). The menu consists of gourmet pizzas, calzones big enough for two, huge burgers served with some of the best fries around, wraps, sandwiches, salads, wings and house specials such as fish tacos, pastas and a wild Alaskan salmon fillet. They also have one of the largest selections of microbrews in Eastern Oregon (17 varieties on tap, eight or nine rotating seasonally).

The Jennings Hotel & Sauna

100 N Main St, 2nd Floor
Inexpensive and up   jenningshotel.com

When visiting beautiful Wallowa County, be sure to stay at the world's first Kickstarter-funded hotel — The Jennings Hotel & Sauna. This is no ordinary hotel. Aside from offering overnight stays, the hotel embraces artists from various locations, allowing them to live in residence while they teach, lecture and work in the community. In fact, everything about this hotel is artsy. Donations from nearly 900 people made the whole thing possible, allowing founder Greg Hennes to work with designers (each assigned to a room) and bring an abandoned city landmark back to life. The Jennings also features a communal kitchen and dining room as well as a library and a beautiful cedar sauna. The Jennings is self-check-in with all bookings done through airbnb.com. Prices start as low as $95 and range up from there.

Joseph Branch Railriders
501 W Alder St (ticket office)   541/786-6149
Seasonal (May 19-Oct 1 for 2018)   jbrailriders.com
The Joseph Branch Railroad was once used to transport lumber, cattle and grain to the Grand Ronde Valley and beyond. Today, Joseph Branch Railriders offers a unique experience riding the rails (no longer used by trains) on a bike-like contraption. Enjoy the fresh air and amazing views of the Wallowa Mountains and the lush meadows, cottonwood and pine trees of the Wallowa Valley. There is a two-hour round trip (Joseph to Enterprise) and a six-hour option (Minam to Wallowa) for the more adventurous. Don't worry, a pedal assist is available as needed. Reservations are recommended, and you'll need to come prepared (water, sunscreen, etc.).

Mad Mary & Co.
5 S Main St   541/432-0547
Daily   madmaryandcompany.com
Mary Wolfe's successful shop is a boon for residents and tourists looking for just the right gift. Mad Mary's is home base for toys, jewelry, gourmet food, home and garden accessories, a year-round selection of Christmas items and more. Across from the retail area is the 1950s-era soda fountain (with old time rock and roll tunes) for malts, milkshakes, sundaes (made to perfection), other creamy concoctions and good ol' hand-dipped ice cream. Mary invites you to stop in for "everything fun and fattening."

Vali's Alpine Restaurant
59811 Wallowa Lake Hwy   541/432-5691
Hours vary with season
Dinner reservations only   valisrestaurant.com
Moderate
Family-owned Vali's has been Wallowa County's place for authentic Hungarian food since 1974. One entree is prepared daily for dinners (seatings at 5 and 7 p.m.) and may include cabbage rolls, goulash, chicken paprika, schnitzel or grilled ribeye steak; a rotating entree special is prepared each Friday. Langos (Hungarian fry bread), sweet and sour cabbage and späetzle are almost as tasty as the entrees. Desserts such as homemade apple strudel, rum ice cream cake and exquisite seasonal goodies are extra special. The selection of beers, wines and cocktails is impressive. Near-famous homemade donuts are fresh on weekends from 9 to 11 a.m. (they frequently sell out early) or

purchase European-style cold cuts at the summer-only takeout deli counter. Dinner reservations required. The business now accepts credit cards.

Valley Bronze

307 W Alder St (foundry)   541/432-7551
18 S Main St (gallery)   541/432-7445
Thu-Sat: 10-5 (gallery)   valleybronze.com

Once a sleepy mountain town, Joseph has become an arts mecca. Dozens of art galleries and studios now fill formerly empty storefronts along Main Street as scores of professional artists and craftspeople have moved to the area. This movement began when Valley Bronze opened its foundry in 1982. They began casting the sculptures created by some of the country's foremost artists and now have worldwide recognition for castings of the highest quality. Working in ferric and precious metals, as well as bronze and aluminum, the company combines a state-of-the-art casting facility with a fully equipped metal fabrication operation. Its projects range from small edition fine art sculpture to multi-million dollar ornamental metal contracts. Call or email to schedule a tour of the foundry, or drop by the gallery during business hours.

Wallowa Lake Lodge

60060 Wallowa Lake Hwy   541/432-9821
Seasonal   wallowalake.com
Inexpensive to moderate

A trip to this gem in "Little Switzerland" offers a family adventure that will not soon be forgotten. This cozy retreat was built in the early 1920s and included an amusement park, bowling alley, dance hall, outdoor movie theater, horse-drawn carousel and other services accessed by boat across the lake. Much has changed, but not the laid-back atmosphere and stunning views of the sparkling lake and Wallowa Mountains. Lodging options are all different and rustic; no in-room telephones or televisions (no pets or smoking either). The lodge's 22 rooms are seasonally available late May through mid-October, as is the lodge's restaurant. In the off-season, the lodge hosts conferences and group events. Eight cabins are open year round; all are fully furnished, most have wood-burning fireplaces. When you go, be sure to ride the Wallowa Lake Tramway (wallowalaketramway. com) to the summit of Mt. Howard (May to October); a convenient cafe serves casual food and drink on the alpine patio; the views are breathtaking. Wear hiking shoes and bring a jacket if you want to explore or walk down the mountain; there are plenty of hiking opportunities nearby, including Aneroid Lake.

LA GRANDE

BELLA Main Street Market
1216 Adams Ave   541/663-9463
Mon-Sat: 9-6; Sun: 11-5
(See main listing in Baker City)

The Potter's Gift House & Gallery
1601 6th St   541/910-0550
Mon-Sat: 10-6; Sun: 11-4   thepottershousegallery.com
Judy and Bob Jensen work from a 120-year-old Victorian beauty that functions as their home, gallery and gift boutique. Each day you'll find Bob at
the potter's wheel creating raku and decorative and functional stoneware
pieces, all lead-free and safe for use in the microwave, oven and dishwash-
er. The Bob Jensen warmer would make a unique and thoughtful gift for
your favorite cook or special order a full set of dinnerware. If you're crafty,
schedule time to participate in making and firing a raku pot of your own
design. Alongside Bob's raku in the gallery are sculptures, ceramics, prints,

---

FESTIVALS AND FAIRS IN EASTERN OREGON
JULY
Chief Joseph Days Rodeo (Joseph, chiefjosephdays.org): PRCA
rodeo, parades, Western entertainment
Miner's Jubilee (Baker City, minersjubilee.com): parade, bull riding,
mining demos

AUGUST
Most **Eastern Oregon County Fairs** are held in August. Check
oregonfairs.org for dates and details.

SEPTEMBER
Alpenfest (Joseph/Wallowa Lake, oregonalpenfest.blogspot.com):
polka and alphorn music, folk dancing, yodeling
Hells Canyon Mule Days (Enterprise, hellscanyonmuledays.com)
Happy Canyon Indian Pageant and Wild West Show
(Pendleton, 541/276-2553, happycanyon.com)
Pendleton Round-Up (Pendleton, 541/276-2553, pendletonroundup.
com): world class PRCA rodeo, parades, Western activities
Wallowa Valley Festival of Arts (Joseph, wallowavalleyarts.org):
fine art, artists' quick draw, live music

jewelry and photography by 20 or so local artists and craftsmen. A fine selection of boutique gifts includes candles, regional gourmet foods, collectible figurines and cottage, Western and lodge decor items.

Ten Depot Street

10 Depot St541/963-8766
Mon-Thu: 4-10:30; Fri: 4-11; Sat: 5-11tendepotstreet.com
Moderate

This corner brick building houses a casual, yet upscale dinner house. Lamb meatballs with Jamaican dipping sauce, house specialty smoked salmon paté or a tasty combination of bites are beyond run-of-the-mill appetizers. Daily soups are homemade and taco and Thai entree salads are prepared with a choice of chicken or beef. Enjoy prime rib, generously portioned steaks and other meats, sandwiches, seafood and pasta. Lentil pecan burgers, pasta with pesto and vegetarian dinners are pleasant choices for non-meat eaters. Tuesday and Thursday evenings offer live music; be sure to check out the turn-of-the-century bar.

MILTON-FREEWATER

Blue Mountain Cider Company

235 E Broadway Ave541/938-5575
Tue-Sat: 11-5 (tasting room)drinkcider.com

This friends-and-family business started in a garage and now sports industry awards displayed in the historic Watermill Building tasting room. Pressed apples are grown locally — and not just any apple, but varieties with high tannin content (Winesap, Pippen, winter banana) to give the best "zing" to the fermentation. The company has a signature method of adding fresh juice with a bit of carbonation prior to bottling, producing a unique and thirst-quenching result. Unusual custom rose ciders with added real juices (cranberry, cherry, peach) are also available.

Petits Noirs

622 S Main St541/938-7118
Thu-Sun: 10-5 (other days by appointment)petitsnoirs.com

This boutique chocolate maker was founded by two New Yorkers who fell in love with the Walla Walla Valley. It specializes in chocolates inspired by the fresh produce grown in the valley and the complex characteristics of the wines produced here. With flavors such as oak chestnut, lavender, rosemary, clove and violet, their chocolates are natural accompaniments to wine. Petits was founded by Lan Wong and James Boulanger. Wong apprenticed with one of New York's finest chocolatiers, and Boulanger is a baker who worked in some of the city's finest artisan bakeries, such as Amy's Bread and Sullivan Street Bakery (both businesses, by the way, are featured in my popular New York guidebook). Their culinary skills and love for fine food combine to make their chocolates and other treats unique.

NORTH POWDER

Anthony Lakes Mountain Resort
47500 Anthony Lakes Hwy   541/856-3277
Seasonal   anthonylakes.com
Far from the megalopolis and subject to snowpack, Anthony Lakes offers great family ski adventures on uncrowded runs that start early to mid-December. Base elevation is 7,100 feet, and you'll find light, dry snow, perfect for powder lovers, groomed cross-country trails, snowboard terrain and Sno-Cat tours to the back side of the mountain. Certified instructors are adept at teaching the entire family. Start or end your day at the lodge with breakfast or lunch in the cafeteria or gather in Starbottle Saloon for a hot toddy and more fun times. Yurts also are available to rent.

ONTARIO

Four Rivers Cultural Center and Museum
676 SW 5th Ave   541/889-8191
Mon-Fri: 9-5; Sat: 10-5   4rcc.com
Nominal
Named for the four rivers that converge in the western Treasure Valley, Four Rivers Cultural Center and Museum represents the flow of people of varied ancestry (American Indian, Basque, European, Hispanic and Japanese) that made this area so culturally diverse. Visitors enter an orientation theater and move through the exhibit gallery with audio dialogue. Exhibits include the arrival of cattlemen and the railroad to the area, as well as internment camps and the various cultures of the community. The Harano Gallery is an amazing exhibit gallery.

Mackey's Steakhouse & Pub
111 SW 1st St   541/889-3678
Lunch, Dinner: Daily   mackeysonline.com
Moderate
Honoring their Irish heritage, Angie and Shawn Grove named this establishment after their grandfather, Thomas Mackey Grove. Irish fare starts with Dublin potato skins (famous Malheur russets, no doubt), Guinness on tap and Killian's Irish Red. Traditional dinner fare includes Guinness-glazed

chicken, chicken with Jameson Irish Whiskey sauce, bangers and mash and shepherd's pie. Other options include steaks with the Mackey's traditional Irish rub, fish and seafood, sandwiches, daily fresh soups and salads. Bring the whole family for dining upstairs or on the patio; the downstairs pub is for the 21-and-over crowd.

OXBOW

Hells Canyon Adventures
4200 Hells Canyon Dam Road   541/785-3352, 800/422-3568
Seasonal: May-Dec   hellscanyonadventures.com
Moderate (lodging)
Come prepared to explore a remote location; Hells Canyon is North America's deepest river gorge, carved by the Snake River on the Oregon/Idaho border and includes 215,000 acres of designated wilderness. Jet boat tours provide dramatically different views of the north and south ends of the canyon — whitewater rapids and sheer rock walls or calm water and wide open terrain. Seasonal day and multi-day packages include jet boat and rafting adventures, fishing charters, shuttles and lodging. Charters are available for steelhead, sturgeon, bass and trout fishing — great family outings. While camping under the stars is a romantic notion, if you're more attuned to a soft bed, try their lodge overlooking the reservoir. Breakfast is included (and lunch on some tours); however, the closest restaurants for lunch or dinner are at least ten miles down the road. GPS or other mapping programs could inevitably lead you astray; best to check the website or call for complete directions.

PENDLETON

Hamley & Co.
30 SE Court Ave   541/278-1100, ext. 1
Mon-Thu, Sat: 9-6; Fri: 9-8; Sun: 10-3 (May-Oct)
Mon-Sat: 9-6 (Nov-April)   hamleyco.com
Beginning in England, generations of the Hamley family passed on the trade of saddle and leather craftsmanship. William Hamley brought his family to America in 1840; after several moves, son J.J. Hamley settled in Pendleton to set up shop in 1905 in the same building that Hamley's occupies today. Parley Pearce and Blair Woodfield acquired ownership of the store a century later to return it to its original glory, and then some. Expect outstanding selections of magnificent leather kits, belts, chaps, saddlery and tack; ranch and fashion apparel for the whole family; hats; silver jewelry, belt buckles and accessories and western gifts for the person or home.

Custom saddles are made on site, true works of art and proudly used by generations of equestrians. Service is topnotch. During Round-Up week, the store is bursting with cowboys, cowgirls and rodeo fans looking to freshen up wardrobes or garner a professional cowboy's autograph. The mezzanine level accommodates one of the best collections of Western art that I've seen anywhere. The company's legacy of community support continues today, and the Hamley name is synonymous with the Pendleton Round-Up.

Hamley Steak House

8 SE Court Ave   541/278-1100, ext. 2
Steakhouse daily: 5-8:30 (Fri, Sat till 9)
Cafe daily: 8 a.m.-4 p.m.
Expensive   hamleysteakhouse.com

Wranglers, Pendleton Whisky and dinner at Hamley Steak House. That, my friends, is the embodiment of an evening in Pendleton. Hamley & Co. entrepreneurs Parley Pearce and Blair Woodfield have created a superb atmosphere for traditional, hearty cooking and a not-to-be-missed saloon (open at 4 p.m. daily). The 14-ounce ribeye melts in your mouth, and the prime rib is the restaurant's most popular entree. Grandma's roast beef heads the list of ranch-cooking favorites, along with chicken and gravy and the fire-roasted salmon. Soups are homemade, sandwiches are more than a mouthful, and burgers start with a half-pound of ground chuck. Check out the surroundings for an original 19th-century bar, authentic tin ceilings, Old West artifacts and faultless local craftsmanship. Sandwiched between the Western store and steakhouse is Hamley Cafe, a great quick stop for breakfast and lunchtime soups, salads and sandwiches, and coffee and pastries anytime. You'll be treated Western-style right with delicious food and faultless service. Every Friday and Saturday during summer months, free concerts are featured on the grassy area in front of the steakhouse. Look for the outdoor stage and seating area.

Montana Peaks Hat Co.

24 SW Court Ave   541/215-1400
Mon, Tue, Fri, Sat
(Seasonal hours and by appointment)   montanapeaks.net

Western wear is de rigueur for spectators, locals and cowboys at the Pendleton Round-Up, and this popular retailer is dedicated to Western head gear. The array of felt hats would have pleased John Wayne, Tom Mix or Hopalong Cassidy; in fact, hat styles are named for these legendary characters. These folks shine when it comes to custom handmade cowboy hats — individualized by shape, fit, color and accessories. Best to call ahead if you're making a special trip to Montana Peaks; the owners practice random acts of kindness and take random days off.

Pendleton Round-Up

Office: 1114 SW Court Ave   541/276-2553
Stadium: 1205 SW Court Ave   pendletonroundup.com

Make your arrangements well ahead of time for the Pendleton Round-Up, an authentic taste of the Old West that features a professional bull-riding rodeo at its heart. Pendleton comes alive the second full week of September as thousands of competitors and spectators from around the world descend on the city. Schools close, businesses expand hours, restaurants and saloons are packed and there's no vacancy at nearly any lodging alternative. Not only are rooms scarce — schoolyards serve as camping and RV parking sites — but rodeo performances, especially Friday and Saturday afternoons, play to sell-out crowds. Afternoon rodeos allow for evening performances of the Happy Canyon Indian Pageant and Wild West Show and for entertainment and frivolity along Main Street (blocked off to traffic). Don't miss the Friday morning Westward Ho! Parade, the Cowboy Breakfasts in Stillman Park, the working tipi village or a visit to the Let 'er Buck Room under the grandstands. This is one of my favorite annual events, best seen from a seat behind the bucking chutes.

Pendleton Underground Tours

37 SW Emigrant Ave   541/276-0730
Seasonal hours   pendletonundergroundtours.org
Reasonable

The influence of bootlegging, gambling, prostitution and Chinese inhabitants at the turn of the 19th century in Eastern Oregon is unknown to

---

EASTERN OREGON CASINO

There's plenty of gaming in Oregon for folks who want a chance at Lady Luck. Casinos are operated by individual Native American tribal councils and have been successful in bringing additional revenues and jobs to Oregon. Here's an overview of Eastern Oregon's:

PENDLETON
Wildhorse Resort & Casino (46510 Wildhorse Blvd, 541/278-2274, wildhorseresort.com): 1,200 slots, table games, bingo, lodging, RV sites, golf, concerts and special events (see write up in Eastern Oregon chapter)

many. A walking tour through what was once the red light district enter-
tains and informs tourists with character re-enactments and interesting
tales of legal and illegal businesses and activities; one of the stops, Cozy
Rooms, is a former brothel. Trained guides lead the curious (age six and
over) along sidewalks, through tunnels and into historic buildings for a
glimpse of Pendleton not necessarily found in history books. Reservations
required.

Pendleton Woolen Mills

1307 SE Court Pl   541/276-6911
Mon-Sat: 8-6; Sun: 9-5   pendleton-usa.com
Pendleton Woolen Mills has been weaving world-class woolen fabrics
since 1909. That's when the Bishop family opened this mill to weave colorful trade blankets for local Native American tribes. The Pendleton line has
grown to include apparel, accessories and home goods. After six generations the Bishop family still owns and operates the company, including
40 Pendleton stores nationwide and two state-of-the-art Pacific Northwest
mills. Take a free informative mill tour (call for exact times). Then visit the
next-door Pendleton Mill Store, stocked with apparel for the family, home
decor, gifts, and the legendary patterned blankets that began the Pendleton story.

Plateau Restaurant

46510 Wildhorse Blvd   541/966-1610
(See detailed listing with Wildhorse Resort & Casino)

Prodigal Son Brewery & Pub

230 SE Court Ave   541/276-6090
Tues-Sat: 11-10; Sun: noon-9   prodigalsonbrewery.com
Moderate
Good beer, good food and good vibes are the basic elements at Pendleton's first craft brewery, smack dab in the middle of town. Ales, porters,
stouts, hefs and seasonal brews are always on tap. Traditional pub fare,
soups, salads and daily specials are made from scratch and the menu
changes to incorporate seasonal regional ingredients. You'll want to save
room for delicious whoopie pie or chocolate and hazelnut tart laced with
whiskey for dessert. The family-friendly restaurant resides in a great old
building with a children's room that features board games, a library and
toys. The noise level certainly adds to the buzz.

Roosters

1515 Southgate
Daily: 7 a.m.-8:30 p.m.
Inexpensive

541/966-1100
roostersdining.com

This house is something to crow about. The Code family owns and operates this farm-themed restaurant, where platters are meant for hearty breakfast (served until 3 p.m.) appetites. You'll find all the usual breakfast items, plus wonderful "corn field" French toast (egg-battered and rolled in cornflake crumbs, then grilled), that will fuel anyone for the better part of a day. Lunch and dinner (served 10 till close) offer comfort-food soups, salads, sandwiches, burgers, pastas, seafood and meats. Their signature chicken noodle soup with fresh homemade noodles is served daily. They even roast the peppers and tomatoes used in their homemade salsa. With such high standards, it's no wonder Roosters is so popular. With easy parking and trailer parking, too.

Sundown Grill & Bar-B-Q

233 SE 4th St
Wed-Sat: 4:30-8 (dinner); Sun: 11-1:30 (brunch)
Moderate

541/276-8500
Facebook

In the historic Raley House, Raphael Hoffman has created fun and affordable dining. The former chef and owner of Raphael's is now serving his signature dishes and grill favorites in a casual dining atmosphere in Pendleton. Same beautiful location with a new menu. Join them for award winning cocktails, grill and barbecue favorites, mouth-watering desserts and the best happy hour in town. Sundown Grill provides on-site and off-site catering for special events, business luncheons, after hours functions, weddings and parties.

Virgil's at Cimmiyotti's

137 S Main St
Tue-Sat: 4 p.m.-close
Moderate and up

541/276-7711
virgilsatcimmiyottis.com

Jennifer Keeton pays tribute to her father in the restaurant's name, originally opened by Anne and Paul Cimmiyotti in 1959. Restorations included attention to the original red velvet wallpaper, black leather booths and crystal chandeliers. The original menu featured steak with a side of spaghetti and while that tradition continues, hand-cut certified Angus ribeye steak is also a house favorite. Although beef takes center stage, seafood, chicken, vegetarian and Italian dishes round out the menu. Housemade chocolate toffee torte and lemon mousse are superb desserts. The bar stays open until midnight on weekends.

Wildhorse Resort & Casino

46510 Wildhorse Blvd   541/278-2274, 800/654-9453
Lodging: Inexpensive to expensive   wildhorseresort.com
Restaurant: Moderately expensive to expensive

Wildhorse Resort is a recognizable landmark as Eastern Oregon's tallest building. Rooms and suites in the ten-story hotel tower are comfortably furnished and attractively priced. Good restaurants, a golf course, RV park, tipi village and various gaming opportunities make this a popular destination. Plateau Restaurant (541/966-1610) features farm-to-table dinners with local ingredients best exemplified in the Pendleton Whisky steak. Plateau is on the upper floor of the casino, where you'll not only enjoy one of the best Kobe beef burgers (white cheddar cheese, mushrooms, shallot ketchup, frizzled onions and hand-cut French fries) in the state, but also sweeping views of the Blue Mountains. Northwest wines, beers and special dining events are worth noting. A sports bar, 24-hour cafe and buffet satisfy casual diners. What else to do? Take in a current flick at the five-screen Cineplex, turn the kiddos loose in the children's entertainment center or head across the parking lot to Tamástslikt Cultural Institute (541/966-9748, tamastslikt.org) for 10,000 years of living history.

Working Girls Hotel

17 SW Emigrant Ave   541/276-0730
Inexpensive   pendletonundergroundtours.org

For a real Old West experience, stay in one of the hotel's four guest rooms or one suite operated by Pendleton Underground Tours. Through Pam Severe's meticulous renovation 20 some years ago, the Victorian decor, hardwood floors, 18-foot ceilings and exposed brick walls remain. The circa-1890 hotel has 21st-century indulgences (like heat and air conditioning); baths are extra large. Open year round; no children or pets. In case you're wondering, yes, this once was one of Pendleton's 18 bordellos.

PRAIRIE CITY

DeWitt Museum & Sumpter Valley Railway Depot

425 S Main St   541/820-3330
Wed-Sun: 10-5 (Mid-May to Mid-Oct)   prairiecityoregon.com

The Sumpter Valley Railway operated between Prairie City and Baker City until 1933. Today you can explore exhibits of this logging, freight and passenger railroad in the original depot building. The museum houses Oregon's most significant collection of narrow gauge railroad artifacts and historical documents. The depot's current collection includes many photographs of life along the rail line, visual depictions of some of the spectacular wrecks on this steep and dangerous section of the railroad, various lanterns, lights and physical artifacts collected along the line. The second floor of the depot provided living quarters for the station agent and today features antiques and memorabilia from the local area and the Dewitt family, arranged much as it might have appeared while the agent's family occupied the quarters. Also consider a Sumpter Valley Railroad excursion in Sumpter (211 Austin St, 541/894-2268, 866/894-2268, sumptervalley-railroad.org).

Hotel Prairie
112 Front St   541/820-4800
Inexpensive to moderate   hotelprairie.com
If you head cross-country on Oregon's designated Journey through Time Scenic Byway, Prairie City is a likely stop. Guests are welcomed into nine rooms, including one full suite with kitchen. Two rooms can create a suite effect; all rooms offer private baths. Built in 1910, the hotel has gone through several transformations, serving various business ventures from 1980 to 2005. In 2005 the current owners stepped in to create a cozy destination hotel and greeted their first guests three years later. Photos of local families, the area and bygone mining, ranching and logging line the walls. Since this is a popular route for bicyclists, the hotel offers secure bicycle storage, packed lunches and catered group meals. The hotel now features a beer and wine lounge (4-9 p.m. May to November), and a charging station for Tesla and other electric vehicles.

Oxbow Restaurant & Saloon
128 W Front St   541/820-4544
Wed-Fri: 4-close; Sat, Sun: noon-close   Facebook
Moderate
Located in an Old West-style building, Carol and Phil Bopp serve burgers, sandwiches, steaks, seafood and such for lunch and dinner. Do not miss the specialty of the house: Carol's homemade pies, made fresh daily and served with a scoop of hard ice cream. The original condition, antique bar (circa 1879) is quite a conversation piece where full-service drink options and a large selection of beers and microbrews are poured.

Pine Shadows Getaway Resort
25923 Green Haven Road   541/820-3736
Seasonal: May 1-Oct 1   pineshadowsgetaway.com
Pine Shadows Getaway is like a secret garden hidden in the foothills of the Strawberry Mountains. The resort, situated at the headwaters of the

John Day River, features three rustic cabins (reservations required) and a tiny cabin perfect for spare children or friends. Each has unique charms and all have special touches such as vintage books in every cabin, covered porches with lounge furniture and barbecues with fire rings. Cabins are fully equipped with modern appliances and stocked with kitchen necessities (even coffee grinders), bathroom amenities, towels and much more. Shady relaxation is the main thing here, but there are plenty of recreational opportunities such as hiking, fishing the John Day River, and biking. The city of John Day is just a 30-minute drive away. (Note: The resort is not equipped for hunters.)

Riverside School House Bed & Breakfast

28076 N River Road   541/820-4731
Moderate   riversideschoolhouse.com
Original chalkboards with a personalized message greet guests as they enter this former one-room schoolhouse. The unusual resting place offers two suites with separate entrances and private baths; rooms are comfortable with classy furnishings. Innkeeper Judy Jacobs delivers the morning's bountiful breakfast at the appointed time with ample suggestions for a day full of local activities. Located on a working cattle ranch, visitors are treated to seasonal opportunities for great hiking, fishing, cycling, snowmobiling, cross-country skiing or horseback riding. Peaceful surrounds include the John Day River meandering through the property, abundant wildlife and vistas of the Strawberry Mountain Range.

RUFUS

Bob's Texas T-Bone

101 E 1st St   541/739-2559
Daily: 6 a.m.-10 p.m.   Facebook
Moderate
The Baunach family has owned a familiar establishment in Rufus (midway between Portland and Pendleton with easy access off I-84) for more than 40 years; first as Frosty's, a local tavern. Long hours make Bob's a convenient dining stop for travelers and gorge dwellers. Portions are generous, the salad bar items are fresh and the menu showcases hand-cut steaks, freshly-ground hamburger, family-recipe sausages, smoked chicken and ribs and seasonal Columbia River salmon. Weekend dinners feature prime rib. Daily lunch specials, homemade soups, hearty sandwiches and burgers give midday diners plenty to choose from including breakfast any time of the day.

EDUCATIONAL OPPORTUNITIES

BAKER CITY
National Historic Oregon Trail Interpretive Center (22267 Hwy 86, 541/523-1843; oregontrail.blm.gov): There's plenty to do at this 500-acre center along the Hells Canyon Scenic Byway. History of the Oregon Trail comes alive with interactive exhibits, multi-media presentations, demonstrations and activities, four miles of interactive trails, special events and concerts. See remnants of a defunct gold mine, wagon wheel ruts and six full-scale replica wagons Open daily 9-4.

BOARDMAN
SAGE Center (101 Olson Road, 541/481-7243; visitsage.com): This innovative and interactive experience of Morrow County and the region's sustainable agriculture includes a simulated hot air balloon ride over the area. Learn how food emanates from the farm to the table and journeys around the world. Hours are Monday through Saturday 10-5 (daily Memorial Day to Labor Day 10-5; Friday, Saturday 10-6).

JOSEPH
Maxville Heritage Interpretive Center (103 N Main St, 541/426-3545; maxvilleheritage.org): In the 1920s and '30s Maxville was a multicultural railroad and lumber town 15 miles north of Wallowa. African-Americans and families worked and lived in the area and children attended Oregon's only segregated school. This story is depicted at this interpretive center through exhibits, historical photos, journals, maps and video and audio interviews. Hours vary, call for days and hours.

PENDLETON
Children's Museum of Eastern Oregon (400 S Main St, 541/276-1066; cmeo.org): Kids of all ages will find something to tickle their fancy here. Among the attractions are an art studio, music wall, simulated fire station, Tommy the Train and a reading corner. Fun and educational toys, puzzles and games are for sale in the gift shop. Currently open Tuesday through Saturday, 10-5; best to call ahead.

SENECA

The Retreat & Links at Silvies Valley Ranch

10000 Rendezvous Lane   541/573-5150, 800/745-8437
Expensive   silvies.us

This is the epitome of luxury in Eastern Oregon (40 miles north of Burns off Highway 395). This private retreat and golf links features luxury cabins, spacious guest rooms, a spa to open in July 2018, fine dining and loads of recreational activities, all on a working cattle ranch. Oh, and did we mention golf? There are two reversible 18-hole courses that share nine greens. Rounds are played from first to 18th one day, and then reversed the next, making for a unique golfing experience, all designed by course architect Dan Hixson. There's also a nine-hole, par-three course. The two-bedroom cabins can be divided into two units, one with a living room, mini-kitchen and hot tub on the patio. They're plush with elaborate decor including fireplace, bedroom skylights, copper bathroom sinks, rain showers and wall mounted TVs. Guest rooms are spacious and can be configured to accommodate large and small groups. Dining options include the stunning Dining Room, the Porch at the Lodge and the Hideout Clubhouse. All serve Western-inspired fare, including organic beef raised on the ranch. Other activities include shooting ranges, hiking, biking, fishing and more. This could be the ideal location for golf trips, romantic getaways, corporate outings and family gatherings.

SUMPTER

Sumpter Valley Railroad

211 Austin St   541/894-2268, 866/894-2268
Weekends/holidays (Memorial Day through Sept)   sumptervalleyrailroad.org
Prices vary

With the march of progress, the narrow gauge Sumpter Valley Railroad that once helped haul ore, lumber, freight and passengers met its demise. Thankfully, a dedicated group of volunteers revived this great iron horse, thus ensuring that the whistle of a steam engine continues to echo through this scenic valley. Volunteers are still the mainstay of this organization. Since July 4, 1976, the railroad has provided nostalgic weekend and holiday excursions through the rugged countryside. The approximate five-mile route from McEwen to the town of Sumpter ends at a reproduction of the original passenger station; stations are located in McEwen and Sumpter. Along the way, restored historic equipment and artifacts from around the country are on display. A trip on the Sumpter Valley Railroad is a fun and affordable activity for the whole family. Also visit the DeWitt Museum & Sumpter Valley Railway Depot in Prairie City (425 S Main St, 541/820-3330; prairiecityoregon.com).

Gerry's Exclusive List

BBQ
Sundown Grill & Bar-B-Q (223 SE 4th St, Pendleton; 541/276-8500)

Bars and Pubs with Good Eats
Barley Brown's Beer (2190 Main St, Baker City; 541/523-4266)
Prodigal Son Brewery & Pub (230 SE Court Ave, Pendleton; 541/276-6090)
Terminal Gravity Brewing and Public House (803 SE School St, Enterprise; 541/426-3000)

Best Sleeps
Bronze Antler Bed & Breakfast (309 S Main St, Joseph; 541/432-0230)
Geiser Grand Hotel (1996 Main St, Baker City; 541/523-1889)
The Retreat & Links at Silvies Valley Ranch (10000 Rendezvous Lane, Seneca; 541/573-5150)
Wildhorse Resort & Casino (46510 Wildhorse Blvd, Pendleton; 541/278-2274)

Breads and Bakery Goods
Sugar Time Bakery (107 N River St, Suite A, Enterprise; 541/426-0362)
Sweet Wife Baking (2080 Resort St, Baker City; 541/403-6028)

Breakfast/Brunch
Bob's Texas T-Bone (101 E 1st St, Rufus; 541/739-2559)
Inland Cafe (2715 10th St, Baker City; 541/523-9041)
Roosters (1515 Southgate, Pendleton; 541/966-1100)
Sundown Grill & Bar-B-Q (233 SE 4th St, Pendleton, 541/276-8500): weekend brunch

Burgers
Embers Brew House (206 N Main St, Joseph; 541/432-2739)
Hamley Steak House (8 SE Court Ave, Pendleton; 541/278-1100)
Plateau Restaurant (Wildhorse Resort & Casino, 46510 Wildhorse Blvd, Pendleton; 541/966-1610)

Casual Dining/Casual Prices
Barley Brown's Beer (2190 Main St, Baker City; 541/523-4266)
Inland Cafe (2715 10th St, Baker City; 541/523-9041)
River Lodge and Grill (6 Marine Dr, Boardman; 541/481-6800)

RJ's Restaurant (Hwy 20 East Hwy 395, Burns; 541/573-6346)
Roosters (1515 Southgate, Pendleton; 541/966-1100)

Coffee and Tea
Hamley Cafe (16 SE Court Ave, Pendleton; 541/278-1100): breakfast, lunch
Jolts & Juice (298 S Oregon St, Ontario; 541/889-4166)

Confections
Arrowhead Chocolates (100 N Main St, Joseph; 541/432-2871)
Petits Noirs (622 S Main St, Milton-Freewater; 541/938-7118)
The Sycamore Tree (2108 Main St, Baker City; 541/523-4840): fudge

Deli
Charley's Deli & Ice Cream (2101 Main St, Suite 101, Baker City; 541/524-9307)

Doughnuts
Vali's Alpine Restaurant (59811 Wallowa Lake Hwy, Joseph; 541/432-5691): seasonal; weekend mornings

Foreign Flavors
HUNGARIAN: **Vali's Alpine Restaurant** (59811 Wallowa Lake Hwy, Joseph; 541/432-5691)
IRISH: **Mackey's Steakhouse & Pub** (111 SW 1st St, Ontario; 541/889-3678)

Ice Cream and Other Frozen Treats
Charley's Deli & Ice Cream (2101 Main St, Suite 101, Baker City; 541/524-9307)
Mad Mary & Co. (5 S Main St, Joseph; 541/432-0547)

Liquid Libations
Blue Mountain Cider Company (235 E Broadway Ave, Milton-Freewater; 541/938- 5575)

Personal Favorites
Geiser Grand Hotel (1996 Main Street, Baker City; 541/523-1687)
Hamley & Co. (30 SE Court Ave, Pendleton; 541/278-1100, ext.1)
Hamley Steak House (8 SE Court Ave, Pendleton; 541/278-1100, ext. 2)
Pendleton Round-Up (Office: 1114 SW Court Ave, Pendleton; 541/276-2553)

Pendleton Woolen Mills (1307 SE Court Pl, Pendleton; 541/276-6911)
Plateau Restaurant (Wildhorse Resort & Casino, 46510 Wildhorse Blvd, Pendleton; 541/966-1610)
The Retreat & Links at Silvies Valley Ranch (10000 Rendezvous Lane, Seneca; 541/573-5150)
Wildhorse Resort & Casino (46510 Wildhorse Blvd, Pendleton; 541/278-2274)

Picnic Fixings
BELLA Main Street Market (2023 Main St, Baker City, 541/523-7490; 1216 Adams Ave, La Grande, 541/663-9463)

Pie
Oxbow Restaurant & Saloon (128 W Front St, Prairie City; 541/820-4544)

Pizza
Paizano's Pizza (2940 10th St, Baker City; 541/524-1000): Eat a 24-inch giant pizza within 30 minutes and get the pizza free plus $100.

Special Occasions
Palm Court (Geiser Grand Hotel, 1996 Main St, Baker City; 541/523-1889)
The Retreat & Links at Silvies Valley Ranch (10000 Rendezvous Lane, Seneca; 541/573-5150)

Steaks
Bob's Texas T-Bone (101 E 1st St, Rufus; 541/739-2559)
Haines Steak House (910 Front St, Haines; 541/856-3639)
Hamley Steak House (8 SE Court Ave, Pendleton; 541/278-1100, ext. 2)
The Snaffle Bit Dinner House (830 S Canyon Blvd, John Day; 541/575-2426)
Virgil's at Cimmiyotti's (137 S Main St, Pendleton; 541/276-7711): with a side of spaghetti

Vegan and Vegetarian Options
Ten Depot Street (10 Depot St, La Grande; 541/963-8766)

Notes

Notes

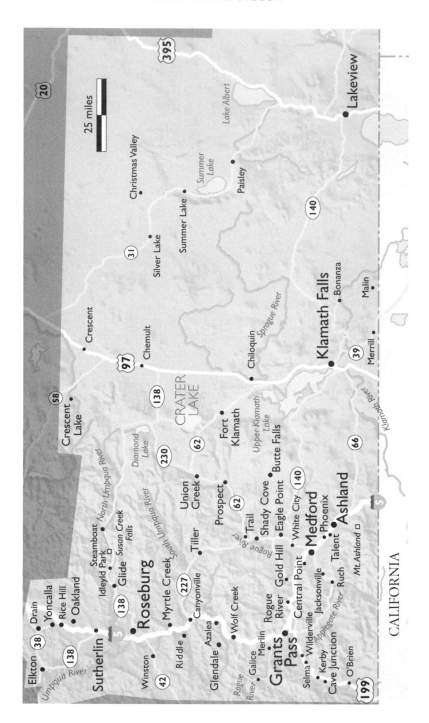

CHAPTER SEVEN

Southern Oregon

ASHLAND

A Midsummer's Dream Bed & Breakfast

496 Beach St   541/552-0605
Moderate   amidsummer.com

In a quiet neighborhood within walking distance to downtown, this classy 1901 Victorian is a fine special occasion getaway. You will be welcomed into your home away from home in a beautifully landscaped setting, with king-size beds and large private bathrooms. A spa tub and soft-as-silk robes, fireplace and wonderful linens add to the pampering. Relax in the common area, which includes a game room (and the only television on the property) with library, wet bar and tea service. Lisa Beach is the consummate host, offering gourmet breakfasts and anything else within her grasp.

Amuse

15 N 1st St   541/488-9000
Seasonal hours   amuserestaurant.com
Moderately expensive

Chefs/owners Jamie North and Erik Brown have impressive culinary backgrounds, and it shows. North made wedding cakes in Napa Valley and was a pastry cook at the legendary French Laundry restaurant; Brown also cooked at Napa Valley restaurants. The Northwest/French menu reflects their talents and utilizes fresh, seasonal ingredients. Cauliflower soup with sweet and sour cabbage, and roasted beets with feta are representative of starters. Flavorful seafood, steaks and roasted game hens are paired with wonderful relishes, butters, fresh produce and palate-pleasing accompaniments. By all means, order the beignets with crème anglaise and heirloom berry jam if they are offered — exquisite. This intimate, elegant restaurant has great service and a delightful summer patio (perfect for pre-theater dining).

Ashland Creek Inn

70 Water St	541/482-3315
Moderate to expensive	ashlandcreekinn.com

This ten-suite boutique hotel is nestled into a private park-like setting; stunning blue shutters and awnings embellish the façade. Each suite is luxuriously decorated to commemorate an international area (Edinburgh, Marrakech, Normandy, Canton, Taos, Devon, Caribe, Matsu, Siena, Copenhagen) visited by owner Graham Sheldon. Beautiful and comfortable rooms have a private entrance, balcony overlooking gurgling Ashland Creek and kitchen or kitchenette. Antiques, original artwork and jetted tubs vary among the units. Relax on the inn's deck and terraced gardens for breakfast or an afternoon glass of wine. Breakfast is a multi-course gourmet production and is served in the elegant dining room or alfresco. The location is handy to downtown shops, restaurants, nightlife and theaters.

Ashland Springs Hotel

212 E Main St	541/488-1700, 888/795-4545
Lodging: Moderate	ashlandspringshotel.com
Restaurant: Moderate	

Listed on the National Register of Historic Places, this hotel exudes charm and elegance. Built as Lithia Hotel in 1925 and later named the Mark Antony, it was restored to grandeur in 2000 by owners Becky and Doug Neuman. The illuminated marquee and curved windows evoke a bygone era and assure guests that great care was given to the renovation. Guests are beckoned to a palm-filled conservatory and English garden featuring a wrought-iron gazebo and old-fashioned rose bushes. All 70 eclectically furnished and tastefully appointed guest rooms offer comfort and charm not found in modern hotels. Free parking and continental breakfast are included in the rates. For breakfast, lunch or dinner, on-site Larks Home Kitchen Cuisine (541/488-5558, larksrestaurant.com) serves farm-to-table gourmet comfort food made from scratch with local organic components, housemade charcuterie and artisan cheeses. The chef is a master at showcasing Oregon wines and splendid local, seasonal ingredients. Dishes such as homemade meatloaf, hearty soups and fresh Pacific Northwest seafood are popular; the pastry chef's creations are divine. Nature-inspired Waterstone Spa (236 E Main St, 541/488-0325, waterstonespa.com) is also part of this downtown resort and offers a full-service rejuvenating and beautifying menu. A variety of thoughtfully developed packages may include tickets to the Varsity Movie Theatre, the Oregon Shakespeare Festival, Oregon Chocolate Festival or wine tasting at local wineries.

Beasy's on the Creek

51 Water St   541/488-5009
Tue-Sat: 5:30-8:30 (seasonal hours)   beasysonthecreek.com
Moderate

No matter the season, Beasy's capitalizes on its picturesque setting. Big windows and a big red fireplace frame the outdoor deck, creek and trees which provide welcome shade to outside diners. This dinner house features steaks, seafood, chicken and several pasta entrees, all with Texas-Mediterranean influences. Several dishes can be spiced up Inca Inca style with the addition of a sauce made with fresh jalapenos, garlic and lime juice. Entrees include a choice of salad or gumbo; add salmon, prawns, crab or chicken to a salad to make it a meal. Be sure to visit Beasy's sister restaurant and bar in Ashland, Harvey's Place (50 E Main St, 541/488-9511).

Callahan's Mountain Lodge

7100 Old Hwy 99 S   541/482-1299, 800/286-0507
Lodging: Moderate to expensive   callahanslodge.com
Restaurant: Moderate

Established in 1947, Callahan's is a full-service restaurant and lodge that has become a Southern Oregon landmark. The picturesque setting is tucked into a wooded canyon ten minutes south of Ashland, just below Mt. Ashland Ski Resort and the Pacific Crest Trail. Nineteen guest rooms are furnished with corner jetted tubs, wood-burning fireplaces and terraces with rockers to while away the afternoon. Lodge amenities include a wine and gift shop, game room, horseshoe pit, rock waterfall features and unscheduled sideshows starring native wildlife. The restaurant is also a destination for breakfast, lunch and dinner. Start the day with basic to fancy egg dishes served with fruit and lodge-made pastries; or opt for crepes and pancakes. House-cut fries go well with lunch wraps and sandwiches. "Western mountain lodge" dinner entrees are sourced from pastures, freshwater and saltwater and are served with artisan bread and a salad dressed with hazelnut-pear vinaigrette. Callahan's is open 365 days a year with nightly live music at dinner. This beautiful location is a favorite of brides and grooms and ideal for gatherings for up to 150 guests.

SOUTHERN OREGON CASINOS

Casinos are operated by individual Native American tribal councils and have been successful in bringing additional revenues and jobs to Oregon. Here's a brief overview of Southern Oregon:

CANYONVILLE

Seven Feathers Casino Resort (146 Chief Miwaleta Lane, 541/839-1111, sevenfeathers.com): 900 slots, table games, bingo, 300 guest rooms, 191 full RV hook-up sites, dining (casual, buffet, steakhouse), concerts and special events

CHILOQUIN

Kla-Mo-Ya Casino (34333 Hwy 97 N, 541/783-7529, klamoyacasino. com): over 300 slots, blackjack, casual dining

Coquina

542 A St	541/488-0521
Tue-Sat: 5-9	coquinarestaurant.com
Expensive	

This fine dining restaurant in Ashland's Railroad District as of spring 2018 was offering a seven-course prix-fixe meal as well as an à la carte menu featuring seasonal and regional cuisine. For starters, try the beets with chèvre, fennel marmalade, oyster mushrooms pancetta, sherry vinaigrette and watercress, among several appetizers. For an entree, consider pheasant with rabbit polenta, parsnips, caper purée and beach mushrooms. (There are also ribeye, halibut and scallop entrees.) The full bar serves classic cocktails, and the wine list focuses on Northwest wines, plus some from Europe. For dessert, try the chocolate torte with cherries.

Country Willows Bed & Breakfast Inn

1313 Clay St	541/488-1590, 800/945-5697
Moderate	countrywillowsinn.com

This charmer has all the atmosphere of bygone days, but with comfortable, modern facilities. The original farmhouse was built more than a century ago and is now in its third decade as a B&B. Features include two-course gourmet breakfasts, top-grade bed linens and magnificent views. Mt. Ashland skiing, hiking and biking trails are close at hand, and theaters and wineries too. Four standard guest rooms are in the main house; four comfortable suites with private deck or patio are located in the renovated barn behind the house. A separate cottage has a king bed and a twin bed,

wet bar and private patio just off the duck pond. A heated outdoor swimming pool and croquet and lawn bocce equipment are accessible in warm
weather. Comfy seating is spread throughout the property; enjoy a cookie
and cup of tea — on the house, of course.

Cowslip's Belle Boutique Vacation Rentals

159 N Main St   541/488-2901, 800/888-6819
Year-round   cowsllp.com
Inexpensive to moderate

Lush gardens surround Cowslip's Belle Boutique Vacation Rentals, making
for a beautiful, aromatic and relaxing stay just two blocks from Ashland's
downtown plaza. Fragrant flowers, gurgling waterfalls, patios and foot
bridges, a koi pond and seasonal flowering trees and plants provide a delightful background to the property; most rooms overlook the manicured
gardens. The Rosebud Suite is situated at the rear of the main house and
has a private, outside entrance; the carriage house is comprised of four
rooms and suites, each with a private outside entrance. All tastefully appointed accommodations sleep one to three guests and include en suite
bathrooms and outdoor seating areas; varying amenities include full kitchens or kitchenettes, gas fireplaces, spa tubs and laundry facilities. Guests
are welcomed with a tray of sherry and biscotti.

Greenleaf Restaurant

49 N Main St   541/482-2808
Daily: 8-8   greenleafrestaurant.com
Inexpensive to moderate

Greenleaf, just a block from the Oregon Shakespeare Festival, features
Mediterranean-style cuisine prized by health-conscious diners and an
Ashland favorite since 1985. Whether you opt for classic Greek dishes or
those inspired by the Pacific Northwest, you're sure to satisfy your hunger
at breakfast (served until noon), lunch or dinner. Breakfast choices include
pancakes, waffles, French toast, omelets and scrambles. Among the lunch
and dinner classics are spanakopita, an organic hummus plate and fresh
Greek salads. Or stay with fish and chips, burgers (made with local beef,
wild salmon and organic tofu) and spaghetti with house sauce and garlic
bread. (There are also gluten-free menus for breakfast, lunch and dinner.)
Northwest beer and wine are on rotation seasonally.

Green Springs Inn & Cabins

11470 Hwy 66   541/890-6435
Moderate   greenspringsinn.com

A relaxed atmosphere awaits at this retreat about 25 minutes east of Ashland. Amenities in the eight lodge rooms may include Jacuzzi tubs, private decks and a fireplace. You can also choose from nine cabins, mainly powered by solar energy, that sleep up to six. Each is furnished with a Jacuzzi tub, fully-equipped kitchen, wood-burning stove, gas grill and large deck. The inn serves three square meals a day from a menu of great selections. For Tesla, Volt and other electric car travelers, Green Springs Inn offers a free Level II charging station.

Hither

376 E Main St   541/625-4090
Daily: 7-3   hithermarket.com
Inexpensive

Hither is rather new to the area, and it offers something new: Everything the cafe uses in the kitchen is sold on its market shelf. It also specializes in naturally fermented wines. For a lighter breakfast (served 7-11:30) the herbed eggs are a hit; on the more filling side the biscuit sandwich is a popular choice. Lunch (11:30-3) offerings include a few salads made of fresh local ingredients, as well as a couple of sandwich options such as an open-face grilled cheese topped with fresh greens, a fried egg and garlic aioli. The freshness and quality of the food is vivid on each plate, and although portions may not be large, the classy presentation, locally sourced ingredients and rich flavors make up for it. Pastries are made fresh daily and are ever-changing, but you're likely to be welcomed by the smell of chocolate chip cookies, custard-filled doughnuts, scones and more. Hither features a different resident coffee roaster every few months.

Larks Home Kitchen Cuisine

212 E Main St   541/488-5558
(See detailed listing with Ashland Springs Hotel)

Lithia Springs Resort

2165 W Jackson Road   541/482-7128, 800/482-7128
Moderate and up   lithiaspringsresort.com

This property is home to a serene, spa-like resort with a beautiful outdoor pool and fitness room. Nearly 40 bungalows, studios and suites with contemporary furnishings in soothing tones are situated around a courtyard on four acres of gardens and mineral springs; for privacy, request the water tower suite overlooking the resort. The springs, once considered holy water by the Native Americans, are purported to restore and heal the body; in-room soaking tubs provide tranquil environs to enjoy those properties. The charming bungalows sleep up to four guests and are furnished with a small kitchenette. An overnight stay includes a complimentary hot breakfast in the breakfast room and afternoon tea and cookies. On-site spa services are provided a la carte or combined with lodging for romantic and relaxing packages. The gardens are spectacular in spring and summer; pergolas, bridges, paths and lush lawns are inviting.

Loft Brasserie & Bar

18 Calle Guanajuato Way   541/482-1116
Tue-Sat: 5:30-close   loftashland.com
Moderately expensive

Jacqueline and Jeremy Vidalo offer contemporary American fare with a French flair in their rooftop restaurant and bar. As much as possible, the food is organic and sourced locally; made from scratch is the rule, not the exception. The bar and lounge (opens at 3) has a fun specialty cocktail list and features local and European wines (from the Rogue to the Rhine). Chef Jeremy heads up the kitchen while Jacqueline runs the front of the house. Their seasonal menus showcase local ingredients such as wild-foraged mushrooms, line-caught local halibut, Pacific oysters, Oregon lamb and more along with comfort classics like Dungeness crab truffle mac and cheese. Dinner reservations are recommended, especially during theater season. Walk-ups to the bar and lounge are welcomed.

Macaroni's Ristorante
and Martino's Restaurant and Lounge

58 E Main St   541/488-3359
Daily: 5-9 (Fri, Sat till 10) dinner
Fri-Sun: open at 11:30 for lunch   martinosashland.com
Moderate

If you choose outdoor seating at Martino's, you'll be as close as you can get to the Angus Bowmer Theatre without a ticket. Martino's is upstairs and Macaroni's is downstairs; owner Marty Morlan offers the same menu throughout the neo-classic house. You won't be disappointed with the Oregon smoked salmon ravioli served in a mushroom, basil and tomato

---

OUTDOOR GUIDES
Oregon Outfitters & Guides (541/617-9090, oregonoutfitters. org) is a non-profit organization that provides a comprehensive list of guide services on their website. The possibilities include adventures on rivers around the state via canoe, drift boat, jet boat and kayak — choose your favorite kind of watercraft. Other undertakings include climbing, hiking, fishing and hunting.

cream sauce or the rigatoni carbonara made with applewood-smoked bacon. Pizza, Caesar salads and other pasta dishes are also on the menu, plus drinks and desserts (try Marty's famous lemon ricotta cheesecake). This location serves after-theater bistro and late-night fare, too, after 10 p.m.

McCall House

153 Oak St   541/482-9296, 800/808-9749
Moderate to expensive   mccallhouse.com

This historic home-turned B&B is a great place to stay if you're visiting for the Oregon Shakespeare Festival, located just a block away. Grand Victorian accommodations such as king beds, claw-foot tubs and fireplaces exemplify McCall House. Other amenities include Wi-Fi, spa towels, private bathrooms, quality linens, robes and general conveniences like a refrigerator, microwave, coffeemaker and more. A selection of wine, champagne and complimentary sherry is offered in the lounge and library. At McCall House, hosts are happy to provide in-room accommodations to suit individual needs, offer expertise on local happenings, arrange transportation or make arrangements for pets at a local kennel, and more. Looking for something more private? McCall House also features five cottages.

Morning Glory Restaurant

1149 Siskiyou Blvd   541/488-8636
Daily: 8-1:30   Facebook
Moderate

Owner Patricia Groth presides over this breakfast and brunch spot that is a local favorite. Inside the 1926 Craftsman bungalow you'll find creative day-starters like shrimp cakes with poached eggs and smoked tomato chutney, plus a host of other egg scrambles and omelets. For the sweet tooth, there's lemon-ricotta stuffed French toast, whole grain pecan waffles, oatmeal pancakes, sourdough blueberry pancakes and other such fare.

Music Coop

268 E Main St   541/482-3115
Daily   musiccooponline.com

In the business since 1975, Trina and John Brenes moved lock, stock and record to Ashland in 2001. Their store is one of the largest record outlets between Sacramento and Portland. There are over 20,000 CD titles, hundreds of box-set CDs and the largest selection of vinyl LPs in Southern Oregon. The selection includes everything from rock, hip-hop, jazz, blues and folk to bluegrass and country music.

Northwest Nature Shop

154 Oak St   541/482-3241, 877/482-3241
Mon-Sat: 10-6; Sun: 11-5   northwestnatureshop.com

Northwest Nature Shop stocks a variety of educational books, hiking guides, binoculars and scientific gear, bird feeders and accessories, cards and gifts, and information about the forests and waterways of the Northwest. Treat the birds and wildlife in your yard to a new bird bath, fountain or feeder and accent your home with clocks and decorative pieces.

Oregon Cabaret Theatre

241 Hargadine St   541/488-2902
Prices vary   theoregoncabaret.com

Forget Shakespeare for a bit and book an amusing evening for your party at the Oregon Cabaret Theatre. Five shows (over 270 performances) change throughout the year, but the intimate venue stays the same. You can opt for gourmet dinner or brunch (reservations necessary) before the curtain goes up; choose from a variety of appetizers, soups, salads and desserts or go for the entertainment only. Menus are prepared by the resident chef and change with each show. The 140-seat theater calls the former First Baptist Church home, magnificently renovated in the 1980s.

Oregon Shakespeare Festival

15 S Pioneer St   800/219-8161
Seasonal   osfashland.org

One of the world's finest venues to celebrate William Shakespeare (along with other performing arts) is in the charming town of Ashland. Established in 1935, the festival boasts the oldest existing full-scale Elizabethan stage in the Western Hemisphere. Throughout the eight-month season, up to 11 plays by Shakespeare and classic and contemporary playwrights are presented in three venues with varying seating capacities. People come from around the globe to Ashland to experience the festival and Southern Oregon. During busy summer months, lodging and restaurants also play to a full house.

Paddington Station

125 E Main St   541/482-1343
Sun, Mon: 10-5:30; Tue-Sat: 9:30-8   paddingtonstationashland.com

Ashland's eclectic emporium has been a Main Street fixture for over 40 years — a fun spot any time of the year. At Paddington Station you'll find three floors of merchandise: gadgets and goodies, toys, clothing, books, kitchen needs, women's fashions, toiletries, stationery, souvenirs and more. Check out equally interesting sister shops, Inspired by Oregon (541/482-1343) and Paddington Jewel Box (541/488-1715), also on Main Street.

The Peerless Hotel

243 4th St   541/488-1082, 800/460-8758
Moderate   peerlesshotel.com

Peerless Restaurant & Bar

265 4th St   541/488-6067
Tue-Sat: 5 till close   peerlessrestaurant.com
Moderate to moderately expensive

Historic accommodations are part of Ashland's claim to fame. The Peer-less, built in 1900, is charmingly restored and located close to the town's central shopping and gallery core. All rooms have hand-painted features and private baths. Amenities include Italian linens and organic body-care products. If you like large bathrooms, ask for the room with two claw-foot tubs. Relax in gorgeous guest rooms decorated with antiques or outside in the private gardens. Breakfast and complimentary evening sherry are provided between mid-February and November. Room service is available from the excellent Peerless Restaurant & Bar right next door. Delicious, made-from-scratch entrees and small plates are served in the dining room, bar and enchanting garden.

Plaza Inn & Suites

98 Central Ave   541/488-8900, 888/488-0358
Moderate   plazainnashland.com

This Shakespearean-theme boutique hotel offers 92 spacious rooms with various options and concierge service. A hot tub and 24-hour fitness center are available, and rooms in the Cascade building are designated for guests with pets. Mornings begin with a continental breakfast and a snack welcomes guests home each early evening. Later (10 p.m. to midnight), a nightcap of freshly-baked cookies, milk and PB&J sandwiches are provided. Many of Ashland's attractions are within easy walking distance.

ScienceWorks Hands-On Museum

1500 E Main St   541/482-6767
Tue-Sun: 10-5   scienceworksmuseum.org
Nominal (under 2 free)

Travelers of all ages can stay curious at this museum with fun, hands-on exhibits and activities that explore energy, anatomy, chemistry and more. Stand inside a bubble in Bubbleology, pedal a stationary bike to turn kinetic energy into electricity and push an electric train around its track, encounter optical illusions and think with your hands in Da Vinci's Garage tinkering room. This museum is home to more than 100 exhibits and hosts themed weekends and ongoing educational science programs for all ages.

IN-N-OUT BURGER
Known for its "gold standard" fast-food burgers, **In-N-Out Burger** doesn't cut corners. In fact, none of their food is frozen or pre-packaged; all patties are 100% pure beef. Everything is made in their own facilities using only the freshest ingredients. Keep it simple with a classic hamburger or cheeseburger, or try one of their not-so-secret menu items (double, triple or quadruple the beef patties; animal or protein style). Of course there are fries and shakes. As of spring 2018 there were two locations in Oregon: 1970 Crater Lake Hwy, Medford, and 124 NW Morgan Lane, Grants Pass.

Smithfields Restaurant & Bar

36 S 2nd St　　　　　　　　　　　　　　　541/488-9948
Daily: 5-10 (dinner); Sat, Sun: 10-2:30 (brunch)　　smithfieldsashland.com
Moderate to moderately expensive

At Smithfields, everything from the meat, fish and produce down to the beer and wine is locally and independently sourced. Brunch features the chef's creative spin on traditional dishes like sweet lemon crepes, shrimp n' grits, biscuits with crimini gravy, flat iron steak Benedict and much more. For dinner, I suggest beginning with the house bacon beignets with maple-chive crème fraiche, or their version of a Caesar salad: grilled romaine, white anchovies, crostini and shaved parmesan with a roasted garlic dressing. Entrees include a fish of the day, cod, steaks, duck, fried chicken, a house burger, a twice-baked goat cheese soufflé and more. This eatery is a phenomenal choice for steak, and although the dishes are upscale, the setting is informal, prices are right and portions are generous. Reservations are recommended. Visit their sister location across the street, Smithfields Pub & Pies (23 S 2nd St, 541-482-7437).

Standing Stone Brewing Co.

101 Oak St　　　　　　　　　　　　　　　541/482-2448
Daily: 11 a.m.-midnight　　　　　　standingstonebrewing.com
Moderate

Residing in the former Whittle Garage Building, this classy pub serves up microbrews, signature pizzas baked in a wood-fired oven and great food until midnight. The restaurant's display kitchen turns out an extensive menu with usual pub grub; burgers are made with beef raised on their One Mile Farm just down the road from the brew pub. There is plenty of seating, a back deck with mountain views and regularly-scheduled live music; kids are welcome.

Weisinger Family Winery

3150 Siskiyou Blvd   541/488-5989
Daily: 11-6 (May-Sep); Wed-Sun: 11-5 (Oct-Apr)   weisingers.com
Established in 1988 by John Weisinger, the Weisinger Family Winery produces limited production craft wines created exclusively from local vineyards. Sourcing only from vineyards within five miles of the winery property, they support local growers and the local economy. The winery specializes in Gewürztraminer, tempranillo, pinot noir, Rhone and Bordeaux varietals, as well as proprietary blends. A one-bedroom Craftsman-style bungalow is adjacent to the vineyard and is equipped with a kitchen and private deck with hot tub and gas grill. Guests receive a welcoming cheese and wine basket and discounts in the tasting room. The tasting room is available by appointment Mondays and Tuesdays from October through April.

Winchester Inn

35 S 2nd St   541/488-1113, 800/972-4991
Lodging: moderate to expensive   winchesterinn.com
Restaurant: expensive
Owners Laurie, Michael and Drew Gibbs have magnificently transformed five buildings and a hilly lot into one of Ashland's finest inns with gorgeous tiered gardens. Drew is the inn's second-generation owner and certified sommelier. Top-drawer amenities in the house and cottages' 11 rooms and ten suites include down feather beds, pillows and comforters; luxury bed linens and Egyptian cotton towels; imported toiletries; guest phones with data ports and voicemail and complimentary Wi-Fi. Afternoon pastries are delivered to guest rooms, and there's an evening turndown service. A sumptuous two-course gourmet breakfast is included with an overnight stay. The nationally-recognized Alchemy Restaurant and Bar (541/488-1115) is excellent. Chef Chaz McKenna has assembled a fine selection of small plates, soups, salads and entrees using local and organic products; dinner menus change according to the season. The newly renovated bar is nestled in the gardens and features craft cocktails and an extensive wine selection. Reservations are recommended for the restaurant; bar seating is first come, first served.

AZALEA

Heaven on Earth Restaurant & Bakery

703 Quines Creek Road   541/837-3700
Daily: 7 a.m.-8 p.m.   heavenonearthbakery.com
Moderate
A slice of paradise is 30 minutes north of Grants Pass at exit 86 where Chris-

tine Jackson makes her restaurant and bakery a requisite visit for folks in Southern Oregon. The rustic eatery is noted for its home-style cooking and use of locally made products. Stop to enjoy or take home some of the tastiest baked goods and gigantic, melt-in-your-mouth cinnamon rolls (including a giant family-size version).

BLY

Aspen Ridge Resort

Fishhole Creek Road 18   541/884-8685, 800/393-3323
Seasonal   aspenrr.com
Moderate

This century-old, 14,000-acre working cattle ranch is about 70 miles east of Klamath Falls and 18 miles southeast of Bly. Log cabins, suites and lodge rooms are rustically elegant; the large cabins sleep six and feature wood-burning stoves, four-poster beds, lofts and full kitchens (no pets please). You can fill the long days with hiking, fishing, horseback riding, biking, swimming and tennis. The resort offers guided horseback rides, during which guests take part in the daily ranch work such as keeping tabs on newborn calves, moving cattle or just checking the herd. Generously portioned country breakfasts and dinners are served in the lodge restaurant, and the on-premises Buffalo Saloon is a favorite for beer, wine and cocktails. Steaks, chicken and baby back ribs are grilled over mesquite on the back deck and served with great-tasting sides; beef tri-tip is the specialty of the house. Reservations are a must for guests and drive-up customers. Wi-Fi is available in the lodge, but there is no cell phone service.

CAVE JUNCTION

The Chateau at the Oregon Caves

20000 Caves Hwy   541/592-3400
Seasonal: May-Sep   oregoncaveschateau.com
Moderate

Built in 1934 by businessmen from Grants Pass, this historic lodge features 23 unique rooms. Standard and deluxe rooms are accented with Monterey-style furniture and contain either two double beds or one queen bed; family suites have two rooms and one bath. A focal point is a stream channeled from the Oregon Caves which runs through the dining room. Dinners include fish, beef, bison, pastas and other Northwest-influenced selections. The vintage coffee shop (where you can take a stool at the counter, order a malt and enjoy the nostalgic 1930s soda fountain) is open for breakfast, lunch and dessert. Oregon Caves memorabilia, snacks and gifts are sold in the Gift Gallery. The lodge will close Sept. 30, 2018, for restorations. The closure could last one or two seasons.

Great Cats World Park
27919 Redwood Hwy   541/592-2957
Daily: 10-6 Memorial Day weekend through Labor Day
Other hours seasonally, or by appointment   greatcatsworldpark.com
Reasonable
Great Cats World Park offers animal demonstrations and educational guided tours, private photography tours and field trips, among many tour options. On this ten-acre park you can get up close and personal with a variety of large and small cats as they exhibit natural behaviors. Resident felines include lions, tigers, leopards, serval, ocelots, lynx and more — over 40 cats in all representing 17 species and subspecies. Snacks are available at the gift shop.

Oregon Caves National Monument
19000 Caves Hwy   541/592-2100
Seasonal: Spring-fall   nps.gov/orca
Nominal
Another of our state's treasures can be found tucked away in the Siskiyou Mountains about 20 miles southeast of Cave Junction. Be forewarned that the last ten miles are narrow, steep and winding (travel trailers and large RVs are not recommended beyond milepost 12). Expect snowfall late fall through spring. That being said, the incentives are magnificent marble caves of re-crystalized limestone, hiking, wildlife and nearby camping. Tours of the caves (fee applies) are offered late March through early November and are weather dependent; there is no fee to visit the surface trails and monument facilities. There are two visitor centers; one at the monument and one in Cave Junction. (Tours can be somewhat strenuous, so children must be at least 42 inches tall.)

Out 'n' About Treehouse Treesort
300 Page Creek Road   541/592-2208
Year-round   treehouses.com
Moderate
Kids of all ages have the time of their lives at this unique bed and breakfast in the trees. It features 13 treehouses and three non-treehouses complete with lavatories in the trees and on the ground. Each space has a specific theme and accommodates two, four or more people on one level or two. Furnishings vary and may include queen or twin beds and bunks, kitchen-

ettes and tables and chairs. The loftiest unit is over 40 feet up a tree and accessed by swinging bridges and platforms. Throughout the 36 private acres are child-size forts, seven swinging bridges, six swings, 20 flights of stairs and four ladders; over a mile of zip lines; a swimming pool; and horses. Breakfast is included in the stay and is served in the main lodge (full breakfast served mid-March through October; continental breakfast served remainder of the year). There are no TVs or landline phones, but you will not be bored. Reservations required.

Wild River Brewing & Pizza Company

249 N Redwood Hwy   541/592-3556
Mon-Thu: 11-9; Fri, Sat 11-10; Sun: noon-9   wildriverbrewing.com
Moderate
(See main listing in Grants Pass)

CENTRAL POINT

Lillie Belle Farms

211 N Front St   541/664-2815, 888/899-2022
Mon-Fri: 9-5 (Sat till 6); Sun: 11-5   lilliebellefarms.com
Jeff Shepherd started selling homemade truffles named after his wife and daughter at local farmers markets. Now 17 years later, Lillie Belle Farms chocolates are known throughout North America. If you've had a taste, you know Jeff takes no shortcuts. From the start he has used the finest ingredients from his own organic farm. Although chocolates can be shipped worldwide (Lillie Belles are available online), there's nothing like a stop at the shop for the freshest berry cordials, bon bons, berry cups, bars, truffles and other specialties. Some look too good to eat, but the available samples make it impossible not to take some home. For heat lovers, there's organic ghost pepper chocolate. For cravers of salty and sweet, the lavender sea salt caramels are a must. For the eat-dessert-first crowd, try a truffle with just the right amount of Rogue Creamery's Smokey Blue cheese, organic milk chocolate and toasted almonds (also in spread form).

Rogue Creamery

311 N Front St (Hwy 99)   541/665-1155, 866/396-4704
Daily   roguecreamery.com
This creamery dates back to 1933. In the 1940s, Rogue Creamery supplied cheddar cheese to the war effort and was the first major supplier of cottage cheese in Oregon. Today under the leadership of David Gremmels, Rogue Creamery continues to produce award-winning blue and cheddar cheese in Central Point. The classic Oregon Blue Vein Cheese was created

in 1954 and was the first blue cheese made in caves on the West Coast. In 2002, Gremmels created Rogue River Blue followed by the world's first smoked blue cheese, Smokey Blue. You'll find artisan cheeses, specialty foods, local wines and craft beers in the cheese shop as well as grilled

FAMILY ACTIVITIES

ASHLAND
Emigrant Lake and Water Slides (5505 Hwy 66, 541/774-8183, emigrantlake.org): water slides Memorial Day through Labor Day, select days
Lithia Park (Winburn Way, 541/488-5340, lithiaparkplayground.com, lithiaparktrailguide.com): 100 acres; playground, band shell, winter ice skating, trails, pond, creek
ScienceWorks Hands-On Museum (1500 E Main St, 541/482-6767, scienceworksmuseum.org): hands-on activities and exhibits, educational science programs

CAVE JUNCTION
Great Cats World Park (27919 Redwood Hwy, 541/592-2957, greatcatsworldpark.com): animal demonstrations and educational guided tours; seasonal
Oregon Caves National Monument (19000 Caves Hwy, 541/592-2100, nps.gov/orca): marble caves, hiking, tours
Out 'n' About Treehouse Treesort (300 Page Creek Road, 541/592-2208, treehouses.com): treehouse lodging; zip lines, Tarzan swing, river rafting, hiking

CENTRAL POINT
Rogue Jet Boat Adventures (meets at Touvelle State Park, 8400 Table Rock Road; 541/414-4182; roguejetadventures.com): reservations required; four trips daily
Rogue Valley Family Fun Center (1A Peninger Road, 541/664-4263, rvfamilyfuncenter.com): go carts, miniature golf, bumper boats, batting cages, arcade

CRATER LAKE
Crater Lake National Park (541/594-3000, nps.gov/crla): one of Oregon's finest attractions

cheese sandwiches to enjoy while watching the cheese makers or chilling on the patio. Each March, the annual Oregon Cheese Festival showcases products from Rogue Creamery and other Oregon cheese producers, plus beer, wine, baked goods and chocolates.

GOLD HILL
House of Mystery at Oregon Vortex (4303 Sardine Creek Left Fork Road, 541/855-1543, oregonvortex.com): a spherical field of force, both above and below ground; March through October
Rogue Valley ZipLine Adventure (9450 Old Stage Road, Central Point, 541/821-9476, rvzipline.com): off Gold Hill Exit 40 (shuttle location/golf course), year-round, reservations required

GRANTS PASS
Hellgate Jetboat Excursions (966 SW 6th St, 541/479-7204, hellgate.com): 2 to 5 hour jet boat excursions with or without brunch, lunch or dinner at the OK Corral; May through September
Wildlife Images Rehabilitation Center (11845 Lower River Road, 541/476-0222, wildlifeimages.org): wildlife and nature educational programs; birds of prey, mammals, reptiles

KLAMATH FALLS
Crater Lake Zipline (29840 Hwy 140, 541/892-9477, craterlakezipline.com): April to October; kids' course; combo zip line and kayak tour
Favell Museum of Western Art and Indian Artifacts (125 W Main St, 541/882-9996, favellmuseum.org): artifacts and art

LAKEVIEW
Warner Canyon Ski Area (98158 Hwy 140, 541/947-5001, warnercanyon.org): old-fashioned ski hill; seasonal

MEDFORD
Kid Time Children's Museum (106 N Central Ave, 541/772-9922, kid-time.org): fun and educational playful exhibits

WINSTON
Wildlife Safari (1790 Safari Road, 541/679-6761, wildlifesafari.net): drive-through wildlife park; play area, petting zoo

CHILOQUIN

Lonesome Duck Ranch & Resort

32955 Hwy 97 N   541/783-2783
Moderately expensive   lonesomeduck.com
Debbie and Steve Hilbert preside over a scenic and fun retreat, combining many things for different family members to enjoy (kids love walking the llamas). In a 200-acre setting on two miles of Williamson River frontage, the possibilities are especially attractive for those who relish the outdoors. Rivers Edge, a full-size log home with two bedrooms, two full baths and a loft area with twin beds is also available. Arrowhead cottage, one of the original ranch houses, features a great stone fireplace, two small bedrooms, kitchen, living and dining rooms. There's a two-night minimum and off-season (November to mid-May) rates are reduced. Each cabin offers superb views. Fly-fishing is first-class, with guides available for half or full days. The Wood River, Klamath Lake, Agency Lake and the Sprague River are nearby; what a thrill to land a trophy rainbow trout! The ranch is near five Klamath Basin refuges, home to more than 430 wildlife species and some 250 bird varieties. Take a tour with ranch manager Marshal Moser, a wildlife biologist and naturalist. You can't help but enjoy the flora and fauna, enhanced by Marshal's expert knowledge. With easy access to Crater Lake, horse facilities, barbecues and kitchens in each unit, what more could you ask for? Photographers: This place is for you.

CRATER LAKE

Crater Lake National Park

Lodging: Moderate to expensive   541/594-3000
Restaurant: Expensive   nps.gov/crla
Oregon's only national park brings visitors from around the world to take in the brilliant blue beauty from the caldera rim. The rim road is open until the snow flies, usually open in its entirety from July through October. The scenery is breathtaking as you wind your way around our nation's deepest lake (1,943 feet), which has two islands (Wizard and Phantom Ship). Visitor centers are located at the rim (typically open June to September) and year-round at park headquarters. A concessionaire operates seasonal ranger-narrated boat tours around the lake and to Wizard Island. Built in 1915 and beautifully renovated in 1995, the 71-room Crater Lake Lodge (888/774-2728, craterlakelodges.com) and restaurant are open mid-May through mid-October. The restaurant features Northwest breakfast, lunch and dinner cuisine. Southwest of the lake, Mazama Village has a campground, cabins, camper store, fuel, restaurant and gift shop. Various fees

apply for vehicles, bicycles and pedestrians entering the park. Allow plenty of time to experience this national treasure.

EAGLE POINT

Butte Creek Mill

402 N Royal Ave   buttecreekmillfoundation.com

Debbie and Bob Russell were making their living and keeping history alive as operators of the last commercial water-powered grist mill west of the Mississippi. The mill had functioned since 1872 and is on the National Register of Historic Places. But on Christmas morning, 2015, the mill burned to the ground in what was deemed an accidental electrical fire. The mill stones were not harmed in the fire, and the basement was largely intact. The mill is now owned by the Butte Creek Mill Foundation, which is fundraising to reconstruct the mill in a historically accurate manner. A reopening is planned for 2019. Your donations can help make that happen. Go to their website to see how you can help.

Oregon Bee Store

14356 Hwy 62   541/826-7621

Seasonal: March-Dec   oregonbeestore.com

For a sweet stop in Southern Oregon, visit second generation Wild Bee Honey Farm for honey and honey products. They also sell gourmet honey from around the world and beautiful beeswax candles in a variety of shapes and sizes. Beekeeping supplies, equipment and instruction are available at the store and online.

ELKTON

The Big K Guest Ranch and Outfitters

20029 Hwy 138W   541/584-2295

Year-round   big-k.com

Moderate

The Big K Guest Ranch offers great hospitality and service at a beautifully constructed rustic lodge. The guest ranch is located within a historic 2,500-acre Century Farm that borders ten secluded miles of the Umpqua River. The classic log structure is perfect for corporate retreats, family reunions, weddings and parties. In addition, there are private, beautifully appointed guest cabins. The full-service resort's offerings include scenic float trips and guided fishing excursions along the famous Umpqua River Loop; ranch-style dining with portions sized to satisfy the loggers and ranchers of our area; and peace, serenity and beauty.

Tomaselli's Pastry Mill & Cafe

14836 Umpqua Hwy — 541/584-2855
Wed-Sun: 6 a.m.-8 p.m. — tomasellispastrymill.com
Inexpensive to moderately expensive

Tomaselli's Pastry Mill & Cafe is a convenient destination for refilling coffee mugs and reenergizing with espresso and homemade bakery goodies on Highway 38 between Drain and Reedsport. You can't go wrong with pastries and breads, but don't overlook Tomaselli's for dinner any night. The gourmet meals may include sautéed duck breast with cherry sauce, praline-glazed Chinook salmon, polenta with beef and Italian sausage, stew or lamb, pork and steak dishes, delicious with wines from local vineyards. There are plenty of great breakfast favorites and combos which are served until noon. Lunch service starts at 11 a.m. with comfort foods, soups, salads, sandwiches and burgers. Wood-fired pizzas are available starting at noon; opt for one of the house specialties or pick your own combination.

GOLD HILL

Rogue Valley ZipLine Adventure

Shuttle location: I-5 exit 40 — 541/821-9476
9450 Old Stage Road, Central Point — rvzipline.com
Expensive

Where to find a challenging family adventure with the best views in Southern Oregon, led by entertaining guides? Answer: In Gold Hill for an exhilarating off-the-ground excursion on an amazing zip line. Actually, the 2,700-foot course consists of five zip lines; the longest is over 1,300 feet. A van picks up parties at a shuttle stop on Old Stage Road in Central Point where they are transported to zip headquarters on private property in gold mining country. From there, participants are outfitted with safety equipment and given important guidelines before hiking to the first platform. Along the way, certified guides impart local history and interesting tidbits about the flora, fauna and landmarks. Allow three to three-and-a-half hours to complete the course. Tours operate all year; sun, rain or snow (although dangerous inclement weather will halt the activities). Post-zipping, visit the general store for snacks and such and catch a ride back to the shuttle stop. What's more fun than a summer afternoon in the trees? A full day (June, July and August) zipping, dipping and sipping. The Zip, Dip & Sip Tour starts on the zip line course followed by a professionally guided seven-mile whitewater rafting trip and lunch at Laurel Hill Golf Course. The last leg is wine tasting at an estate winery. Reservations required for all trips; group discounts available.

GRANTS PASS

Flery Manor Bed & Breakfast

2000 Jumpoff Joe Creek Road   541/476-3591
Moderate   flerymanor.com

A bed and breakfast combined with an art studio is the Flery's unusual hosting formula. This attractive mountainside destination is near the Rogue River and has three suites and two additional nicely decorated rooms; some feature a fireplace and Jacuzzi. Guests enjoy a well-stocked library, and a piano is available for those with a musical flair. Original recipe, three-course organic breakfasts (many times with ingredients fresh from the home garden) feature innovative egg dishes. Guests are invited to experience the art studio where they may dabble in clay, paint, music, photography, writing or other creative art forms. Enjoy a walk or hike around the property to view the ponds, waterfalls and streams and perhaps catch a glimpse of the two resident black swans; more exhilarating hiking trails are on adjacent private property. Less strenuous time may be spent in the hammock or the gazebo enjoying the sights and sounds of nature.

The Haul

121 SW H St   541/474-4991
Wed-Sun: 11-10 (till midnight Fri, Sat); Mon: 11-9   thehaulgp.com
Moderate

The Haul serves Neapolitan-inspired pizzas cooked in a 700-degree, wood-fired Italian pizza oven. In addition, the menu features small plates, sandwiches, soups, salads and burgers. Food is fresh and locally sourced, and there are numerous vegan options. Draft beers come exclusively from Conner Fields Brewing, for which The Haul is the tasting room. The drink menu also includes cocktails, hard cider, wine, bottled beer and non-alcoholic options. The Haul's warehouse-like setting resembles something you would find in Portland and welcomes customers with its casual, yet intimate, atmosphere. Small tables and picnic benches fill the restaurant. Order service is available at the counter with a bar downstairs and a full bar upstairs open to the public on the weekends and also available for special events and private parties. Check out their website for live music events.

Taprock Northwest Grill

971 SE 6th St   541/955-5998
Daily: 8 a.m.-10 p.m.   taprock.com
Moderate

This beautiful lodge-inspired restaurant sits at the edge of the Rogue River along Highway 99. A man-made waterfall, wildlife sculptures and ample outdoor lighting are welcoming touches. The restaurant serves breakfast, lunch and dinner and has seating for 300 inside, plus more on the wrap-around deck and at the hand-hewn bar. The menu reflects its Northwest theme with farm-fresh egg dishes, salmon, Dungeness crab and other seafood, sandwiches, burgers, steaks and pastas. Salads are farm-to-table fresh and offered in two sizes. Start your morning with breakfast favorites of Dungeness crab cake Benedicts, berry French toast and flat iron steak and eggs.

Weasku Inn

5560 Rogue River Hwy   541/471-8000, 800/493-2758
Moderately expensive   weasku.com

Even the pronunciation of this inn's name is welcoming: We-Ask-U Inn. This historic lodge has been home away from home for guests since 1924. Restoration to the lodge and the original A-frame cabin were completed in 1998 retaining the authentic feel and decor. The 11 riverfront cabins and a three-bedroom river house are nicely appointed; stone fireplaces and Jacuzzi tubs in some cabins. Additional amenities include a deluxe continental breakfast, afternoon appetizer reception and nightly freshly-baked cookies and milk. Hollywood legends such as Clark Gable, Carole Lombard and Walt Disney left Tinseltown behind to vacation at this tranquil Rogue River retreat.

Wild River Brewing & Pizza Company

595 NE E St   541/471-7487
Daily: 10-10 (Fri, Sat till 11)   wildriverbrewing.com
Moderate

The main location is a family-oriented restaurant that features a showcase brewery and in addition to pizza, serves pasta, European-inspired classics, sandwiches and other meals. Down the street (533 NE F St, 541/474-4456), the pub's friendly atmosphere is a good place to grab a pint and watch a sporting event on the big screen. They also serve great burgers, pub fare and entrees from the full-service menus at their other locations in Brookings, Cave Junction and Medford.

IDLEYLD PARK

Steamboat Inn

42705 N Umpqua Hwy   541/498-2230, 800/840-8825
Moderate and up   thesteamboatinn.com

Although this charming retreat is known far and wide by fishermen, others will be just as engaged with the many attractions offered. For over a

> **WINE TOURS**
>
> Tour the Southern Oregon Wine Region with **Wine Hopper Tours** (855/550-9463, winehoppertours.com), carefully tailored for the connoisseur in each of us. The tours, departing from Ashland and Medford, provides in-depth education of the region's history and a hands-on tasting experience that is not found in a self-guided tour. Travel in style aboard a Mercedes Benz tour van to learn about the wine-making process and spend some time in the barrel room of a featured winery. Custom group trips are also available.

half-century, anglers have made Steamboat their base camp for some of the best steelhead fishing anywhere. The eight cabins and two suites on the river are breathtaking; the sounds of the rippling water will put even the most restless sleeper into seventh heaven. Also available (and particularly well suited for families) are five hideaway cottages and three 1960s three-bedroom ranch houses. The main building has a charming library and a huge dining table where guests have experienced wonderful meals for generations. For over 20 years, great winemakers and wonderful chefs have combined their talents to provide remarkable winemakers' dinners at Steamboat Inn. Hikers can explore a multitude of waterfalls on some of the most fantastic trails in Oregon. Proprietors Melinda and Travis Woodward are gracious, friendly, guest-oriented hosts. Take fly-fishing instruction, a whitewater raft trip or simply relax and enjoy the river and forest. This is one of Oregon's best.

JACKSONVILLE

Bybee's Historic Inn

883 Old Stage Road   541/899-0106, 877/292-3374
Moderate   bybeeshistoricinn.com

Experience living history in a classical revival manse built in 1857 by William M. Bybee, a Jackson County farmer, freight driver, settler, stockman, politician and leader. Today, six beautiful guest rooms are tastefully appointed with period antiques and fabric-covered walls and supplied with modern technological amenities; the Americana room on the first floor offers a separate entrance and is wheelchair accessible. Each room in this bed and breakfast inn contains a private bathroom that is outfitted with a two-person Jacuzzi tub (unheard of in the 1850s), walk-in shower or claw-foot tub and luxurious robes, towels and quality bed linens (line-dried in the summer sunshine). Outside, enjoy the manicured three acres with a game of bocce ball and croquet or settle onto one of the porches and patios with a complimentary glass of wine, ice cream or homemade treat. Breakfasts, included with an overnight stay, are a three-course gourmet experience prepared to guests' dietary requests. Bybee's Historic Inn, a National Historic Landmark, also features murder mystery dinners and is a spectacular setting for outdoor weddings, showers and other gatherings.

Elan Guest Suites and Gallery

245 W Main St   541/899-8000
Moderate   elanguestsuites.com
This classy boutique hotel includes a first-floor art gallery, garden walkway and secure parking garage with luggage lift. Three stylish and contemporary suites are appointed with private balconies, wood and tile floors, fully-equipped kitchens and state-of-the-art entertainment systems. Guests are sure to appreciate the original artwork that enhances each suite. Complimentary coffee and fresh-baked breakfast treats are provided by nearby Good Bean Coffee Co. Elan Gallery features special art exhibits and is open daily to guests. Pure panache.

Schoolhaus Brewhaus

525 Bigham Knoll Drive   541/899-1000
Mon-Thu: 3-9; Fri, Sat: 10:30-9; Sun: 10:30-8   theschoolhaus.com
Moderate
Housed in a former Jacksonville schoolhouse (circa 1908), the restaurant and biergarten (which stays open later) are enhanced with Bavarian scenes, historic photos and other German decor. The menu offers authentic German listings with English explanations — fondues, schnitzels, schweinebraten, knodels and so much more. Celebrate Oktoberfest, Winterfest and MaiFest with good German food, good German beer and good friends.

Gary West Meats

690 N 5th St   800/833-1820
Mon-Sat: 10-6; Sun: 11-5
(summer and holidays; other hours seasonal)   garywest.com
Gary's grandparents were pioneers in the Applegate area, and Gary is well-schooled in the special flavors of old-time foods that make for memorable ranch meals. A break at this jerky factory and tasting room is fun and different from the usual snack stops. You'll be treated to tasty elk, bison and Angus beef samples. If you're in a buying mood, there are jerky samplers; a great selection of Oregon wines; baskets featuring wild game, sausage and other unusual gifts; hams and buffalo strips. Gary's meats are also available online.

Gogi's Restaurant

235 W Main St   541/899-8699
Wed-Sun: 5-9   gogisrestaurant.com
Moderate

Brothers Gabriel Murphy and Jonoah Murphy pull much of the seasonal produce from their small farm in the Applegate Valley. Intimate dining in chic environs features international cuisine, made in-house using local organic ingredients as much as possible. For starters, try crispy pork belly served with creamy polenta and pickled watermelon rind, soup of the day or crisp salad. Dinner entrees include double-cut New York steak, braised lamb shank, confit of duck leg, seafood and other very good choices. Outstanding service, fine wines and creative cocktails complete the impressive dining experience.

Jacksonville Inn

175 E California St   541/899-1900, 800/321-9344
Rooms: Moderate; Cottages: Moderately expensive   jacksonvilleinn.com

This historic bed and breakfast (circa 1861) is tastefully decorated with period antiques and reproductions. There are eight rooms with private bathrooms at the inn. The original honeymoon cottage, a small restored historic house, is two blocks away; and three replicate cottages, including the Presidential Cottage where President and Mrs. George W. Bush stayed, were built at the same location. Each is private and luxurious. A full breakfast is included with an overnight stay and is served in the inn's dining room. Guests choose from a variety of favorites, such as house-made granola, waffles and eggs Benedict. Sunday brunch starts with champagne or sparkling cider. Then try fresh fruit, house-baked pastries, eggs, meats and scalloped potatoes (another favorite), or select a special of the day. Lunch and dinner are served in the dining room and bistro, as well as on a lovely garden patio. Dinners with fresh, local and seasonal ingredients include the inn's special grilled chicken, fish and seafood, flavorful steaks, prime rib, and more. Vegetarian and gluten-free meals are available, and the wine list is extensive. Keep the restaurant in mind for off-site catering, banquets (private dining rooms are available) and picnic baskets to take to Britt Festival concerts. Proprietors Linda and Jerry Evans also operate one of the top wine and gift shops in the U.S., stocked with over 2,000 wine selections.

Jacksonville's Magnolia Inn

245 N 5th St   541/899-0255
Moderate   magnolia-inn.com

Magnolia Inn offers nine well-appointed vintage rooms with en suite baths and a veranda overlooking the property's English garden. Delightful hosts

Susan and Robert Roos oversee the morning's continental breakfast; a guest kitchen and dining area are located on the second floor. The check-in area is stocked with something for the taking from Susan's treasure trove of baked goods.

Mustard Seed Cafe

130 N 5th St   541/899-2977
Tue-Sat: 7-2   Facebook
Inexpensive
You can count on this tiny eatery for a good meal at easy prices and with warm service. What to order? Cinnamon rolls, various scrambles and omelets and corned beef hash for breakfast (served 7-11); burgers, sandwiches and onion rings for lunch (served 11-2) or selections from the special value breakfast and lunch menus. If you can't decide, ask one of the regular customers for their suggestions.

Pot Rack

140 W California St   541/899-5736
Daily: 10-5
Aptly named, this shop sells pot racks (and pots, pans and cooking utensils to hang on them). You'll find brand name cookware, bakeware, useful and obscure gadgets, colorful table accessories, table linens, aprons, cutlery, gifts and more to inspire your culinary bent. Their wedding registry makes it easy to decide on gifts for newlyweds.

Terra Firma Gift

135 W California St   541/899-1097
Mon-Sat: 10:30-6; Sun: 11-5   terrafirmahome.com
Merchandise at this gift emporium is best described as fun stuff. The main floor has a unique selection of some of this and some of that — soap by the loaf, candles, jewelry, hardware, housewares, home decor and affordable gifts for your home or best friend. A clearance area for furniture from their home and design location in Medford is located on the second floor.

KLAMATH FALLS

Crystalwood Lodge

38625 Westside Road   866/381-2322
Moderate   craterlakelodgingatcrystalwoodlodge.com
When you pack up the family and the pet dog (or cat or bird or hamster) begs to come along, it's no problem if the destination is Crystalwood

Lodge. Near the south entrance to Crater Lake National Park and adjacent to the Upper Klamath National Wildlife Refuge, this lodge sits on 130 acres in the center of wonderful fly-fishing, canoeing, golf, hiking, horseback riding, cross-country skiing, snowshoeing, dog sledding, biking and other outdoor activities. Nearby you can visit Train Mountain, a narrow-gauge train ride covering 36 miles through the forest. You can also take in Crater Lake Zipline, Oregon's longest zipline, which gives you up to three hours of fun flying from tree to tree. Rooms are named after checkpoints in the Iditarod Sled Dog Race, and the owner's sled dog kennel is available for guest tours. Crates (home-away-from-home pet houses) are provided in every room, a dog-washing facility is near at hand and pet day care is available. In lieu of meal service, guests have access to a fully-outfitted kitchen facility, walk-in cooler, freezer and grill. Lodging, gathering and meeting space is available year-round along with optional catered meals to groups for reunions, retreats, weddings, workshops and such. The lodge primarily hosts groups, but individuals may rent if space is available.

Favell Museum of Western Art and Indian Artifacts
125 W Main St   541/882-9996
Tue-Sat: 10-5   favellmuseum.org
Nominal
The museum features over 100,000 Native American artifacts and contemporary Western art by some of the country's most notable artists. Collections include pottery dating back 1,000 years, baskets representing numerous tribes across the Western U.S., points (arrowheads) dating back 13,500 years, sandals found in caves that date back nearly 12,000 years, the oldest known atlatl with a boatstone attached (a leverage device that increases the power of a thrown spear), and Inca textiles displayed with the tools used to weave them. The museum's Western art collection includes oils by Charles Russell and John Clymer and a collection of Edward Curtis photographs. Each fall the museum hosts The Favell Museum Art Show & Sale.

The Klamath Grill
715 Main St   541/882-1427
Mon-Fri: 6-2:30; Sat, Sun: 7-2   klamathgrill.com
Inexpensive
It's always fun to check out the local hot spots for breakfast and lunch, and a good place to start in K-Falls is at this Main Street restaurant. Pancakes (ten varieties), waffles, stuffed French toast, pigs in a blanket and egg dishes are breakfast staples. If you're in the mood for lunch, hot and cold sandwiches, burgers and salads are tasty options.

TRAVEL ASSISTANCE
Should you ever need roadside assistance as you visit some of the great places in this edition, your **AAA** (800/444-8091, oregon. aaa.com) membership can be a godsend. These folks are available to members 24/7 for vehicle and bicycle roadside service. Travel planning services include maps and tour books for hundreds of destinations, routes and current road conditions; helpful seminars on packing and special offers for cruises and more. Show your AAA card and get discounted rates on hotels, car repair and rental, florists, dining, attractions, computers, eyewear, movie tickets—over 160,000 participating businesses. AAA has insurance professionals and can assist with a variety of insurance options. Offices are conveniently located across the state.

Lake of the Woods Mountain Lodge & Resort

950 Harriman Route   541/949-8300, 866/201-4194
Lodging: Moderate   lakeofthewoodsresort.com
Restaurant: Moderate to expensive

Spend the day at the lake, then head inside your cozy cabin to rest and rejuvenate for another day of fishing, waterskiing, hiking, scuba diving or winter activities. One- and two-bedroom vintage cabins at Lake of the Woods have varying amenities (full kitchen or kitchenette, jetted tub, electric Fire-View heaters). Park model cabins have a bedroom and living rooms with a sofa sleeper or trundle bed, full kitchens and bathrooms. Units may also have sleeping lofts, covered porches or bunk rooms. The Lake House Restaurant is open for breakfast, lunch and dinner and the Marina Pizza Parlor serves lunch and dinner (pizza, wraps, salads, sandwiches) daily during the summer (in winter, the pizza parlor is open Friday through Sunday). A full-service marina offers paddle board and boat rentals, fuel and moorage. Lake of the Woods Resort operates the Forest Service campgrounds also. For campground reservations, go to rec.gov.

Mermaid Garden Cafe

501 Main St   541/882-3671
Mon-Fri: 10:30-2   Facebook
Inexpensive

A mythical marine creature may seem out of place in Klamath Falls, but not at the Mermaid Garden Cafe, where mermaid figurines and kitsch decorate Kelly Hennessey's popular establishment. Lunch consists of paninis, wraps, soups, made-to-order salads (choose from a selection of greens, homemade salad dressings and two dozen additions) and a weekly pizza special. Winning menu items include a New Jersey sloppy joe, turkey curry wrap and a spicy portabella panini (each accompanied by a green salad, Thai cabbage slaw or Southwestern potato salad). This is a hot spot in downtown K-Falls.

Mia & Pia's Pizzeria & Brewhouse

3545 Summers Lane   541/884 4880
Sun-Thu: 11-10; Fri, Sat: 10:30 a.m.-11 p.m.   miaandpiasklamathfalls.com
Moderate to moderately expensive
Dozens of beers and ales are on tap at Mia & Pia's. The brewhouse is the outgrowth of a family business started nearly four decades ago. Much of the equipment and hardware is reclaimed from their prior dairy business and is in daily use at the pizzeria and brewhouse. Some 30 pizza varieties are available, or dream up your own creation. Other good eats include appetizers, burgers, broasted chicken, spaghetti, soups, salads and sandwiches. These folks will bring their beer truck to your event for a never-to-be-forgotten party. Remember to fill your growler, and watch their Facebook page for information on events and entertainment.

Rocky Point Resort

28121 Rocky Point Road   541/356-2287
Lodging: year-round (moderate)   rockypointoregon.com
Restaurant: Memorial Day-Labor Day (moderate)
If you want to be near to nature and enjoy a comfy bed and shower each evening, consider a stay at this rustic resort (about 40 minutes from Crater Lake, 45 minutes from Medford and 30 minutes from Klamath Falls) on the northwest shore of Upper Klamath Lake. You have a choice of cabins, guest rooms, RV spaces — even tent sites (cabins and guest rooms year-round, RV and tent sites closed in winter). The resort's popular restaurant is open for breakfast, lunch and dinner Memorial Day through Labor Day (management plans to operate the restaurant year-round, so do call ahead for hours). Overnighters are welcome to use the well-kept public restrooms, showers, laundry facilities and fish-cleaning station; pick up supplies at the marina store, where you can also rent canoes, boats and kayaks or fuel your watercraft.

Running Y Ranch Resort

5500 Running Y Road   541/850-5500
Lodging: Moderate and up   runningy.com
Restaurant: Moderately expensive
Running Y Ranch Resort is Southern Oregon's premier full-service destination resort. The 82-room lodge features updated guest rooms and

amenities, the Ruddy Duck Restaurant (541/850-5582) overlooking Payne Canyon, and Oregon's only Arnold Palmer Signature Golf Course. The resort offers vacation homes with two, three or four bedrooms, and a ten-bedroom home overlooking the lake. Non-golfers have plenty to do, too: Fishing, birding, hiking, kayaking and Crater Lake Zip Line are close at hand. Winter visitors don't have to travel far for snowshoeing or skating at on-property Ice Sports (541/850-5758). Additional amenities include the Sandhill Spa (541/850-5547), seasonal horseback riding (541/840-9999), a miniature golf course and a sports and fitness center with a year-round swimming pool, sauna and spa.

MEDFORD

4 Daughters Irish Pub

126 W Main St   541/779-4455
Mon-Thu: 11-10; Fri, Sat: 11-midnight
Sun: 10-10   4daughtersirishpub.com
Moderate
This property goes back to the early 1900s; it has been a barbershop, theater, billiards parlor and cigar club. Named for the owner's four daughters, this pub is appropriately furnished with a game room that includes pool and darts. The extensive menu includes small bites, soups and salads, burgers, beer-battered fish and chips, Guinness meatloaf, shepherd's pie and wonderful homemade desserts. Plenty of Irish drink specialties and beers are available. Brunch is served Sundays from 10 a.m. to 1 p.m.

Bambu

970 N Phoenix Road   541/608-7545
Lunch: Mon-Fri, 11:30-2; Dinner: Mon-Thu, 5-9 (Fri, Sat till 9:30)   tigerroll.com
Moderate
The menu at Bambu takes you on a whirlwind tour of Asian cuisine, including flavors from Japan, China, Vietnam, Thailand, Korea, Indonesia, the Philippines and Hawaii. Whether you come in for lunch or dinner, you will find small plates such as tiger rolls, Polynesian coconut prawns, soups, salads, and variations of fish, shrimp, pork, poultry, noodles and curry dishes consisting of fresh vegetables, shrimp, seafood and chicken. Pair dinner with a Southern Oregon wine for the ultimate experience and, of course, don't forget dessert. Reservations are recommended at this intimate eatery.

Downtown Market Co.

231 E Main St   541/973-2233
Market: Mon-Fri: 9-4; Sat, Sun: 9:30-1:30
Kitchen: Mon-Fri: 11-3; Sat, Sun: 9:30-1:30   downtownmarketco.com
Moderate

Nora LaBrocca's love of food led her to open this downtown market with her husband Brian Witter. Brought up in Southern California, her family raised beef, poultry and game birds for chic Los Angeles area restaurants and hotels. Lunch is served Monday through Friday at Downtown Market, and the menu changes every other week bringing fresh soups, salads, sandwiches, pastries and more to the tables. The market also hosts Over Easy, a weekend brunch service led by Chef Braden Hitt, whose menu changes weekly. The market offers a full bar, wine, beer, and its scratch made basil lemonade. Two ground-floor outdoor patios are pleasantly furnished to feel like a big city rooftop.

EdenVale Winery

2310 Voorhies Road   541/512-2955
Daily: 11-6; Fri, Sat till 7 (Apr-Oct)
Daily: 11-5; Fri, Sat till 6 (Nov-Mar)   edenvalewines.com

Whether you are a wine connoisseur or a history buff, the beautiful grounds, historic gardens and tasteful tasting room of EdenVale Winery are worth a visit (the property is on the National Register of Historic Places). In the spirit of the Pear Blossom Festival, a taste of organic pear cider straight from their pear orchard is a must. EdenVale also offers red and white blends and an extensive list of international award winning varietals such as cabernet, syrah, temparillo, merlot, malbec, grenache, chardonnay, pinot noir and dessert viognier. Light fare is available for pairings. Stay for a sunset on the patio as you take in the Cascade Mountain range and picturesque views of the property.

Elements Tapas Bar & Lounge

101 E Main St   541/779-0135
Daily: 4-midnight (Fri, Sat till 1 a.m.)   elementsmedford.com
Moderate

At this historic downtown building you'll find Spanish wines and great drinks from the full bar to accompany outstanding food, crafted as much as possible from local produce. Try red grapes encrusted with Rogue Creamery smoked blue cheese and crushed pistachios, Spanish olives, mushroom catalan, roasted beet salad and other delectable choices. Traditional Spanish paellas with vegetables and assorted meats and seafood are made to order from scratch, which allows adequate time to share tasty tapas. And there's a new emphasis on seasonal dishes.

Inn at the Commons

200 N Riverside Ave   541/779-5811
Lodging: Moderate   innatthecommons.com
Restaurant: Moderately expensive to expensive

Hospitality entrepreneurs Becky and Doug Neuman purchased the former
Red Lion Hotel, renamed it and created a destination property that is warm
and comfortable. All 118 guest rooms and suites are outfitted with the latest technology; many rooms offer courtyard views and balconies. The inn
has an outdoor pool and Jacuzzi (open seasonally), and guests are treated
to a complimentary hot breakfast buffet. Larks Restaurant (541/774-4760)
features farm-to-table gourmet fare for lunch and dinner. The inn is Medford's biggest venue for large meetings and conventions with space for up
to 600 people.

Jaspers Cafe

2739 N Pacific Hwy   541/776-5307
Mon-Thu: 11-7; Fri, Sat: 11-8; Sun: 11-6   jasperscafe.com
Inexpensive

It's no secret that I enjoy great hamburgers with all the trimmings and, of
course, crispy French fries. If you're in Southern Oregon, Jaspers Cafe is the
place to go. The menu lists classic, gourmet, extreme gourmet and outra-
geous and wild burgers. Choices include beef in combination with game
meats (antelope, elk, kangaroo, bison). Over 20 flavors of hand-scooped
shakes and malts reign supreme on the drink menu. And if you're ever in
Bluff Dale, Texas, you'll find a Jaspers Cafe there, too.

José Mexican Express

101 S Riverside Ave   541/690-7535
Mon-Sat: 10:30-6:30
Inexpensive

This place may look like a little food cart, but it is a gem offering big, authentic flavors and generous portions that always include fresh, seasonal
organic vegetables and handmade corn tortillas. The carne asada and fish
tacos are popular choices. Other options include enchiladas, nachos, burritos, chili rellenos and more.

Porters

147 N Front St   541/857-1910
Daily: 5-close (bar opens at 4)   porterstrainstation.com
Moderately expensive

Named a National Historic Landmark, Medford's beautifully-restored railroad depot has been home to this dinner restaurant for over a decade.

The century-old building is magnificent with original Craftsman-style architecture. Details include over 40,000 red roof tiles, hand-chiseled granite corbels, massive wood beams, working radiators, and a ticket-making machine. Dinner features outstanding Southern Oregon produce, meats and cheeses, beer and wine, and an excellent selection of fish and seafood. For

FESTIVALS & FAIRS IN SOUTHERN OREGON

FEBRUARY-OCTOBER
Oregon Shakespeare Festival (15 S Pioneer St, Ashland; 800/219-8161, osfashland.org)

JUNE
Summer Arts Festival (Fir Grove Park, 1624 W Harvard Ave, Roseburg; 541/672-2532, uvarts.com); high quality juried art, entertainment, food

JUNE, JULY, AUGUST
Britt Music & Arts Festival (350 1st St, Jacksonville; 541/779-0847, brittfest.org): Three months of concerts and performances under the stars in the Britt Pavilion and the Britt Performance Garden; classical, folk, pop, country and blues musicians and comedians. The relaxed venue offers seating on the lawn (bring a blanket) and reserved seating near the stage. Various cultural and fun events occur in conjunction with the concerts; early purchase of single performance tickets is highly recommended.

JULY/AUGUST
Douglas, Jackson, Josephine, Klamath and Lake County Fairs are held. Check oregonfairs.org for dates and details.

OCTOBER
Klamath Basin Potato Festival (Merrill, 541/891-3178, klamathbasinpotatofestival.com): most activities at or near the civic center; music, food, parade, spud bowl

DECEMBER
Klamath Falls Snowflake Festival (Klamath Falls, 541/850-1813, klamathsnowflake.com): parade, bazaar, music, food, family activities; various venues

an appetizer I recommend the Thai lettuce cups with chicken, or a bowl of seafood chowder (among many starters and shareable plates). Standout entrees include slow-cooked rosemary-roasted prime rib and the seared ahi tuna with sesame and black pepper. Jack Daniels bread pudding and a lemon-marionberry tartlet are among more than a half dozen irresistible desserts. Porters has a smoke free dining patio and a cigar friendly bar patio, too. All aboard!

Wild River Brewing & Pizza Company

2684 N Pacific Hwy   541/773-7487
Daily: 10:30-10 (Fri, Sat till 11)   wildriverbrewing.com
Moderate
(See main listing in Grants Pass)

MERLIN

Morrison's Rogue Wilderness Adventures

325 Galice Road   541/479-9554, 800/336-1647
Seasonal: May-Oct   rogueriverraft.com
For over 45 years, Morrison's Rogue Wilderness Adventures has offered raft supported lodge-to-lodge hiking trips, multi-day camping and lodging rafting trips, lodge-to-lodge steelhead fishing adventures, single day rafting trips, multi-day rentals and shuttles and more. Experience a trip to create lifetime memories.

Morrison's Rogue Wilderness Lodge

8500 Galice Road   800/826-1963
Seasonal: May-Oct   morrisonslodge.com
Inexpensive to very expensive
Located on a picturesque stretch of the Rogue River, 16 miles downstream from Grants Pass, Morrison's Rogue Wilderness Lodge offers some of the best whitewater rafting and steelhead fishing in Oregon. The lodge was built in 1945 as a fishing lodge and welcomes guests to updated accommodations in the main log lodge, nearby river-view cabins (circa 1965 to 1976) and beautiful creekside units built since 2007. Guests can choose from nine river-view cottages (with fireplaces, private decks and covered parking) or four rooms in the main lodge. All lodging options feature conveniences like air conditioning, television, Wi-Fi, private baths and more. Two multi-bedroom suites and four cottages are just a brief walk away on Taylor Creek. The property includes a heated swimming pool, putting green and volleyball, tennis and basketball courts. Morrison's is also known for delicious four-course, prix-fixe dinners served outdoors.

The nightly menu may feature prime rib of beef, salmon filet, pork chops, lamb or a chicken dish; housemade orange dinner rolls are a real treat. Fishing season runs from the end of August until the first part of November. Reservations required.

OAKLAND

MarshAnne Landing Winery

1/5 Hogan Road   541/459-7998
Wed-Sun: 11-5 (March-Dec,
other times by appointment)   marshannelanding.com
Fran and Greg Cramer's small winery produces cab and syrah blends, merlot, pinot noir, syrah, chardonnay, viognier, and other proprietary blends. The tasting room showcases bronze sculptures, paintings, pottery, glasswork, jewelry and fiber art from local artists. Special events are scheduled throughout the year in the tasting room and on the deck overlooking the vineyard. Check out their music schedule, which features classical, opera and jazz concerts. It is also a prime wedding and private function venue.

PROSPECT

Prospect Historic Hotel
(Bed & Breakfast Inn, Motel and Dinner House)

391 Mill Creek Dr   541/560-3664, 800/944-6490
B&B: Moderate   prospecthotel.com
Motel: Inexpensive to moderate
Restaurant: Moderate
This historic 1880s stagecoach-stop hotel in Prospect is the closest full-service lodging to Crater Lake and the Rogue River. It is also the jumping-off point for many outdoor activities. Ten bed-and-breakfast rooms are in the Nationally Registered Historic Hotel; the full hearty breakfast is a delightful start to the morning. All rooms have private bathrooms, handmade quilts and period furnishings. Behind the hotel, 14 modern motel units are outfitted with TVs, coffeemakers, refrigerators and microwaves (some kitchenettes); these units are ideal for families and guests with pets. The dinner house is open May through October as well as most holidays and serves dinners complete with salad, freshly-baked bread and dessert. Karen and Fred Wickman are the owners; Karen oversees the dinner house while Fred serves as jack-of-all-trades for the inn. Explore five acres of park-like grounds and three waterfalls just a short stroll away, then relax with a local wine or beer on the veranda.

VIEW FROM A LOOKOUT

For a unique getaway experience, U.S. Forest Service fire lookouts and cabins (firelookout.org/lookout-rentals) are available for seasonal (and economical) campouts. Amenities (bathrooms, cooking facilities, running water) vary by location, so be sure to read descriptions carefully before renting; most are remote and require packing in your gear. Availability varies seasonally and whether they are used by the Forest Service for active fire detection. Here's a sampling of locations:

Deschutes National Forest
Green Ridge Lookout

Fremont-Winema National Forest
Aspen Cabin
Bald Butte Lookout
Hager Mountain Lookout
Drake Peak Lookout

Malheur National Forest
Fall Mountain Lookout

Rogue River-Siskiyou National Forest
Bolan Mountain Lookout
Lake of the Woods Lookout
Onion Mountain Lookout
Snow Camp Lookout

Umpqua National Forest
Pickett Butte Lookout

Willamette National Forest
Indian Ridge Lookout

ROGUE RIVER

Pholia Farm

9115 W Evans Creek Road
Seasonal
Lodging: Inexpensive

541/582-8883
pholiafarm.com

Learn all you never knew about Nigerian dwarf dairy goats and the rich milk they produce at Gianaclis and Vern Caldwell's farm. The breed's milk boasts the highest butterfat of all goats, which translates into extraordinary Old World-style cheeses. Classes are offered in artisanal cheesemaking and herdsmanship for novice goat owners (although the farm no longer sells goat cheese). The dairy is off-grid, as is the Caldwell's home (solar, micro-hydro generator and backup bio-diesel generator supply electricity). It's best to call ahead if you are going to this off-the-beaten-path enterprise. If you'd like to spend the night at the farm, inquire about guest quarters in the refurbished 1970 Airstream Land Yacht (airbnb.com).

ROSEBURG

Abacela Vineyard and Winery

12500 Lookingglass Road   541/679-6642
Daily: 11-6 (till 5 in winter)   abacela.com
When Earl Jones and his wife, Hilda, adopted Oregon as their home in the early 1990s, Oregon's small wine industry had already earned an international reputation for great pinot noir. But the Joneses had come to do something different. Their Abacela Vineyard planted its first vines, tempranillo grapes, in 1995, a variety that although previously grown in America had only been used for jug wine or distilled for its alcoholic content. Today, varietal tempranillo is produced by over 200 wineries throughout the U.S., and Abacela can rightly be considered a pioneer in that effort. That goes for varietal malbec, syrah and grenache, too, which in addition to tempranillo are now the leading red varieties in the warm-climate regions of Oregon. Earl and Hilda are passionate about their wines and award-winning Umpqua Valley winery, and a visit will show you why. Take a winery tour or enjoy an elegant private tasting (by appointment) in the Vine & Wine Center, which also offers magnificent views. Wines are available online and through the Abacela wine club, too.

Brix Grill

527 SE Jackson St   541/440-4901
Daily: 7 a.m.-8 p.m.   Facebook
Moderate
In downtown Roseburg is a trifecta of historic buildings joined together to encompass Brix Grill (an eatery), Brix Chill (a lounge) and Brix Gather (an event center). The real crab cake Benedict is delicious for breakfast, and there are other gourmet selections, too. For lunch there are soups, sandwiches, salads and specials. For dinner choose from steaks, seafood, crab cakes, burgers, pasta dishes, chicken and superb salads; there is also a full bar.

Delfino Vineyards

3829 Colonial Road   541/673-7575
Daily: 11-5   delfinovineyards.com
Cottage: Expensive

Terri and Jim Delfino's enterprise includes a five-star, one-bedroom guest cottage nestled in the picturesque 160-acre site; in-room breakfast basket or fixings to make your own breakfast and a bottle of Delfino Vineyards wine are included. During your stay, amble over to the tasting room, hike the wooded trails, soak in the hot tub, take a dip in the lap pool or snuggle up by the cottage's fireplace. For two couples or a family (no guests younger than 14, please), the cottage has a queen sofa bed; two-night stay minimum.

Dino's Ristorante Italiano

404 SE Jackson St   541/673-0848
Tue-Thu: 5-9 (till 9:30 Fri, Sat)   dinosristorante.com
Moderate

Since 1998 this family-operated restaurant has cooked up authentic Italian cuisine made from fresh, local and organic ingredients whenever possible. Traditional pastas like lasagna and spaghetti Bolognese are offered alongside other dishes enriched with seafood, chicken and beef. Menu options also feature soups, salads, pizza and antipasti like calamari fritte. Whole wheat and gluten-free pastas are available on request. Desserts include classic tiramisu and a limoncello version. Dino and his chef wife are quite the duo. The atmosphere is casual and laid back, just like the Italians do it. If you share the same passion for food as they do, visit their Facebook page to find information about cooking classes, specials and closures.

SILVER LAKE

Cowboy Dinner Tree

East Bay Road   541/576-2426
Thu-Sun: June-Nov; Fri-Sun: Nov-June   cowboydinnertree.net
Moderate

This dinner stop in the heart of Oregon's High Desert country is a unique experience. When you call (reservations are a must), place your order for either a 26-ounce top sirloin steak (think roast) or whole chicken. The trimmings, such as hearty soup, salad, baked potato and homemade dessert, will make you happy you journeyed this far. Angel and Jamie Roscoe continue in her parent's footsteps. Just like her mother, Angel prepares homemade sweet yeast rolls from a secret family recipe. On a busy evening, she'll turn out 80 pans of the melt-in-your-mouth bread. Jamie prepares chickens for the rotisserie and spice-rubbed steaks for the grill. If you want to call it a night at sundown, reserve one of the two rustic cabins (no TV or telephone); the package deal includes dinner. Interesting cowboy memorabilia accents the dining room and cabins. No credit or debit cards, please.

TALENT

New Sammy's Cowboy Bistro

2210 S Pacific Hwy   541/535 2779
Wed-Sat: noon-1:30 (lunch); 5-9 (dinner)   newsammyscowboybistro.com
Moderately expensive

Venture off I-5 about three miles north of Ashland for one heck of a dining experience. For nearly 30 years Charlene and Vernon Rollins have been filling satisfied customers' plates with awesome food. Chef Charlene consistently produces healthy, organic meals with homemade breads, entrees made with seasonal ingredients and amazing desserts. Vernon takes care of the front of the house. The restaurant's garden supplies herbs and vegetables; other local producers provide meats and such, including whole suckling pigs. The Rollins' talents have caught the eye of prestigious food magazines, and Charlene has been nominated by the James Beard Foundation for her culinary accomplishments. Reservations are definitely in order.

WINSTON

Wildlife Safari

1790 Safari Road   541/679-6761
Daily: 9-5 (March 13-Nov 7); 10-4 (Nov 8-March 12)   wildlifesafari.net
Reasonable

This spectacular 600-acre drive-through wildlife park continues to attract families eager to observe more than 500 animals roaming natural habitat. It is committed to research, education and conservation. About 90 species of mammals, birds and reptiles (some threatened or endangered) indigenous to Africa, Asia and North and South America are showcased. To the delight of youngsters, many brush up next to visitors' autos. Before or after your safari (the drive-through takes about an hour and a half), explore the village with unique animals, train rides and a petting zoo, as well as a cafe, gift shop, play area and gardens. Private encounters such as helping feed the bears and tigers are by reservation. No pets on the drive-through, please (kennels available).

Gerry's Exclusive List

BBQ
Cowboy Dinner Tree (East Bay Road, Silver Lake; 541/576-2426)
Smithfields Restaurant & Bar (36 S 2nd St, Ashland; 541/488-9948)

Bars and Pubs with Good Eats
Elements Tapas Bar & Lounge (101 E Main St, Medford; 541/779-0135)
The Haul (121 SW H St, Grants Pass; 541/474-4991)
Standing Stone Brewing Co. (101 Oak St, Ashland; 541/482-2448)
Wild River Brewing & Pizza Company (16279 Hwy 101 S, Brookings, 541/469-7454; 249 N Redwood Hwy, Cave Junction, 541/592-3556; 595 NE E St, Grants Pass, 541/471-7487; (pub) 533 NE F St, Grants Pass, 541/474-4456; 2684 N Pacific Hwy, Medford, 541/773-7487)

Best Sleeps
Callahan's Mountain Lodge (7100 Old Hwy 99 S, Ashland; 541/482-1299)
Jacksonville Inn (175 E California St, Jacksonville; 541/899-1900)
Steamboat Inn (42705 N Umpqua Hwy, Idleyld Park; 541/498-2230)
Winchester Inn (35 S 2nd St, Ashland; 541/488-1113)

Breads and Bakery Goods
Heaven on Earth Restaurant & Bakery (703 Quines Creek Road, Azalea; 541/837-3700)
Tomaselli's Pastry Mill & Cafe (14836 Umpqua Hwy, Elkton; 541/584-2855)

Breakfast/Brunch
4 Daughters Irish Pub (126 W Main St, Medford; 541/779-4455): brunch
Heaven on Earth Restaurant & Bakery (703 Quines Creek Road, Azalea; 541/837-3700)
Jacksonville Inn (175 E California St, Jacksonville; 541/899-1900)
The Klamath Grill (715 Main St, Klamath Falls; 541/882-1427)
Morning Glory Restaurant (1149 Siskiyou Blvd, Ashland; 541/488-8636): breakfast, brunch
Smithfields Restaurant & Bar (36 S 2nd St, Ashland; 541/488-9948)

Burgers
The Haul (121 SW H St, Grants Pass; 541/474-4991)

In-N-Out Burger (124 NW Morgan Lane, Grants Pass; 1970 Crater Lake Hwy, Medford)
Jaspers Cafe (2739 N Pacific Hwy, Medford; 541/776-5307): Popper burger
Jimmy's Classic Drive-In (515 NE E St, Grants Pass; 541/479-3850): Cryin Shame burger
Taprock Northwest Grill (971 SE 6th St, Grants Pass; 541/955-5998)

Casual Dining/Casual Prices
Mermaid Garden Cafe (501 Main St, Klamath Falls; 541/882-3671)
Mustard Seed Cafe (130 N 5th St, Jacksonville; 541/899-2977)
Tomaselli's Pastry Mill & Cafe (14836 Umpqua Hwy, Elkton; 541/584-2855)

Cheese
Rogue Creamery (311 N Front St, Central Point; 541/665-1155)

Coffee and Tea
Dobrá Tea (75 N Main St, Ashland; 541/708-0264): Bohemian-style tearoom
Dutch Bros Coffee (numerous locations throughout the Northwest; Grants Pass is the headquarters)
Mellolo Coffee Roasters (3651 Lear Way, Medford, 541/858-2552; 229 W Main St, Medford, 541/734-3271)
Rogue Valley Roasting Co. (917 E Main, Ashland; 541/488-5902)

Confections
Branson's Chocolates (1662 Siskiyou Blvd, Ashland; 541/488-7493): chocolates, truffles
Lillie Belle Farms (211 N Front St, Central Point; 888/899-2022)

Fireside
Beasy's on the Creek (51 Water St, Ashland; 541/488-5009)

Fish and Seawood
Amuse (15 N 1st St, Ashland; 541/488-9000)
Gogi's Restaurant (235 W Main St, Jacksonville; 541/899-8699)
Porters (147 N Front St, Medford; 541/857-1910)

Foreign Flavors
ASIAN: Bambu (970 N Phoenix Rd, Medford; 541/608-7545)
ENGLISH: Smithfields Pub & Pies (23 S 2nd Street, Ashland; 541/482-7437)

FRENCH: Amuse (15 N 1st St, Ashland, 541/488-9000); **Loft Brasserie & Bar** (18 Calle Guanajuato Way, Ashland, 541/482-1116)
GERMAN: Schoolhaus Brewhaus (525 Bigham Knoll Dr, Jacksonville; 541/899-1000)
IRISH: 4 Daughters Irish Pub (126 W Main St, Medford; 541/779-4455)
ITALIAN: Macaroni's Ristorante and Martino's Restaurant and Lounge (58 E Main St, Ashland; 541/488-3359)
MEDITERRANEAN: Greenleaf Restaurant (49 N Main St, Ashland; 541/482-2808)
SPANISH: Elements Tapas Bar & Lounge (101 E Main St, Medford; 541/779-0135)

Game
Gary West Meats (690 N 5th St, Jacksonville; 800/833-1820)
Jaspers Cafe (2739 N Pacific Hwy, Medford; 541/776-5307)

Ice Cream and Other Frozen Treats
K&R Drive Inn (201 John Long Rd, Oakland; 541/849-2570): Exit 148, Rice Hill; Umpqua Dairy products
Zoey's Cafe & All Natural Ice Cream (199 E Main St, Ashland; 541/482-4794)

Meats
Gary West Meats (690 N 5th, Jacksonville; 800/833-1820)

Outdoor Dining
Beasy's on the Creek (51 Water St, Ashland; 541/488-5009)
Loft Brasserie & Bar (18 Calle Guanajuato, Ashland; 541/482-1116)
Standing Stone Brewing Co. (101 Oak St, Ashland; 541/482-2448)
Taprock Northwest Grill (971 SE 6th St, Grants Pass; 541/955-5998)

Personal Favorites
The Haul (121 SW H St, Grants Pass; 541/474-4991)
Smithfields Restaurant & Bar (36 S 2nd St, Ashland; 541/488-9948)
Steamboat Inn (42705 N Umpqua Hwy, Idleyld Park; 541/498-2230)

Pie
Punky's Diner & Pies (953 Medford Center, Medford; 541/494-1957)
Smithfields Pub & Pies (23 S 2nd Street, Ashland; 541/482-7437)

Pizza
The Haul (121 SW H St, Grants Pass; 541/474-4991)

Kaleidoscope Pizzeria & Pub (3084 Crater Lake Hwy, Medford; 541/779-7787)
Mia & Pia's Pizzeria & Brewhouse (3545 Summers Lane, Klamath Falls; 541/884-4880)
Tomaselli's Pastry Mill & Cafe (14836 Umpqua Hwy, Elkton; 541/584-2855)
Wild River Brewing & Pizza Company (16279 Hwy 101 S, Brookings, 541/469-7454; 249 N Redwood Hwy, Cave Junction, 541/592-3556; 595 NE E St, Grants Pass, 541/471-7487; (pub) 533 NE F St, Grants Pass, 541/474-4456; 2684 N Pacific Hwy, Medford, 541/773-7487)

Sandwiches
Downtown Market Co. (231 E Main St, Medford; 541/973-2233)
Mia & Pia's Pizzeria & Brewhouse (3545 Summers Lane, Klamath Falls; 541/884-4880)

Soups
Downtown Market Co. (231 E Main St, Medford; 541/973-2233)
Larks Home Kitchen Cuisine (Ashland Springs Hotel, 212 E Main St, Ashland; 541/488-5558)

Southern
Smithfields Restaurant & Bar (36 S 2nd St, Ashland; 541/488-9948)

Special Occasions
Amuse (15 N 1st, Ashland; 541/488-9000)
Coquina (542 A St, Ashland; 541/488-0521)
Gogi's Restaurant (235 W Main St, Jacksonville; 541/899-8699)
New Sammy's Cowboy Bistro (2210 S Pacific Hwy, Talent; 541/535-2779)
Porters (147 N Front St, Medford; 541/857-1910)

Steaks
Cowboy Dinner Tree (50962 E Bay Road, Silver Lake; 541/576-2426): by reservation only
Gogi's Restaurant (235 W Main St, Jacksonville; 541/899-8699)
Porters (147 N Front St, Medford; 541/857-1910)
Smithfields Restaurant & Bar (36 S 2nd St, Ashland; 541/488-9948)

Notes

Index